The Pocket Encyclopaedia of World Aircraft in Colour
BOMBERS

PATROL AND RECONNAISSANCE AIRCRAFT

1914–1919

The Pocket Encyclopaedia
of World Aircraft in Colour

BOMBERS
PATROL AND RECONNAISSANCE AIRCRAFT
1914–1919

by
KENNETH MUNSON, Associate R.Ae.S.

Illustrated by
JOHN W. WOOD

Norman Dinnage
Brian Hiley
William Hobson
Alan Holliday
Tony Mitchell
Allen Randall

Additional notes by
IAN D. HUNTLEY, A.M.R.Ae.S.

BLANDFORD PRESS
POOLE   DORSET

ISBN 0 7137 0632 8

Colour printed by The Ysel Press, Deventer, Holland
Printed and bound in England by
Richard Clay (The Chaucer Press) Ltd, Bungay, Suffolk

PREFACE

So far as the colour plates in this volume are concerned, we owe an incalculable debt of gratitude to Ian D. Huntley, A.M.R.Ae.S., whose extensive researches have provided the basis for all of the colour work in this volume. A short account of Ian Huntley's researches – and a few of the results that they have yielded – appear in the Appendices. These, if read in conjunction with the notes on page 15, should obviate a number of misconceptions which apparently confused some readers of the first edition.

For help or reference material of other kinds, I am indebted to material published by the American journal *Air Progress*, by Harleyford Publications Ltd. and by Profile Publications Ltd. Individual assistance with the original edition, also much appreciated, was given by Messrs. Charles F. Andrews of BAC, Bo Widfelt of the Swedish Aviation Historical Society and Lt. Col. N. Kindberg of the Royal Swedish Air Force; this revised edition has benefited in no small measure from material kindly made available subsequently by Chaz Bowyer, Jack Bruce, Roland Eichenberger and Douglas Pardee. To them all I am delighted to express again my thanks, both for their kindness and for the helpful spirit in which their assistance was offered.

Kenneth Munday

May 1976

INTRODUCTION

It is difficult to establish with certainty when bombs were first dropped from an aeroplane in the furtherance of a military campaign, but the earliest recorded occasion was on 1 November 1911, when Giulio Gavotti of the Squadriglia di Tripoli, flying a Rumpler Taube of the Italian Air Service, released four small bombs over the North African townships of Tagiura and Ain Zara. At any rate it is certain that, as a type, the use of the aeroplane as a bomber antedated the fighter by several years, for machines capable of such activity were in service or being designed some time before the outbreak of World War 1.

One of the leading types at this time was the French Voisin, and the first bombing attack of the war was made by Voisins of the Aviation Militaire which bombed the Zeppelin hangars at Metz-Frascaty on 14 August 1914. During the early part of the war Germany and Austro-Hungary relied almost exclusively upon the Zeppelin airship as their main vehicle for bombing raids, and many of the first offensive sorties made by the Allies were directed at the factories or airfield sites where these 'monsters of the purple twilight' were built or housed. Before the end of 1914 a few successful bombing raids were also carried out by aircraft of the Royal Naval Air Service. It is probably fair to say that their morale value was higher than that of the actual destruction caused, for they were made mostly by small aircraft carrying only a modest load of the lightest bombs.

The Voisin was almost the only aeroplane in service with any of the warring nations that really deserved to be regarded as a bomber, and in September 1914 this was recognised by the Aviation Militaire, which began to reorganise its Voisin squadrons specifically to carry out bombing activities. (It was, incidentally, a French Voisin that scored the first air-to-air combat victory of the war, when its observer shot down a German Aviatik 2-seater on 5 October 1914.) France's first steps towards the creation of a bombing force were soon followed by the formation, in the Imperial Russian Air Service, of Tsar Nicholas II's 'Squadron of Flying Ships' (or

E.V.K.), equipped with the giant Sikorsky Ilya Mouromets. The Ilya Mouromets was the first (and, at that time, still the only) four-engined bomber in the world. This enormous machine, which had flown for the first time in January 1914, was a development of the record-setting *Le Grand*, also designed by Igor Sikorsky early in 1913. The E.V.K. made its first bombing raid with these machines on 15 February 1915 from its base at Jablonna in Poland.

Two months before this, Commodore Murray F. Sueter of the British Admiralty's Air Department had set the wheels in motion to produce what he called a 'bloody paralyser of an aeroplane' to bomb targets in Germany, although the bomber that resulted from this specification, the Handley Page O/100, was not to enter service until nearly the end of 1916.

In the meantime, in May 1915 the Aviation Militaire began a sustained bombing campaign using its squadrons of Voisin aircraft, the strength of which was eventually built up to a total of some six hundred aircraft. Both Britain and Italy bought Voisin and Breguet bombing types from France and began to build them under licence as well. Russia, too, essayed the licence production of the Voisin, with local modifications, but with unfortunate results.

On 24 May 1915 another protagonist joined the conflict on the side of the Allies. Italy's combined total of military and naval aeroplanes at this time was little more than a hundred, and a high proportion of these were of French origin. They did include, however, a number of examples of the excellent Caproni Ca 2 bombers with the range and reliability to undertake the long, hazardous flight across the Alps to targets in Austro-Hungary, and the first such raid by these aircraft was carried out on 20 August 1915.

For the first half of the war, the Zeppelins continued to be Germany's chief vehicles for heavy bombing, but thereafter they were used mostly by the German Naval Air Service while the military arm turned to using aeroplanes. Daylight raids on Great Britain, using A.E.G. and Gotha twin-engined bombers, began early in 1917. During the summer these attacks were stepped up to such an intensity that the R.F.C. and R.N.A.S. were obliged to recall aircraft that they could ill afford to spare from the Western Front in order to expand the number of Home Defence squadrons. These fighters, some of them makeshift conversions of 2-seat types, resisted the German raiders to such good effect that they were at first obliged to attack only by night and finally to abandon the raids altogether in May 1918.

The Gothas typified the German bombers of the period and were the principal types to be used, but they were abetted by smaller numbers of the similar Friedrichshafen G types and, in the later stages, by the bigger Zeppelin (Staaken) R types. Allied bombers of the later war years included later and improved models of the Caproni series and the Ilya Mouromets, together with such excellent new types as the Breguet 14, D.H.4 and Handley Page O/400. Some other bomber types, notably the D.H.9 and the R.E.8, were produced in far greater numbers which their combat value did not merit. In June 1918 Britain established the Independent Force in Europe, a strategic bombing force equipped in the main with Handley Page bombers, to undertake the bombing of targets in the German homeland. The United States of America had come into the war on 6 April 1917, and for most of 1918 the American Expeditionary Force, equipped predominantly with fighters and bombers of French origin, made an important contribution to the bombing offensive which was sustained until the end of the war.

The load-carrying abilities of the bomber aeroplane had increased to such an extent by the end of World War 1 that, from the little 20-lb. or 10-kg. weapons that had been the norm in 1914, high explosive 'block-busters' weighing 1,650 lb. (nearly 750 kg.) had been developed and used. The weapons in most general use were those weighing around 100 kg. – 250 lb., but the Handley Page V/1500, which was all ready to go into action when the Armistice was signed, was able to carry two bombs each weighing 3,300 lb. (1,497 kg.). The small-size bombs were often carried by observation 2-seaters, more for their 'nuisance' value than anything else, but occasionally these could be used in other ways with spectacular results. One such occasion was the destruction of the Zeppelin LZ.37 in June 1915 by Flight Sub-Lieutenant Warneford of the R.N.A.S., who flew along the length of the dirigible dropping six of these tiny bombs into the airship's envelope. Warneford was awarded the Victoria Cross for his action, which was the first time a Zeppelin had been brought down by an attack from another aircraft. So far as armament was concerned, the guns carried by bombing, patrol or reconnaissance aircraft were primarily for defensive purposes. The Parabellum, the standard German observer's weapon, was the pre-war LMG.08 version of the Maxim infantry machine-gun; its standard Allied equivalent was the Lewis.

One variation of the orthodox bomber evolved during 1914–18 was the torpedo bomber, but such aircraft as a class did not contribute a significant amount towards the progress of the war. Successful launches of torpedoes were made from several different aircraft types, but the actual amount of shipping sunk or damaged by this form of attack was small in comparison with that accounted for by ordinary high explosive bombs.

The use of water-borne aircraft in patrolling the seas and defending naval shore stations was an important element in the conduct of the war as a whole. Germany, alone of the major combatants, eschewed the value of the flying-boat for these purposes, but she did employ a considerable variety of floatplanes, both on board seaplane carriers or other naval vessels and at naval shore stations, for defensive or patrol duties. Their British counterparts included such useful workhorses as the Fairey Campania, Short 184 and Sopwith Baby.

The Lohner, Macchi, Tellier and F.B.A. flying-boats, of Austrian, Italian and French origin respectively, were mostly medium-sized 2-seaters with a modest defensive armament and a small bomb load. They were among the less glamourised aircraft of World War 1, but they carried out a vast amount of routine but valuable work. The large flying-boat appeared first in the form of the indifferent Curtiss 'America' series from the U.S.A., which Squadron Commander John Porte of the R.N.A.S. transformed into the Felixstowe F.2A, a thoroughly efficient and seaworthy long range patroller that set a pattern for flying-boat evolution lasting for two decades and more after the war ended. Porte was one of a select band of naval officers who made an incalculable contribution to the development of marine aviation during these formative years; another was Squadron Commander E. H. Dunning, who lost his life in August 1917 while carrying out a test landing in a Sopwith Pup in connection with the evolution of deck take-off and landing techniques.

World War 1 was the background for the first true air war, and in this as in all subsequent conflicts the glamour attached itself chiefly to the fighter and bomber aircraft involved. But in 1914–18 the real workhorses in every air service were the 2-seat observation and reconnaissance machines. Right from the outset of World War 1 the aeroplane's principal – indeed, its only – value had been thought in most official circles to be that of observing and reporting the progress of the war on the ground, rather than making a positive contribution to that progress. Even when this way of thinking had been proved to be wrong, the value of the reconnaissance machine remained undiminished.

Aircraft of both sides were sent over enemy lines during the first few months of the war to report the progress of troop movements or the accuracy of their own side's artillery fire. At first, the majority of aircraft used for this role were unarmed, but before the war was many weeks old some observers began to take into the air with them service revolvers, cavalry carbines, duck rifles and all manner of other, often bizarre, weapons with which to 'have a go' at any enemy machine they chanced to meet while out on a patrol. Once this practice had started, other observers were obliged to equip themselves with similar means of protection or retaliation; and from the first few sporadic encounters of this kind the foundations were laid of the arts and skills of aerial fighting. On the one hand this led, naturally enough, to the evolution of the fighter as a specialised combat type. At the same time it created the need to evolve faster, more manoeuvrable and better-armed observation types that could defend themselves adequately against attack from fighters or other 2-seaters.

It must be remembered that at this period of the war the standard arrangement of most 2-seaters was to place the observer in the front cockpit. In a tractor biplane, the most common configuration, he therefore had the engine block in front of him, bracing struts and wires on either side and the pilot behind him. Consequently, when weapons began to be carried he had little worthwhile field of fire at all, and his field of view for carrying out his observation duties was not very much better. Moreover, the risk of a bullet fracturing a bracing wire – or, more important, a control wire – was always present. Yet, despite the difficulties, several successes were achieved with hand-held guns operated from the front cockpit in this fashion.

First to break out of the rut was Germany, which introduced its new category of C type armed 2-seaters in the spring of 1915. In these machines the observer more logically occupied the rearmost of the two cockpits, where he had a much wider field of view and the freedom to fire a gun in almost every direction except directly below. The hand-held rifle or other weapon was replaced by a ring-type mounting for a machine-gun that could be rotated to right or left, elevated or depressed, and from then onward the German armed 2-seater was an opponent to be reckoned with for as long as the war continued. Most of the German and Austrian C types had a fair degree of manoeuvrability, and some of them could give even the best Allied fighters a run for their money. Late-war fighters of the calibre of the S.E.5a found the best of them, the D.F.Ws. and L.V.Gs, more than worthy opponents in the hands of a good crew. Some of the high altitude photographic C types, like the later Rumplers, could climb to heights above 20,000 feet (6,100 metres), well above the ceiling of most Allied fighters. For such missions they qualified for heated flying suits and oxygen breathing apparatus to be issued to the crews – both comparative rarities in other classes of wartime aircraft.

Germany, having a large domestic aircraft industry, was able to undertake the development of a wide variety of reconnaissance 2-seaters, but on the Allied side such types were less diversified. The Italian SAML and Ansaldo scouts were among the best, the latter (a single-seater) being probably the fastest reconnaissance aircraft used by any combatant during the entire war. Russia's only original contribution was the indifferent Anatra, while France relied to a large extent on pre-war Farmans or Caudrons or unspectacular Spad and Nieuport designs until the Salmson 2 appeared early in 1918. Britain pinned its faith for too much of the war upon the unfortunate B.E.2 series designed at the Royal Aircraft Factory, which were the principal prey of the Fokker monoplanes and later German biplane fighters. From the structural and design viewpoints the B.E. was a fine, well-thought-out piece of engineering with many desirable flying qualities. Unfortunately, what did not get through to the men with influence over its production and employment was the fact that the very qualities that made it such an excellent, safe and stable flying machine were the direct cause of its downfall against the German fighters. Its stability made it virtually impossible for the B.E.2 to outmanoeuvre the agile enemy single-seaters, its speed was not great enough nor its ceiling high enough for it to outrun or outclimb them; and by clinging obstinately to the outmoded practice of putting the observer in the front seat surrounded by a 'cage' of struts, wires and engine its sponsors severely limited what little defensive firepower it had. It was not to be wondered at that the wretched B.Es. were shot down in their dozens.

In order to study the aircraft of 1914–18 in a proper perspective it is helpful if one appreciates some of the conditions under which they and their crews had to carry out their combat duties. In nearly every case crews had to fly in unheated flying suits, in open cockpits, at altitudes where the intense cold affected not only their own physical efficiency but the lubrication and cooling systems of their engines and guns. Gun stoppages were still an all-too-frequent occurrence, even in excellent late-war designs with otherwise good performance, and often an engagement had to be broken off by one or other participant because of a jammed gun or some similar circumstance. While on the ground, the aircraft were usually either pegged down in the open, or, at best, stored in canvas field hangars, and the depredations to their fabric from the bitter Russian cold, the miserable dampness of the Western Front or the blistering Middle Eastern heat can well be imagined. Performance figures recorded for individual types are those obtaining under more or less ideal flying conditions, but for much of the time such conditions were not enjoyed.

THE COLOUR PLATES

As an aid to identification, the sixty-seven colour plates which follow
have been arranged on a visual basis, within the broad sequence:
tractor monoplanes, pusher biplanes, tractor biplanes, flying-
boats and seaplanes. The Curtiss H-4/12/16, Fairey Campania and
Felixstowe F.2A/F.3 seaplanes, which appeared in the original
edition of this volume, can now be found in the *Flying Boats and
Seaplanes since 1910* volume in the series. The 'split' plan view is
adopted to give upper and lower surface markings within a single
plan outline. The reference number of each aircraft corresponds to
the appropriate text matter, and an index to all types appears on
pages 186 and 187.

To clarify some apparent misconceptions arising from the first
edition:

(*a*) It should not be assumed, from the 'split' plan view presentation, that the unseen portion of the plan view of a camouflaged
aircraft is a 'mirror image' of the half that is portrayed.

(*b*) It should not be assumed that all colour plates are intended
to show standard colour schemes or a pristine 'ex-works' state of
finish. Indeed, several plates deliberately show 'weathered' aircraft.

(*c*) Note (*b*) above applies particularly to the British khaki/
P.C.10 colouring (see Appendix 2) for which, within the limitations
of the colour reproduction process, an attempt has been made to
illustrate this finish in a wide variety of conditions, from an ex-
works aircraft with maximum 'green shift' (e.g. page 59) to a much-
weathered aircraft (e.g. page 64).

BLÉRIOT XI (France)

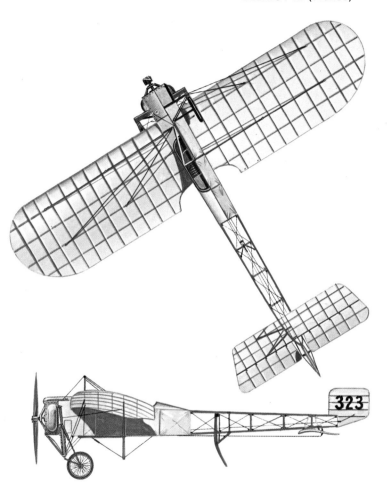

1

Blériot XI-2 *Artillerie,* possibly an aircraft of No. 3 Squadron R.F.C., 1914. *Engine:* One 70 h.p. Gnome 7 A rotary. *Span:* 29 ft. 2½ in. (8·90 m.). *Length:* 25 ft. 7 in. (7·80 m.). *Wing area:* 161·3 sq.ft. (15·00 sq.m.). *Take-off weight:* 882 lb. (400 kg.). *Maximum speed:* 55·9 m.p.h. (90 km./hr.) at sea level. *Service ceiling:* 6,562 ft. (2,000 m.). *Endurance:* 3 hr. 30 min.

AGO C.II (Germany)

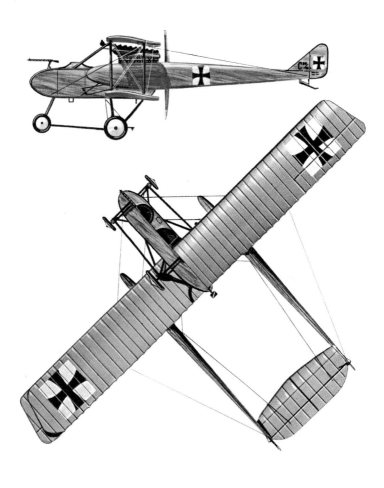

2

Ago C.II of the Imperial German Military Aviation Service, summer 1915.
Engine: One 220 h.p. Benz Bz.IV water-cooled in-line. *Span:* 47 ft. 6⅞ in.
(14·50 m.). *Length:* 32 ft. 3⅜ in. (9·84 m.). *Wing area:* approx. 510·2 sq.ft.
(47·40 sq.m.). *Take-off weight:* 2,998 lb. (1,360 kg.). *Maximum speed:* 85·1
m.p.h. (137 km./hr.) at sea level. *Service ceiling:* approx. 14,764 ft. (4,500
m.). *Range:* 360 miles (580 km.).

BREGUET BrM.5 (France)

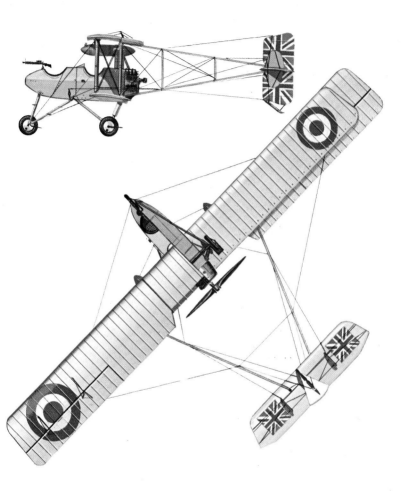

3

The machine illustrated is believed to be a French-built pre-series Type 5 supplied as a pattern for the Grahame-White-built Type XIX in late summer 1915. *Data apply to the production G.W. XIX. Engine:* One 250 h.p. Rolls-Royce I (Eagle) water-cooled Vee-type. *Span:* 57 ft. 8⅛ in. (17·58 m.). *Length:* 26 ft. 0¾ in. (7·94 m.). *Wing area:* 621·1 sq.ft. (57·70 sq.m.). *Take-off weight:* 4,740 lb. (2,150 kg.). *Maximum speed:* 85·7 m.p.h. (138 km./hr.) at sea level. *Service ceiling:* 14,108 ft. (4,300 m.). *Range:* 435 miles (700 km.).

VOISIN 5 (France)

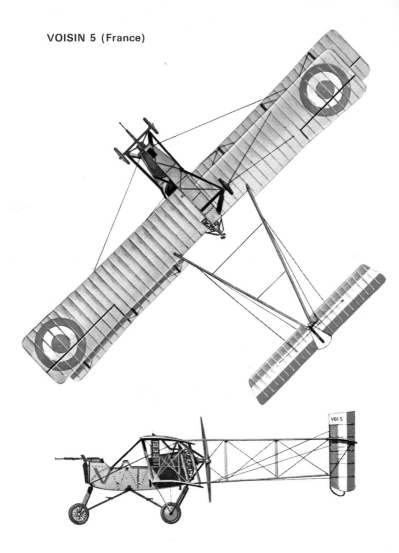

4

Voisin Voi.5B.2 (Type LA.S) of the French *Aviation Militaire, ca.* summer 1916.
Engine: One 150 h.p. Salmson (Canton-Unné) 9 P water-cooled radial. *Span:*
48 ft. 4¼ in. (14·74 m.). *Length:* 31 ft. 2 in. (9·50 m.). *Wing area:* 484·4
sq.ft. (45·00 sq.m.). *Take-off weight:* 3,020 lb. (1,370 kg.). *Maximum speed:*
69·6 m.p.h. (112 km./hr.) at sea level. *Service ceiling:* 11,483 ft. (3,500 m.).
Endurance: 3 hr. 30 min.

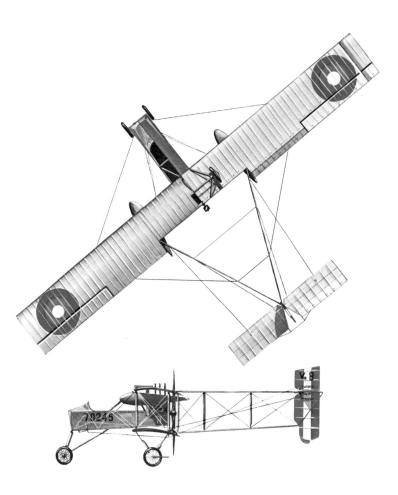

5

Voisin Voi.8Bn.2 (Type LA.P) bombing trainer of the American Expeditionary Force, France, *ca.* April 1918. *Engine:* One 220 h.p. Peugeot 8 Aa water-cooled in-line. *Span:* 59 ft. 0¾ in. (18·00 m.). *Length:* 33 ft. 11½ in. (10·35 m.). *Wing area:* 678·1 sq.ft. (63·00 sq.m.). *Take-off weight:* 4,101 lb. (1,860 kg.). *Maximum speed:* 73·3 m.p.h. (118 km./hr.) at sea level. *Service ceiling:* 14,108 ft. (4,300 m.). *Endurance:* 4 hr. 0 min.

FARMAN HF.23 (France)

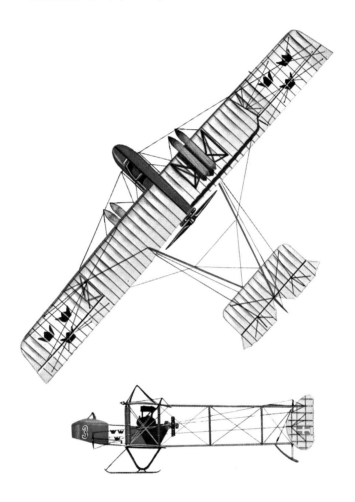

6

Södertälje-built Henry Farman HF.23 (SW.11) of the Royal Swedish Naval Aviation, 1914. *Engine:* One 80 h.p. Gnome 7 A rotary. *Span:* 49 ft. $2\frac{1}{2}$ in. (15·00 m.). *Length:* 29 ft. $2\frac{1}{2}$ in. (8·90 m.). *Wing area:* approx. 360·6 sq.ft. (33·50 sq.m.). *Take-off weight:* 1,499 lb. (680 kg.). *Maximum speed:* 55·9 m.p.h. (90 km./hr.) at sea level. *Service ceiling:* 9,022 ft. (2,750 m.). *Endurance:* 3 hr. 30 min.

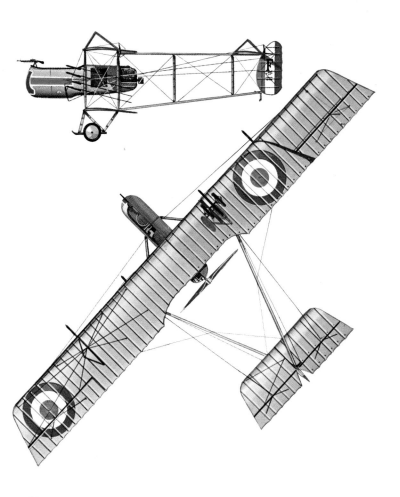

7

Farman F.40 of the French *Aviation Militaire,* 1916. *Engine:* One 160 h.p. Renault water-cooled Vee-type. *Span:* 57 ft. $11\frac{5}{8}$ in. (17·67 m.). *Length:* 30 ft. $4\frac{1}{8}$ in. (9·25 m.). *Wing area:* 559·7 sq.ft. (52·00 sq.m.). *Take-off weight:* 2,469 lb. (1,120 kg.). *Maximum speed:* 83·9 m.p.h. (135 km./hr.) at 6,562 ft. (2,000 m.). *Service ceiling:* 13,123 ft. (4,000 m.). *Endurance:* 2 hr. 20 min.

FRIEDRICHSHAFEN G.III (Germany)

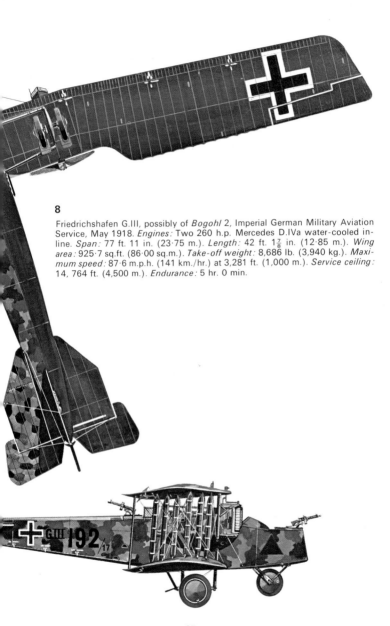

8

Friedrichshafen G.III, possibly of *Bogohl* 2, Imperial German Military Aviation Service, May 1918. *Engines:* Two 260 h.p. Mercedes D.IVa water-cooled in-line. *Span:* 77 ft. 11 in. (23·75 m.). *Length:* 42 ft. 1$\frac{7}{8}$ in. (12·85 m.). *Wing area:* 925·7 sq.ft. (86·00 sq.m.). *Take-off weight:* 8,686 lb. (3,940 kg.). *Maximum speed:* 87·6 m.p.h. (141 km./hr.) at 3,281 ft. (1,000 m.). *Service ceiling:* 14, 764 ft. (4,500 m.). *Endurance:* 5 hr. 0 min.

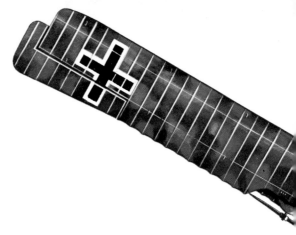

9

Gotha G.V of the Imperial German Military Aviation Service, April 1918. *Engines:* Two 260 h.p. Mercedes D.IVa water-cooled in-line. *Span:* 77 ft. $9\frac{1}{8}$ in. (23·70 m.). *Length:* 40 ft. $6\frac{1}{4}$ in. (12·35 m.). *Wing area:* 963·4 sq.ft. (89·50 sq.m.). *Take-off weight:* 8,763 lb. (3,975 kg.). *Maximum speed:* 87 m.p.h. (140 km./hr.) at sea level. *Service ceiling:* 21,325 ft. (6,500 m.). *Range:* 522 miles (840 km.).

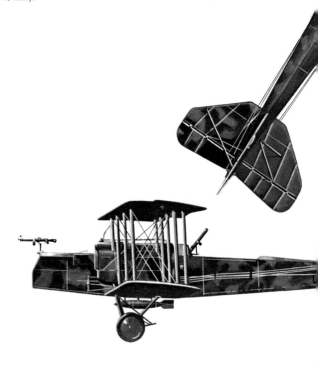

D.F.W. B.I (Germany)

10

D.F.W. B.I of the Imperial German Military Aviation Service, 1915. *Engine:* One 100 h.p. Mercedes D.I water-cooled in-line. *Span:* 45 ft. $11\frac{1}{8}$ in. (14·00 m.). *Length:* 27 ft. $6\frac{2}{3}$ in. (8·40 m.). *Wing area:* approx. 369·2 sq.ft. (34·30 sq.m.). *Take-off weight:* 2,238 lb. (1,015 kg.). *Maximum speed:* 74·6 m.p.h. (120 km./hr.) at sea level. *Service ceiling:* approx. 9,843 ft. (3,000 m.). *Endurance:* approx. 4 hr. 0 min.

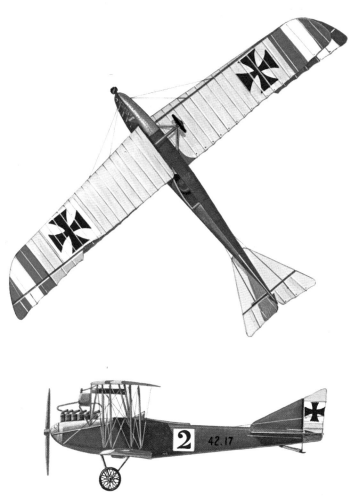

11

Lloyd-built C.II of the Austro-Hungarian Air Service, 1915. *Engine:* One 145 h.p. Hiero water-cooled in-line. *Span:* 45 ft. $11\frac{1}{8}$ in. (14·00 m.). *Length:* 29 ft. $6\frac{1}{3}$ in. (9·00 m.). *Wing area:* approx. 374·0 sq.ft. (34·75 sq.m.). *Take-off weight:* approx. 2,976 lb. (1,350 kg.). *Maximum speed:* approx. 79·5 m.p.h. (128 km./hr.) at sea level. *Service ceiling:* 9,843 ft. (3,000 m.). *Endurance:* approx. 2 hr. 30 min.

HANSA-BRANDENBURG C.I (Austro-Hungary)

12

Hansa-Brandenburg C.I of the Imperial German Military Aviation Service, *ca.*
spring 1916. *Data for Phönix-built Series 23. Engine:* One 160 h.p. Austro-
Daimler water-cooled in-line. *Span:* 43 ft. $0\frac{1}{2}$ in. (13·12 m.). *Length:* 26 ft.
$10\frac{3}{4}$ in. (8·20 m.). *Wing area:* 467·8 sq.ft. (43·46 sq.m.). *Take-off weight:*
2,337 lb. (1,060 kg.). *Maximum speed:* 77·6 m.p.h. (125 km./hr.) at sea level.
Service ceiling: 19,029 ft. (5,800 m.). *Endurance:* approx. 3 hr. 0 min.

ALBATROS B.II (Germany)

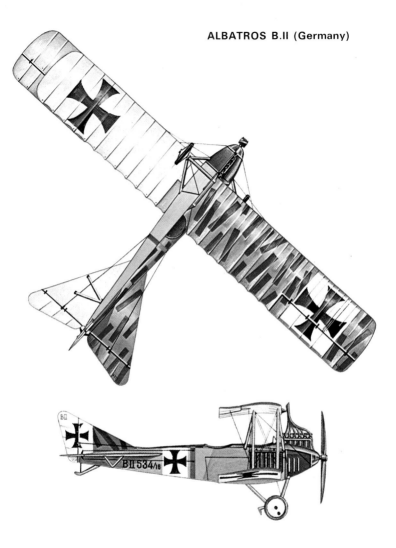

13

Albatros B.II of the Imperial German Military Aviation Service, *ca*. April 1916. *Engine:* One 100 h.p. Mercedes D.I water-cooled in-line. *Span:* 42 ft. 0 in. (12·80 m.). *Length:* 25 ft. 0⅜ in. (7·63 m.). *Wing area:* 431·8 sq.ft. (40·12 sq.m.). *Take-off weight:* 2,361 lb. (1,071 kg.). *Maximum speed:* 65·2 m.p.h. (105 km./hr.) at sea level. *Service ceiling:* 9,843 ft. (3,000 m.). *Endurance:* 4 hr. 0 min.

AVIATIK B.II (Austro-Hungary)

14

Austrian Aviatik B.II of the Austro-Hungarian Air Service, *ca.* early 1916.
Engine: One 120 h.p. Austro-Daimler water-cooled in-line. *Span:* 45 ft. 11$\frac{1}{8}$
in. (14·00 m.). *Length:* 26 ft. 3 in. (8·00 m.). *Wing area:* approx. 349·8 sq.ft.
(32·50 sq.m.). *Take-off weight:* 1,918 lb. (870 kg.). *Maximum speed:* 67·7
m.p.h. (109 km./hr.) at sea level. *Service ceiling:* 8,202 ft. (2,500 m.). *Endurance:* 4 hr. 0 min.

LOHNER C.I (Austro-Hungary)

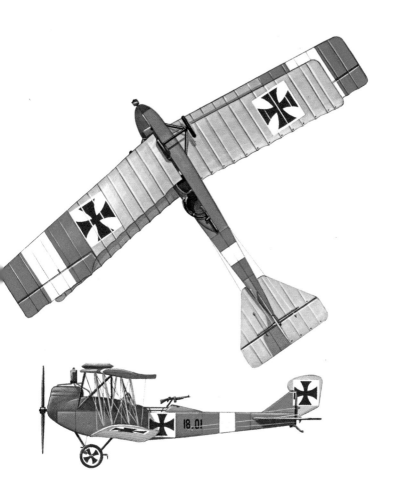

15

Lohner-built C.I of the Austro-Hungarian Air Service, 1916. *Engine:* One 160 h.p. Austro-Daimler water-cooled in-line. *Span:* 44 ft. 1½ in. (13·45 m.). *Length:* 29 ft. 3 in. (9·22 m.). *Wing area:* approx. 413·3 sq.ft. (38·40 sq.m.). *Take-off weight:* approx. 2,998 lb. (1,360 kg.). *Maximum speed:* 85·1 m.p.h. (137 km./hr.) at sea level. *Service ceiling:* 11,483 ft. (3,500 m.). *Endurance:* approx. 3 hr. 0 min.

ALBATROS C.I (Germany)

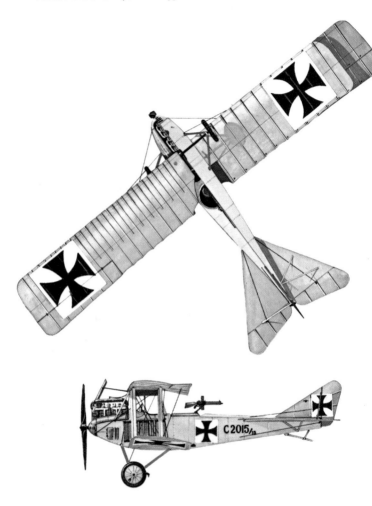

16

Albatros C.I of the Imperial German Military Aviation Service, late 1915. *Engine:* One 160 h.p. Mercedes D.III water-cooled in-line. *Span:* 42 ft. $3\frac{7}{8}$ in. (12·90 m.). *Length:* 25 ft. 9 in. (7·85 m.). *Wing area:* 434·9 sq.ft. (40·40 sq.m.). *Take-off weight:* 2,624 lb. (1,190 kg.). *Maximum speed:* 87 m.p.h. (140 km./hr.) at sea level. *Service ceiling:* 9,843 ft. (3,000 m.). *Endurance:* 2 hr. 30 min.

LEBED'-XII (Russia)

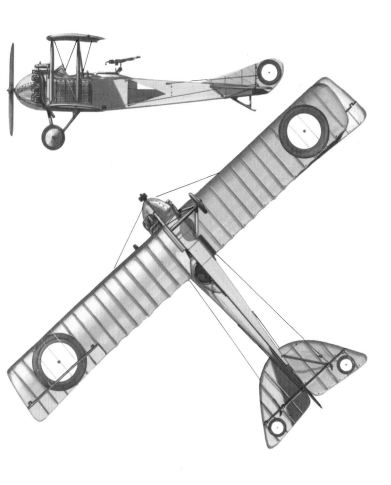

17

Lebed'-XII of the Imperial Russian Air Service, *ca.* summer 1917. *Engine:* One 150 h.p. Salmson (Canton-Unné) 9 P water-cooled radial. *Span:* 43 ft. 1¾ in. (13·15 m.). *Length:* 26 ft. 1½ in. (7·96 m.). *Wing area:* 452·1 sq.ft. (42·00 sq.m.). *Take-off weight:* 2,672 lb. (1,212 kg.). *Maximum speed:* 82·6 m.p.h. (133 km./hr.) at sea level. *Service ceiling:* 11,483 ft. (3,500 m.). *Endurance:* 3 hr. 0 min.

ALBATROS C.III (Germany)

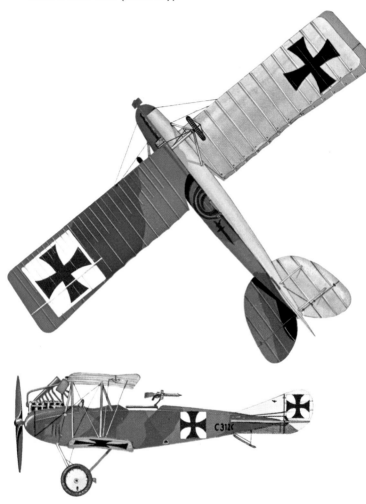

18

Albatros C.III of the Imperial German Military Aviation Service, *ca.* summer 1916. *Engine:* One 160 h.p. Mercedes D.III water-cooled in-line. *Span:* 38 ft. 4⅝ in. (11·70 m.). *Length:* 26 ft. 3 in. (8·00 m.). *Wing area:* 397·2 sq.ft. (36·90 sq.m.). *Take-off weight:* 2,983 lb. (1,353 kg.). *Maximum speed:* 87 m.p.h. (140 km./hr.) at sea level. *Service ceiling:* 11,155 ft. (3,400 m.). *Endurance:* 4 hr. 0 min.

DORAND ARL.1 (France)

19

Dorand ARL.1.A2 of the French *Aviation Militaire, ca.* late 1916. *Data are for AR.1.A2. Engine:* One 190 h.p. Renault 8 Bd Vee-type. *Span:* 43 ft. 6½ in. (13·27 m.). *Length:* 29 ft. 11¾ in. (9·14 m.). *Wing area:* 542·1 sq.ft. (50·36 sq.m.). *Take-off weight:* 2,756 lb. (1,250 kg.). *Maximum speed:* 95 m.p.h. (153 km./hr.) at 6,562 ft. (2,000 m.). *Service ceiling:* 18,045 ft. (5,500 m.). *Endurance:* 3 hr. 0 min.

RUMPLER C.I (Germany)

20

Rumpler C.I of the Imperial German Military Aviation Service, 1915. *Engine:*
One 160 h.p. Mercedes D.III water-cooled in-line. *Span:* 39 ft. 10⅓ in. (12·15
m.). *Length:* 25 ft. 9 in. (7·85 m.). *Wing area:* 384·3 sq.ft. (35·70 sq.m.).
Take-off weight: 2,932 lb. (1,330 kg.). *Maximum speed:* 94·4 m.p.h. (152
km./hr.) at sea level. *Service ceiling:* 16,568 ft. (5,050 m.). *Endurance:* 4
hr. 0 min.

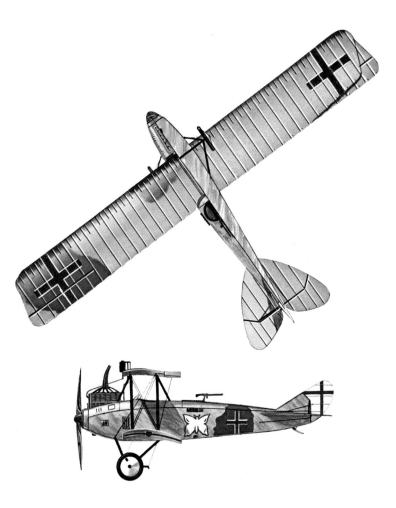

21

D.F.W. C.V of the Imperial German Military Aviation Service, captured by U.S. forces in July 1918. *Engine:* One 200 h.p. Benz Bz.IV water-cooled in-line. *Span:* 43 ft. 6½ in. (13·27 m.). *Length:* 25 ft. 10 in. (7·87 m.). *Wing area:* 457·5 sq.ft. (42·50 sq.m.). *Take-off weight:* 3,153 lb. (1,430 kg.). *Maximum speed:* 96·3 m.p.h. (155 km./hr.) at 3,281 ft. (1,000 m.). *Service ceiling:* 20,997 ft. (6,400 m.). *Endurance:* 4 hr. 30 min.

A.E.G. C.IV (Germany)

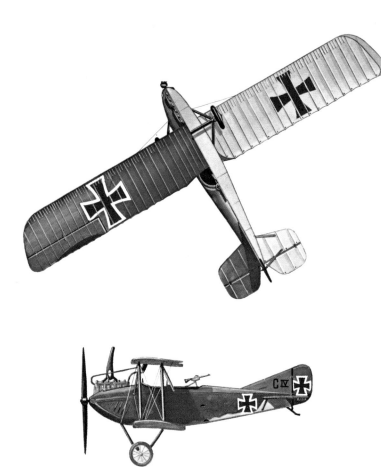

22

A.E.G. C.IV of the Imperial German Military Aviation Service, 1916. *Engine:* One 160 h.p. Mercedes D.III water-cooled in-line. *Span:* 44 ft. 1$\frac{7}{8}$ in. (13·46 m.). *Length:* 23 ft. 5$\frac{1}{2}$ in. (7·15 m.). *Wing area:* 419·8 sq.ft. (39·00 sq.m.). *Take-off weight:* 2,469 lb. (1,120 kg.). *Maximum speed:* 98·2 m.p.h. (158 km./hr.) at sea level. *Service ceiling:* 16,404 ft. (5,000 m.). *Endurance:* 4 hr. 0 min.

HALBERSTADT C.V (Germany)

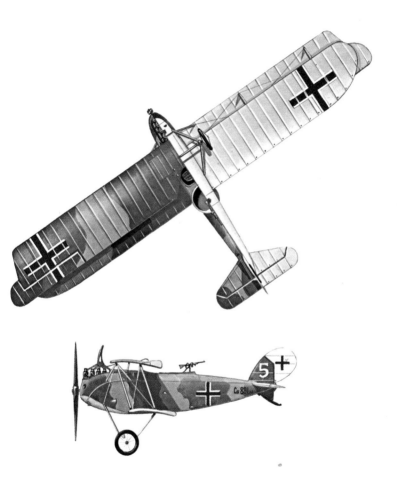

23

Halberstadt (possibly Aviatik-built) C.V of the Imperial German Military Aviation Service, *ca.* summer 1918. *Engine:* One 220 h.p. Benz Bz.IV water-cooled in-line. *Span:* 44 ft. 8⅓ in. (13·62 m.). *Length:* 22 ft. 8½ in. (6·92 m.). *Wing area:* 462·8 sq.ft. (43·00 sq.m.). *Take-off weight:* 3,009 lb. (1,365 kg.). *Maximum speed:* 105·6 m.p.h. (170 km./hr.) at sea level. *Service ceiling:* 16,404 ft. (5,000 m.). *Endurance:* 3 hr. 30 min.

RUMPLER C.IV (Germany)

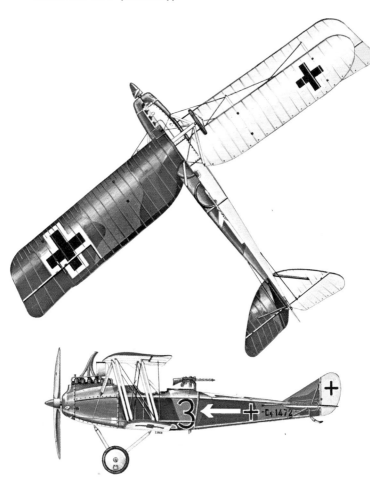

24

Rumpler C.IV of the Imperial German Military Aviation Service, late 1917. *Engine:* One 260 h.p. Mercedes D.IVa water-cooled in-line. *Span:* 41 ft. 6⅜ in. (12·66 m.). *Length:* 27 ft. 7⅛ in. (8·41 m.). *Wing area:* 360·6 sq.ft. (33·50 sq.m.). *Take-off weight:* 3,373 lb. (1,530 kg.). *Maximum speed:* 106·3 m.p.h. (171 km./hr.) at 1,640 ft. (500 m.). *Service ceiling:* 20,997 ft. (6,400 m.). *Endurance:* 3 hr. 30 min.

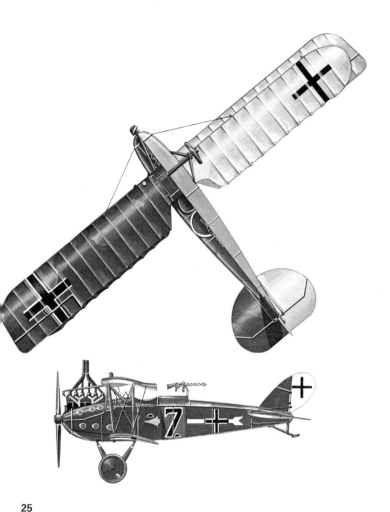

25

L.V.G. C.VI of the Imperial German Military Aviation Service, 1918. *Engine:* One 200 h.p. Benz Bz.IV water-cooled in-line. *Span:* 42 ft. $7\frac{3}{4}$ in. (13·00 m.). *Length:* 24 ft. $5\frac{1}{3}$ in. (7·45 m.). *Wing area:* 372·4 sq.ft. (34·60 sq.m.). *Take-off weight:* 2,888 lb. (1,310 kg.). *Maximum speed:* 105·6 m.p.h. (170 km./hr.) at sea level. *Service ceiling:* 21,325 ft. (6,500 m.). *Endurance:* 3 hr. 30 min.

ALBATROS C.XII (Germany)

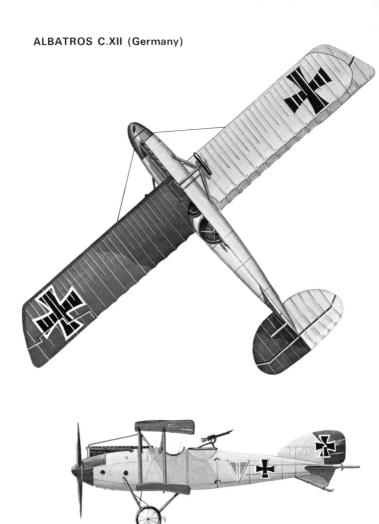

26

Albatros C.XII of the Imperial German Military Aviation Service, 1918. *Engine:* One 260 h.p. Mercedes D.IVa water-cooled in-line. *Span:* 47 ft. 1¾ in. (14·37 m.). *Length:* 29 ft. 0⅜ in. (8·85 m.). *Wing area:* 459·6 sq.ft. (42·70 sq.m.). *Take-off weight:* 3,616 lb. (1,640 kg.). *Maximum speed:* 108·7 m.p.h. (175 km./hr.) at sea level. *Service ceiling:* 16,404 ft. (5,000 m.). *Endurance:* 3 hr. 15 min.

ROLAND C.II (Germany)

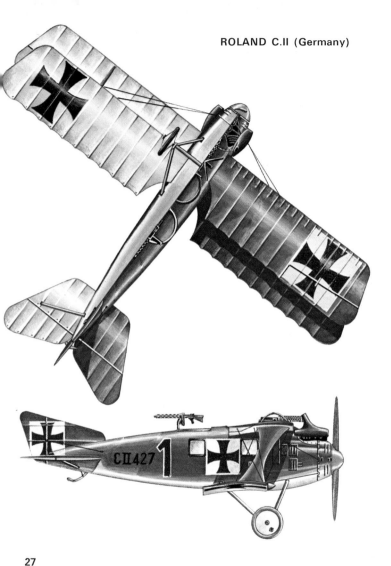

27

L.F.G. (Roland)-built C.II of an unidentified *Feld Flieger Abteilung,* Imperial German Military Aviation Service, Western Front, late 1916. *Engine:* One 160 h.p. Mercedes D.III water-cooled in-line. *Span:* 33 ft. 10¾ in. (10·33 m.). *Length:* 24 ft. 8⅛ in. (7·52 m.). *Wing area:* 279·9 sq.ft. (26·00 sq.m.). *Take-off weight:* 2,886 lb. (1,309 kg.). *Maximum speed:* 102·5 m.p.h. (165 km./hr.) at sea level. *Service ceiling:* 13,123 ft. (4,000 m.). *Endurance:* 4 hr. 0 min.

PHÖNIX C.I (Austro-Hungary)

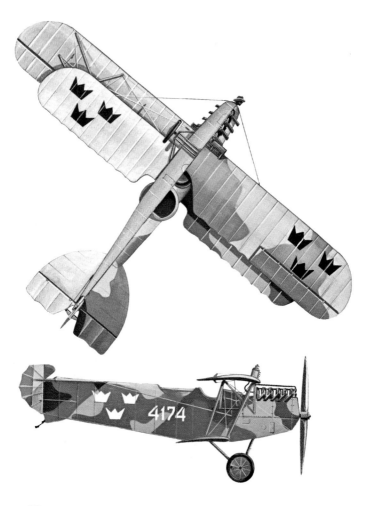

28

Swedish-built C.I *(Phönix-Dront)* of the Royal Swedish Army Aviation, 1919. *Engine:* One 220 h.p. Benz Bz.IV water-cooled in-line. *Span:* 36 ft. $1\frac{1}{8}$ in. (11·00 m.). *Length:* 24 ft. $8\frac{1}{8}$ in. (7·52 m.). *Wing area:* approx. 249·2 sq.ft. (23·15 sq.m.). *Take-off weight:* 2,436 lb. (1,105 kg.). *Maximum speed:* 110 m.p.h. (177 km./hr.) at sea level. *Service ceiling:* 17,716 ft. (5,400 m.). *Endurance:* approx. 3 hr. 30 min.

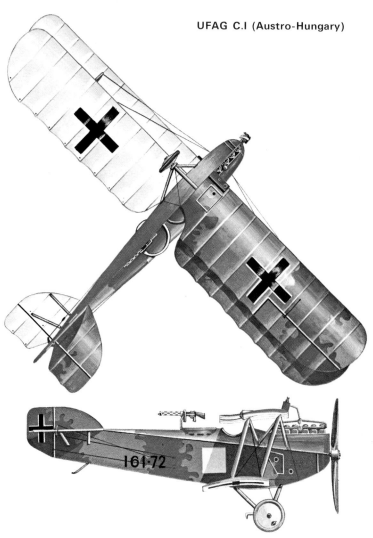

UFAG C.I (Austro-Hungary)

29

Ufag-built C.I of the Austro-Hungarian Air Service, *ca.* autumn 1918. *Engine:*
One 230 h.p. Hiero water-cooled in-line. *Span:* 35 ft. 2 in. (10·72 m.). *Length:*
23 ft. 7½ in. (7·20 m.). *Wing area:* approx. 290·6 sq.ft. (27·00 sq.m.). *Take-off
weight:* approx. 2,315 lb. (1,050 kg.). *Maximum speed:* 118·1 m.p.h. (190
km./hr.) at sea level. *Service ceiling:* 16,076 ft. (4,900 m.). *Endurance:* approx.
3 hr. 30 min.

ANATRA DS (Russia)

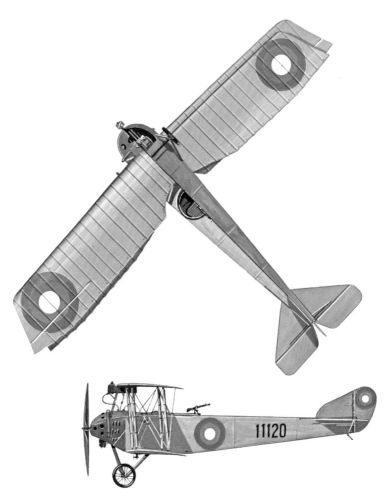

30

Anatra DS of the Imperial Russian Air Service, *ca.* spring 1917. *Engine:* One 150 h.p. Salmson (Canton-Unné) water-cooled radial. *Span:* 37 ft. $5\frac{1}{2}$ in. (11·42 m.). *Length:* 26 ft. $6\frac{7}{8}$ in. (8·10 m.). *Wing area:* 398·3 sq.ft. (37·00 sq.m.). *Take-off weight:* 2,566 lb. (1,164 kg.). *Maximum speed:* 89·5 m.p.h. (144 km./hr.) at sea level. *Service ceiling:* 14,108 ft. (4,300 m.). *Endurance:* 3 hr. 30 min.

JUNKERS J.I (Germany)

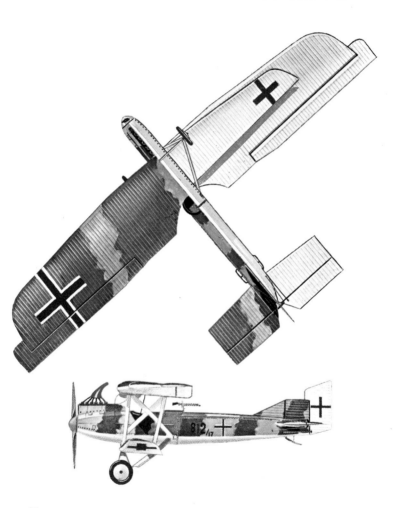

31

Junkers J.I of the Imperial German Military Aviation Service, *ca.* early 1918.
Engine: One 200 h.p. Benz Bz.IV water-cooled in-line. *Span:* 52 ft. $5\frac{7}{8}$ in.
(16·00 m.). *Length:* 29 ft. $10\frac{1}{4}$ in. (9·10 m.). *Wing area:* 531·7 sq.ft. (49·40
sq.m.). *Take-off weight:* 4,797 lb. (2,176 kg.). *Maximum speed:* 96·3 m.p.h.
(155 km./hr.) at sea level. *Operational ceiling:* approx. 5,000 ft. (1,524 m.).
Range: 193 miles (310 km.).

ANSALDO S.V.A.5 (Italy)

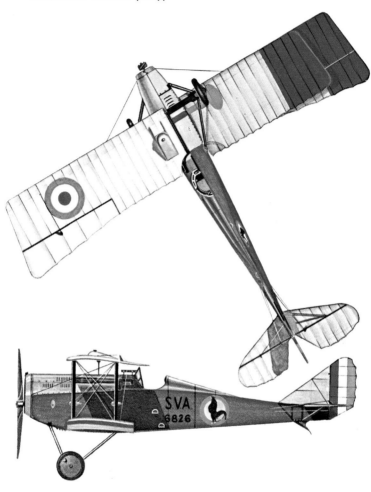

32

Ansaldo S.V.A.5 of the 3° *Gruppo Aeroplani, Corpo Aeronautica Militare,* Italian Front, June 1918. *Engine:* One 220 h.p. SPA 6A water-cooled in-line. *Span:* 30 ft. 1½ in. (9·18 m.). *Length:* 26 ft. 8 in. (8·13 m.). *Take-off weight:* 2,150 lb. (975 kg.). *Maximum speed:* 136·7 m.p.h. (220 km./hr.) at sea level. *Service ceiling:* 16,404 ft. (5,000 m.). *Endurance:* 6 hr. 0 min.

S.I.A. 7B (Italy)

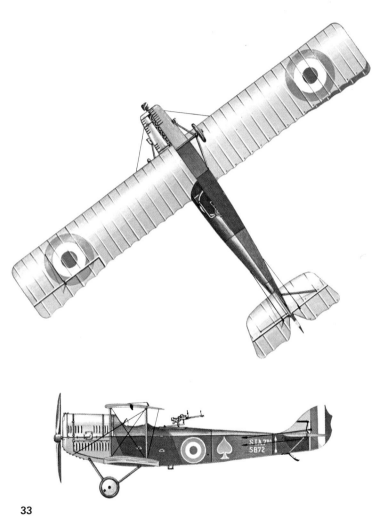

33

S.I.A. 7B.1 of the *Corpo Aeronautica Militare, ca.* December 1917. *Engine:*
One 260 h.p. Fiat A-12 water-cooled in-line. *Span:* 43 ft. 8⅜ in. (13·32 m.).
Length: 29 ft. 8⅔ in. (9·06 m.). *Wing area:* 430·6 sq.ft. (40·00 sq.m.). *Take-off
weight:* 2,425 lb. (1,100 kg.). *Maximum speed:* 124·3 m.p.h. (200 km./hr.)
at sea level. *Service ceiling:* 22,966 ft. (7,000 m.). *Endurance:* 4 hr. 0 min.

POMILIO PE (Italy)

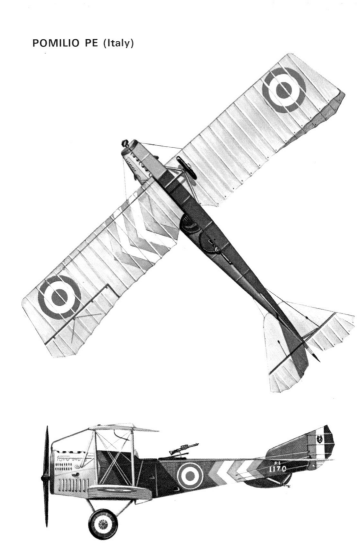

34

Pomilio PE of the *Corpo Aeronautica Militare, ca.* spring 1918. *Engine:* One 300 h.p. Fiat A-12*bis* water-cooled in-line. *Span:* 38 ft. 8⅝ in. (11·80 m.). *Length:* 29 ft. 4 in. (8·94 m.). *Wing area:* 495·1 sq.ft. (46·00 sq.m.). *Take-off weight:* 3,388 lb. (1,537 kg.). *Maximum speed:* 120·5 m.p.h. (194 km./hr.) at sea level. *Service ceiling:* 16,404 ft. (5,000 m.). *Endurance:* 3 hr. 30 min.

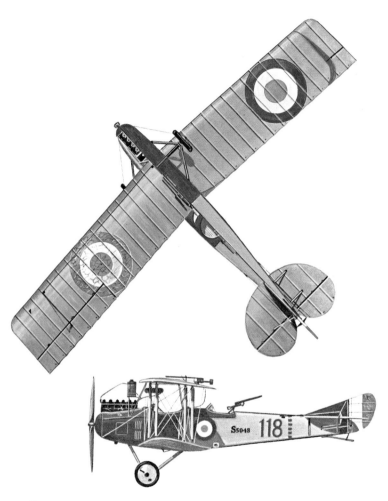

35

SAML S.2 of the 118a *Squadriglia da Ricognizione, Corpo Aeronautica Militare,* Middle East, *ca.* late 1917. *Engine:* One 300 h.p. Fiat A-12*bis* water-cooled in-line. *Span:* 39 ft. 8$\frac{3}{8}$ in. (12·10 m.). *Length:* 27 ft. 10$\frac{2}{3}$ in. (8·50 m.). *Wing area:* 419·8 sq.ft. (39·00 sq.m.). *Take-off weight:* 3,075 lb. (1,395 kg.). *Maximum speed:* 100·7 m.p.h. (162 km./hr.) at sea level. *Service ceiling:* approx. 16,404 ft. (5,000 m.). *Endurance:* 3 hr. 30 min.

B.E.2b (U.K.)

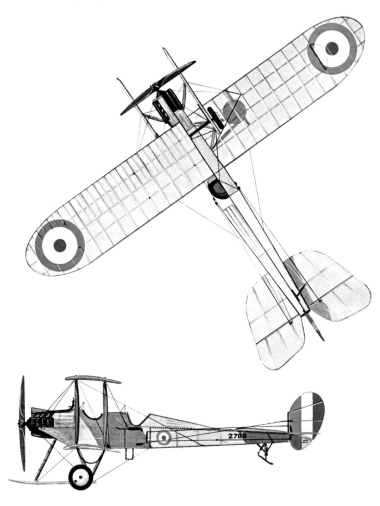

36

Joucques-built B.E.2b, possibly an aircraft of No. 16 Reserve Squadron R.F.C., Beaulieu, late 1916. *Engine:* One 70 h.p. Renault air-cooled Vee-type. *Span:* 35 ft. 0½ in. (10·68 m.). *Length:* 29 ft. 6½ in. (9·00 m.). *Wing area:* 352·0 sq.ft. (32·70 sq.m.). *Take-off weight:* 1,600 lb. (726 kg.). *Maximum speed:* 70 m.p.h. (112·7 km./hr.) at sea level. *Service ceiling:* 10,000 ft. (3,048 m.). *Endurance:* 3 hr. 0 min. *(Weight and performance data are for basically similar B.E.2a).*

B.E.2c (U.K.)

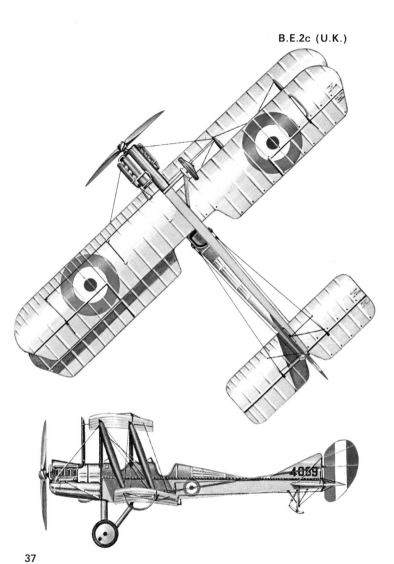

37

Bristol-built B.E.2c of No. 13 Squadron R.F.C., prior to leaving for France, October 1915. *Engine:* One 90 h.p. R.A.F.1a air-cooled Vee-type. *Span:* 37 ft. 0 in. (11·28 m.). *Length:* 27 ft. 3 in. (8·31 m.). *Wing area:* 371·0 sq.ft. (34·47 sq.m.). *Take-off weight:* 2,142 lb. (972 kg.). *Maximum speed:* 72 m.p.h. (115·9 km./hr.) at 6,500 ft. (1,981 m.). *Service ceiling:* 10,000 ft. (3,048 m.). *Endurance:* 3 hr. 15 min.

B.E.2e (U.K.)

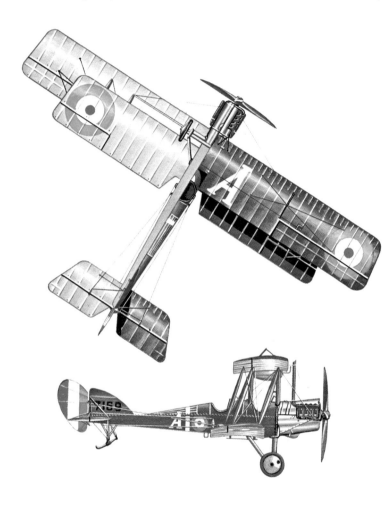

38

Bristol-built B.E.2e of an unknown R.F.C. squadron, France, October 1916. *Engine:* One 90 h.p. R.A.F.1a air-cooled Vee-type. *Span:* 40 ft. 9 in. (12·42 m.). *Length:* 27 ft. 3 in. (8·31 m.). *Wing area:* 360·0 sq.ft. (33·46 sq.m.). *Take-off weight:* 2,100 lb. (953 kg.). *Maximum speed:* 82 m.p.h. (132 km./hr.) at 6,500 ft. (1,981 m.). *Service ceiling:* 10,000 ft. (3,048 m.). *Endurance:* 4 hr. 0 min.

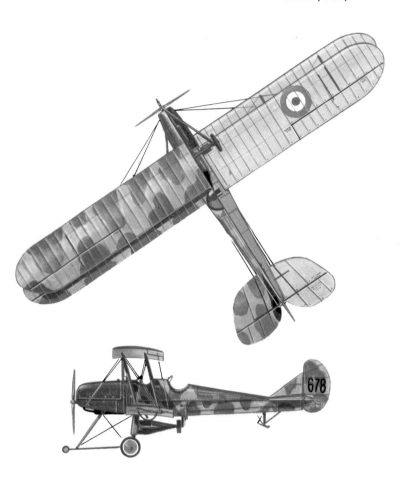

39

Royal Aircraft Factory-built R.E.5, possibly an aircraft of No. 7 Squadron R.F.C., France, *ca*. April/May 1915. *Engine:* One 120 h.p. Beardmore-built Austro-Daimler water-cooled in-line. *Span:* 44 ft. 6 in. (13·56 m.). *Length:* 26 ft. 2 in. (7·98 m.). *Wing area:* 400·0 sq.ft. (37·16 sq.m.). *Typical take-off weight:* 2,300 lb. (1,043 kg.). *Maximum speed:* 78 m.p.h. (125·5 km./hr.) at sea level. *Service ceiling:* 15,000 ft. (4,572 m.). *Endurance:* 4 hr. 30 min.

R.E.7 (U.K.)

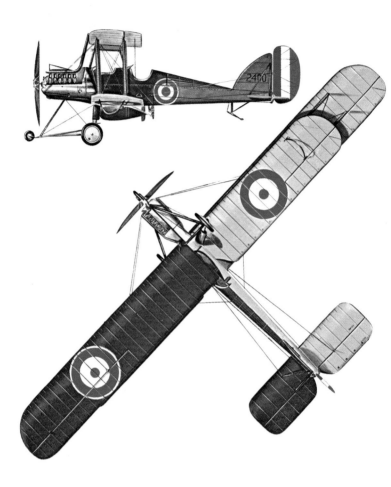

40

Siddeley-Deasy-built R.E.7 at the Royal Aircraft Factory, Farnborough, 1915, with 336-lb. bomb. *Engine:* One 150 h.p. R.A.F.4a air-cooled Vee-type. *Span:* 57 ft. 0 in. (17·37 m.). *Length:* 31 ft. 10½ in. (9·72 m.). *Wing area:* 548.0 sq.ft. (50·91 sq.m.). *Take-off weight:* 3,449 lb. (1,564 kg.). *Maximum speed:* 84·9 m.p.h. (136·6 km./hr.) at sea level. *Service ceiling:* 6,500 ft. (1,981 m.). *Endurance:* 6 hr. 0 min.

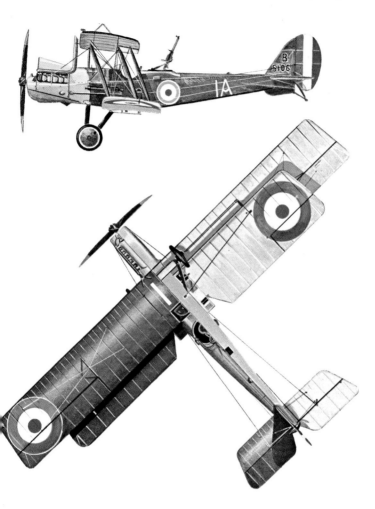

41

Daimler-built R.E.8 of 'A' Flight, No. 59 Squadron R.A.F., Vert Galand, May 1918. *Engine:* One 150 h.p. R.A.F.4a air-cooled Vee-type. *Span:* 42 ft. 7 in. (12·98 m.). *Length:* 27 ft. 10½ in. (8·50 m.). *Wing area:* 377·5 sq.ft. (35·07 sq.m.). *Take-off weight:* 2,678 lb. (1,215 kg.). *Maximum speed:* 102 m.p.h. (164·2 km./hr.) at 6,500 ft. (1,981 m.). *Service ceiling:* 13,500 ft. (4,115 m.). *Endurance:* 4 hr. 15 min.

1½-STRUTTER (U.K.)

42

Sopwith-built Type 9700 (converted from Type 9400) of No. 3 Wing R.N.A.S., Luxeuil, France, *ca.* September 1916. *Engine:* One 130 h.p. Clerget 9 B rotary. *Span:* 33 ft. 6 in. (10·21 m.). *Length:* 25 ft. 3 in. (7·70 m.). *Wing area:* 346·0 sq.ft. (32·14 sq.m.). *Take-off weight:* 2,342 lb. (1,062 kg.). *Maximum speed:* 102 m.p.h. (164·2 km./hr.) at 6,500 ft. (1,981 m.). *Service ceiling:* 13,000 ft. (3,962 m.). *Endurance:* approx. 4 hr. 0 min.

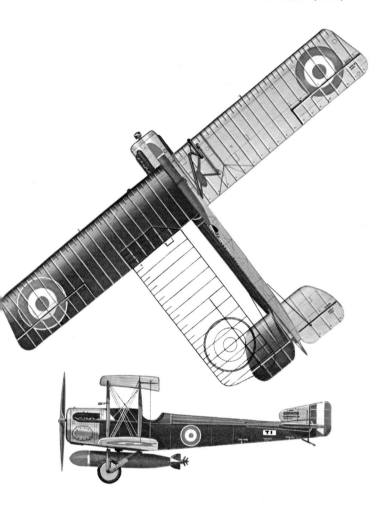

43

Sopwith T.1 Cuckoo prototype in R.N.A.S. colours, at the Isle of Grain, July 1917. *Engine:* One 200 h.p. Hispano-Suiza water-cooled Vee-type. *Span:* 46 ft. 9 in. (14·25 m.). *Length:* 28 ft. 6 in. (8·69 m.). *Wing area:* 566·0 sq.ft. (52·58 sq.m.). *Take-off weight:* 3,572 lb. (1,620 kg.). *Maximum speed:* 103·5 m.p.h. (166·6 km./hr.) at 6,500 ft. (1,981 m.). *Service ceiling:* 15,600 ft. (4,755 m.). *Endurance:* 3 hr. 45 min.

D.H.4 (U.K.)

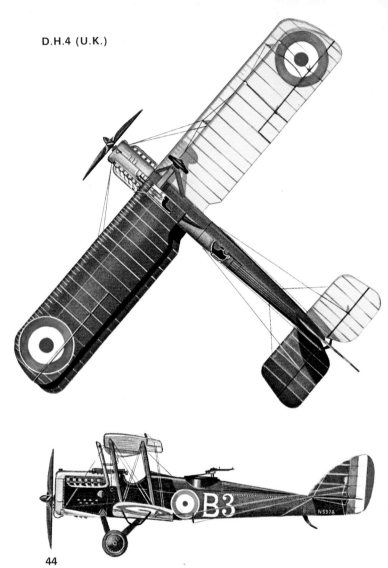

44

Westland-built D.H.4 of No. 5 Wing R.N.A.S., Dunkirk, *ca.* summer 1917. *Engine:* One 250 h.p. Rolls-Royce III (Eagle III) water-cooled Vee-type. *Span:* 42 ft. 4⅝ in. (12·92 m.). *Length:* 30 ft. 8 in. (9·35 m.). *Wing area:* 434·0 sq.ft. (40·32 sq.m.). *Take-off weight:* 3,313 lb. (1,503 kg.). *Maximum speed:* 117 m.p.h. (188·3 km./hr.) at 6,500 ft. (1,981 m.). *Service ceiling:* 16,000 ft. (4,877 m.). *Endurance:* 3 hr. 30 min.

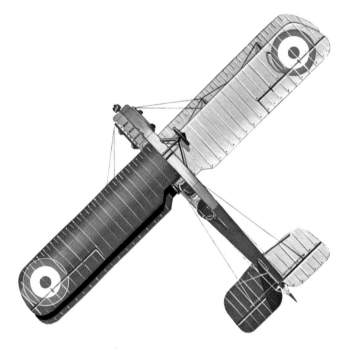

45

Mann, Egerton-built D.H.9A of No. 205 Squadron R.A.F., autumn 1918.
Engine: One 400 h.p. Liberty 12 water-cooled Vee-type. *Span:* 45 ft. $11\frac{1}{2}$
in. (14·00 m.). *Length:* 30 ft. 3 in. (9·22 m.). *Wing area:* 434·0 sq.ft. (40·32
sq.m.). *Take-off weight:* 4,645 lb. (2,107 kg.). *Maximum speed:* 123 m.p.h.
(197·9 km./hr.) at sea level. *Service ceiling:* 16,750 ft. (5,105 m.). *Endurance:*
5 hr. 15 min.

F.K.8 (U.K.)

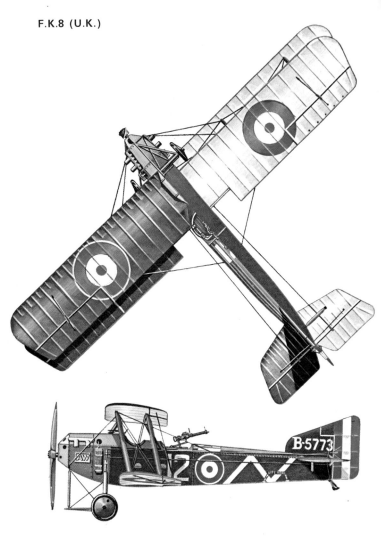

46

Armstrong Whitworth-built F.K.8 flown by 2nd Lt. A. A. McLeod and Lt. A. W. Hammond of No. 2 Squadron R.F.C., France, March 1918. *Engine:* One 160 h.p. Beardmore water-cooled in-line. *Span:* 43 ft. 6 in. (13·26 m.). *Length:* 31 ft. 0 in. (9·45 m.). *Wing area:* 540·0 sq.ft. (50·17 sq.m.). *Take-off weight:* 2,811 lb. (1,275 kg.). *Maximum speed:* 93 m.p.h. (149·7 km./hr.) at 8,000 ft. (2,438 m.). *Service ceiling:* 13,000 ft. (3.962 m.). *Endurance:* 3 hr. 0 min.

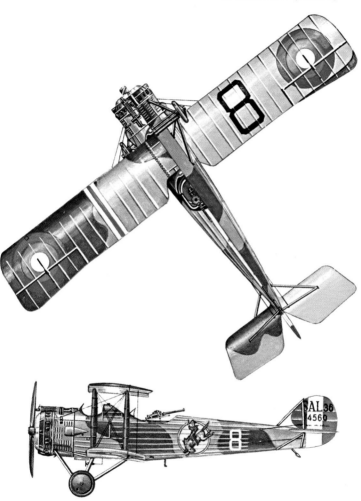

47

Salmson 2A.2 of the 88th Aero Squadron, 1st Observation Group of the American Expeditionary Force, Marne, August 1918. *Engine:* One 260 h.p. Salmson (Canton-Unné) 9 Z water-cooled radial. *Span:* 38 ft. 6½ in. (11·75 m.). *Length:* 27 ft. 10⅔ in. (8·50 m.). *Wing area:* 401·2 sq.ft. (37·27 sq.m.). *Take-off weight:* 2,954 lb. (1,340 kg.). *Maximum speed:* 116 m.p.h. (187 km./hr.) at sea level. *Service ceiling:* 20,505 ft. (6,250 m.). *Endurance:* 3 hr. 0 min.

SPAD XI (France)

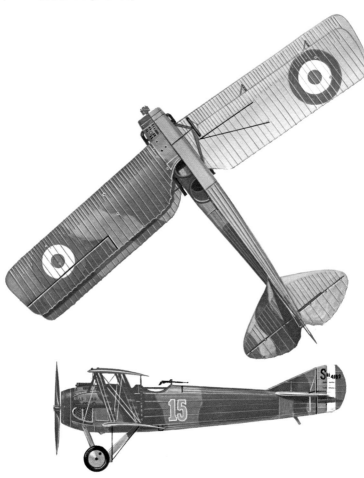

48

Spad XIA.2 of the French *Aviation Militaire,* early 1918. *Engine:* One 235 h.p. Hispano-Suiza 8 Bc water-cooled Vee-type. *Span:* 36 ft. $10\frac{1}{8}$ in. (11·23 m.). *Length:* 25 ft. $5\frac{1}{8}$ in. (7·75 m.). *Wing area:* approx. 307·8 sq.ft. (28·60 sq.m.). *Take-off weight:* 2,310 lb. (1,048 kg.). *Maximum speed:* 109·4 m.p.h. (176 km./hr.) at 6,562 ft. (2,000 m.). *Service ceiling:* 22,966 ft. (7,000 m.). *Endurance:* 2 hr. 15 min.

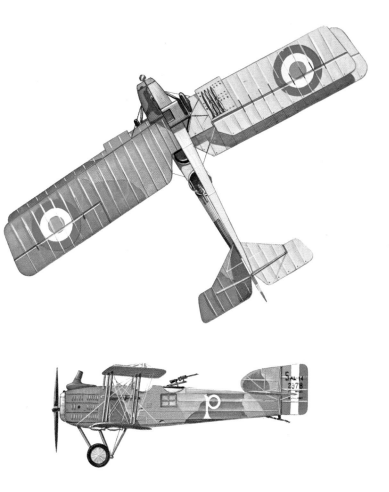

49

Breguet Br.14B.2 of an unidentified *Escadrille de Bombardement,* French *Aviation Militaire,* late 1917/early 1918. *Engine:* One 300 h.p. Renault 12 Fcx water-cooled Vee-type. *Span:* 47 ft. 1½ in. (14·364 m.). *Length:* 29 ft. 1¼ in. (8·87 m.). *Wing area:* 540·3 sq.ft. (50·20 sq.m.). *Take-off weight:* 3,891 lb. (1,765 kg.). *Maximum speed:* 110 m.p.h. (177 km./hr.) at 6,562 ft. (2,000 m.). *Service ceiling:* 19,029 ft. (5,800 m.). *Endurance:* 2 hr. 45 min.

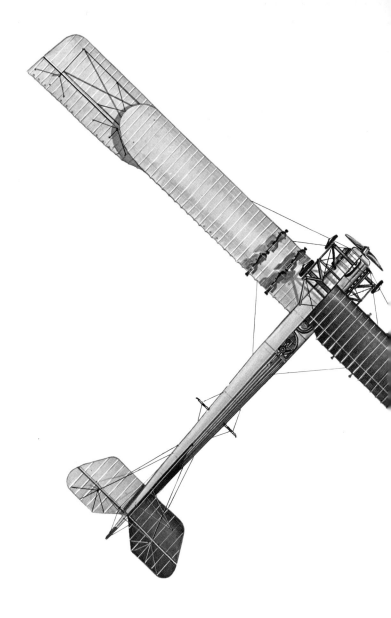

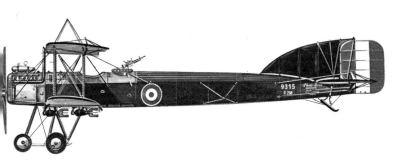

50

Short-built Bomber, possibly an aircraft of No. 7 Squadron R.N.A.S., Belgium, *ca.* late summer 1916. *Engine:* One 250 h.p. Rolls-Royce Eagle III water-cooled Vee-type. *Span:* 85 ft. 0 in. (25·91 m.). *Length:* 45 ft. 0 in. (13·72 m.). *Wing area:* 870·0 sq.ft. (80·83 sq.m.). *Take-off weight:* 6,800 lb. (3,084 kg.). *Maximum speed:* 77·5 m.p.h. (124·7 km./hr.) at 6,500 ft. (1,981 m.). *Service ceiling:* 9,500 ft. (2,896 m.). *Endurance:* 6 hr. 0 min.

LETORD TYPE 5 (France)

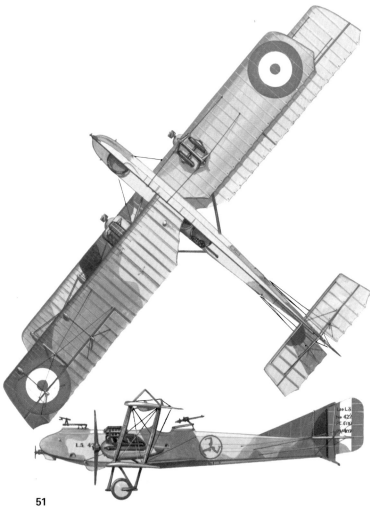

51

Letord Type 5 of the French *Aviation Militaire, ca.* late spring/early summer 1917. *Engines:* Two 220 h.p. Lorraine-Dietrich 8 Fb Vee-type. *Span:* 59 ft. 0¾ in. (18·00 m.). *Length:* 36 ft. 7¾ in. (11·17 m.). *Wing area:* 669·5 sq.ft. (62·20 sq.m.). *Take-off weight:* 5,390 lb. (2,445 kg.). *Maximum speed:* 99·4 m.p.h. (160 km./hr.) at 6,562 ft. (2,000 m.). *Service ceiling:* 16,404 ft. (5,000 m.). *Endurance:* 3 hr. 0 min.

CAUDRON R.11 (France)

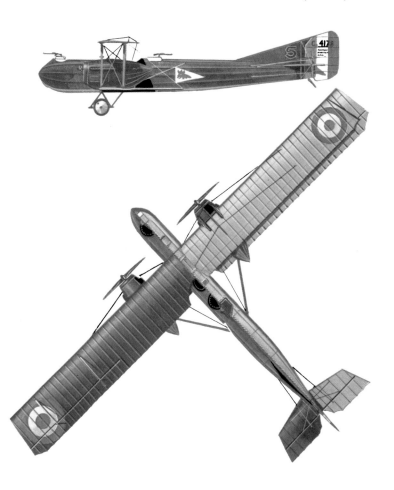

52

Caudron R.11 Bn.3 of the French *Aviation Militaire, ca.* summer 1918. *Engines:*
Two 215 h.p. Hispano-Suiza 8 Bdawater-cooled Vee-type. *Span:* 58 ft. 9½
in. (17·92 m.). *Length:* 36 ft. 9¾ in (11·22 m.). *Wing area:* 583·9 sq.ft. (54·25
sq.m.). *Take-off weight:* 4,773 lb. (2,165 kg.). *Maximum speed:* 113·7 m.p.h.
(183 km./hr.) at 6,562 ft. (2,000 m.). *Service ceiling:* 19,521 ft. (5,950 m.).
Endurance: 3 hr. 0 min.

53

A.E.G. G.IV of the Imperial German Military Aviation Service shot down by the French, May 1918. *Engines:* Two 260 h.p. Mercedes D.IVa water-cooled in-line. *Span:* 60 ft. 2¾ in. (18·35 m.). *Length:* 32 ft. 3¾ in. (9·85 m.). *Wing area:* 721·2 sq.ft. (67·00 sq.m.). *Take-off weight:* 8,003 lb. (3,630 kg.). *Maximum speed:* 90·1 m.p.h. (145 km./hr.) at 4,921 ft. (1,500 m.). *Service ceiling:* 13,123 ft. (4,000 m.). *Endurance:* approx. 4 hr. 30 min.

O/400 (U.K.)

54

Handley Page O/400 of the R.N.A.S., early 1918. *Engines:* Two 360 h.p. Rolls-Royce Eagle VIII water-cooled Vee-type. *Span:* 100 ft. 0 in. (30·48 m.). *Length:* 62 ft. 10¼ in. (19·16 m.). *Wing area:* 1,648·0 sq.ft. (153·10 sq.m.). *Take-off weight:* 13,360 lb. (6,060 kg.). *Maximum speed:* 97·5 m.p.h. (156·9 km./hr.) at sea level. *Service ceiling:* 8,500 ft. (2,591 m.). *Endurance:* 8 hr. 0 min.

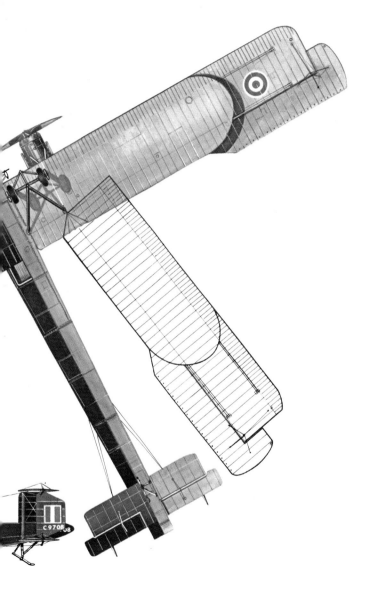

V/1500 (U.K.)

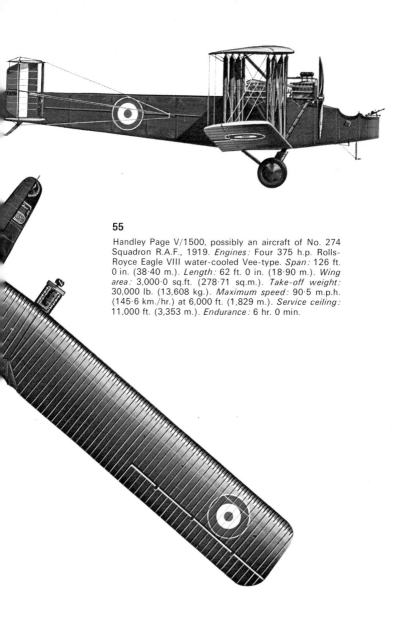

55

Handley Page V/1500, possibly an aircraft of No. 274 Squadron R.A.F., 1919. *Engines:* Four 375 h.p. Rolls-Royce Eagle VIII water-cooled Vee-type. *Span:* 126 ft. 0 in. (38·40 m.). *Length:* 62 ft. 0 in. (18·90 m.). *Wing area:* 3,000·0 sq.ft. (278·71 sq.m.). *Take-off weight:* 30,000 lb. (13,608 kg.). *Maximum speed:* 90·5 m.p.h. (145·6 km./hr.) at 6,000 ft. (1,829 m.). *Service ceiling:* 11,000 ft. (3,353 m.). *Endurance:* 6 hr. 0 min.

56

Vickers-built Vimy IV prototype (see text) as tested at Martlesham Heath, October 1918. *Engines:* Two 360 h.p. Rolls-Royce Eagle VIII water-cooled Vee-type. *Span:* 68 ft. 0 in. (20·73 m.). *Length:* 43 ft. 6½ in. (13·27 m.). *Wing area:* 1,330·0 sq.ft. (123·56 sq.m.). *Take-off weight:* 12,500 lb. (5,670 kg.). *Maximum speed:* 103 m.p.h. (165·8 km./hr.) at sea level. *Service ceiling:* 7,000 ft. (2,314 m.). *Range:* approx. 900 miles (1,448 km.).

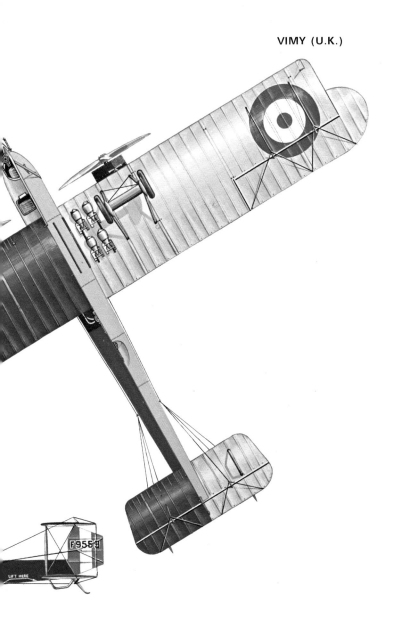

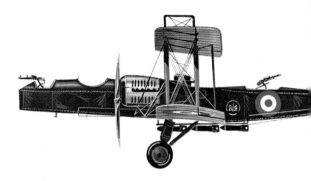

57

Blackburn-built Kangaroo, believed to be an aircraft of No. 246 Squadron, R.A.F. Seaton Carew, April 1918. *Engines:* Two 255 h.p. Rolls-Royce Falcon II water-cooled Vee-type. *Span:* 74 ft. 10$\frac{1}{4}$ in. (22·82 m.). *Length:* 46 ft. 0 in. (14·02 m.). *Wing area:* 880·0 sq.ft. (81·75 sq.m.). *Take-off weight:* 8,017 lb. (3,636 kg.). *Maximum speed:* 100 m.p.h. (160·9 km./hr.) at sea level. *Service ceiling:* 10,500 ft. (3,200 m.). *Endurance:* 8 hr. 0 min.

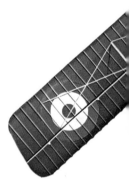

KANGAROO (U.K.)

81

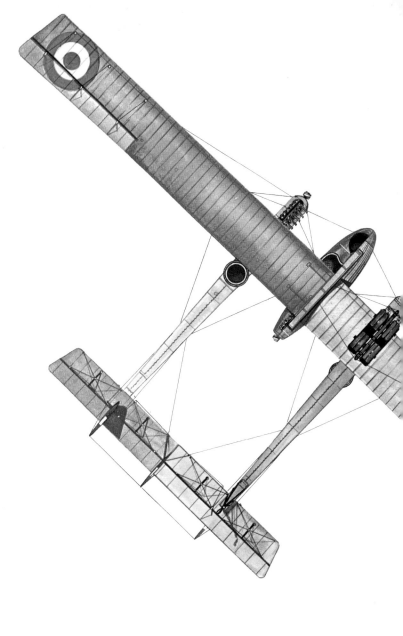

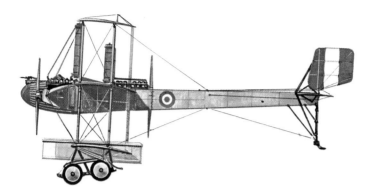

58

Caproni Ca 4 (Ca 42) of the *Corpo Aeronautica Militare,* 1918. *Engines:* Three 270 h.p. Isotta-Fraschini water-cooled Vee-type. *Span:* 98 ft. 1$\frac{1}{8}$ in. (29·90 m.). *Length:* 49 ft. 6$\frac{1}{2}$ in. (15·10 m.). *Wing area:* 2,152·8 sq.ft. (200·00 sq.m.). *Take-off weight:* 16,535 lb. (7,500 kg.). *Maximum speed:* 87 m.p.h. (140 km./hr.) at sea level. *Service ceiling:* 9,843 ft. (3,000 m.). *Endurance:* 7 hr. 0 min.

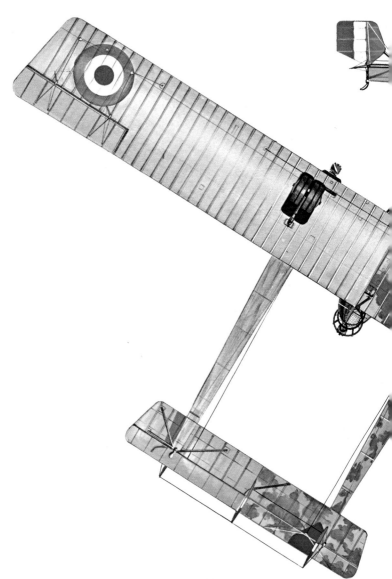

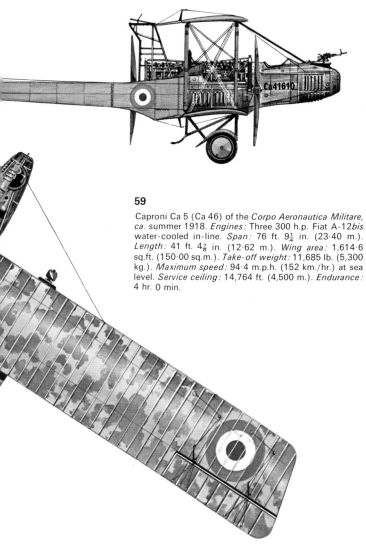

CAPRONI Ca 5 (Italy)

59

Caproni Ca 5 (Ca 46) of the *Corpo Aeronautica Militare,*
ca. summer 1918. *Engines:* Three 300 h.p. Fiat A-12*bis*
water-cooled in-line. *Span:* 76 ft. $9\frac{1}{4}$ in. (23·40 m.).
Length: 41 ft. $4\frac{7}{8}$ in. (12·62 m.). *Wing area:* 1,614·6
sq.ft. (150·00 sq.m.). *Take-off weight:* 11,685 lb. (5,300
kg.). *Maximum speed:* 94·4 m.p.h. (152 km./hr.) at sea
level. *Service ceiling:* 14,764 ft. (4,500 m.). *Endurance:*
4 hr. 0 min.

SIEMENS-SCHUCKERT R.I (Germany)

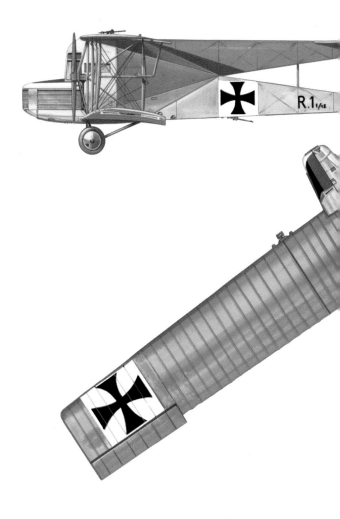

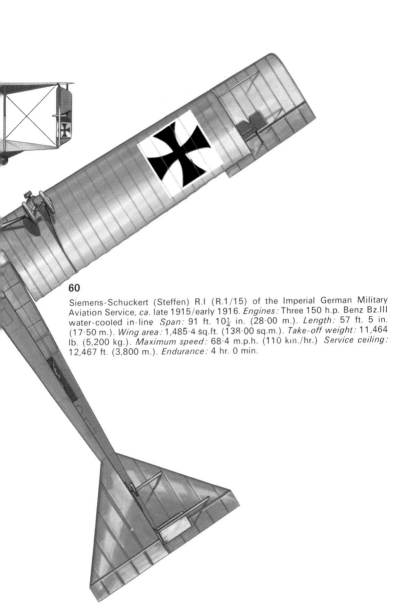

60

Siemens-Schuckert (Steffen) R.I (R.1/15) of the Imperial German Military Aviation Service, *ca.* late 1915/early 1916. *Engines:* Three 150 h.p. Benz Bz.III water-cooled in-line *Span:* 91 ft. 10¼ in. (28·00 m.). *Length:* 57 ft. 5 in. (17·50 m.). *Wing area:* 1,485·4 sq.ft. (138·00 sq.m.). *Take-off weight:* 11,464 lb. (5,200 kg.). *Maximum speed:* 68·4 m.p.h. (110 km./hr.) *Service ceiling:* 12,467 ft. (3,800 m.). *Endurance:* 4 hr. 0 min.

61

O.A.W.-built R.VI salvaged after crashing at Betz on 1 June 1918. *Engines:* Four 260 h.p. Mercedes D.IVa water-cooled in-line. *Span:* 138 ft. 5¾ in. (42·20 m.). *Length:* 72 ft. 6⅛ in. (22·10 m.). *Wing area:* 3,573·6 sq.ft. (332·00 sq.m.). *Take-off weight:* 25,265 lb. (11,460 kg.). *Maximum speed:* 80·8 m.p.h. (130 km./hr.) at sea level. *Service ceiling:* 12,467 ft. (3,800 m.). *Endurance:* 7–10 hr. according to load.

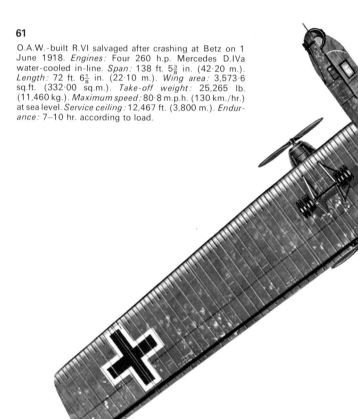

ZEPPELIN (STAAKEN) R.VI (Germany)

ILYA MOUROMETS (Russia)

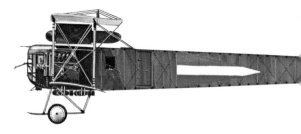

62

Sikorsky *Ilya Mouromets* Type V of the *Eskadra Vozdushnykh Korablei,* Imperial Russian Air Service, 1916. *Engines:* Four 150 h.p. Sunbeam water-cooled Vee-type. *Span:* 97 ft. 9$\frac{1}{8}$ in. (29·80 m.). *Length:* 57 ft. 5 in. (17·50 m.). *Wing area:* 1,345·5 sq.ft. (125·00 sq.m.). *Take-off weight:* 10,141 lb. (4,600 kg.). *Maximum speed:* 68·4 m.p.h. (110 km./hr.) at 6,562 ft. (2,000 m.). *Service ceiling:* 9,514 ft. (2,900 m.). *Endurance:* 4 hr. 0 min.

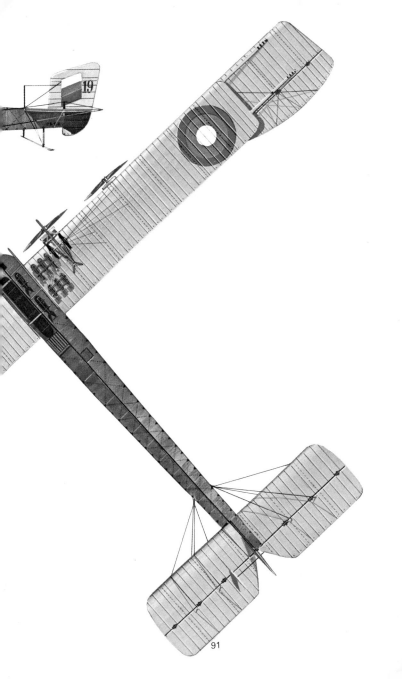

CAUDRON G.IV (France)

63

Caudron G.IVA.2 of the French *Aviation Militaire, ca.* spring 1916. *Engines:*
Two 80 h.p. Le Rhône 9 C rotaries. *Span:* 55 ft. 4½ in. (16·88 m.). *Length:*
23 ft. 7½ in. (7·20 m.). *Wing area:* 396·1 sq.ft. (36·80 sq.m.). *Take-off weight:*
2,910 lb. (1,320 kg.). *Maximum speed:* 81 m.p.h. (130 km./hr.) at sea level.
Service ceiling: 13,123 ft. (4,000 m.). *Endurance:* 4 hr. 0 min.

LOHNER L (Austro-Hungary)

64

Lohner L flown by Sub-Lt. Walter Zelezny of the Austro-Hungarian Navy, September 1916. *Engine:* One 160 h.p. Austro-Daimler water-cooled in-line. *Span:* 53 ft. 1¾ in. (16·20 m.). *Length:* 33 ft. 7⅞ in. (10·26 m.). *Wing area:* 570·5 sq.ft. (53·00 sq.m.). *Take-off weight:* 3,748 lb. (1,700 kg.). *Maximum speed:* 65·2 m.p.h. (105 km./hr.) at sea level. *Service ceiling:* 16,404 ft. (5,000 m.). *Endurance:* approx. 4 hr. 0 min.

F.B.A. Type C (France)

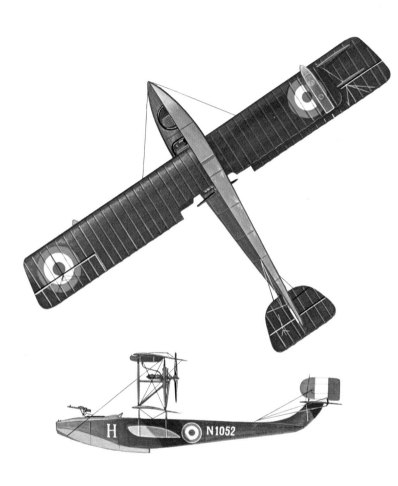

65

Norman Thompson-assembled F.B.A. Type C of the R.N.A.S., spring 1916.
Engine: One 130 h.p. Clerget rotary. *Span:* 44 ft. 11¾ in. (13·70 m.). *Length:*
28 ft. 10⅛ in. (8·79 m.). *Wing area:* 322·9 sq.ft. (30·00 sq.m.). *Take-off weight:*
2,072 lb. (940 kg.). *Maximum speed:* 68·4 m.p.h. (110 km./hr.) at sea level.
Service ceiling: approx. 11,483 ft. (3,500 m.). *Range:* 186 miles (300 km.).

66

Blackburn-built Baby of the R.N.A.S. coastal air station, Felixstowe, late 1917.
Engine: One 130 h.p. Clerget 9 B rotary. *Span:* 25 ft. 8 in. (7·82 m.). *Length:*
23 ft. 0 in. (7·01 m.). *Wing area:* 240·0 sq.ft. (22·30 sq.m.). *Take-off weight:*
1,715 lb. (778 kg.). *Maximum speed:* 98 m.p.h. (157·7 km./hr.) at sea level.
Service ceiling: approx. 7,600 ft. (2,316 m.). *Endurance:* 2 hr. 0 min.

FF33 (Germany)

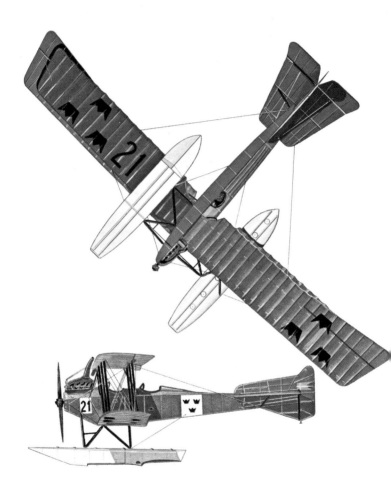

67

Friedrichshafen FF33J of the Royal Swedish Naval Aviation, 1919. *Engine:* One 150 h.p. Benz Bz.III water-cooled in-line. *Span:* 54 ft. 11½ in. (16·75 m.). *Length:* 34 ft. 3⅜ in. (10·30 m.). *Wing area:* 565·1 sq.ft. (52·50 sq.m.). *Take-off weight:* approx. 3,704 lb. (1,680 kg.). *Maximum speed:* 72·1 m.p.h. (116 km./hr.) at sea level. *Service ceiling:* approx. 11,485 ft. (3,500 m.). *Endurance:* 5 hr. 0 min.

1 Blériot XI

The frail-looking tractor monoplane in which Louis Blériot crossed the English Channel in July 1909 was developed, with more powerful Gnome rotary engines in place of the original 25 h.p. Anzani, into one of the foremost military and civil aeroplanes of the period before World War 1. Blériot XIs established various speed, height and endurance records during 1910–11, and their aerobatic capabilities were well demonstrated by Alphonse Pégoud, who successfully looped an aeroplane of this kind in 1913. Military Blériot XIs were in service in France and Italy from 1910, the latter seeing action with the Italian forces in North Africa in 1911. The R.F.C.'s Military and Naval Wings and, later, the R.N.A.S. received their first Blériots in 1912.

During the first year of World War 1 the Blériots were among the most widely used of Allied observation types. They served with at least eight escadrilles of the French Aviation Militaire, with Nos. 1, 3, 6, 7, 9 and 16 Squadrons R.F.C. in France, and when Italy entered the war in May 1915 her air force had six squadriglie equipped with Blériot XIs. There were five basic variants of the standard shoulder-wing monoplane. Two of them, the XI Militaire and XI Artillerie, were single-seaters with 50 h.p. Gnome engines; the XI-2 Artillerie and XI-2 Génie were 2-seaters with 70 h.p. Gnomes; and the 3-seat XI-3 had a 140 h.p. Gnome. They differed in such matters as undercarriage, elevators, rudders and control pylons. The single-seat XI Militaire and the XI-2 Génie also served with the Belgian Aviation Militaire. Some single-seat Militaires were flown as 'nuisance' bombers with up to 25 kg. (55 lb.) of small bombs carried along the sides of the fuselage. Rifles or revolvers were the only armament carried by the crew. In addition to those in front-line service, many Blériot XIs were used by the French, British and Italian air forces as training aircraft.

A parasol-winged version was designated XI-B.G.: this was flown by French escadrilles and by both British air services. A few floatplane Blériots are believed to have served with the British and Italian Navies.

Known British serial number allocations indicate that twenty-one parasol Blériots and up to forty-eight Blériot XIs of other kinds were in R.F.C. service; and sixteen parasols and twenty-six Blériot XIs with the R.N.A.S. In addition, there were allocations for ten (R.N.A.S.) and eleven (R.F.C.) 'Blériot tractor' aircraft, which may be assumed to have been aircraft of one type or the other.

2 Ago C types

The Ago Flugzeugwerke, formed in 1912 from the former Aerowerke Gustav Otto, produced its first C type biplane, the C.I, in mid-1915. This, and the later C.II and C.III, shared a similar configuration, being pusher-engined 2-seaters with two slender oval-section fuselage booms supporting the tail unit. The C.I, originally powered by a 150 h.p. Benz Bz.III and later by a 160 h.p.

Mercedes D.III, entered service in summer 1915 in small numbers on the Western Front. Designed by the Swiss engineer August Haefeli, it was characterised by having small, comma-type rudders and prominent H. & Z. side radiators on the nacelle, in the nose of which was mounted a free-firing Parabellum machine-gun for use by the observer. For a pusher type the C.I was quite fast and had an operational endurance of 4 hours. One example of a twin-float version, the C.IW, was delivered to the German Navy for evaluation. Late in 1915 the C.I was superseded by the C.II, which had the more powerful Benz Bz.IV engine with a wing radiator, small triangular fins and plain rudders and various other aerodynamic improvements. This remained in service throughout 1916 and the first half of 1917 and, like its predecessor, was a useful aeroplane with good handling qualities. A variant of the Ago C.II was built by Haefeli, at Thun in 1915–16, as the DH-1 for the Swiss Air Force. For reasons that remain unexplained, the Ago pushers seem to have acquired an early reputation for being much larger and more heavily manned and gunned than in fact they were. A version did exist, however, with an enlarged wing span of 18·30 m. (60 ft. 0½ in.), and a few of these were built in landplane and C.IIW floatplane forms for use by the German Navy. Conversely, the Ago C.III was a smaller edition, powered by a Mercedes D.III, but only a few of these were built.

Ago's next C type was the C.IV, and this departed completely from the previous designs in being a tractor biplane with equal-tapered, equal-span wings of identical pattern, double ailerons and very slight wing stagger. The C.IV was powered by a 220 h.p. Bz.IV engine, had a synchronised forward-firing Spandau gun for the pilot and a ring-mounted Parabellum gun in the observer's cockpit. The prototype bore a comma-type rudder only, but a small fixed fin was introduced on production aircraft, giving a continuously rounded tail contour. The Ago C.IV was a fast and efficient aeroplane of its type, but it entailed long and costly constructional methods that limited the number built. The maximum number of C.IVs in service at any time was seventy in September 1917; this is thought to represent little more than a quarter of the total output, some of which were subcontracted to Schütte-Lanz and Rathgeber. The C.VII and C.VIII were experimental developments of the C.IV with, respectively, revised wing bracing and a different engine installed. Neither went into quantity production.

3 Breguet 4 and 5

After a series of tractor aeroplanes Louis Breguet designed his BU3 (later BR54) prototype in mid-1914 as a pusher biplane in deference to official insistence that French 2-seater aircraft should carry their observers in front, where they had the maximum possible field of view and of fire. Powered originally by 200 h.p. Canton-Unné, and later by 220 h.p. Renault engines, one hundred aircraft of a slightly modified type were built by André and Edouard Michelin at their Clermont-Ferrand factory and presented to the Aviation Militaire. They were known as BUMs (with Canton-Unné engines), BLMs (with Renault engines) or simply as Breguet-Michelins, this last name also being applied to later developments from the design. In summer 1915 the French government issued a specification for a bomber capable of carrying a 300 kg. (661 lb.) load over a range of 600 km. (373 miles), and to meet this Breguet developed the BU3 into the SN3. The SN3 differed from the BU3 in having unequal-span wings and a modified undercarriage. It won the competition, which was held in October 1915, and in its production form was known as the Breguet Concours; military designations, applied later, were Type 4B.2 and Type 5Ca.2, the latter signifying a cannon armament. Both entered production early in 1916 at the Breguet and Michelin factories, with the 220 h.p. Renault 12 as their standard powerplant. The 4B.2 was armed with a single Hotchkiss or Lewis machine-gun in the front cockpit, and could carry up to forty 7·25 kg. bombs in Michelin automatic bomb racks beneath the lower wings outboard of the main landing wheels. The Breguet 5Ca.2 was basically similar, but mounted a 37 mm. cannon in the front cockpit and a rearward-firing machine-gun over the top wing. Its purpose was to act as escort for the 4B.2 bombers, but in practice the heavy cannon was usually replaced by a standard machine-gun. The Breguet Type 6 was a further development of the Type 4 with a 225 h.p. Salmson A9 radial engine and smaller radiators.

The Breguet pushers had a good range with a useful load, but required a long take-off, were difficult to land and were far too slow for day bombing. They were transferred to night operations from October 1916. The type served with at least five Escadrilles de Bombardement, one of which was still equipped with this type of Breguet in January 1918. The R.N.A.S. purchased approximately forty-six Breguets, of various models, from France; an additional thirty, with 250 h.p. Rolls-Royce engines, were ordered from Grahame-White Aviation under the designation G.W. XIX, but only ten of these were completed. British Breguets served with No. 3 Wing in France, and in the Aegean area.

4 **Voisin 1 to 6**
In spite of their frail appearance, the Voisin pusher biplanes, first designed in 1914, were in fact extremely weather-worthy and battle-worthy aeroplanes, as was demonstrated convincingly by their continuous employment throughout the whole of World War 1. The basis of their success was the strongly made steel airframe and the ability to take advantage of successively more powerful engines as the war progressed.

The Voisin 1 (Type L) appeared early in 1914 and was powered by a 70 h.p. Gnome rotary engine. The

Voisin 2 was essentially similar except that it was fitted with an 80 h.p. Le Rhône. These two types were already in service with four escadrilles of the French Aviation Militaire in August 1914 and initially were employed for artillery observation on the Western Front. From November 1914, however, they began to be used for daylight bombing, carrying about 60 kg. (132 lb.) of bombs in or on the sides of the 2-seat crew nacelle.

Also a pre-war design, the Voisin 3 (Type LA) had flown in February 1914 and was to become the most widely built Voisin type. It differed from the earlier machines in having a 120 h.p. Salmson (Canton-Unné) 9 M radial engine and unequal-span wings. It also carried a Hotchkiss machine-gun in the front of the nacelle, for the use of the observer, and the first enemy aircraft to fall to a French crew was shot down by Voisin V.89 on 5 October 1914. Although used at first for daylight operations, the Voisin 3 was transferred to night bombing from September 1915 and some aircraft of this type were also in service with the Marine Nationale. About eight hundred Voisin 3s were built for the Aviation Militaire, and a small quantity, equipping one escadrille, was supplied to Belgium; substantial numbers were delivered to Russia, and in 1915–16 the Società Italiana Transaerea built one hundred and twelve Voisin 3s which served with five squadriglie of the Corpo Aeronautica Militare and were powered by Fiat, Isotta-Fraschini or Renault engines. Both British ser-

vices purchased French-built Voisins locally, the R.N.A.S. having at least twenty-one and the R.F.C. at least twenty-three; a further fifty Voisins were built in the United Kingdom by Savages Ltd. for the R.F.C. Later-production aircraft were known as Type LA.S, the suffix letter indicating surélevé (raised), in which the engine was installed at a slight downward angle to improve its thrust properties. Two hundred examples were also completed of the Voisin 4 (Types LB and LB.S). This was basically similar to the Type 3, but had slightly staggered wings and a more rectangular nacelle, in the nose of which a 47 mm. Hotchkiss cannon was installed. This version was used primarily for ground strafing, and sometimes for escort duty. The LB version flew for the first time in March 1915 and the LB.S towards the end of the year. Both the Voisin 3 and 4 were also used in D.2 form as 2-seat dual-control trainers.

A more powerful version of the Type 3 LA.S was the Type 5 LA.S, which appeared late in 1915. It differed from the Voisin 3 in having a 150 h.p. Salmson radial engine, an enlarged cut-out in the upper trailing edge and a strengthened undercarriage. Three hundred and fifty Voisin 5s were built. The Voisin 6 was virtually identical to the 5 except in having a slightly modified 155 h.p. version of the Salmson engine.

5 Voisin 8 to 10
The second most widely built Voisin biplane was the Voisin 8,

developed from the Voisin 7 and enlarged and strengthened in an attempt to sustain a viable performance in the later war years by using a 220 h.p. Peugeot engine. A ready point of distinction between the Voisin 8 and the earlier models was the installation of two streamlined fuel tanks beneath the upper wings. The Voisin 8 was produced initially in Type LA.P form as a night bomber, going into service late in 1916. It was armed with one or two machine-guns, and the bomb load was increased to 180 kg. (396 lb.), carried beneath the wings and in the nacelle. The LB.P was a 'canon' version, slightly smaller and heavier and mounting a 37 mm. or 47 mm. Hotchkiss cannon in the front cockpit. It entered service in August 1916 for ground-attack and escort duties, but was not employed in very great numbers. One thousand one hundred and twenty-three Voisin 8s were built; one of these was sent to the United States for evaluation in 1917 and was followed by the purchase of eight more in April 1918 for use as trainers. Twenty Voisin 8s were delivered to the Marine Nationale and the remainder to the Aviation Militaire, which still had fifty-one in service in August 1918. The Voisin 9 was a lighter-weight reconnaissance version of the Voisin 8 LA.P.

Early in 1918 the Voisin 10 appeared as a replacement for the Voisin 8. The latter's Peugeot engine had been somewhat unreliable, and in the Voisin 10 its place was taken by the 300 h.p. Renault, which gave much less trouble and

more efficiently sustained the aircraft's performance at altitude. It also enabled the bomb load to be increased to about 300 kg. (661 lb.), although at some reduction in the aircraft's range. Nine hundred Voisin 10s were built, two of which were purchased by the A.E.F. in July 1918, the rest being delivered to the Aviation Militaire from the beginning of the year. A 'canon' version, with a 37 mm. Hotchkiss, was designated LB.R (the bomber version being known as the LA.R), but was not employed on any scale.

6 Farman HF.20 series

The Henry Farman HF.20, which first appeared in 1913, was based on the earlier HF.16 design and had been produced in some numbers for military service well before the outbreak of World War 1 together with the generally similar HF.21, HF.22 and HF.23. These were all wooden-framed, 2-seat pusher biplanes designed to the same basic configuration and varying chiefly in their dimensions. The HF.21 had a greater span but a shorter fuselage than the HF.20; while the HF.22 and HF.23 had a longer fuselage than either the HF.20 or HF.21.

In August 1914, aircraft of the HF.20/21/22 type were in service with Escadrilles 1, 7, 13, 19 and 28 of the French Aviation Militaire; with Escadrilles 1 and 2 of the Belgian Aviation Militaire; with Nos. 1, 2 and 3 Squadrons R.N.A.S.; Nos. 3, 5, 6 and 7 Squadrons R.F.C.; and with the air forces of Romania and Russia. They were built under licence in Belgium by

Jero; in Italy by Savoia, with float landing gear and 100 h.p. Colombo engines; and in the United Kingdom by the Aircraft Manufacturing Co. and Grahame-White Aviation among other manufacturers. Usual powerplant was a 70 h.p. or 80 h.p. Gnome, or 80 h.p. Le Rhône rotary, although Anzanis or other engines of different ratings were fitted occasionally. Six HF.22s were supplied to the Netherlands in 1913, where a further fourteen were built in 1915 by the Spijker motor-car company; one or two of these were allocated to the Dutch Navy, the remainder serving with the Dutch Army Air Service. British Farmans operated in France with both the R.F.C. and the R.N.A.S., and with No. 3 Wing R.N.A.S. in the Dardanelles. Many R.N.A.S. Farmans were also operated as floatplanes.

The major variant of the design was the HF.27, which had a steel-tube airframe, a shorter nacelle, equal-span wings and a simplified 4-wheel undercarriage without landing skids. It was a slightly bigger aeroplane than the previous Henry Farmans, and usually powered by a 140 or 160 h.p. Canton-Unné engine. It had a 4-hour endurance and could carry a maximum bomb load of about 250 kg. (551 lb.). Farman HF.27s were employed operationally on the Western Front, in the Dardanelles, Mesopotamia, East and South-West Africa. Those of the R.N.A.S. were used both in France and at Mudros in the Aegean (with No. 2 Wing). Several of the R.N.A.S. Farman HF.27s were transferred to the R.F.C., equipping

Nos. 26 and 30 Squadrons. Six British-built HF.27s were supplied to Romania.

A precise breakdown of the Farmans in British service is almost impossible to achieve since many serial allocations did not specify the individual type. However, from known serial batches it can be confirmed that the R.N.A.S. received more than one hundred and fifty Henry Farmans, of which about half were French-built. Similarly, R.F.C. serial numbers can be traced for more than four hundred and seventy Henry Farmans, almost all of which were built in the United Kingdom, by Airco, Grahame-White or other manufacturers.

7 Farman F.40 series

Towards the end of 1915 Henry and Maurice Farman produced a joint design incorporating the better features of their earlier, separate designs. The basic model for this series was the F.40, a 2-seat pusher biplane with the crew nacelle mounted mid-way between the unequal-span wings. It was powered by a 160 h.p. Renault engine. The F.40 series was preceded in December 1915 by the F.30, a simplified version with more angular nacelle and flying surfaces and powered by a 160 h.p. Canton-Unné radial engine. The F.30 was produced primarily for Russia, where it was also built under licence, although an F.30B.2 version with a 260 h.p. Salmson radial may have been built in small numbers for the Aviation Militaire.

The F.41 differed from the F.40

in having shorter-span wings, a nacelle similar to that of the Maurice Farman MF.11bis and an 80 or 110 h.p. Renault. The F.60 and F.61 corresponded respectively to the F.40 and F.41 except for their 190 h.p. Renault powerplants. The other major production version was the F.56, which had a 170 h.p. Renault but was otherwise similar to the F.41; the F.46 was produced specifically for training, with large front skids like those on the MF.7.

The Farmans entered service early in 1916 and were used widely for reconnaissance and bombing, serving with forty-seven escadrilles of the Aviation Militaire on the Western Front and in Macedonia. Only a small bomb load could be carried by the Farmans, whose sole defence was a single Lewis gun in the front cockpit. The type was virtually outclassed from the time it entered service, but it was not declared obsolete until early 1917 and even then continued to be used for night bombing until the arrival of Breguet 14s at the end of the year. A few Farmans were employed for 'balloon-busting', armed with Le Prieur rockets carried on the interplane struts. During 1918 all Farmans were withdrawn from the front line to training establishments. Farman F.41s and F.60s served with two escadrilles of the Belgian Aviation Militaire: thirty F.40s were purchased by the A.E.F. for training purposes; and a small number of Farmans were used by No. 5 Wing R.N.A.S. in France.

The Farman F.50, despite its designation, was not a variant of the F.40 design. It was a twin-engined tractor biplane bomber, with a wing span of 75 ft. 0 in. (22·86 m.), two 250 h.p. Lorraine-Dietrich engines and a possible load of eight 75 kg. (165 lb.) bombs. The F.50 appeared in 1918, and a small number had been delivered to French Escadrilles de Bombardement, including F.114 and F.119, before the Armistice. Two others were purchased by the A.E.F. in March 1918. After the war two F.50s were supplied to the Marine Nationale, another went to Japan and a small batch were demilitarised and used for a short while as passenger-carrying aircraft.

8 Friedrichshafen G types

Although better known for its wartime series of naval seaplanes, the Flugzeugbau Freidrichshafen did produce during World War 1 a range of G type twin-engined bombers. They were slightly smaller than the contemporary and more widely used Gotha G types, from which they could be distinguished by the shape of their wingtips and horizontal tail surfaces. The first type to appear was the G.I (FF30), which was completed late in 1914. It was a 3-bay biplane with two 150 h.p. Bz.III pusher engines, a compound tail assembly, and was armed with a single Parabellum defensive machine-gun in the nose. This apparently did not go into production, and it was not until 1916 that the G.II (FF38) appeared, a 2-bay, single-tailed aircraft with two 200 h.p. Bz.IV pusher engines and a Parabellum gun in each of the nose and rear cockpits. The G.II went into limited production by the parent company and the Daimler Motoren-Werke, entering service towards the end of 1916. It continued to serve throughout the following year, but its 150 kg. (330 lb.) bomb load was modest by current standards and it was supplanted by the G.III (FF45), a larger aeroplane capable of carrying a heavier load.

The G.III first appeared early in 1917, and was again a 3-bay design. All flying surfaces, including the double ailerons, were balanced, but only the elevators were overhung. A 3-man crew was carried, and the defensive armament consisted of single or twin Parabellum guns in each of the front and rear cockpits; the rear gunner was protected from the pusher propellers of the Mercedes D.IVa engines by wire mesh guards on either side of him. Bomb load of the G.III for normal ranges was 500 kg. (1,102 lb.), of which 100 kg. (220 lb.) was carried internally and the remainder on racks under the fuselage. The Friedrichshafen G.III was in service at about the same time as the Gotha G.V (i.e. from mid-1917 until the end of the war), operating chiefly as a night bomber against targets in France and Belgium, although some accompanied the Gothas in their attacks on the United Kingdom. From early 1918 they were joined by the G.IIIa, which differed principally in having a compound tail unit. Production of the G.III/IIIa was shared by Daimler and Hansa, who built two hundred and forty-

five and ninety-three aircraft respectively.

Later variants, appearing in modest numbers during 1918, included the G.IVa, G.IVb and G.V. All were short-nosed developments without a front gun position, the G.IVa being a pusher type like the earlier Friedrichshafens, while the G.IVb and G.V had engines driving tractor propellers. The Friedrichshafen G types equipped Bombengeschwadern 1, 2 and 5, and served in Macedonia as well as on the Western Front.

9 Gotha G.I to G.V

The first Grossflugzeug (large aeroplane) built by the Gothaer Waggonfabrik A.G. was the G.I, evolved by Oskar Ursinus and Major Friedel of the German Army from a prototype flown for the first time in January 1915. A few of these were built by Gotha under licence, in simplified and improved form. They were intended for ground-attack and general tactical duties and were employed on the Western and Eastern Fronts. The G.Is were characterised by a slim fuselage attached to the upper wings, while the two 160 h.p. Mercedes D.III engines were mounted close together on the lower wings.

Although following the same basic concept, the Gotha G.II was an entirely new design, evolved at Gotha under the Swiss engineer Hans Burkhard and flown for the first time in March 1916. The fuselage and engines (220 h.p. Mercedes D.IVs) were mounted conventionally on the lower wings; overall span was increased, and auxiliary front wheels were added to the landing gear to avoid the risk of nosing over. The Gotha G.II carried a crew of three and a defensive armament of two machine-guns; the first production example was completed in April 1916. The G.II entered service in the autumn, but was soon withdrawn from operations (on the Balkan Front) after repeated failures of the engine crankshafts. It was replaced by the G.III from October 1916 on the Balkan and Western Fronts, a new model with reinforced fuselage, an extra machine-gun and 260 h.p. Mercedes D.IVa engines. An initial twenty-five G.IIIs were ordered, and in December 1916 fourteen were in service at the Front.

First major production model was the G.IV, chosen to carry out raids on the United Kingdom: an initial fifty G.IVs were ordered from Gotha, and eighty were built by Siemens-Schuckert and about a hundred by L.V.G. The G.IV went into service about March 1917, and began to make daylight raids on southern England towards the end of May. The G.IV retained the Mercedes D.IVa, but differed appreciably in having a tunnel hollowed out of the rear fuselage so that the rear gunner could cover the 'blind spot' below and to the rear of the bomber. Normally this was done with the standard rear-mounted gun, but a fourth gun could be carried for the purpose at the expense of part of the bomb load. The G.IV, with an all-plywood fuselage, and ailerons on top and bottom wings, was stronger yet easier to fly than its predecessors, though its performance remained much the same as for the G.III, and Germany was obliged to switch it to night attacks against Britain from September 1917. By this time it was beginning to be replaced by the new G.V, which had entered service in August; this version continued the night bombing of England until the following May. At the peak of their employment, in April 1918, thirty-six Gotha G.Vs were in service. Their typical bomb load on cross-Channel raids was six 50 kg. (110 lb.) bombs – about half their maximum load. Final versions in service were the G.Va/Vb. These differed from one another only in internal details, but could be distinguished from the G.V by their biplane tail assembly and shorter nose. The G.Va/Vb went into production in March 1918 and into service in June; by August there were twenty-one G.Vbs at the Front.

In general, the Gotha bombers were agile for their size, well defended and difficult to shoot down. More were lost to anti-aircraft fire than in aerial fighting, but far more still were lost in landing accidents. Forty of the Siemens-built G.IVs were completed as trainers, most of them with 180 h.p. Argus As.III or 185 h.p. N.A.G. engines. About thirty of the L.V.G. G.IVs were later transferred to Austro-Hungary, where they were refitted with 230 h.p. Hieros and employed on the Italian Front. A seaplane development of the G.I, the Gotha-Ursinus UWD, was completed late in 1915.

It was handed over to the German Navy in January 1916 and used on operations.

10 D.F.W. B.I and C.I

In the years preceding World War 1 one of the types built by the Deutsche Flugzeug-Werke was the Etrich Taube, and some indication of its influence was apparent in the banana-shaped wings of D.F.W.'s own MD 14 design that appeared in mid-1914. This was an elegant, stable and pleasant-to-fly aeroplane, with 3-bay bracing of the modest-span wings and small, looped skids underneath the lower extremities. Other characteristics of the MD 14 included the large H. & Z. side radiators and a downward-pointing engine exhaust manifold on the starboard side.

Upon the outbreak of war the MD 14 was impressed for military service and given the military designation B.I. Powered by a 100 h.p. Mercedes D.I engine, it was employed during the early months of hostilities for observation work on both the Eastern and Western Fronts. Like all B types, it carried no fixed defensive armament, the only weapons being a rifle or re-volver carried by the observer, who in the fashion of the time occupied the front seat. With the arrival in service of armed 2-seaters in 1915, the B.Is were reallocated to training duties, for which their pleasant flying qualities made them an excellent choice. The D.F.W. MRD biplane, which became the military B.II, was externally similar to the B.I; this may have been a dual-control model produced especially for the training role.

In 1915 the D.F.W. KD 15 (military designation C.I) entered service in replacement of the un-armed B types. It was powered by a 150 h.p. Benz Bz.III; the observer still occupied the front seat, but the centre-section of the top wing now incorporated a cut-out enabling him to stand up and operate a free-firing Parabellum machine-gun mounted over the top wing. Like its predecessor, the C.I served on the Eastern and Western Fronts, and about one hundred and thirty of these aircraft are thought to have been completed. The T 25, or C.II, was a rather smaller aeroplane with modified tail surfaces, straight-edged staggered wings and more conventional crew seating with a Schneider ring for a Parabellum gun in the rear cockpit. Reports indicate that the C.II was somewhat un-stable, and it may not actually have entered service. Total production of B types by the Deutsche Flugzeug-Werke is thought to have reached about one hundred machines.

11 Lloyd C types

The C type 2-seat reconnaissance aircraft built by the Ungarische Lloyd Flugzeug und Motoren-fabrik are among the lesser-known aircraft of World War 1, despite the fact that between four and five hundred aircraft of this type were built and used quite extensively by both Austro-Hungarian air serivces during the first half of the war.

They originated before the out-break of war with the C.I (Series

41), one example of which was flown to an altitude of 6,170 m. (20,243 ft.) at Vienna in the summer of 1914. Aircraft of this type were already in military service when the war commenced. They were followed early in 1915 by the Lloyd C.II (Series 42), whose general appearance was typical of the Lloyd machines up to the time of the C.V. One hundred C.IIs were completed, fifty by Lloyd and fifty by W.K.F. They were powered by 145 h.p. Hiero engines and had a communal cockpit for the 2-man crew; the wing span was slightly larger than that of the C.I. The C.IIs were at first unarmed, but later aircraft in service were fitted with a Schwarzlose machine-gun for the observer. In 1916 the C.III appeared, being basically similar to the C.II except for its more powerful 160 h.p. Austro-Daimler engine in a somewhat deeper cowling. W.F.K. built fifty C.IIIs (Series 43.51), and they were employed on the Italian and Romanian Fronts in 1916–17. Some were fitted with a second machine-gun mounted on top of the wings. Little is known about the C.IV: it is thought to have been a single-bay version of the C.III, built by Lloyd and W.K.F. as Series 44 and 44.51, but its operational employment has not been confirmed.

The final Lloyd C type was the C.V (Series 46), with smaller dimensions, an aerodynamically refined airframe including a spinnered propeller and a taller fin with a rounded rudder. Powered by 185 h.p. Austro-Daimlers in the first fifty aircraft and 220 h.p. locally built Benz Bz.IVs in the second fifty, the C.V was some 32 km/hr. (20 m.p.h.) faster than the C.III. It was also built in Series 82 form by W.K.F. with 200 h.p. Bz.IV engines, but by the time the C.V appeared, later and more efficient reconnaissance aircraft were in service, and the Lloyd C types were transferred to training duties.

12 Hansa-Brandenburg C.I

Although it was employed almost exclusively by the Austro-Hungarian air services during World War 1, the Hansa-Brandenburg C.I or Type LDD was designed by Ernst Heinkel of the parent company in Germany, and may have owed something to the earlier Brandenburg FD (B.I) of 1914, three of which were supplied to Austro-Hungary. A characteristic of both designs was the inward-sloping interplane bracing struts.

The Brandenburg C.I was a 2-seat armed reconnaissance biplane of conventional appearance, having the typical communal cockpit favoured in Austrian aircraft at that time, in which the observer occupied the rear position and was provided with a free-firing Schwarzlose machine-gun. On later production C.Is a synchronised Schwarzlose was installed in front of the cockpit on the port side for use by the pilot. From the early spring of 1916 until the end of World War 1 the Brandenburg C.I was employed widely on reconnaissance, artillery observation and light bombing. Its normal war load was 60 kg. (132 lb.), but some aircraft were operated with a maximum load of 100 kg. (220 lb.), consisting of one 80 kg. (176 lb.) and two 10 kg. (22 lb.) bombs. Visual and photographic reconnaissance missions were undertaken. The C.I was simple and stable to fly, had good take-off and landing qualities and a gradually improving performance in the air as successive production batches were fitted with engines of increased power.

In all, one thousand three hundred and eighteen C.Is were built, in eighteen series, by Brandenburg (eighty-four), Phönix (four hundred) and Ufag (eight hundred and thirty-four). Phönix built C.Is with 160 h.p. Austro-Daimlers (Series 23 and 26), 185 h.p. Austro-Daimlers (Series 27), 210 h.p. Austro-Daimlers (Series 29), 200 h.p. Hieros (Series 29·5, 129, 229 and 329) and 230 h.p. Hieros (Series 429). The Ungarische Flugzeugfabrik A.G. (Ufag) built Brandenburg C.Is with 160 h.p. Austro-Daimlers (Series 61, 64, 67 and 68), 160 h.p. Mercedes D.IIIs (Series 63), 200 h.p. Austro-Daimlers (Series 269), 200 h.p. Hieros (Series 69), 220 h.p. Benz Bz. IVas (Series 169) and 230 h.p. Hieros (Series 369).

13 **Albatros B types**

The unarmed 2-seat Albatros biplanes that served Germany in one capacity or another throughout World War 1 were probably the best reconnaissance machines in German service at the outbreak of war. Their design had been undertaken by Ernst Heinkel early in 1914, and the original version had entered production in a small way before the war started. They were impressed for war service, given the military designation B.I and allocated to Feld Flieger Abteilung (Field Reconnaissance) units in August 1914. Production was not especially standardised, and the B.I appeared in 1-, 2- and 3-bay forms with either a 100 h.p. Mercedes D.I or 120 h.p. D.II engine, the radiator for which was mounted above the cylinder block. As was the fashion at the time, the pilot sat in the rear cockpit while the observer occupied the front seat under the cabane trestle. No fixed defensive armament was carried, but during the early months of the war the observer usually armed himself with a rifle or carbine. Two batches of Albatros B.Is (Series 23 and 24) were built in Austria-Hungary by Phönix.

A second Albatros 2-seater had also flown during 1914, and in the summer it set an altitude record of 4,500 m. (14,764 ft.). A 2-bay biplane with a shorter span than the B.I, the B.II, as this version became known, was powered at first by a 100 h.p. Mercedes D.I. The Albatros B.II was one of the most widely used reconnaissance and observation types during the first year of the war, and was the subject of an extensive production programme. To improve the downward view for both pilot and observer, small cut-outs were made in the lower-wing roots. A small batch of B.Is and B.IIs (Series 21) was supplied to Austro-Hungary, and it is thought that some or all of these may have been fitted with a rudimentary mounting for a machine-gun in the front cockpit. Later production B.IIs were of the B.IIa model, with a strengthened and aerodynamically improved airframe, dual controls and a 120 h.p. engine – either the Mercedes D.II or the Argus As.II.

The final Albatros B type was the B.III, which was built in small numbers in 1915 for reconnaissance work with both the German Army and Navy. This retained more or less the same fuselage as the B.II, but had shorter-span wings and a new, high-aspect-ratio vertical tail and curved tailplane similar to those later employed on the C.III.

With the introduction of the C category of armed 2-seaters in summer 1915, the B types became obsolete as observation aircraft. However, the Albatros machines' excellent flying qualities made them ideally suited to a training role, and they were extensively employed in this capacity throughout the remainder of the war. Production of the Albatros B series was undertaken by the B.F.W., L.F.G., Linke-Hofmann, Merkur, Kondor and Refla companies in Germany, in addition to those built by the Ostdeutsche Albatros Werke. Some Albatros B types were in military service in Sweden in 1918–19.

14 Austrian Aviatik B.II and B.III

In 1914–15 the German Automobil und Aviatik A.G. of Leipzig built a small, 2-seat reconnaissance aircraft designated B.I, powered by a 100 h.p. Mercedes D.I engine,

which was employed in small numbers on the Western Front for observation during the early months of World War 1. The company's Austrian subsidiary, the Oesterreich-ische-Ungarische Flugzeugfabrik Aviatik of Vienna, in 1915 built a variation of this design with similar-pattern fuselage and wings, a characteristic of which were the strut-braced outer sections. Chief points of distinction between the German and Austrian Aviatiks were the horn-balanced, overhung elevators and rudder of the latter. The Austrian B.II was built in a small series (Series 32) in 1915, powered by a 120 h.p. Austro-Daimler engine. It carried no defensive armament other than the observer's rifle or revolver, but was able to carry a pair of 10 kg. bombs for 'nuisance' raids.

It was followed by the B.III (Series 33), which was ostensibly an improved version. This was powered by a 160 h.p. Austro-Daimler, with a box radiator mounted over the engine instead of the B.II's side radiators. The wings were of increased span, with raked-back tips; the fin was strut-braced; and instead of the B.II's separate cockpits, the B.III featured a long, communal cockpit in which the pilot now sat in the front seat and the observer at the rear had a Schwarzlose machine-gun on a flexible mounting. Like the B.II, the B.III had an excellent range, and was used in some numbers for long-distance reconnaissance on the Russian Front. It could carry three 10 kg. bombs. Unfortunately, the B.III's flying qualities were nowhere near as good as those of its predecessor: it did not respond very quickly to its flight controls, and this caused it to swing about when flying in windy conditions, earning it such nicknames as 'gondola' and 'rocking-chair'.

Because of its unsatisfactory flying tendencies, a second series of B.II aircraft were built – the Series 34. These retained the former basic B.II airframe, but incorporated the 160 h.p. Austro-Daimler engine with its box radiator and the machine-gun installation of the B.III. Bomb load was increased to three 20 kg. bombs. In its Series 34 form the B.II was considerably more stable in flight, faster than the B.III and could climb to twice the altitude of the original B.II. Though they were not outstanding machines, the Austrian Aviatiks performed useful service in theatres where their long range was an asset, but by early 1916 they had been withdrawn from the front line and relegated to training duties.

15 Lohner B and C types
The Jakob Lohner Werke of Vienna is best known for the range of marine aircraft that it produced during 1914–18, but, like its lesser-known compatriot, Lloyd, it also produced a range of 2-seat reconnaissance biplanes during the early part of the war. The first of these, the Lohner Type B, was in fact a 1913 design, several of which had been built before the outbreak of war with 100 h.p. Austro-Daimler engines. Some of them were given individual names, all beginning with the letter B. After the outbreak of war, production was

increased, and the type was designated B.I. It was built by Lohner (as Series 11) and by the government factory at Fischamend (as Series 73), some aircraft having 120 h.p. engines. Although unarmed, the B.Is were used in some numbers during the early months of hostilities for observation and communications work. The Lohner Type C, or B.II, differed chiefly in having a longer fuselage, balanced rudder and an 85 h.p. Hiero engine. This type was built by Lohner, Fischamend and Ufag with Series numbers 12, 74 and 12.41 respectively.

The third B type to enter service was the B.IV (Lohner Type E), which equipped several Fliegerkompagnien in 1915. It was powered by a 100 h.p. Mercedes D.I engine, had a further-extended fuselage and a neater undercarriage. It was the first B type to be properly armed, having a Schwarzlose machine-gun in the rear for use by the observer. Built by Lohner (Series 15) and Ufag (Series 15.51), the B.IV was of limited value to the Austro-Hungarian air service since it could only maintain its performance effectively at altitudes below 2,000 m. (6,562 ft.). Later, in 1915, the B.IV was followed by the B.VII (Lohner Type I), which had a much more powerful engine and a far better performance. This version was built by Lohner as Series 17 with the 150 h.p. Austro-Daimler, and by Ufag as Series 17.51 with the 160 h.p. Austro-Daimler. The rear-mounted Schwarzlose machine-gun was retained as standard equipment.

Although numerically earlier, the

Lohner B.VI (Type H) did not enter service until 1916, after the appearance of the B.VII. Powered by a 145 h.p. Rapp engine, the B.VI had a shorter fuselage than its predecessors and lower wings of extended span. The sweepback of both upper and lower planes was reduced, and the interplane bracing simplified. The B.VI was built by Lohner as Series 16.10. The same basic airframe, with a 160 h.p. Austro-Daimler engine, was used in the construction of the Lohner C.I, or Type K. This entered service early in 1916 and remained in use throughout that year, being built by Lohner only as Series 18.

16 Albatros C.I

For the first few months of World War 1 the opposing forces in France carried out reconnaissance and observation of one another's troop movements and artillery concentrations by means of aircraft that carried no formal armament either for offence or defence. At best, they could defend themselves if attacked only by revolvers or rifles carried by the observer, and since he customarily occupied the front cockpit in tractor-type biplanes, he was prevented by the surrounding engine cylinders, wing struts and bracing wires from making very effective use of such weapons. However, in the spring of 1915 Germany introduced a new category of warplane, the armed 2-seat C class, which not only had more powerful engines but also transferred the observer to the rear position, where he had a much more effective field of fire to the sides, rear and above the aircraft, and armed him with a free-firing machine-gun.

One of the first such types to appear in service was the Albatros C.I. This aeroplane was, essentially, a slightly scaled-up version of the unarmed B.II, powered in its prototype form by a 150 h.p. Benz Bz.III engine. Apart from being better defended, by its ring-mounted Parabellum gun, the C.I also offered a better field of view to both crew members by virtue of a distinctive dual-curve cut-out in the upper trailing edge and rectangular cut-outs in the lower-wing roots. Standard production C.Is were 2-bay biplanes with 160 h.p. engines – either the Mercedes D.III or the Argus As.III. They were strongly built, and inherited the same fine stability and flying qualities that had characterised the earlier B.II. From late spring 1915 the Albatros C.I was used in substantial numbers, both on the Western Front and in Russia, chiefly for photographic or visual reconnaissance and artillery observation duties. It could also be used for light bombing, with a load of some 70 kg. (154 lb.) of bombs stowed vertically in a space between the two cockpits. The Albatros C.I's performance, for its time, was sufficiently good to permit it to be used aggressively, as well as on more passive duties, and among those who gathered valuable early fighting experience in Albatros-built C.Is were Oswald Boelcke and Manfred von Richthofen. Albatros-built C.Is could be distinguished by the prominent side radiators flanking the front cockpit; the C.Ia, built by B.F.W. and L.F.G. (Roland), replaced these by a single leading-edge box-type radiator. Comparatively few C.Ias were built, as by this time the improved C.III was ready for production. However, a dual-control variant, the C.Ib, appeared in 1917, built by Merkur for the training role. It is not certain whether these were newly built aircraft or conversions of C.I/Ias, but after their replacement by more up-to-date Albatroses and other C types the C.I series continued to give useful service in the training role.

One C.I was built with an experimental 3-bay enlarged wing cellule and a long, communal cockpit; a standard C.I wing unit and undercarriage were also used in the construction of the experimental C.II early in 1916. This was a pusher type with a 150 h.p. Benz Bz.III, but did not go into production.

17 Lebed'-XI, XII and XIII

Vladimir Alexandrovich Lebedev learned to fly in France in 1909, and three years later became head of the PTA (Petersburg Aviation Company). Later, while still at St. Petersburg, the company was renamed as the Aktsionernoe Obitsestvo Vozdukhoplavaniya V.A. Lebedeva (V.A. Lebedev Aeronautics Company), its early products including licence-built versions of Deperdussin, Farman, Morane, Nieuport, Sopwith and Voisin designs for the Imperial Russian Air Service. Among these early aircraft was also the Lebed'-VII of 1915, a small 2-seat scout with a close resemblance to the Sopwith Tabloid; two examples of the Lebed'-VIII, of similar appearance to the Albatros B.II; and the Lebed'-IX, based on an L.V.G. design. During 1915 a captured Albatros B.II was sent to the Lebedev factory for evaluation, and from an amalgamation of the best features of this and the Lebed'-VIII there first emerged the Lebed'-XI, a 2-seat reconnaissance aircraft having a 47 ft. 6¾ in. (14·50 m.) wing span and, initially at least, a 150 h.p. Sunbeam engine.

Apart from a tendency to 'float' when landing, it was pronounced superior in most respects to the Albatros design, and it was presumably this criticism which led to the development of the Lebed'-XII, which first flew on 28 December 1915 and had the wing span reduced to 43 ft. 1¾ in. (13·15 m.). An order for two hundred and twenty-five Lebeds was placed on 19 April 1916, by the Central Military Technical Board, and it is known that two hundred and sixteen Lebed'-XIIs (plus a substantial quantity of spares) were completed. The remainder, possibly, were either Lebed'-XIs (or LM I twin-float equivalents), in which 150 h.p. Benz or Salmson engines were installed as powerplants.

The first production Lebed' (Type XI?) was flown on 4 August 1916, and service acceptance trials were completed some two months later. The Lebed'-XII was a 2-seat reconnaissance aircraft, armed with a single 7·62 mm. Colt machine-gun on a pillar mounting in the rear (observer's) cockpit and with four racks for small bombs beneath the lower wings. Bomb load was of the order of 165–220 lb. (75–100 kg.), according to whether a 140 or 150 h.p. Salmson engine was installed. Both the bomb racks and the gun mounting of the early production aircraft were the work of Lebedev's chief designer, Schulnik, but were found unsatisfactory in service and were later replaced by fittings of Kolpakov design. Unfortunately, these were not the Lebed'-XII's only unsatisfactory features. The centre of gravity, especially when carrying a bomb load, was badly positioned, and combined with excessive wing flexing to create a marked tendency to go into dives from which recovery was often impossible; and the occupants were repeatedly overcome by fumes from the side-mounted radiators.

Modifications made during the summer of 1917, at which time about eighty Lebed'-XIIs had been delivered, led to the Lebed'-XIIbis (140 h.p. Hispano-Suiza V8 engine) and Lebed'-XIII (150 h.p. Salmson). The former offered no great improvement over its predecessor, but a contract for two hundred Lebed'-XIIIs was placed, though it is uncertain whether all were completed. Other 1917 variations on the Albatros/Lebed'-XII theme included the Lebed'-XVII, mounting a fixed, forward-firing gun for the pilot; and the Lebed'-XXIV, with either a 200 h.p. Hispano-Suiza or 230 h.p. Fiat engine. Between 1914 and 1917 inclusive the Lebedev factories (including new ones opened in 1917 at Penze and

Taganrog) produced a total of six hundred and seventy-four aircraft of all types, including foreign designs and prototypes of the indigenous Lebed'-XIV and Lebed'-XVI twin-engined bombers.

18 **Albatros C.III**

Well and widely as the Albatros C.I series of biplanes served the Flieger Abteilungen, the C.IIIs which followed them were even more successful. As the C.I had been evolved from the B.II unarmed 2-seater, so the C.III was a similarly scaled-up version of the Albatros B.III, repeating the latter's curved tailplane and low-aspect-ratio fin. These revised tail surfaces improved the already excellent flying qualities of the aircraft, making it more stable longitudinally and better able to manoeuvre in combat with Allied fighters.

The C.III prototype, like that of the C.I, was powered by a 150 h.p. Bz.III engine, and this unit was installed in some production C.IIIs. The standard powerplant was the well-tried and thoroughly reliable Mercedes D.III of 160 h.p. The Albatros C.III was the most widely built Albatros C type, the production programme being shared between Albatros, O.A.W., D.F.W., Hansa, Linke-Hofmann, L.V.G. and Siemens-Schuckert. The Parabellum gun on a Schneider ring mounting in the observer's cockpit was a standard installation; most C.IIIs were also provided with a synchronised forward-firing Spandau gun on the starboard side of the engine block. The C.III went into service late in 1915, and it continued to serve on the Western Front, in Macedonia and in Russia throughout 1916 and the early part of 1917. Its duties included visual and photographic reconnaissance; it could undertake light bombing duties with about 90 kg. (198 lb.) of bombs stowed internally between the cockpits. Without a bomb load, radio equipment could be installed in the C.III for use in artillery co-operation work. In addition to its pleasant handling qualities, the C.III was a compact, sturdily built aeroplane whose ply-covered fuselage enabled it to withstand a considerable amount of battle damage. After its withdrawal from front-line operations early in 1917 it continued to render useful service as a trainer until the end of the war.

Single examples were built in 1916 of the C.IV, which was basically a C.III airframe with a completely new single-bay wing cellule, and of the W.2, a twin-float version of the C.III, which was handed over to the German Navy in June. No series production of either version was undertaken. A few Albatros C.VIs were built: these had stronger but lighter C.III-type airframes fitted with 180 h.p. As.III engines, giving a slight improvement in overall performance.

19 Dorand AR types

Designed in 1916 by Capitaine Georges Lepère, chief designer of the Section Technique de l'Aéronautique, the AR 2-seat reconnaissance biplane was named after the S.T.Aé's director, Lt. Col. Dorand, who had issued the requirement for

its development as a replacement for the Aviation Militaire's ageing Farman F.40s. Referred to variously as the AR.1 or ARL.1, the interpretation of its designation is obscure. The 'L' has been taken by some to indicate manufacture by the Letord company, though evidence to support this is conflicting, to say the least; an alternative, and plausible, explanation is that the prefix letters originally stood for 'Avion Renault' and later for 'Avion Renault ou Lorraine'. Major production was undertaken by the government-owned factory of the S.T.Aé. at Chalais-Meudon, near Paris; additional quantities are believed to have been produced by Farman Frères and, possibly, others. Flight testing was completed in the autumn of 1916, and the first AR.1A.2s began to join operational French squadrons on the Western Front in the following spring, serving there until early 1918.

In all, AR.1s and/or AR.2s served with some eighteen French escadrilles, five of which also flew their Dorands on the Italian Front. The indications are that both aircraft warranted only a low priority in the demand for available powerplants, and Lt. Col. Dorand is on record as saying that they 'performed as well as could be expected, considering the engines installed'.

Normal powerplants of the AR.1 and AR.2 were, respectively, the 190 h.p. Renault 8 Bd or the 200 h.p. Renault 8 Gdy, with the 185 or 240 h.p. Lorraine-Dietrich (ARL.1 and ARL.2) as the usual alternatives, although other Renault variants were also employed. Frontal radiators were fitted to the AR.1/ARL.1, and wing radiators to the AR.2/ARL.2. Both types had the pronounced backward wing stagger that characterised aircraft bearing the Dorand name, the AR.2 being somewhat smaller with a wing span of only 39 ft. 4½ in. (12·00 m.) and area of 484·4 sq. ft. (45·00 sq. m.). Bomb load of either type, carried in the fuselage, was of the order of 176 lb. (80 kg.), and armament comprised a single synchronised forward-firing Vickers machine-gun for the pilot and one or two Lewis guns, on a movable mounting in the rear cockpit, for the observer.

In 1917 the American Expeditionary Force ordered twenty-two AR.1s and a hundred and twenty AR.2s, delivery of these beginning in December 1917 and February 1918 respectively. From the beginning of 1918 until May or June of that year the Dorands flew on operational service with the 12th Aero Squadron of the A.E.F., until replaced by Salmson 2s; thereafter they were employed almost entirely for training duties, and were redesignated Type X in 1919. Many AR.1s and AR.2s gravitated to the French civil register after the war, some as 2/3-passenger transports with Compagnie Aérienne Française in France (which had about two dozen) and Réseau Aérien Transafricain (which had four); others were used for joyriding or training flights.

20 Rumpler C.I

Although mainly concerned with the production of Taube monoplanes in the periods immediately before and after the outbreak of World War 1, the Rumpler Flugzeug-Werke also produced a 2-seat reconnaissance biplane, the B.I, with a 100 h.p. Mercedes D.I engine; about two hundred of these aircraft were built by Rumpler and Pfalz and served on the Eastern and Western Fronts in 1914–15. Early in 1915 Rumpler was one of the first German companies to produce a C type, the C.I, which was to become one of the longest-serving C types of the whole war. It was a well-built aeroplane, and intelligently designed to enable the crew to carry out their various duties with the maximum efficiency. The C.I went into production and service in 1915, its standard engine being the 160 h.p. Mercedes D.III with a semicircular radiator in the centre of the upper leading edge. Its 2-bay wings were slightly swept back, and had cutouts in the lower wing roots to improve the view downward. An extensive production programme was undertaken by the parent company and the Germania, Hannover, Märkische and Albert Rinne factories. Early production C.Is were armed only with a Parabellum gun on a Schneider ring mounting in the rear cockpit, but a synchronised Spandau was fitted on later aircraft on the port side of the front fuselage. A subsequent version designated C.Ia was powered by the 180 h.p. Argus As.III.

The Rumpler C.I served on the Eastern and Western Fronts, in Macedonia, Palestine and Salonika. In all theatres it was an extremely efficient machine, both for reconnaissance and for light 'nuisance' bombing raids with up to 100 kg. (220 lb.) of small bombs. Visual and photographic reconnaissance was carried out, except in the Middle Eastern theatres where the climate affected the photographic materials. In October 1916 there were two hundred and fifty Rumpler C.Is in service on all Fronts; the type was still in production for part of 1917 and some C.Is were still with front-line units as late as February 1918. Thereafter they were used on training duties, for which their pleasant handling and flying qualities made them eminently suitable; one batch was built especially for the training role by the Bayerische Rumpler-Werke with 150 h.p. Bz.III engines and no gun ring in the rear cockpit. A development, the Rumpler C.II, was projected, but apparently none were actually built.

21 D.F.W. C.V

The Deutsche Flugzeug-Werke's C.V, one of the finest German 2-seat types to be used during World War 1, was preceded in service by the C.IV of generally similar appearance. Authorities differ in regard to the extent in which the C.IV was produced, and its operational record was certainly overshadowed by that of the more widespread C.V. However, it is certain that among the two thousand three hundred and forty C types produced by D.F.W. during the war period the C.IV and C.V were the predominant models. The basic airframe, designed by Heinrich Oele-

rich, was common to both aircraft, the C.IV having a neatly installed 150 h.p. Benz Bz.III engine with a radiator mounted flush in the top wing. Its rudder and elevator surfaces were non-balanced, and the fin and tailplane structures were more triangular than those of the C.V. The C.IV first appeared in spring 1916 and was subsequently built by both D.F.W. and Aviatik for both German air services.

The C.V (factory designation T 29) was built by Aviatik, Halberstadt and L.V.G., in addition to the parent company. It differed principally in having the uprated Bz.IV engine (some later aircraft were fitted with 185 h.p. N.A.G. C.IIIs) and was at first fitted with Windhoff side radiators. A single box-type leading-edge radiator was fitted to later C.Vs, and the propeller was fitted with a small spinner. Tail contours were more rounded, and the elevator and rudder surfaces balanced. The C.V went into service on the Western Front in late summer 1916, subsequently appearing in Italy, Macedonia and Palestine. It continued to be used in France throughout 1917 and the early part of 1918, and about six hundred C.Vs were still in service on all Fronts when the war ended. The type handled well and was very popular with its crews, and its performance, at high or low level, was excellent for an aeroplane in its class. Its duties included artillery co-operation and infantry contact patrol, and visual and photographic reconnaissance. The C.V possessed a high degree of manoeuvrability, and with an experienced crew aboard could out-manoeuvre even the late-war Allied fighters. Major J. T. McCudden, V.C., in his book *Five Years in the Royal Flying Corps*, admits having to give best to a D.F.W. that evaded his every attempt in his S.E.5a to shoot it down in 1917.

Of the C.Vs that fell into Allied hands at the time of the Armistice some twenty-five to thirty were acquired by Belgium, where the type was used for some time for pilot training. On 17 June 1919 a D.F.W. C.V established a world altitude record for an aeroplane of its class by flying to 9,620 m. (31,561·7 ft.). The C.VI, which appeared in 1918, remained a prototype only. This aircraft had a 220 h.p. Bz.IVa engine, overhung, balanced ailerons and a redesigned tail unit.

22 A.E.G. C and J types

In 1914–15 the Allgemeine Elektrizitäts Gesellschaft built a small series of unarmed reconnaissance and training biplanes under the designations B.I, B.II and B.III. The first C type (armed 2-seater) was the C.I, based on the B.II, powered by a 150 h.p. Benz Bz.III and having a Bergmann machine-gun in the rear cockpit. In autumn 1915 this was followed by the smaller C.II, a more compact aeroplane capable of carrying four 10 kg. (22 lb.) bombs. The C.III, which also appeared late in 1915, was apparently influenced by the Roland C.II, for it had a deep, clumsy fuselage that completely filled the interplane gap. No production of the C.III was undertaken.

The principal A.E.G. C type to appear was the C.IV, produced in 1916 to meet the need to expand German field reconnaissance and contact patrol units. Externally it generally resembled the C.II, but had wings of much greater span. Its 160 h.p. Mercedes D.III was enclosed in a typical A.E.G. cowling, with the cylinders exposed and a large 'rhino horn' exhaust manifold rising well clear of the top wing. More attention was evidently paid to its structure than to its stream-lining, for Allied reports on captured machines commented favourably on the high standard of welding in its steel-tube airframe. The C.IV entered service in early spring 1916, mainly on escort and reconnaissance duties, and a small number were still operational when the war ended. They were armed with a single Spandau gun offset to starboard in front of the cockpit, with a Parabellum gun on a Schneider ring mounting for the observer; the latter could accommodate up to 90 kg. (198 lb.) of bombs in his cockpit. The only figures available apply collectively to all A.E.G. armed 2-seaters; these record a total output of six hundred and fifty-eight C types, and a peak employment of one hundred and seventy at the Front in June 1917. Probably about five hundred of these would have been C.IVs. Variants included the C.IVN night bomber with longer-span wings, a Bz.III engine and a carrying capacity of six 50 kg. (110 lb.) bombs; it appeared in 1917. The C.V and C.VII both appeared in 1916, the former having a 220 h.p. Mercedes D.IVa and the latter a Mercedes D.III and sweptback upper wings of smaller span. The C.VIII, appearing in July 1917, had an even shorter span, an improved cowling for its Mercedes engine and redesigned tail surfaces. It was also seen in triplane form later in the year.

The major variant, based on the standard C.IV airframe, was that produced for armoured ground-strafing duties from early 1918. The engine and crew positions were encased in some 390 kg. (860 lb.) of armour plating, and to power this heavier machine a 200 h.p. Bz.IV was installed. Initial version was the J.I; with small, lower-wing ailerons added this became the J.Ia; and with balanced, overhung top ailerons, elevators and rudder it was known as the J.II Six hundred and nine A.E.G. J types were built, but they were not an outstanding success. Instead of the normal forward-firing gun, these aircraft had twin Spandaus mounted in the floor of the rear cockpit to fire forward and downward at about 45 degrees; but the guns were difficult to aim properly when the aircraft was flying low. At least one machine flew experimentally as a single-seater, with six of these downward-firing guns.

Production of the C.IV was subcontracted to Fokker, who may have built some of the C.IVa machines reported to have had 180 h.p. Argus As.III engines.

23 Halberstadt C.V

Two principal types were employed by the German Air Force in 1918 for photographic reconnaissance work: of these, the Rumpler C.VII was undoubtedly the superior machine, but its companion, the Halberstadt C.V, was also built and used in substantial numbers. The Halberstadt company's previous C types began with the C.I, a 1916 adaptation, with a rotary engine, of the unarmed B.II. It is doubtful whether this went into production. The C.III, which appeared late in 1917, was the first long-range photographic type designed by Karl Theiss. It was powered by a 200 h.p. Benz Bz.IV and an unusual feature of its design was the attachment of the lower wings to a small 'keel' on the underside of the fuselage. The C.III formed the basis for the C.V, in which a simpler and more conventional attachment was employed for the lower wings.

Powerplant of the C.V was the high-compression version of the Bz.IV developing 220 h.p. and giving a much better performance at altitude. The wings were of wide span, with 2 bays of bracing struts and overhung, balanced ailerons on the upper sections. The fuselage was essentially a scaled-up version of that used in the C.IV, but with separate cockpits for the 2-man crew. Reconnaissance cameras were aimed downward through a trap in the floor of the rear cockpit; the top of the cockpit was built up with the traditional ring mounting for a Parabellum machine-gun. The pilot was furnished with a synchronised

Spandau gun immediately in front of his cockpit on the port side; C.Vs also normally carried wireless equipment. The prototype C.V appeared early in 1918, undergoing its official trials in the spring. Its front-line career lasted from summer 1918 until the Armistice. Production was undertaken by the Aviatik, B.F.W. and D.F.W. companies in addition to those built by Halberstadt.

Variants appearing during 1918 included the C.VII, C.VIII and C.IX. The C.VII (245 h.p. Maybach Mb.IV) and C.IX (230 h.p. Hiero) remained in the prototype stage, though the latter may have been intended for Austro-Hungarian production. The C.VIII, officially tested in October 1918, was a single-bay biplane, slightly smaller than the C.V and powered by an Mb.IV engine; it had a ceiling of 9,000 m. (29,528 ft.), which it could reach in 58 minutes, and was probably intended for series production if the war had continued; however, only the prototype had been completed when the war ended.

24 Rumpler C.IV to C.VII

The C.IV, the second of Dr. Edmund Rumpler's C type designs to go into large-scale production, was preceded by the generally similar C.III, seventy-five of which were recorded in service in February 1917. The C.III was a 1916 design, powered by a 220 h.p. Benz Bz.IV. When the more powerful Mercedes C.IVa became available it was developed into the C.IV, which was one of the most efficient, as well as most elegant, German 2-seaters to

appear on the Western Front. It had the staggered, sweptback wings of 'libellule' planform that characterised subsequent Rumpler C types, and its horizontal tail surfaces were of 'wing-nut' shape. The fuselage was reasonably well streamlined, with attention paid to nose-entry in the neat cowling of the 260 h.p. D.IVa engine and the small conical spinner over the propeller hub. In place of the small, comma-type rudder of the C.III, the C.IV's vertical tail surfaces were of the triangular fin and plain rudder form used on the earlier C.I. The Rumpler C.IV carried the normal 2-seater armament of the period, i.e. a forward-firing synchronised Spandau gun and a ring-mounted Parabellum. The reconnaissance cameras were aimed through a trap in the floor of the rear cockpit. Light 'nuisance' raids were often undertaken, with a small load usually consisting of four 25 kg. bombs on underwing racks. The C.IV had an excellent performance for an aeroplane in its class, especially at high altitude; it could climb to 5,000 m. (16,404 ft.) in 38 minutes, and at its maximum altitude was still fast enough to elude Allied fighters. Rumpler C.IVs saw service in Italy and Palestine as well as on the Western Front; they were built by the Bayerische Rumpler-Werke and Pfalz Flugzeugwerke, those built by the latter concern having linked double ailerons.

The Rumpler C.V was a variant of the C.III airframe fitted with a Mercedes D.IVa, but apparently it did not go into production. There is no record of a C.VI, the next production version being the C.VII, which appeared late in 1917. The C.VII had a 240 h.p. Maybach Mb.IV engine which, although of a lower nominal rating, had a higher compression ratio than the Mercedes D.IVa that enabled it to maintain its output at greater heights. The C.VII was slightly smaller than the C.IV; it was built in two standard forms, the long-range reconnaissance version with radio equipment and a normal 2-gun armament and the C.VII (Rubild). In the latter version the front gun was dispensed with, and instead the aircraft carried additional photographic gear and oxygen breathing apparatus for the crew members, who were also provided with electrically heated flying suits. These assets were extremely necessary, for the C.VII (Rubild) could fly to, and maintain its speed at, even greater heights than those reached by the C.IV. Service ceiling of the C.VII (Rubild) was 7,300 m. (23,950 ft.), which it could reach in 50 minutes. At heights in the region of 20,000 ft. (6,000 m.) it could fly as fast as such Allied fighters as the S.E.5a. Both the Rumpler C.IV and C.VII remained in German Air Force service until the Armistice.

25 L.V.G. C types

Like many other German manufacturers, the Luft-Verkehrs Gesellschaft built a small series of B type unarmed 2-seaters during the early part of World War 1 which formed the basis for armed reconnaissance aircraft when the C category was introduced in spring 1915. The L.V.G. C.I, based on the B.I, has the distinction of being the first 2-seat operational German aircraft in which the observer was provided with a Schneider ring mounting and a Parabellum machine-gun. The first four L.V.G. C types were designed by Franz Schneider. Only limited production was undertaken of the C.I (150 h.p. Bz.III), this being followed late in 1915 by the C.II, the basis for which was the unarmed B.II. The L.V.G. C.II was produced in substantial numbers by the parent company, and by the Ago and Otto works, and was powered by a 160 h.p. Mercedes D.III. It was used extensively for visual and photographic reconnaissance work, and also for light bombing. One aircraft of this type made an audacious daylight raid on London on 28 November 1916, dropping six 10 kg. bombs on Victoria railway station. The raid was not an unqualified success, since the aircraft was obliged to force-land in Allied territory on the return journey. In spring 1916 there were some two hundred and fifty C.I/C.II types in service and some late-production C.IIs had a forward-firing Spandau gun in addition to the usual Parabellum. It is thought that only one example of the C.III was completed, a smaller but slightly heavier version of the C.II in which the observer occupied the front seat. An enlarged version of the C.II appeared in 1916: this was the C.IV, powered by a neatly cowled 220 h.p. Mercedes D.IV and having a balanced rudder.

A major step forward in design and performance was made with the appearance in mid-1917 of the L.V.G. C.V. This was later to serve in considerable numbers alongside the D.F.W. C.V; the external resemblance of these two types to one another is explained by the fact that the engineer responsible for the L.V.G. machine was formerly the chief designer of D.F.W. Among the largest German 2-seaters to be used during the war, the L.V.G. C.V was a neat, compact aircraft with 'libellule' shaped wings and overhung upper ailerons. It had a neatly installed 200 h.p. Benz Bz.IV engine with a leading-edge box-type radiator, and a spinnered propeller. Armament consisted of a single forward-firing Spandau gun and a rear-mounted Parabellum, and up to 115 kg. (254 lb.) of bombs could be carried beneath the lower wings. The C.V was in widespread use by autumn 1917, eventually serving in Palestine as well as on the Western Front. It was an excellent all-rounder, being used for artillery observation, photographic reconnaissance and light bombing. It usually operated with an escort, although it was quite able to give a good account of itself in combat when necessary.

In 1918 the C.V was joined by the C.VI, of which about one thousand were built by L.V.G. The C.VI incorporated a number of modifications, apparently designed both to improve performance and to simplify production. It had a deeper, slightly smaller fuselage, in which the engine was less neatly cowled, and the propeller had no spinner. The wings, which were slightly staggered, had plain ailerons and a flush-mounted centre-section radiator. This last feature, which could be hazardous for the occupants if punctured during combat, was replaced in some aircraft by Windhoff radiators on the sides of the fuselage. The crew members' view from their respective cockpits was considerably better in the C.VI than in the C.V, where their outlook was restricted by a confusion of cabane struts, engine cylinders and radiator. Larger and rounder horizontal tail surfaces were also fitted to the C.VI. A variant of the C.VI which appeared in 1918 was the C.VIII; apparently only one was completed, with a high-compression Bz.IVü engine of 240 h.p., linked double ailerons and other minor improvements.

26 Albatros C.V, C.VII, C.X and C.XII

Up to and including the C.IV, the early Albatros C types were fundamentally descendants of the unarmed B series designed by Ernst Heinkel. The first entirely newly designed C type was the C.V, the joint handiwork of Thelen and Schubert. Appearing in spring 1916, it utilised a wing cellule resembling, but slightly larger than, that of the Albatros C.III, but the new cigar-shaped fuselage, spinnered propeller and rounded tail unit reflected the same approach to streamlining as that practised on the early Albatros single-seat fighters. The C.V was powered by an almost fully cowled

220 h.p. Mercedes D.IV with, in the original C.V/16 form (i.e. built in 1916), prominent Windhoff radiators on either side of the front fuselage. It was fitted with a synchronised Spandau machine-gun for the pilot, mounted on the starboard side of the engine, with a ring-mounted Parabellum gun in the observer's cockpit. A bomb load of up to 175 kg. (386 lb.) could be carried. The C.V/16 was not a particularly elegant aeroplane, and was a cumbersome one to fly; in this respect the C.V/17 was some improvement, having a flush-mounted wing radiator, balanced and tapered ailerons on the top wings and elliptical tips to the lower ones. Four hundred and twenty-four C.Vs were completed by Albatros, but only a fraction of these were in service at any one time between early spring 1916 and the beginning of 1917. Apart from their indifferent flying qualities the C.Vs were repeatedly beset by engine crankshaft failures, and when production of the D.IV engine was abandoned, that of the Albatros C.V also came to an end. One C.V/16 was built experimentally with clumsy I-type interplane struts, but these did not improve the type's performance.

The next production Albatros C type was the C.VII, which went into service late in 1916. Albatros had in mind a C.V development using the 260 h.p. Mercedes D.IVa engine, but pending the availability of this powerplant the C.VII was produced as an interim measure for long-range reconnaissance and artillery observation. It was powered by a 200 h.p.

Benz Bz.IV, installed in typical Germanic fashion with the cylinder heads exposed, and the airframe was a mixture of C.V/16 and C.V/17 components. The lower wings and side radiators of the C.V/16 were combined with the upper wings of the C.V/17. Like other compromise designs before it (and since), the C.VII flew and fought very well, and was successful enough to be built in considerable numbers. It was still in service late in 1917, its peak period of employment having been in February of that year when three hundred and fifty were in service on all Fronts. Production of the C.VII was shared between Albatros, O.A.W. and B.F.W.

In mid-1917 the fully developed version of the C.V appeared in the form of the C.X, powered by the long-awaited Mercedes D.IVa engine. The C.X was appreciably larger than its predecessors, and showed even greater similarity of outline to the Albatros D types. The flush-mounted wing radiator was reinstated in new wings of increased span with double ailerons. With these aerodynamic improvements and the greater power and reliability of the D.IVa engine, the C.X had an excellent altitude performance and usually carried oxygen equipment for the crew in addition to wireless and/or a light bomb load. Production was shared between the parent company, O.A.W., Linke-Hofmann, B.F.W. and L.F.G. (Roland), and by October 1917 there were three hundred C.Xs in service. The type remained with front-line reconnaissance and artillery co-operation units until mid-1918.

The Albatros C.XII (the C.XI remained a project only) appeared early in 1918 as a successor to the C.X, and continued to serve until the Armistice. In this ultimate form it could probably claim to be the most handsome German 2-seater on the Western Front, its elegant, rakish lines and the addition of a small fin beneath the rear fuselage emphasising still more the design resemblance between the Albatros C and D types. The final production Albatros C type was the C.XV, evolved from the C.XIV prototype of 1917. This was a smaller and much less elegant aeroplane, with a hump-backed fuselage, short-span staggered wings and a 220 h.p. Bz.IVa engine. It went into production in 1918, but only a few had entered service when the war ended.

Post-war designations of the C.V, C.VII, C.X, C.XII and C.XV were, respectively, L.14, L.18, L.25, L.27 and L.47.

27 L.F.G. (Roland) C.II

The Roland C.II 2-seater was an extremely advanced design, and one of the best German aircraft on the Western Front during the second half of 1916. It was the smallest C type used by Germany during the war period, being less than 50 kg. (110 lb.) over the weight limit for the lighter CL category. The design, by Dipl. Ing. Tantzen, featured an extremely strong, ply-covered semi-monocoque fuselage, beautifully streamlined and completely filling the interplane gap. The wings had a single 'I' srut and a minimum of external bracing wires. An excellent view of the upper hemisphere was enjoyed by both crew members, but the view downward past the nose, already poor, was restricted further by the large side radiators, and made the C.II a difficult aeroplane to land.

The first C.II was flown in October 1915, but the first handful of production aircraft were not delivered until March 1916 and had only a rearward-firing Parabellum gun in the observer's cockpit. Some squadrons met the need for a forward-firing gun by installing captured Lewises above the centre-section, but on later C.IIs a fixed, synchronised Spandau was provided. The first C.IIs in service were flown by the Kampfgeschwadern involved in the fighting at Verdun and the Somme in spring 1916, and their performance was well above that of contemporary German 2-seaters. In fact, the Roland C.II was as fast as the opposing Nieuport and Pup fighters, although it was less manoeuvrable and took half an hour to reach its fighting altitude of 3,000 m. (9,843 ft.). A number were lost in landing accidents due to the poor frontal view, and some weakness was found in the outer wing sections. This led to the introduction, from August 1916, of the C.IIa, with revised and reinforced wingtips. Late in 1916 the C.II was used for night bombing with four 12·5 kg. (28 lb.) bombs beneath the fuselage. In mid-year Capt. Albert Ball, who scored his first confirmed victory over a Roland

C.II, had called it 'the best German machine now', yet it never served at the front in outstanding numbers; the Roland's meticulous streamlining demanded careful and therefore costly constructional methods, which restricted the total built. Peak employment of the C.II/IIa came in December 1916, when sixty-four were at the Front. It was withdrawn slowly during the first half of 1917, after which the majority were employed for training, though some were retained for combat duty on quieter sectors of the Western Front and in Russia. Total production is estimated at between two hundred and fifty and three hundred, some two hundred of these by the parent company and the remainder by Linke-Hofmann. Some late-production aircraft had an enlarged vertical tail. In 1916 a single C.III was produced: this was a C.II development with 2-bay wings, parallel interplane struts, revised tail surfaces and a 200 h.p. Benz Bz.IV engine.

28 Phönix C.I

As explained in the description of the Ufag C.I (page 125), that aircraft and the Phönix C.I 2-seaters which appeared in Austro-Hungarian service in 1918 shared a common descent from the Hansa-Brandenburg C.II 'star-strutter' designed by Ernst Heinkel in Germany. Both were chosen for production, the Phönix machine in Series 121, and aircraft 121.01 and 121.02 were utilised as prototypes. They differed principally in their cabane strutting and radiator positions, and 121.02

was subsequently brought up to production standard with a centrally mounted 'Hifa' radiator in the top leading edge. Production Series 121 aircraft were powered by 230 h.p. Hiero engines and, except for the additional crew position, bore a strong resemblance to the Phönix D.I fighter. The unequal-span wings had distinctive, backward-curving tips and were braced by parallel pairs of 'V' struts. The deep, narrow fuselage left a minimum of gap below the top wing, thus giving the pilot an excellent view forward and upward. From the elevated gun position in the rear cockpit the observer also had a first-class field of view and of fire. Armament consisted of a synchronised forward-firing Schwarzlose machine-gun under the port-side engine panels, firing through an aperture in the front of the cowling; a second free-firing Schwarzlose gun was installed in the rear cockpit. A modest bomb load of 50 kg. (110 lb.) could be carried beneath the lower wings. The Phönix C.I went into service in spring 1918 and was used until the end of the war on both visual and photographic reconnaissance work. About one hundred and ten were built for the Fliegerkompagnien. They were somewhat slower than the Ufag 2-seaters, but had better take-off characteristics, climbing powers and performance at altitude.

After the war thirty aircraft of this type were built in Sweden by the Army Aircraft Workshops at Malmslatt, with 220 h.p. Benz Bz.IV engines in place of the Austrian powerplants. They went into service early in 1919 with the Royal Swedish Army Aviation under the title S 21 Dront and continued to be used until well into the 1920s.

29 Ufag C.I

Examples of the Hansa-Brandenburg C.II 2-seat 'star-strutter' designed by Ernst Heinkel were completed in Austro-Hungary in 1916 by both the Phönix Flugzeugwerke and the Ungarische Flugzeugfabrik A.G. Each company developed its own C.I derivative of this aeroplane, which were flown in comparative trials in January 1917. Both were powered by 230 h.p. Hiero engines; the Ufag C.I differed from its compatriot in having parallel interplane struts, equal-span, round-tipped wings with a moderate stagger and a squarish, balanced rudder. Each aircraft had an elevated gun ring in the rear cockpit for a single Schwarzlose machine-gun.

Flight trials revealed that each aircraft had some features superior to the other, and it was finally decided to put both into production. The Ufag C.I had a somewhat poorer ceiling and take-off than the Phönix, but it was appreciably faster and more manoeuvrable. Consequently, in service, while both types carried out general observation duties, the Ufag was used for lower-level missions such as artillery co-operation, while the Phönix C.I, with its higher ceiling, was chosen for photographic reconnaissance. In its production form the Ufag C.I had a smaller tailplane, and a plain rudder with a triangular fixed fin

that improved the aircraft's directional stability. One or two synchronised forward-firing guns could be mounted in the front of the fuselage. Possibly because of production priority afforded to the Phönix single-seat fighters, the two C types did not go into service much before spring 1918, but for the remaining period of the war they carried out useful work and a small batch of Ufag C.Is were supplied to Romania after the war ended. It may be supposed that the Ufag was considered the better machine, since it was also manufactured under licence by Phönix as well as by the parent company. Phönix-built Ufag C.Is, at least thirty-six of which were completed, were designated Series 123, while Ufag's own machines were known as Series 161; more than one hundred were built by Ufag.

30 Anatra D and DS

The first major task of the Anatra aircraft factory at Odessa was the production of Voisin-type bombers. Based on the Voisin LA.S, with local modifications designed by Lt. V. Ivanov of the Imperial Russian Air Service, up to one hundred and fifty of these aircraft were built with the designation VI (Voisin Ivanov) with 150 h.p. Salmson (Canton-Unné) engines between March 1915 and March 1916. Unfortunately they were a wretched failure, many crashes occurring due to extremely poor stability and a lack of lateral control; a modified version was test-flown by Ivanov early in 1917 and received qualified approval, but the crashes continued and the VI was finally dismissed as 'quite unfit for fighting purposes'.

Early in 1916 Anatra produced a design of its own, the Type D, a 2-seat reconnaissance tractor biplane with a 100 h.p. Gnome Monosoupape engine. An initial order for eighty Anatra Ds, placed in April 1916, was supplemented by later orders for a further seven hundred. The first of them went into service that summer, when inevitably they inherited the unfortunate reputation of the VI. This they did not deserve, although they were variously reported as being nose-heavy and liable to lose power due to inefficient engine cooling. A shortage of raw materials, particularly good-quality timber, led to makeshift constructional methods which caused many machines to break up in the air when flown under combat conditions. Production was curtailed after only two hundred and five Anatra Ds had been completed. Their peak period of employment came in spring 1917: seventy-six were at the Front in April, but this figure had dwindled to forty by June and the type disappeared from front-line service by the end of the year. Despite its shortcomings, a well-built Anatra D in the hands of a competent pilot was by no means an unsatisfactory aeroplane. It could climb to 2,000 m. (6,560 ft.) in 15 minutes, and was armed with one or two defensive machine-guns.

The Russian aircraft industry was always hampered by aero-engine supply problems, and some Anatra

Ds were fitted with 130 h.p. Clerget rotary engines.

A developed version which appeared in service from mid-1917 was the Anatra DS, with a 150 h.p. Salmson (Canton-Unné) radial engine (which gave it its popular name of 'Anasal'). The DS was armed with a synchronised forward-firing gun and a ring-mounted gun in the rear cockpit. Production of the DS was curtailed by the November Revolution, by which time about a hundred had been completed.

31 Junkers J.I

The J.I, which must vie with the Airco D.H.6 as the most angular aeroplane of World War 1, was the only one of Hugo Junkers' many all-metal aircraft of the war period to be completed as a biplane. It was evolved to replace the interim A.E.G. and Albatros J types for infantry contact patrol and support duties with the Flieger Abteilungen, and made its first flight early in 1917. As such, its function was to fly at low level over the trenches and forward infantry positions to report troop concentrations and movements by means of a W/T link; and its metal construction afforded it excellent protection from ground fire, which was often heavy. The 5 mm. armoured shell which enclosed the 200 h.p. Benz Bz.IV engine and the crew positions alone weighed some 470 kg. (1,036 lb.), and in later examples the rear fuselage section was also metal-skinned. Other distinctive features of the design included the enormous span of the upper wings and the uncommonly short-legged undercarriage.

Production J.Is differed from the prototype in having overhung, balanced ailerons and rudder and a redesigned vertical fin. The airscrew spinner was frequently omitted from aircraft in service, some of which carried a camera in the rear of the fuselage. Manufacture of J.Is was shared between the Junkers and Fokker factories: a total of two hundred and twenty-seven were built, the first being completed in October 1917. They entered service at the beginning of 1918, and soon proved efficient at their job. Frequently the J.Is would drop ammunition and food supplies to their own forward troops during the course of a mission. The J.I's size and weight necessitated long take-off and landing runs, and it was rather heavy to handle – factors which led the J.I to be nicknamed Möbelwagen (Furniture Van). Nevertheless, its crews appreciated its strength and the protection it offered, and it was generally regarded as the best German armoured type to appear during the war. Usual armament consisted of two Spandau machine-guns installed under the front engine decking, with a single ring-mounted Parabellum gun in the rear cockpit. Early in their service some J.Is carried, instead of W/T equipment, two extra downward-firing Parabellum guns, manned by the observer, but it was found difficult to aim these successfully at low level while the aircraft was flying fast, and the practice was soon abandoned. At the peak of their employment one hundred and eighty-nine Junkers J.Is were in service at the Front.

32 Ansaldo S.V.A. series

The outstanding S.V.A. biplanes that rendered such excellent service to the Italian Air Force in the final year of World War 1 were largely the handiwork of Umberto Savoia and Rudolfo Verduzio. The design was begun in 1916 as a single-seat fighter, its development being undertaken by Ansaldo as a private venture. However, it showed such promise that, with massive backing from the Italian government, the Ansaldo company was able to expand to such an extent that the S.V.A. series became the second most widely built Italian type of 1914–18.

The S.V.A. prototype, which flew for the first time on 3 March 1917, was an elegant machine with a slender, ply-covered fuselage and thin-section wings braced with a Warren-type interplane truss. It had a range, speed and climb far in excess of any other aircraft in Italian service at that time, but because it lacked the manoeuvrability of the contemporary Hanriot HD.1 the Italian Air Force decided instead to employ it in the reconnaissance and light bombing roles. Production began in autumn 1917, the first Ansaldo-built version apparently being the S.V.A.4, which entered service in February 1918. (A short-span version built by A.E.R. was designated S.V.A.3; it was used in small numbers for home defence and occasional reconnaissance from spring 1918.) The

S.V.A.4 was powered by a 220 h.p. S.P.A. 6A engine and carried a usual armament of twin forward-firing synchronised Vickers guns; one of the guns could be omitted when a reconnaissance camera was installed. A seaplane version was known as the I.S.V.A.

The major single-seat version was the S.V.A.5, with minor variations and the same powerplant as the S.V.A.4. The two types were soon in use, both for bombing raids across the Alps to Austria and Germany and along the length of the Adriatic. They also provided much extremely valuable photographic intelligence during the summer and autumn campaigns in 1918 which led to the Austrian surrender. A few S.V.A. landplanes formed part of the mixed equipment of one Italian naval squadron, being evaluated as potential torpedo bombers, and fifty twin-float I.S.V.As. were produced in 1918 for defending naval bases and patrolling the Italian coastline.

Alternative engines tested in the S.V.A. during 1917 included the 220 h.p. Lorraine-Dietrich and the 250 h.p. Isotta-Fraschini V-6. The latter unit was chosen for two 2-seat variants that appeared in 1918. These were the S.V.A.9, an unarmed trainer, and the S.V.A.10, for reconnaissance and bombing. The S.V.A.10, which entered service around August/September 1918, carried a single forward-firing Vickers gun and a Lewis gun on a flexible mounting in the rear cockpit.

The S.V.A.'s long-range capabilities were demonstrated repeatedly during the final months of the war; in September 1918 the prototype made a flight of 900 miles (1,448 km.) non-stop. In February 1919 two S.V.As. (of seven starters) completed an 11,250 mile (18,105 km.) flight from Rome to Tokyo in 109 flying hours. By the end of 1918, one thousand two hundred and fifty had been built (including I.S.V.As.), and this total had increased to two thousand before production ended in 1928. The S.V.As. remained in Italian service for many years, both at home and in North Africa. In 1923 six squadrons were still equipped with them, and they did not finally pass out of service until the mid-1930s. Many were used by Italian civil flying schools and clubs in the 1920s; others were flown as sporting and racing aircraft in Italy and the United States; and military S.V.As. were exported to Argentina, Ecuador, Peru and Latvia.

33 S.I.A. 7 and 9 and Fiat R-2

The Società Italiana Aviazione of Turin, a subsidiary of the famous Fiat motor-car building concern, was occupied during the first year or two of Italy's involvement in World War 1 with the production of foreign aircraft under licence. However, in 1917 it produced a native design, by Savoia and Verduzio (who also designed the Ansaldo scouts). This was the S.I.A. 7B, a 2-seat armed reconnaissance biplane powered by a 260 h.p. Fiat A-12 engine. As the S.I.A. 7B.1 it entered service with the Corpo

Aeronautica Militare in November 1917, and was armed with a Revelli machine-gun on a Nieuport-type mounting in the rear cockpit with a second gun of the same type mounted over the top wing to fire forward outside the propeller arc. A light bomb load of some 60 kg. (132 lb.) could be carried beneath the lower wings. The S.I.A. 7B.1 was a manoeuvrable aeroplane, with good level and climbing speeds, but its career was marred by a succession of structural failures of the wing cellule, which resulted in the type being withdrawn from front-line service in July 1918. Five hundred and one S.I.A. 7B.1s were built; two were sent to the United States for evaluation in 1917, and in February 1918 the A.E.F. purchased a further nineteen for use on the Italian Front.

A later and supposedly stronger version, the S.I.A. 7B.2, was powered by the 300 h.p. Fiat A-12bis, and had the rear fuselage deepened in order to bring the two cockpits on a level with the top of the engine cowling. This considerably improved the crew members' field of view compared with the S.I.A. 7B.1, in which the high engine decking seriously obstructed the view to the front. The S.I.A. 7B.2 inherited the same speed, climbing and endurance powers of its predecessor, and one aircraft of this type flew non-stop from Turin to London, a distance of some 1,200 km. (746 miles). Unfortunately it also inherited the same wing weaknesses that had plagued the 7B.1, and both types were withdrawn from the front line at the same time. The S.I.A. 7B.2 had been in service for only about two months, and only seventy-one of these aircraft were built.

An enlarged bomber/reconnaissance development flew for the first time late in 1917. This was the S.I.A. 9B, also a 2-seater, but powered by the large 700 h.p. Fiat A-14 and capable of carrying a 350 kg. (772 lb.) bomb load. The S.I.A. 9B was in service by February 1918, but despite its useful performance with a reasonable war load, it, too, was subject to the same structural weaknesses as the earlier models. The Italian Army air service refused to operate it, and only sixty-two S.I.A. 9Bs, of five hundred ordered, were completed. These flew with three squadriglie of the Italian Navy.

The weakness of the basic design was finally overcome in 1918, after S.I.A. had become Fiat Aviazione, and the airframe was redesigned by Celestino Rosatelli. The result was the Fiat R-2, a much improved and slightly smaller form of the S.I.A. 7B.2, retaining the same powerplant and having provision for single or twin Lewis guns in the rear cockpit in addition to the wing-mounted Revelli gun. Five hundred R-2s were ordered, entering production in autumn 1918, but only one hundred and twenty-nine were completed by the Armistice. The Fiat R-2 thus saw little operational service during World War 1, but it continued as a standard reconnaissance and bomber type with the post-war Italian Air Force until 1925.

34 Pomilio P types

The most widely produced aircraft of Italian design during World War I were the P series of armed 2-seaters built by the Fabbrica Aeroplani Ing. O. Pomilio of Turin during 1917–18. The first of these to enter service (in March 1917) was the PC, powered by a 260 h.p. Fiat A-12 in a rather Germanic cowling that left the cylinder heads exposed. Pilot and observer sat in close-mounted, separate cockpits, the former having a Revelli machine-gun fixed over the top wing to fire at an angle outside the propeller arc, and the latter with another Revelli on a Nieuport-type mounting. The PC was fast enough to dispense with fighter escort on its reconnaissance missions, but it suffered from pronounced instability, which was the cause of frequent accidents. To eliminate this the next model, the PD, introduced a small, curved underfin incorporating the tail-skid; other changes included a revised engine cowling, in which the cylinder heads were enclosed in louvred panels, and a box radiator in front of the top wing replacing the vertical radiator in front of the PC's cockpit.

By far the most successful variant was the PE, which went into service in February 1918. This had a 300 h.p. A-12bis engine with a frontal radiator, a slightly enlarged upper fin and a bigger tailplane. The PE was armed with a synchronised, forward-firing machine-gun and a Scarff ring in the rear cockpit for one or two Lewis guns. It could climb to 3,000 m. (9,843 ft.) in 16 minutes.

The Pomilio P types flew with thirty squadriglie of the Corpo Aeronautica Militare, of which eighteen squadriglie had PDs or PEs during 1918. One hundred and twelve PEs were marshalled for the Battle of Vittorio Veneto on 20 October 1918. Total output of the three types reached one thousand six hundred and sixteen: five hundred and forty-five PCs and PDs during 1917, and one thousand and seventy-one PDs and PEs during 1918. Final variant was the PY, generally similar to the PE but with squared-off top decking to improve the observer's field of fire; only seven PYs were built. The Pomilio brothers then sold their business to Ansaldo and emigrated to the United States, where they continued their aeronautical activities. They designed two types evaluated by the U.S. Signal Corps, the FVL-8 and BVL-12. The former was a single-seat fighter with a 280 h.p. Liberty 8 engine, the latter a 2-seat bomber with a 400 h.p. Liberty 12. Six FVL-8s and five BVL-12s were completed.

35 S.A.M.L. S.1 and S.2

The German Aviatik B.I armed 2-seater was the subject of extensive licence production in Italy during World War I. The first three versions to appear were designated A.1 (100 h.p. Fiat A-10), A.2 (120 h.p. Le Rhône) and A.3 (110 h.p. Colombo). The majority, however, were powered with 140 h.p. Salmson (Canton-Unné) radial engines, but 160 h.p. Isotto-Fraschini V-4Bs were installed in some late-production examples. Five hundred and sixty-eight Aviatiks were built in Italy during 1915–18, and four hundred and ten of these were completed by the Società Aeronautica Meccanica Lombarda of Monza. Until early 1917 these were employed extensively by the Italian reconnaissance squadrons; thereafter they were transferred to training duties, on which they continued to serve until 1930.

From the beginning of 1917 they began to be replaced in the reconnaissance role by an Italian product, the S.A.M.L. S.1, designed by the Swiss engineer Robert Wild, who had previously been responsible in Germany for the Aviatik B.I and B.II. The S.A.M.L. S.1 was basically an enlarged, 3-bay development of the Aviatik, with a 260 h.p. Fiat A-12 engine and a rotatable 6·5 mm. Revelli machine-gun on a tripod mounting in the rear cockpit. The S.1 was primarily a reconnaissance type, though it could carry up to 40 kg. (88 lb.) of small bombs. It served principally with the I Armata of the Corpo Aeronautica Militare at Trentino on artillery-spotting and occasional bombing duties. From the summer of 1917 it was joined in service by the S.2, which had shorter-span, 2-bay unstaggered wings with dihedral on the lower planes; a fully curved rudder in place of the flat-topped rudder of the S.1; and a second Revelli machine-gun mounted over the top wing to fire at an angle outside the propeller arc.

The S.A.M.L. 2-seaters were strongly built, reliable aircraft with good handling qualities, and were well liked by the crews who flew them. Between 1916 and 1918 six hundred and fifty-seven S.1s and S.2s were completed, serving with sixteen Squadriglie da Ricognizione in Italy, Albania and Macedonia. Some S.2s carried camera equipment instead of a bomb load, and others were fitted with dual controls and employed for training. The first S.2s had the same powerplant as the S.1, but in later machines the more powerful 300 h.p. A-12bis was installed. Some aircraft of this type survived the war and later saw action again during Italy's military campaigns in North Africa.

36 Royal Aircraft Factory B.E.2, B.E.2a and B.E.2b

The first B.E. type* produced by the Army Aircraft Factory was the B.E.1, designed by Geoffrey de Havilland and F. M. Green in the second half of 1911. Ostensibly, it was supposed to be a reconstruction of a Voisin biplane; in fact, almost its only connection with the Voisin was the latter's 60 h.p. Wolseley engine, and even this was changed for a 60 h.p. Renault some time after the B.E.1's first flight on 1 January 1912. The B.E.1 later served with the R.F.C., with the official serial number 201.

* Under the Army Aircraft Factory designation system adopted in November 1911 the letters B.E. signified Blériot Experimental. However, this was merely to indicate that the B.E. types were general-purpose 2-seat tractor biplanes; they had no design or other connection with aircraft of Blériot origin.

The B.E.2, which appeared in February 1912, was a developed version with equal-span unstaggered wings and a 70 h.p. Renault; it was a 2-seater, with the pilot in the rear cockpit. On 12 August 1912 the B.E.2 was flown to a new British altitude record of 10,560 ft. (3,218·7 m.), and later that month it demonstrated its superiority to the Cody biplane that had officially won the Military Trials at Larkhill. A token order for four B.E.2s had been placed with Vickers nearly three months before this, and the first of these machines was delivered to the R.F.C. in February 1913. Other orders followed, and most production aircraft at this time were delivered as B.E.2as, with unequal-span wings, additional decking round the front cockpit and a modified fuel system. Before the outbreak of World War 1 the B.E.2/2a was in service with three R.F.C. squadrons, and at least one such aircraft was in the possession of the R.N.A.S. in September 1913.

Following the outbreak of war, the B.Es. served in France with Nos. 2, 4, 6, 8, 9 (Wireless) and 16 Squadrons R.F.C., and with the former R.N.A.S. Eastchurch Squadron in the Ostend/Dunkirk area. They were joined by the B.E.2b, which differed in its elevator and rudder controls and had redesigned top-decking and cockpit contours to give better protection to the crew. The first air V.C. of the war was awarded, posthumously, to Lt. W. B. Rhodes-Moorhouse of No. 2 Squadron, who, despite his wounds, brought his B.E. back suc-

cessfully from a bombing attack on the railway station at Courtrai on 26 April 1915. Another officer of No. 2 Squadron had, on 13 August 1914, piloted the first British aircraft (a B.E.2a) to land in France after the outbreak of war. The B.Es. of the R.N.A.S. were used quite often for bombing, carrying a single 100 lb. bomb or three smaller ones under the fuselage. Early B.Es. carried no fixed defensive armament, their only protection being rifles or revolvers carried by the observer. These often fired incendiary bullets in efforts to shoot down enemy airships. The early B.Es. saw almost all of their operational service in France, although small numbers of R.F.C. machines were flown in Egypt and one or two R.N.A.S. aircraft took part in the Dardanelles campaign.

There are one hundred and sixty-four known serial number allocations for B.E.2/2a/2b aircraft, completed by nine British manufacturers; undoubtedly more than these were built, but surviving records make it impossible to give more precise figures. Final B.E.2b deliveries were made in late autumn 1916, by which time the type had been obsolete for at least a year. Late-production aircraft, and earlier machines withdrawn from front-line service, however, served a further useful period in a training capacity.

37 Royal Aircraft Factory B.E.2c and B.E.2d

Throughout its early existence the Royal Aircraft Factory and its antecedents were concerned – one might even say obsessed – with the evolution of an inherently stable aeroplane. They believed, quite rightly, that such an aeroplane would be easier and safer to fly; doubtless they were also influenced by the War Office's opinion that aircraft were only of use for reconnaissance, for which a steady-flying machine was even more desirable. Unhappily, while combat experience in France was almost every day proving this attitude to be wrong, from an operational standpoint, the Factory either was not told (or, if it was, it chose to ignore) the fact that it was the very stability of the B.E. that was contributing to its downfall. Against the nimble, front-gunned Fokker monoplane fighters the B.E.2 was virtually helpless: it was far too stable to outmanoeuvre the enemy, too slow to run away from him and, since it needed 45 minutes to reach its modest ceiling of 10,000 ft. (3,048 m.), had no hope at all of outclimbing him.

The B.E.2 type had been the principal mount of one of the Factory's leading experimental fliers, Edward Busk, during his researches into the matter of inherent stability. The main results of his findings took expression in the B.E.2c, which was first flown in early summer of 1914. This version had equal-span wings with marked forward stagger and double ailerons in place of the warp control of the earlier B.Es.; vertical fin area was also increased. A few B.E.2cs reached France late in 1914, but the first unit fully equipped with them (No. 8 Squadron) did not arrive until April 1915. By this time the R.A.F.1a engine (developed from the Renault of earlier B.E.2cs) had become the standard power-plant, and a plain Vee-type undercarriage replaced the earlier wheel-and-skid arrangement. Bomb load of Renault-powered B.E.2cs comprised four 25 lb. Cooper bombs suspended beneath the nose; R.A.F. 1a-engined aircraft carried two 112 lb. or ten 20 lb. bombs under the wings; with the heavier load they were usually flown solo from the rear cockpit. The B.E.2c ultimately served on the Western Front with No. 1 Wing R.N.A.S. and with more than a dozen R.F.C. squadrons. It was also flown as a bomber or reconnaissance type in Macedonia and the Middle East, and Naval B.E.2cs served as bombers and anti-submarine aircraft in the Dardanelles and the Aegean. From spring 1916 the B.E.2d began to join it in service. This had a large gravity fuel tank beneath the top wing, which increased its range with a similar load to the B.E.2c, but it took nearly twice as long as the B.E.2c to reach 10,000 ft. The new version was somewhat better defended, the observer occupying its rear cockpit armed with a free-firing Lewis gun. A few B.E.2ds were supplied to Escadrille 6 of the Belgian Aviation Militaire, being fitted with 150 h.p. Hispano-Suiza engines.

Notwithstanding its unhappy reputation as 'Fokker fodder' in France, the B.E.2c enjoyed rather more success at home. Here its stability made it a good gun platform for night fighting, and, flown solo from the back seat, with an upward-firing Lewis gun above the top wing, it achieved some success as a Home Defence fighter, including the destruction of seven airships. The lesson of the losses in France, however, was not learned: its only result seemed to be to step up production, and the type was still in front-line service when the last B.E.2c was delivered in July 1917. A precise figure cannot be given, but a total output of B.E.2c/2d in the region of one thousand three hundred aircraft seems likely. These two models remained in service until the Armistice, latterly in a training capacity.

38 Royal Aircraft Factory B.E.2e

The final production model in the ill-starred B.E.2 series, the B.E.2e, was a little faster and was lighter on the controls than its predecessors, but was no real improvement. Indeed, it had a poorer climb than the B.E.2c and, inexplicably, reverted to the outmoded back-to-front seating arrangement, thus severely limiting the use that the observer could make of his defensive machine-gun. Structurally, it differed appreciably from previous models, having single-bay wings with blunt, raked tips and a pronounced difference in span between the upper and lower planes. The tailplane and elevator tips were also raked back, and a larger, more curved vertical fin was fitted.

Some B.E.2c/2d contracts were amended to specify B.E.2es, the first examples of the new model being delivered to the R.F.C. in July 1916. They subsequently served in virtually all of the squadrons that had flown earlier B.E.2 variants, and served in Macedonia and India as well as on the Western Front. About ninety-five R.F.C. B.E.2es were transferred to the R.N.A.S. for training duties; some of these were powered by 75 h.p. Rolls-Royce Hawk engines. In August 1918 the U.S. Navy bought twelve B.E.2es for use as trainers.

It is well-nigh impossible to give a production breakdown for the B.E.2 series. The building programme was so widespread, and many contracts either remain unconfirmed or specified a mixture of two or more variants. In addition to the Royal Aircraft Factory, at least twenty-two other British manufacturers are known to have participated in the production programme, the major contributors being the British & Colonial Aeroplane Co., Ruston Proctor & Co., Vickers Ltd., Vulcan Motor & Engineering Co., and G. & J. Weir. Serial allocations can be confirmed for three thousand five hundred and thirty-five B.E.2-type aircraft, but almost certainly more than this number were built. This suggests that a B.E.2e figure upward of one thousand eight hundred, of which about half are believed to have been employed on training duties, is a reasonable approximation.

39 Royal Aircraft Factory R.E.5

The R.E.5 was the first of the Royal Aircraft Factory's Reconnaissance

Experimental biplanes to be put into production, twenty-four being built with the money received by the War Office from the Admiralty in autumn 1913 as payment for the Army airships taken over by the Navy. The R.E.5 appeared in 1914 as a large 2-seat, 2-bay biplane with wings of equal span, chord and profile and a marked dihedral. Ailerons were fitted to both top and bottom wings. The R.E.5 was powered by the Beardmore version of the 120 h.p. Austro-Daimler engine, enclosed in a long, bull-nosed cowling. The observer, who had nothing but small-arms for protective armament, occupied the front cockpit, and a normal bomb load of 60 lb. (27 kg.) could be carried.

The R.E.5 was flown operationally in France by No. 2 Squadron R.F.C. from September 1914 and by No. 7 Squadron from April 1915. Capt. J. A. Liddell of the latter squadron was awarded the V.C. for bringing back a badly damaged R.E.5 in July. One R.E.5 bomber was also used by the R.N.A.S., operating from Dunkirk, in September 1914. The keynote of the previous R.E. designs had been stability in the air, and one of the R.E.1s was flown extensively by Edward Busk at Farnborough during his researches into the nature of inherent stability. The R.E.5 inherited the reliability and straight-forward handling qualities of its predecessors, and was sturdily built. Unfortunately this lack of agility and the absence of a protective armament detracted seriously from the R.E.5's operational value, and its career was short-lived.

The sixth production R.E.5 was converted to a single-seater and given extended-span wings for high-altitude flying trials: this aircraft reached a height of 17,000 ft. (5,182 m.) in June 1914. Another machine, similarly modified, was employed at Farnborough for flight trials of the Factory's 336 lb. bomb and its carrying gear, and formed the basis for the subsequent R.E.7.

40 **Royal Aircraft Factory R.E.7**

Shortly after the outbreak of World War 1 the Royal Aircraft Factory designed a new 336 lb. bomb, and this weapon, and its carrying gear, were air-tested on a modified R.E.5 in 1915. The R.E.7, whose design was also completed in 1915, was designed primarily as a carrier for this weapon. Its prototype was similar to the R.E.5 test aircraft, but had an even greater wing span and area.

Orders were placed for five hundred R.E.7s, but only just over half of this total were built: one hundred by Siddeley-Deasy, fifty each by Napier and Coventry Ordnance Works and fifty-two by the Austin Motor Co. As a temporary measure early production R.E.7s were fitted with 120 h.p. or 160 h.p. Beardmore engines, but as soon as supplies of the 150 h.p. R.A.F.4a became available this was adopted as the standard powerplant. Deliveries began late in 1915, and the first unit to be equipped fully with R.E.7s, No. 21

Squadron R.F.C., arrived with them in France in January 1916. No. 21 remained the only squadron to be equipped wholly with R.E.7s, although a few were also flown by No. 12 Squadron, and at least one (a 3-seater) was on the strength of No. 20 Squadron. For most of their service in France the R.E.7s were misemployed on escort or reconnaissance duties, for which they were too slow and inadequately armed. They did not undertake bombing until early summer 1916, and by August their replacement by B.E.12s had already begun. As an alternative to the large Farnborough bomb, the R.E.7 could carry two 112 lb. weapons and a few small bombs to an equivalent total weight. It was armed with only a single Lewis machine-gun on a makeshift mounting in the front cockpit.

After their withdrawal from front-line duty the R.E.7s were employed at training establishments until 1918, their work including target towing. A few were converted into 3-seaters, with a ring-mounted machine-gun in the third cockpit, and others were used in experimental installations of the 190 h.p. Falcon I, 200 h.p. R.A.F.3a and 225 h.p. Sunbeam engines. Six R.E.7s were allocated to the R.N.A.S.

41 Royal Aircraft Factory R.E.8

The design of the R.E.8, undertaken late in 1915, was to provide the R.F.C. with a better-defended replacement for the later B.E.2

variants. In its production form it certainly carried a more effective armament, but the stubborn adherence by the Royal Aircraft Factory to the concept of inherent stability meant that the R.E.8, like its predecessors, could easily be outmanoeuvred by the more nimble German fighters. Two prototypes (7996 and 7997) were completed, the first flying on 17 June 1916 and the second about three weeks later. They were powered by R.A.F.4a engines, which remained the standard installation in production R.E.8s, and had B.E.2e-type wings with marked stagger and dihedral.

Production began in August 1916, the first few machines having, like the prototypes, a drum-fed Lewis gun mounted low down in the cockpit and firing between propeller blades fitted with bullet deflector plates. A ring-mounted Lewis was provided in the rear cockpit. Standard front armament of the R.E.8 soon became a Vickers gun, mounted under the port-side engine panels and synchronised at first with Challenger and later with Constantinesco gear. Deliveries began in November 1916, the first aircraft arriving in France later that month with No. 56 Squadron R.F.C. Due to the inexplicable reduction in fin area on production R.E.8s, the aeroplane made a catastrophic start to its career when several were lost in spinning and other accidents or from fires that broke out when they crash-landed. As a result, the upper and lower fin areas were enlarged slightly on later machines.

The R.E.8 was the most widely

used British 2-seater on the Western Front, four thousand and ninety-nine being completed by seven British manufacturers. These included twenty-two supplied to Escadrille 6 of the Belgian Aviation Militaire that were later re-engined with 150 or 180 h.p. Hispano-Suizas. R.E.8s equipped sixteen R.F.C./R.A.F. squadrons in France, and the type was in service throughout 1917–18. Their duties included observation, reconnaissance, ground-support patrols, night bombing (with two 112 lb. bombs or equivalent smaller bombs) and ground attack (with four 65 lb. bombs). Despite the fact that they were outclassed by enemy fighters, they served the Allied cause well for a much longer period than should have been necessary, and fifteen R.A.F. squadrons still had R.E.8s at the time of the Armistice. They were used by two British squadrons in Italy, two in Mesopotamia and four in Palestine; three Home Defence units also had some R.E.8s. A few remained in R.A.F. service for a short time after the war.

Variants included the R.E.8a, with a 200 h.p. Hispano-Suiza and its Vickers gun on top of the front fuselage; it is thought that only one R.E.8a was built. The R.E.9 and R.T.1 were both potential R.E.8 replacements, utilising many components of the latter aircraft. Several R.E.8s were converted to R.E.9s with equal-span wings and variously modified control surfaces; Siddeley-Deasy built six R.T1s with a variety of powerplants, unequal-chord wings and a Lewis gun over the top plane.

42 Sopwith 1½-Strutter

The 1½-Strutter was used widely during World War 1 by British, French and other Allied air forces on a range of duties that included fighter / reconnaissance, bombing, ground strafing, coastal patrol, anti-submarine work and photographic reconnaissance. Its capable performance of all these activities, often in the face of superior opposition, is its own tribute to a remarkable aeroplane. Historically, the 1½-Strutter is significant on two counts: it was the first British service aircraft with an efficient synchronised forward-firing armament, and it was chosen to equip the first-ever strategic bombing force.

The prototype (3686), completed in December 1915, was a 2-seat biplane with a 110 h.p. Clerget 9 Z engine. It went into production for the R.N.A.S. at the beginning of 1916, the 2-seat version being known as the Admiralty Type 9400. Initially the 1½-Strutter was armed with a Vickers machine-gun for the pilot and a Lewis gun in the rear cockpit. Various synchronising gears were installed, one of the most common being the excellent Scarff-Dibovsky. Later 1½-Strutters had a Scarff ring for the observer's gun in place of the original Nieuport mounting. The 1½-Strutter entered service in April 1916 with No. 5 Wing R.N.A.S. in France, where its first task was to escort French bombers. Later that year it was used as a bomber in its own right, with No. 3 Wing R.N.A.S. This unit was formed in spring 1916 with aircraft converted as single-seaters

(Admiralty Type 9700) carrying four 65 lb. bombs internally and having an excellent combat radius. At about this time the R.F.C. made heavy demands on 1½-Strutter production, with the result that No. 3 Wing did not make its first raids until the summer, and did not really get going until October 1916. Meanwhile No. 70 Squadron had become the R.F.C.'s first Strutter unit, employing them in the Battle of the Somme in summer 1916. Additional War Office orders for 1½-Strutters were placed, and the type subsequently flew with Nos. 43 and 45 Squadrons in France.

Between fourteen and fifteen hundred 1½-Strutters were built by eight British manufacturers; these included fifty-eight 'Ship Strutters' that served aboard H.M.S. *Argus*, *Furious*, *Vindex* and other major Naval vessels. Some of these aircraft also performed useful experimental work in trials of ditching and deck arrester gear and in taking off from platforms aboard Naval vessels. A small batch (later increased to over fifty aircraft) supplied to the French government early in 1916 was the prelude to an extensive French building programme in which some four and a half thousand 1½-Strutters were completed by four French manufacturers. They served extensively with the Aviation Militaire, most of them as single-seat bombers at first. French-built machines were supplied to three Belgian escadrilles, and to Russia. In spring 1918 the largest purchase from the French production line was made by the A.E.F., which bought

five hundred and fourteen, primarily for use as trainers, but a few were used operationally. Twenty-one were later transferred to the U.S. Navy. Five aircraft which 'strayed' into Holland were interned and later served with the Dutch Army Air Service, and others found their way to Japan, Lithuania and Romania.

During the middle months of 1917 the R.F.C. 1½-Strutters were replaced by Camels, and many were brought back for Home Defence night-fighter duties. In these single-seaters the pilot occupied the rear cockpit and was provided with one or two Lewis guns on an over-wing Foster mounting in place of the Vickers front gun. British and French Strutters served in Macedonia, Italy and the Aegean area, and in spring/summer 1917 the R.N.A.S. employed some at home and in the Mediterranean for coastal patrol and anti-submarine work.

The 1½-Strutter was not an easy aeroplane to service, and its Clerget engines (130 h.p. in later aircraft) gave quite a lot of trouble, but these good-looking aeroplanes were straightforward to fly and achieved an impressive operational record.

43 Sopwith Cuckoo

The Admiralty, and especially the then Capt. Murray F. Sueter, were convinced well before the outbreak of World War 1 of the potential value of the aeroplane as a torpedo carrier. Prior to 1916 all such activities had been carried out by seaplanes, which depended upon calm water in order to operate; but in

October 1916 Sueter officially asked Sopwith to investigate the possibility of a single-seat land-based aircraft carrying one or two 1,000 lb. torpedoes and having a 4-hour endurance.

The Sopwith prototype carried the factory designation T.1 (it was serialled N74 later) and flew for the first time in June 1917. (The single-seat B.1 bomber was developed concurrently with the T.1 and flew two or three months earlier, but did not go into production.) The Sopwith T.1 had 3-bay fold-back wings, with its cockpit located aft of the trailing edge, and a short-legged undercarriage between whose Vees the torpedo was slung close under the fuselage. The T.1 underwent official trials in July 1917, an order for one hundred following in August and another, for fifty, in November. The prototype was originally powered by a 200 h.p. Hispano-Suiza, but these engines were required urgently for S.E.5a fighters; N74 was therefore re-engined with a 200 h.p. Sunbeam Arab, and this became the standard unit for production Mk.I aircraft. The two original contractors, Fairfield and Pegler, had had no previous aircraft manufacturing experience, and did not deliver their first aircraft until September and October 1918; to overcome these delays, additional orders were placed with Blackburn early in 1918; the first machine from this company was delivered in July, by which time the type had been named Cuckoo. A total of three hundred and fifty Cuckoos were ordered, but with the curtailment of some contracts after the Armistice only about one hundred and fifty were actually completed, ninety of them by November 1918. Sixty-one of these were on R.A.F. charge on 31 October.

The first squadron of Cuckoos had embarked in H.M.S. *Argus* only twelve days before this, and hence was too late for combat service. Three other Cuckoos were aboard H.M.S. *Furious*. After the Armistice the Cuckoo served aboard H.M.S. *Eagle* and with Nos. 185, 186 and 210 Squadrons. Some aircraft were built as Mk.IIs with 200 h.p. Wolseley Viper engines, and in October 1919 Cuckoo N7990 was flown with a 275 h.p. Rolls-Royce Falcon III. This gave the best performance of any Cuckoo variant, but no further development was undertaken. In 1921 six Mk. II Cuckoos formed part of the equipment taken by the British Air Mission to Japan, where they laid the foundations of that country's later pre-eminence in the production of torpedo-carrying aircraft. The Cuckoo finally disappeared from R.A.F. service in April 1923.

44 Airco D.H.4

The D.H.4 was the first British aeroplane to be designed from the outset for high-speed day bombing, although as its career progressed it was employed on a variety of other duties as well. It was designed by Geoffrey de Havilland around the 160 h.p. B.H.P. engine, which powered the first prototype when it flew in August 1916. Before this took place, however, fifty D.H.4s had already been ordered with 250 h.p. Rolls-Royce III or IV (later Eagle III or IV) engines, and an engine of this kind was installed in the second prototype which flew later that summer. The D.H.4 proved to be a comfortable aeroplane, light on the controls and easy to fly; its main operational drawback was the installation of the fuel tank between the two cockpits, where it was vulnerable to enemy gunfire and inhibited communication between the pilot and observer.

Detail airframe improvements, including a ring mounting for the observer's Lewis gun, were made on the second prototype and retained in production aircraft, which were delivered from early 1917. The pilot had a forward-firing Vickers synchronised with Constantinesco gear. The fifty D.H.4s ordered from Westland for the R.N.A.S. had twin Vickers front guns and an elevated Scarff ring to improve the observer's field of fire. Subsequent D.H.4 production was on such a large scale that insufficient Rolls-Royce engines could be supplied; among the alternatives installed were 200 h.p. Puma or Adriatic engines (variations of the B.H.P.), the 200 h.p. R.A.F.3a, 260 h.p. Fiat A-12 and 375 h.p. Eagle VIII. With the last-named powerplant the D.H.4 had a superlative performance, including a maximum speed of 143 m.p.h. (230 km/hr.). Later production aircraft, irrespective of powerplant, had larger-diameter propellers and correspondingly longer-legged undercarriages.

First R.F.C. deliveries were made to No. 55 Squadron, which arrived in France in March 1917 and carried out its first raid during the following month. The first R.N.A.S. unit of D.H.4s was No. 2 Squadron, which became operational at about the same time, and D.H.4s eventually served with Nos. 18, 25, 27, 49, 55 and 57 Squadrons of the R.F.C./R.A.F., and Nos. 2, 5, 6, 11 and 17 Squadrons of the R.N.A.S./R.A.F. on the Western Front. Maximum bomb load of the D.H.4 was two 230 lb. or four 112 lb. bombs or an equivalent weight of smaller weapons. The R.N.A.S. on the whole made more varied use of its D.H.4s' ability to out-fly and climb above enemy fighters, and hence to be capable of operating without an escort. They were used for artillery spotting, anti-submarine patrol and photographic reconnaissance in addition to bombing. Apart from their employment in France, D.H.4s of one or other British service were operated in Russia, Macedonia, Mesopotamia, the Aegean and the Adriatic, and also at home for coastal patrol and training duties. Experimental British variants included two long-range D.H.4s, fuelled for 14 hours flying, which were intended to photograph shipping in the Kiel Canal; they were not after all used for such a mission, but later became night fighters with twin over-wing Lewis guns. Two other D.H.4s were fitted, although not tested, with $1\frac{1}{2}$-pdr. Coventry Ordnance Works guns. One seaplane version was tested, and other landplane D.H.4s carried out trials with flotation gear and parachutes.

The D.H.4 was withdrawn from

R.A.F. service soon after the Armistice, when several were supplied to Belgium, Canada, Chile, Greece, Iran, New Zealand, South Africa and Spain. With some of these countries they remained in service until the early 1930s. British civil D.H.4s included the D.H.4A 2-passenger cabin transport and the D.H.4R racer of 1919, which had a 450 h.p. Napier Lion engine that gave it a top speed of 150 m.p.h. (241·4 km/hr.). One thousand four hundred and forty-nine British-built D.H.4s were built by seven manufacturers; fifteen others were built by SABCA in Belgium in 1926.

The largest D.H.4 production, however, took place in the United States, and it was the only American-built British warplane to see combat service during World War 1. A pattern aircraft was sent to America in July 1917, where it was fitted with a 400 h.p. Liberty 12 engine and flown on 29 October. Four thousand eight hundred and forty-six 'Liberty Planes', designated DH-4A, were built in the United States: three thousand one hundred and six by Dayton-Wright, one thousand six hundred by the Fisher Body Division of General Motors and one hundred and forty by Standard Aircraft Corporation. Contracts for a further seven thousand five hundred and two DH-4As were cancelled after the Armistice. Only some 30 per cent of the American-built machines reached France before hostilities ended, but they served with thirteen squadrons of the A.E.F. from August 1918 and with four squadrons of the U.S.

Naval Northern Bombing Group. The Americans were never happy with the DH-4A: it was semi-obsolete by the time it entered service with them, and had had to be considerably redesigned and reworked to adapt it to American production methods. The improved DH-4B was ready too late (October 1918) to replace it in France, but during the 1920s a considerable building and conversion programme (of DH-4As) kept the DH-4B, DH-4M and other variants in U.S. service until 1932. Two hundred and eighty-three DH-4As were transferred to the U.S. Navy and Marine Corps during and after World War 1. American-built DH-4As were armed with two Marlin or Browning machine-guns in front and two Lewises in the rear cockpit; their maximum bomb load was 332 lb. (151 kg.).

45   Airco D.H.9 and D.H.9A

The D.H.9 arose from a decision taken in 1917 to more than double the number of squadrons in the R.F.C., most of the new units being intended to undertake the daylight bombing of Germany. Basically it was a good design, with pleasant handling qualities, but it was beset by troubles from the engines installed, all derivatives of the B.H.P. As a result, its performance was inferior to the D.H.4 it was meant to replace. In November 1917 the prototype (A7559), a modified D.H.4, was tested concurrently with the first production D.H.9. The prototype was flown 'clean' with a 230 h.p. Galloway Adriatic engine, whereas the first production machine was tested under full military load conditions with a 230 h.p. Siddeley Puma, installed in rather Germanic fashion with its cylinder heads exposed. During autumn 1917 contracts for nine hundred D.H.4s were amended to specify D.H.9s, and subsequent large-scale production of the new bomber was ordered. By the end of 1918 three thousand two hundred and four D.H.9s had been completed, and ultimate production reached more than four thousand, with fifteen British manufacturers taking part in the programme. The majority of D.H.9s had Siddeley Puma engines, although a small batch of Short-built aircraft were fitted with the 260 h.p. Fiat A-12. Armament consisted of a forward-firing Vickers gun with Constantinesco synchronising gear, and a Scarff-mounted Lewis gun in the rear cockpit. Camera or wireless equipment was also installed, and the D.H.9 could (though it seldom did) carry its load of two 230 lb. or four 112 lb. bombs internally; they were more often suspended from racks beneath the fuselage or lower wings.

The first unit to re-equip with D.H.9s was No. 103 Squadron, which began to receive its first aircraft in December 1917; but D.H.9 operations in France were first carried out, in March 1918, by No. 6 Squadron. Over the next few months there was a rapid build-up of D.H.9 squadrons on the Western Front, and they put in a lot of hard work. However, their effectiveness, already hampered by a mediocre performance, was restricted still further by repeated engine failures which rendered many attempted raids abortive. The fact that the D.H.9 achieved as much as it did was due more to the perseverance and initiative of its air and ground crews than to the aeroplane itself. On the credit side it must be admitted that, once free of its bomb load, the D.H.9 was quite a good fighting aircraft. In this respect at least it was better than the D.H.4, chiefly because the pilot's and observer's cockpits were placed closer together, permitting closer collaboration. As early in the D.H.9's career as November 1917 Trenchard had appealed for its cancellation, but his plea was already too late: production was then well advanced, and it was the D.H.9 or nothing. The type ultimately equipped twelve R.F.C./R.A.F. squadrons in France, and others in the Mediterranean, Middle East and Russian theatres, remaining in service until the Armistice. In 1917–18, D.H.9s were used in many different ways as testbed aircraft. Some flew with the 430 h.p. Napier Lion or the high-compression 290 h.p. version of the Puma, or other engines; others tested engine control, cooling, fuel and silencer systems; parachutes; and at least one was used in deck-landing trials. In 1918 two engine-less D.H.9s were supplied to the United States, where a vast production programme was planned using the 400 h.p. Liberty 12 engine. In fact, only four USD-9s were completed, the remainder of the fourteen thousand that had been ordered being cancelled after the Armistice.

Eighteen D.H.9s were supplied to the Belgian Aviation Militaire in 1918. After the end of the war the D.H.9 continued in R.A.F. service in modest numbers, and at least one aircraft was refitted as an ambulance; another nine aircraft, interned in Holland, were also returned to the R.A.F. Extensive D.H.9 sales were made to nearly a score of countries in Europe, South America and the Far East; in the early 1920s thirty were built by SABCA in Belgium, and several hundred were completed later in Spain with 300 h.p. Hispano-Suiza engines. The D.H.9 also figured prominently on the commercial front as a mail and passenger transport, and one, as G-EAAA, became the first aircraft on the new British civil register.

Proof that the basic airframe design was a sound one was provided by the D.H.9A, which was fundamentally a refined version fitted with a dependable powerplant. Following the installation of a 400 h.p. Liberty 12 in C6122, three thousand Liberty engines were ordered from the United States in 1917. Only one thousand and fifty of these actually reached Britain, early in 1918, but these were sufficient to power the eight hundred and eighty-five D.H.9As completed during the war period. The D.H.9A had wings of larger area to offset the bigger, heavier engine, and its fuselage was appropriately redesigned, with the engine fully cowled and given a frontal radiator. Armament and bomb load were the same as for the D.H.9. The first squadron deliveries of D.H.9As were made in June 1918 to No. 110, although they did not become operational in France until the end of August. By the time of the Armistice four squadrons in France were flying D.H.9As, but two of these only received their aircraft in November and hence the type saw little combat service during World War 1, although two squadrons on the Russian Front also had D.H.9As. The type remained in widespread production after the war, nearly two thousand five hundred being built by a dozen British manufacturers, among whom Westland and de Havilland predominated. D.H.9As served with the R.A.F. at home, in the Middle East and India as general-purpose aircraft, and remained in service until 1931, latterly in a training role.

46 Armstrong Whitworth F.K.3 and F.K.8

The F.K.3, proposed by Frederick Koolhoven as a simplified alternative to the B.E.2c for reconnaissance/bombing duties, was evolved in the late summer of 1915 and accepted by the War Office for substantial production. The production version reversed the crew position from those in the prototype, so that the observer could occupy the rear cockpit with a spigot-mounted machine-gun. In this respect, and in its speed and ceiling, the F.K.3 was undoubtedly superior to the B.E.2c, although it carried a smaller bomb load and had a poorer rate of climb. Its flying qualities were far superior to those of the Factory machine. Four hundred and ninety-nine production F.K.3s were built, four hundred of them by Hewlett & Blondeau and the rest by the parent company. The only operational squadron to employ F.K.3s was No. 47 in Macedonia, which used them from September 1916 until early 1918, primarily on patrol and reconnaissance duties but sometimes in the bombing role. For the latter purpose it had to be flown as a single-seater in order to carry a war load of 112 lb. (51 kg.). Standard powerplant of the F.K.3 was the 90 h.p. R.A.F.1a Vee-type engine. Most F.K.3s were employed as trainers, for which they were ideally suited, and they were used by several training establishments in the United Kingdom and Egypt.

The F.K.8 was basically a scaled-up version of the F.K.3, making its maiden flight in May 1916 and being delivered to R.F.C. units towards the end of that year. First operational F.K.8 squadron was No. 35, which arrived in France with them in January 1917; Nos. 2, 8, 10 and 82 Squadrons also received F.K.8s, and they partially equipped Nos. 17 and 47 Squadrons in Macedonia and No. 142 Squadron in Palestine. At home the F.K.8 was flown by No. 50 Home Defence Squadron and several training establishments. The F.K.8 was a contemporary of the R.E.8, and was generally considered superior to the Factory design. Early F.K.8s were powered by 120 h.p. Beardmores, but the 160 h.p. model soon became the standard unit. The 'Big Ack', as

it was known (the F.K.3 being the 'Little Ack'), was armed with a synchronised Vickers gun for the pilot and a Lewis gun on a Scarff mounting in the rear cockpit; it could carry a 160 lb. (72·6 kg.) bomb load. The F.K.8 was well built, well defended and regarded highly by its crews, and was used widely on reconnaissance, patrol, day and night bombing and ground attack throughout 1917 and 1918. The aircraft illustrated was attacked by eight Fokker Dr.Is on 27 March 1918, and its fuel tank and rear cockpit set ablaze while the aircraft was still loaded with bombs and ammunition. Although both crew members were seriously wounded, they accounted for four of the Fokkers before McLeod successfully brought the F.K.8 down in no man's land, a feat for which he received a well-earned V.C.

Known orders for the F.K.8 include six hundred and fifty from Armstrong Whitworth and nine hundred from Angus Sanderson & Co., but a hundred or more of the latter may not have been completed before production ended in July 1918. On 31 October 1918 there were six hundred and ninety-four F.K.8s on R.A.F. charge; over 40 per cent of these were then in store and less than two hundred in front-line service in France. The F.K.8 did not long survive the war, but a few appeared on the British civil register and others in Australia. During 1917–18, experimental installations were made in F.K.8s of the 150 h.p. Lorraine-Dietrich, 150 h.p. R.A.F.4a and 200 h.p. R.A.F.4d engines.

47 Salmson 2

The Société des Moteurs Salmson, as its name indicates, was formed primarily for the production of aero-engines, and in particular it built large numbers of the 9-cylinder water-cooled Canton-Unné radial which powered several types of aircraft in French, British and Russian service during the first half of World War 1. The company's first aeroplane venture, the Salmson-Moineau SM-1, was not a success, but early in 1917 it produced a 2-seat biplane known as the Salmson D with a 130 h.p. Clerget rotary engine. This did not go into production, but its derivative, the Salmson 2, using a Canton-Unné engine, became one of the more successful French types of the later war years.

Designed as a 2-seat 'heavy' observation aircraft, the Salmson 2 was of conventional appearance except that it had neither a vertical fin nor a fixed tailplane. It was a good-looking aeroplane, with a rounded fuselage and a distinctively louvred cowling for the radial engine; the equal-span wings had double ailerons. The Salmson 2 went into production towards the end of 1917 and entered service with the French Aviation Militaire in early 1918 with the military designation 2A.2. Three thousand two hundred Salmson 2s were built, and they served with twenty-two French escadrilles on the Western Front and two others in Italy. Seven hundred and five Salmsons were purchased by the A.E.F. as an interim type pending delivery of the DH-4A 'Liberty plane'. Eleven squadrons of the A.E.F. flew the Salmson 2 during the final months of the war. The duties assigned to the Salmson 2 were primarily those of visual and photographic reconnaissance, the rear cockpit having a trap in the floor for the aiming of cameras. The aircraft could carry two dozen small fragmentation bombs for ground strafing, and was occasionally used also as a light day bomber. Forward armament consisted of a single synchronised Vickers machine-gun mounted slightly to port on top of the engine cowling; some American machines were later fitted with Marlin guns instead. A Scarff ring in the rear cockpit could mount single or twin-yoked Lewis guns for the observer's use. Like the D.H.4, the Salmson 2's main drawback was the wide separation of the two cockpits, which made communication and collaboration between the crew members difficult when in combat. Nevertheless, the Salmson 2, although it did not possess a particularly outstanding performance, was a sturdily built machine with an extremely reliable engine and was capable of receiving and meting out considerable punishment. Lt. W. P. Erwin of the 1st Aero Squadron A.E.F. destroyed eight enemy aircraft using only the front gun of his Salmson 2. The Salmson was not especially fast, but it had a useful rate of climb, being able to reach 5,000 m. (16,404 ft.) in $27\frac{1}{2}$ minutes.

48 Spad XI

The first 2-seater to be designed by Louis Béchereau, creator of the

Spad fighters, was the Spad VIII, although this did not proceed beyond the design stage. Its subsequent development, however, led to the Spad XI, which appeared in September 1916. Externally it resembled the Spad VII single-seater, except that the 2-bay wings had slight stagger and sweepback to balance the longer fuselage with its additional cockpit.

The Spad XIA.2 went into service in 1917, but its early production was affected by teething troubles with the reduction gear of its 235 h.p. Hispano-Suiza engine. It was armed with a single forward-firing synchronised Vickers gun, offset to starboard, in front of the pilot, while one or two Lewis guns could be installed on the ring mounting in the rear cockpit. A light bomb load of about 70 kg. (154 lb.) could be carried under the lower wings. Although sensitive on the controls, the Spad XI could have been a useful aircraft under the right conditions; unfortunately it was easily affected by uneven distribution of loads such as ammunition, cameras, photographic flares or bombs, and acquired a reputation for poor controllability. The same factor also affected its climbing powers, for in anything but a shallow climb the engine readily stalled. In 'clean' condition the Spad XI could climb to 4,000 m. (13,123 ft.) in 17½ minutes. At least one machine was fitted with a 220 h.p. direct-drive Renault engine, but the Hispano remained standard. Despite its shortcomings, the Spad XI served with at least fifteen escadrilles of the French Aviation Militaire and three Belgian escadrilles during 1917 and early 1918; the Belgian Spads remained in service until the Armistice.

In January 1918 a new version appeared. This was the Spad XVIA.2, powered by a 235 h.p. direct-drive Lorraine-Dietrich 8 Fb. The Spad XVI was faster, but had a poorer ceiling than the Spad XI and was no real improvement. With its introduction into service, however, the French government then sold thirty-five surplus Spad XIs to the A.E.F., two of whose squadrons flew the type during the summer of 1918. The A.E.F. also bought six Spad XVIs, and another was supplied to Belgium in 1918. A later version of the Spad XVI had twin guns fore and aft and a 250 h.p. Lorraine-Dietrich 8 Bb, but in March 1918 an explosion at the factory producing these aircraft seriously affected production, and in July all 2-seat Spads in French service were withdrawn from the Front.

49 Breguet 14

Louis Breguet began the design of his Type XIV in mid-1916, and himself flew the prototype at Villacoublay on 21 November. It was a big, capable-looking 2-seater, powered by a 220 h.p. Renault engine with a large frontal radiator and heavily louvred side panels. Another feature was the wide use of duralumin in its construction. Initial production version was the Br.14A.2 reconnaissance model, five hundred and eighty of which were ordered in March/April 1917; by this time a prototype of the Br. 14B.2 bomber version had also been delivered. From then onward production of the Breguet 14 quickly gathered momentum: by the end of 1917 more than two thousand were on order from six French manufacturers; some five and a half thousand were ordered during the war period, and more than eight thousand were built before production ended in 1926.

The B.2 differed from the A.2 in having transparent side panels to the observer's cockpit, lower-wing flaps of nearly full span and Michelin bomb racks protruding from the lower leading edges. Both versions entered service in summer 1917, and carried a similar armament: a single, forward-firing Vickers gun for the pilot and twin Lewis guns on a ring mounting in the observer's cockpit. Some 14A.2s mounted an over-wing Lewis in place of the forward Vickers gun, and an additional downward-firing Lewis could be mounted on the B.2 to protect the aircraft below and behind. Up to thirty-two 8 kg. bombs could be carried by the Br.14B.2; the A.2 could also carry a small load of four small bombs if required.

Breguet 14s served with seventy-one French escadrilles on the Western Front (including seventeen Escadrilles de Bombardement). They also equipped five escadrilles in Serbia, three in Greece, six in Morocco and eight in Macedonia. Two Belgian escadrilles and several A.E.F. squadrons also flew Breguet 14s. Aircraft supplied to the A.E.F. in 1918 included two hundred and twenty-nine Br.14A2s, forty-seven Br.14B.2s and one hundred Br.14E.2 unarmed trainers. As indicated by the numbers built, the Breguet 14 was widely used for day and night bombing during the final year of the war. Various alternative or experimental engine installations included improved versions of the Renault (one with a turbosupercharger), the Fiat A-12bis, Lorraine-Dietrich and Liberty 12. Variants included the unsuccessful Br.14H floatplane and the Br.14S ambulance, which was used in modest numbers in 1918 and extensively in the middle 1920s. The Br.16Bn.2 was an enlarged night-bomber development built in some numbers; also produced, but too late for war service, was the Br.17C.2, a 2-seat escort version with a 400 h.p. Renault 12K engine and twin forward-firing Vickers guns.

The Breguet 14 had a long and varied post-war career. The double crossing of the Mediterranean by Roget and Coli in January 1919 was the first of many endurance flights; other Br. 14s were used as mail and passenger transports; and in addition to a long post-war career with the French Aviation Militaire, the Breguet 14 was supplied to nearly a dozen foreign air forces in Europe, South America and the Far East.

50 Short 184 and Bomber

On 28 July 1914 a torpedo was successfully launched for the first time from a British aircraft, a 160 h.p. Short seaplane, and almost immediately after this the Admiralty issued an official requirement to Short Bros. for an aeroplane designed specifically for this duty. The resultant prototype was given the serial number 184, from which the aircraft derived its official designation. It was powered by a 225 h.p. Sunbeam Mohawk engine, which caused it to be referred to often, but erroneously, as the 'Short 225', even when later-production examples were fitted with engines of greater power. The prototype was completed early in 1915, being a 3-bay biplane with fold-back wings and its 14 in. torpedo slung low between the twin floats. The second prototype, 185, was completed shortly afterwards, and both of these machines later served operationally aboard the seaplane carrier *Ben-my-Chree* in the Dardanelles from June 1915. On 12 August 1915 one of these aircraft, flown by Flt. Commander C. H. K. Edmonds, accomplished the first-ever sinking of a ship (a Turkish merchantman) by means of an air-launched torpedo.

The Short 184 was not one of the war's more spectacular aircraft; when loaded down with its torpedo it was difficult to take off in all but the calmest sea and was tricky to fly successfully; eventually the torpedo role was abandoned in favour of employment on reconnaissance, anti-submarine patrol and bombing. Nevertheless, the 184 served from mid-1915 until the end of the war, performing a great amount of humdrum but useful work in practically every combat theatre. About nine

hundred Short 184s were built, by the parent company and nine other British manufacturers, and three hundred and twelve of them were still in service on 31 October 1918. By then nearly all of them were powered with Sunbeam Maori I, II or III engines, although the 225 h.p. Mohawk had been standard in early-production batches. Other power-plants used in lesser degree included the 240 h.p. Sunbeam Gurkha, 240 h.p. Renault or 250 h.p. Rolls-Royce Eagle. Short 184s were employed at U.K. coastal stations and aboard seaplane carriers of the Royal Navy in the North Sea, Mediterranean and Far East. One of the two 184s carried by H.M.S. *Engadine* made the only reconnaissance carried out during the Battle of Jutland on 31 May 1916. A typical bomb load for the 184 Type A, the standard Mohawk version, was four 100 lb. bombs. The Type D which appeared in 1917 was flown from the rear seat as a single-seater, with up to nine 65 lb. bombs in place of the observer. The Type B, first built by Mann, Egerton, had short-span lower wings, kingpost bracing above the outer-section top wings and reinforced strut bracing for the floats. A version known as the Improved 184 had modified aileron controls. Short 184s were armed with a single defensive Lewis gun in the rear cockpit on a Whitehouse or (later) a Scarff ring mounting. Two 184s were supplied to the French government for evaluation during the war, and in late 1917 and early 1918 two prototypes were completed of the Short N.2B, a potential Maori-engined replacement; no production of this was, however, undertaken, and the Short 184 continued to serve until the end of the war. Indeed, it continued in service for a while after the war, carrying out mine-detection patrols in British waters. A small number were flown commercially for joy-riding by British civil owners, and others were sold to Chile, Estonia, Greece and Japan. Some of those in foreign service did not retire until the early 1930s.

In response to a bomber competition held in 1915, Short Bros. produced a landplane adaptation of the 184 (prototype serial number 3706). This also had a Mohawk engine and was a 2-bay machine with constant-chord top wings, a rather clumsy 4-wheel undercarriage and the observer situated in the front cockpit. Eighty-three production Short Bombers (they never received an official name) were built by Shorts and four other companies, earlier examples following the style of the 184 in having a short fuselage and later machines being given much extended rear fuselages. Production aircraft had 3-bay interplane bracing and a more conventional crew seating with the observer in the rear cockpit, armed with a free-firing Lewis gun. The 250 h.p. Rolls-Royce Eagle was the standard engine except in the fifteen aircraft built by Sunbeam, who installed their own 225 h.p. Mohawk. Typical bomb load comprised four 230 lb. or eight 112 lb. bombs, carried beneath the lower wings. Deliveries

of Short Bombers began in early spring 1916 to No. 3 Wing R.N.A.S. – which, however, did not become operational with them until October. This was because, in answer to an urgent R.F.C. request, fifteen Short Bombers were handed over to that service in preparation for the Battle of the Somme. The remaining R.N.A.S. aircraft were employed operationally until April 1917, when they were replaced by Handley Page O/100s.

51 Letord Types 1 to 9

The Letord Type 1 originated in 1916 to meet a requirement issued by Lt. Col. Dorand, director of the Section Technique de l'Aéro-nautique at Chalais-Meudon, for a twin-engined 3-seat replacement for the Caudron R.4 reconnaissance aircraft. Although designed by the S.T.Aé's chief designer, Capitaine Georges Lepère, series production was entrusted to Établissements Letord, a company formed in 1908 to manufacture balloons and air-ships, which had aircraft factories at Lyon-Villeurbane and, conveniently, at Chalais. No fewer than seven aircraft types (three each for reconnaissance and night bombing and one escort fighter) stemmed from this basic design configuration, all having the characteristic 'trade-mark' of backward-staggered wings (with varying upper and lower spans) and most of them powered by variants of the Hispano-Suiza V8 engine.

All had a basic four-wheel main landing gear; the Types 1, 3 and 4 had an additional wheel under the front of the fuselage to prevent a nose-over.

First to appear was the Let.1A. 3 reconnaissance version, with a pair of 150 h.p. Hispano-Suiza 8 A engines; one hundred and seventy-five of these were ordered in October 1916, entry into service beginning some six months later. Higher-powered Hispano-Suiza 8 Ba engines of 200 h.p. were generally fitted to the Let.2A. 3, though the 170 h.p. Lorraine-Dietrich 8 A was installed in some examples, and also in the third reconnaissance model, the Let.4A. 3. First of the night bombers was the Let.3Bn. 3 of 1917, similar to the 2A. 3 with Hispano-Suiza 8 Ba engines but having equal-span 4-bay wings of 55 ft. 9¼ in. (17·00 m.) span and greater area and an under-nose wheel. Gross weight was 5,291 lb. (2,400 kg.) and maximum speed 93 m.p.h. (150 km/hr.).

The Letord Type 3 was also built in a 3Ca. 3 escort fighter version, with a 'canon' armament, this in turn leading to a more definitive escort version, the Let.6Ca. 3, which had 220 h.p. Hispano-Suiza 8 Be engines and was flight tested in January 1918. The second and third bomber versions were the Types 5 and 7. Fifty-one Type 5s were built, these having unequal-span wings, two 220 h.p. Lorraine-Dietrich 8 Fb engines and no nosewheel. Normal armament consisted of single machine-guns on movable mountings in the front and rear cockpits and a maximum bomb load of 441 lb. (200 kg.); some Let.5Bn. 3 aircraft had an additional gun mounted under the nose to fire to the rear.

Only one Letord Type 7, first flown in 1918, is known to have been built. Developed from (and larger than) the Type 3, it had a 62 ft. 4 in. (19·00 m.) span, with two 275 h.p. Lorraine engines mounted on the lower mainplanes. At a gross weight of 6,305 lb. (2,860 kg.), its maximum speed was 89 m.p.h. (143 km./hr.). Letords of one type or another equipped at least eight escadrilles of the French Aviation Militaire, and some served also with Dorand or Caudron squadrons. A final wartime type, quite outside the foregoing family of designs, was the Letord Type 9, completed only shortly before the Armistice. Much larger than the Lepère-designed Types 1 to 7, it had non-staggered wings of 85 ft. 1¼ in. (25·94 m.) span and 1,453·1 sq. ft. (135·00 sq. m.) area, a biplane tail unit, and a crew of 2. Powered by two 400 h.p. Liberty 12 engines, it had a gross weight of 12,171 lb. (5,521 kg.) and could reach a speed of 90 m.p.h. (145 km./hr.), but it was too late to perform any war service.

52 Caudron R.4 and R.11

Compared with the frail-looking Farman and Voisin bombers then in French service, the prototype Caudron R.4 had, when it first appeared in June 1915, quite a 'solid' and modern appearance for its time. The prefix letter indicated that it had been designed by René Caudron of Caudron Frères, and it was intended for use as a 3-seat bomber. The R.4, although based on Gaston Caudron's G.VI, was virtually a new design, having a single, covered fuselage, single tail assembly and two 130 h.p. Renault engines mounted midway between the 3-bay wings. The undercarriage consisted of a twin-wheel unit beneath each lower wing, in line with the engine, and a fifth wheel under the front of the fuselage to prevent the aircraft from nosing over on landing. The pilot occupied the middle one of the three cockpits, with gunners in each of the front and rear positions equipped with one or two Lewis machine-guns on ring mountings. The R.4 had been designed to carry up to 100 kg. (220 lb.) of bombs, but when fully loaded it was considerably underpowered and its performance was too poor for successful operation. However, in an R.4A.3 form, as a 3-seat reconnaissance aeroplane, it rendered extremely useful service to the Aviation Militaire as a photographic reconnaissance aircraft from spring 1916 until April 1917. It then began to be replaced by the Letord Type 1, another twin-engined biplane broadly resembling the R.4 in general layout, but with a somewhat better performance.

To replace the R.4, Caudron evolved the R.11, which first appeared in March 1917. This was a smaller and lighter machine with shorter-span, 2-bay wings, enlarged fin and rudder and more powerful engines. At first, 200 h.p. Hispano-Suiza 8 Bda engines were installed, but the higher-rated 215

h.p. Hispano was substituted as soon as supplies became available. Some aircraft were fitted with 235 h.p. Hispano-Suiza 8 Beb engines, not necessarily to their advantage. The Caudron R.11 was built originally as a reconnaissance aircraft, but also served in the Bn. 3 category (Bombardement de nuit, 3-seat), in which capacity it could carry a 120 kg. (265 lb.) load. Night-bombing R.11s entered service early in spring 1918, but although their performance was markedly superior to that of the R.4s, the basic design was now nearly three years old and the R.11's effective bomb load was modest by 1918 standards. The R.11 really found its métier in July 1918 when, classified as Cau.11A.3, it was assigned to escort the Breguet 14 bomber squadrons. It may have been at this stage that a fifth gun was added to the defensive armament. Twin Lewis guns were mounted in each of the front and rear cockpits of the R.11, and the fifth gun was installed below the front gunner's position and fired by him downward and to the rear to protect the aircraft from attacks from below. Eight escadrilles of the Aviation Militaire were equipped with Cau.11A.3s, and for the remaining four months or so of World War 1 these 'flying gunboats' accompanied attacks by all French bombing squadrons against enemy targets. The R.F.C. and United States Air Service each evaluated two examples of the R.11. Total production of the R.11 was approximately five hundred.

A variant which is often confused

with the R.4 and R.11 is the Caudron Cau.23Bn.2, an enlarged, 4-bay, 2-seat night bomber which appeared in 1918. A contemporary of the Breguet 16 and Farman F.50, it was powered by two 250 h.p. Salmson (Canton-Unné) 9Z engines and had a much more angular fuselage with a blunter nose. No reliable evidence has been found that this aircraft went into series production before the Armistice.

53   A.E.G. G types

The series of twin-engined G types produced by A.E.G. in 1915–18 differed from most other German Grossflugzeuge in having a tractor, rather than a pusher, engine arrangement. The first in the series appeared early in 1915, before the introduction of the Grossflugzeug category, and was given the Kampfflugzeug (combat aeroplane) designation K.I. The K.I, later redesignated G.I, was a 3-seater powered by two 100 h.p. Mercedes D.I engines; comparatively few were built. In July 1915 the G.II appeared, a slightly bigger machine with 150 h.p. Benz Bz.IIIs, two or three defensive machine-guns and a 200 kg. (441 lb.) bomb load. It, too, was built in comparatively limited numbers, some G.IIs having two small auxiliary rudders. Both the G.I and G.II were flown by Schlachtstaffeln (Battle Flights) as well as by regular bombing formations. In the early summer of 1916 the G.III, which had first appeared at the end of the previous year, went into service. This had a much increased wing span, balanced and

overhung control surfaces and two 220 h.p. geared and handed Mercedes D.IV engines. The G.III was armed with two defensive machine-guns and could carry a 300 kg. (661 lb.) bomb load. Again, only small numbers were built, twenty G.IIIs being in service in October 1916; they served in Macedonia as well as on the Western Front.

The most widely built G type was the G.IV, which entered service late in 1916. This had a basically similar airframe to the G.III, but utilised the more reliable direct-drive Mercedes D.IVa. A crew of three or four men was carried, and the bomb load was about 350 kg. (772 lb.); a Parabellum gun was installed in each of the front and rear cockpits. Lacking both the range and the lifting power of the Friedrichshafen and Gotha G types, the A.E.Gs. were flown mainly as day and night tactical bombers over comparatively short ranges up to about 700 km. (435 miles). With extra fuel tankage in place of a bomb load, they were also employed on long-range reconnaissance and photographic missions. The A.E.G. G.IV remained in fairly widespread use until the Armistice, appearing on the Western Front, in Salonika, Italy, Romania and Macedonia. Experimental variants included the G.IVb, with a 3-bay extended-span wing cellule, and the G.IVk, with a biplane tail unit, armoured engine nacelles and nose section mounting a 20 mm. Becker cannon.

Final production version was the G.V, which first appeared in May 1918. It retained the same powerplant as the G.IV, but had a much enlarged wing span of 27·24 m. (89 ft. 4½ in.), a 600 kg. (1,323 lb.) bomb load and a maximum endurance of 6 hours. The G.Vs were built too late to see any combat service, but a number were employed post-war with Deutsche Luft-Reederei as 6-passenger transports in 1919. Most of them went into commercial service with the minimum of conversion, but a few machines were converted to have passenger cabins. Total wartime production of the G series reached five hundred and forty-two machines; by far the greater proportion of these, perhaps as many as four hundred, were G.IVs, of which fifty were still in service in August 1918.

54   Handley Page O/100 and O/400

In December 1914 the Air Department of the Admiralty confirmed in writing its requirement for a 'bloody paralyser of an aeroplane' for the bombing of Germany. It was to be a 2-seat aircraft, with a speed not less than 75 m.p.h. (120·7 km/hr.) and capable of carrying a minimum load of six 112 lb. bombs. By March 1915 forty such aircraft had been ordered, and the first machine (1455) was flown for the first time on 18 December 1915. It had been intended to install 120 h.p. Beardmore engines in the first Handley Page O/100, but the prototype was fitted with two 250 h.p. Rolls-Royce Eagle IIs, and these engines powered forty of the forty-six O/100s subsequently built by

Handley Page. The other six were built with 320 h.p. Sunbeam Cossacks. The O/100 prototype had an enclosed crew cabin, and the engine nacelles and front part of the fuselage were encased in 1,200 lb. (544 kg.) of armour plating; but these features were omitted from production aircraft. To enable them to be housed in standard British field hangars, the wings of the Handley Page bombers were designed to fold back along the sides of the fuselage. The O/100 exceeded its specification by being able to carry sixteen 112 lb. or eight 250 lb. bombs internally. It accommodated a 4-man crew, with positions for single or twin Lewis machine-guns in nose and dorsal locations and a fifth Lewis firing downward and to the rear through a trap in the floor. The O/100 went into service with No. 3 Wing R.N.A.S. on the Western Front in November 1916. It subsequently equipped Nos. 14 and 16 Naval Squadrons, and some O/100s were still in service when the war ended. For the first few months of their employment in France they were used for daylight sea patrols off the Flanders coast, but from March/April 1917 they began to concentrate on the night bombing of major German installations, such as U-boat bases, railway stations and industrial centres. Two O/100s were used in Palestine by the forces under General Allenby and T. E. Lawrence in their campaigns against the Turks; another O/100, based at Mudros in the Aegean, took part in bombing raids on Constantinople and against the German battle cruiser *Goeben*. This machine was at one time flown by Flt. Lt. J. W. Alcock, later the pilot of the 1919 trans-Atlantic Vimy.

The O/100 was followed into service by the much more numerous O/400, whose prototype (3138) was a converted O/100 airframe. The basic difference between the two bombers was that the fuel tanks were transferred from the engine nacelles to the fuselage, thus giving the O/400 much shorter nacelles. Successively higher-powered Eagle IV, VII or VIII engines were installed in most O/400s, though some aircraft were fitted with the 260 h.p. Fiat A-12bis or the 275 h.p. Sunbeam Maori. One machine was flown with two tandem pairs of 200 h.p. Hispano-Suiza engines to evaluate the engine layout proposed for the later V/1500. Nearly eight hundred O/400s were ordered during the war period, of which about five hundred and fifty were built in the United Kingdom. In addition, one hundred and seven O/400s were assembled from components built in the United States by the Standard Aircraft Corporation and powered with 350 h.p. Liberty 12Ns. A further eight Standard-built O/400s were completed for the U.S. Army after the war, but the rest of the one thousand five hundred ordered were then cancelled. In April 1917, more or less concurrently with the transfer of the O/100 to night operations, the O/400 became operational as a day bomber in France, itself transferring to night bombing from the following October. Handley Page O/400s served with No. 58 Squadron

R.A.F., Nos. 97 and 115 Squadrons of the Independent Force and Nos. 207, 214, 215 and 216 Naval Squadrons. Two hundred and fifty-eight O/400s were on R.A.F. charge on 31 October 1918. One aircraft operated with No. 67 Squadron (No. 1 Squadron, Australian Flying Corps) in Palestine. During the last two months or so of the war the loads carried by O/400s included the 1,650 lb. bomb. In spring 1918 two aircraft were crudely converted into 12-passenger transports for the purpose of flying ferry pilots back from France to England.

The Handley Page O/400 remained in R.A.F. service until 1920, eight of them being allocated to No. 1 (Communications) Wing as V.I.P. transports, carrying officials to and from the Paris Peace Conference between January and September 1919. Four O/400s were converted and operated by Handley Page Transport Ltd. in 1919–20 for route-proving on overseas air routes later flown by Imperial Airways. The O/400 was further developed into the O/700 transport, ten or a dozen of which were supplied to China late in 1919 and two or three more to South Africa. The O/700 was further developed into the O/10 and O/11 transports, eight and five of which were built respectively.

55 **Handley Page V/1500**

The V/1500 was too late for the war and too large for the peace, but it has several claims to a place in aviation history. It was the first British four-engined bomber to go into

154

production, was also the largest British aircraft produced during 1914–19 and was Britain's first truly strategic bomber. It was built to an Air Ministry requirement for an aeroplane with a 600 mile (966 km.) combat radius, and thus capable of bombing Berlin from bases in East Anglia. Design was begun in October 1917, and the first prototype flew in May 1918. This was powered by two tandem pairs of 375 h.p. Rolls-Royce Eagle VIII engines, and had no front gun position. In mid-1918, after the crash of the first prototype, a second machine was completed in which a front gunner's cockpit was provided; each pair of engines was enclosed in a single nacelle, and other aerodynamic improvements were made. Production V/1500s differed from this machine in having uncowled motors, modified radiators and an enlarged tail unit. As in the O/400, single or twin Lewis gun positions were provided in the nose and dorsal positions, and a fifth gun fired downward and rearward through the fuselage floor. A sixth Lewis gun was installed on a ring mounting in the extreme tail – the first time such a feature had been incorporated in the design of a British aeroplane. The V/1500 had provision to carry up to thirty 250 lb. bombs or two of the large 3,300 lb. weapons; a load of about 1,000 lb. (454 kg.) would have been carried on flights to Berlin. In the event, however, the V/1500 was not to make such a flight. Although orders had been placed for two hundred and fifty-five V/1500s before the war ended,

only three of these had been delivered (to No. 166 Squadron on 8 November 1918). They were bombed-up and standing by for two days before the signing of the Armistice rendered their mission unnecessary. After the end of the war several contracts were cancelled and only about three dozen V/1500s were built: Handley Page at least twenty-two, Beardmore at least seven and Harland & Wolff probably completed four others. Most of these aircraft were powered by Eagle VIIIs, but the final Handley Page machine had 450 h.p. Napier Lions, with which it flew on 3 September 1919, and at least one of the Beardmore V/1500s had 500 h.p. Galloway Atlantics.

In December 1918/January 1919 a V/1500 named H.M.A. (His Majesty's Airliner) *Old Carthusian* made the first flight from England to India (Martlesham to Karachi). This aircraft was later used to help expedite a peace settlement in northwestern India by bombing Kabul in May 1919 – the only time a V/1500 ever dropped bombs in anger. Another machine (F7140) was shipped to Newfoundland in 1919, where it was assembled in readiness for an attempted non-stop Atlantic crossing. The attempt was delayed because of overheating troubles with the engines, and by the time these had been dealt with the crossing had been accomplished by the Vimy flown by Alcock and Brown; F7140 abandoned its attempt and instead carried out a demonstration tour of the United States and Canada. The V/1500 was too large, too complex and too costly to become a successful commercial aeroplane, and none came on to the British civil register. One was, however, used briefly by Handley Page Transport Ltd. in 1919 on a London–Brussels service. This may have been the same aircraft that carried 40 passengers over London at 6,500 ft. (1,981 m.) in 1919.

56 Vickers Vimy

A contemporary of the Handley Page V/1500, the Vimy was designed as a twin-engined bomber with range enough to attack Berlin from bases on the Western Front. It was designed by R. K. Pierson as the F.B.27, and three prototypes were ordered in August 1917. The first of these (B9952), powered by 200 h.p. Hispano-Suiza engines, was flown on 30 November 1917; it was later re-engined with 260 h.p. Salmson radials. Changes introduced on the second machine, which was completed in April 1918, included 260 h.p. Maori engines and a third machine-gun, to defend the aircraft below and to the rear. The third aircraft, which appeared a few weeks later, had an airframe more representative of the ultimate production Vimy and was powered by 300 h.p. Fiat A-12bis engines. This prototype was unfortunately destroyed in September 1918, but in the following month a fourth prototype (F9561) appeared, with 360 h.p. Eagle VIII engines and enlarged rudders.

An initial one hundred and fifty Vimys were ordered from Vickers in March 1918, contracts with other manufacturers following until, by the Armistice, more than a thousand were on order. These were to have had a wide variety of alternative engines, but in the event the great majority of those built were Eagle-powered and most of the remainder had Fiats. One hundred and forty-three Vimys were completed by Vickers, twenty-five by Westland, at least sixteen by the Royal Aircraft Establishment and at least forty by Morgan & Co.; contracts with other manufacturers were cancelled towards the end of the war. On 31 October 1918 only three Vimys were on R.A.F. charge, and only one of these was stationed with the Independent Force in France; the war ended before this Vimy was used operationally.

Main squadron deliveries of the Vimy commenced in July 1919, and they served with nine R.A.F. flights or squadrons at home and overseas, and with several training units in Britain and Egypt. They began to be withdrawn from bomber squadrons in 1924, but many continued in use for training (including parachute training) until the 1930s. About eighty aircraft in this category were re-engined with uncowled Bristol Jupiter or Armstrong Siddeley Jaguar radial engines during the last few years of their service. Standard armament of the production Vimy consisted of four 0·303 in. Lewis machine-guns, but the rear upper gun was usually omitted from peacetime aircraft. Maximum internal and external bomb load for the Fiat-powered

Vimy was 4,408 lb. (2,000 kg.), and for the Eagle-powered model 4,804 lb. (2,179 kg.). The Eagle-Vimy is generally referred to as the Mk.IV, although confusion exists over the correct nomenclature for Vimy variants both during and after the war; the Fiat-Vimy is variously described as the Mk.II or Mk.III.

Two notable distance flights were made by specially modified Vimys in 1919. In June the first non-stop trans-Atlantic crossing by Capt. John Alcock and Lt. Arthur Whitten-Brown was made over the 1,890 miles (3,032 km.) between St. Johns, Newfoundland, and Clifden, in the Irish Republic. In November/December Vimy G-EAOU, piloted by Capt. Ross Smith and his brother Lt. Keith Smith, made the first flight from Britain to Australia by Australians in a British aircraft; the distance of 11,130 miles (17,912 km.) was covered in just under 136 flying hours.

57 Blackburn Kangaroo

One of the lesser-known aircraft of World War 1, the Kangaroo had its origins in the Blackburn Type G.P., a twin-engined, twin-float seaplane whose prototype (1415) first appeared in July 1916. This machine carried a crew of three, was powered by 150 h.p. Sunbeam Nubian engines and had fold-back wings. It was followed by a second machine (1416), sometimes known as the S.P., which first appeared with 190 h.p. Rolls-Royce engines and introduced a number of modifications including a greater use of metal in its construction.

The twenty Kangaroos originally ordered were apparently also intended as seaplanes for the R.N.A.S. as maritime patrol bombers. However, it was evidently decided that a landplane version would have more flexibility of operation, and the aircraft were accordingly renumbered and built with wheeled undercarriages for the R.F.C. The War Office also placed a separate order for four Kangaroos. Production Kangaroos still retained the facility to fold their wings, but introduced several minor airframe modifications and were powered by 250 h.p. Rolls-Royce Falcons (which may have been tested in one of the prototypes). The first Kangaroo underwent official acceptance trials in January 1918, and deliveries began to No. 246 Squadron R.A.F., based at Seaton Carew, Co. Durham, in April. The Kangaroo carried a 4-man crew; front and rear Scarff rings each mounted a single Lewis machine-gun, and four 230 lb. bombs or an equivalent weight of smaller bombs could be carried internally. Racks could be fitted under the centre of the fuselage for additional bombs. The Kangaroo's long, slender fuselage was liable to twist under stress, but for an aircraft of its size it was light on the controls, and all crew members enjoyed an excellent view from their respective cockpits. Completion of all twenty-four aircraft has not been verified, but the four ordered by the R.F.C. and at least twelve of the larger batch are known to have been delivered. About ten Kangaroos served with No. 246

Squadron during the final six months of the war, when they sank one U-boat (in August 1918) and damaged four other 'probables'. At least fourteen Kangaroos were in existence at the Armistice.

After the war the R.A.F. Kangaroos were repurchased by Blackburn (except for three sold to Grahame-White in May 1919 for joy-riding activities); these were variously modified. Some were operated by Blackburn on behalf of the R.A.F. for training purposes until 1929; others served as passenger or freight carriers, others with the North Sea Aerial Navigation Co. (a Blackburn subsidiary); one Kangaroo was used in an attempt (unfortunately unsuccessful) to fly from England to Australia in November 1919; and one or two others took part in various racing events during the 1920s. The origin of the name Kangaroo is obscure: although generally adopted, it had no official standing and no apparent visual justification. There may have been a connection with the 'kangaroo bicycle', an early form of hobby-horse with a sloping spine, but this is purely conjecture.

58 & 59 Caproni Ca 1 to Ca 5

The belief still persists in many quarters that Britain and Germany, with their Handley Pages and Gothas, were the first to make widespread use of the aeroplane for heavy bombing. In fact, both Italy and Russia had evolved aircraft suitable for this type of operation well before the outbreak of World War 1, and Italian Ca 2s had made several long-range bombing raids on Austro-Hungarian targets well before the Handley Page O/100 had even flown.

The first Caproni giant was designed in 1913, setting the pattern for future developments. It had a central nacelle and two slender fuselage booms supporting the tail unit: the crew and all three of the engines were located within the nacelle. An 80 h.p. Gnome rotary engine drove a pusher propeller at the rear of the nacelle while two other 80 h.p. Gnomes drove tractor propellers at the front of the booms by means of a transmission gear. This arrangement proved rather clumsy in operation, and the prototype, which first flew in October 1914, had the two tractor engines installed with direct drive. The first production version was powered by three 100 h.p. Fiat A-10 in-line engines, all driving tractor propellers, and was designated Ca 1. One hundred and sixty-two Ca 1s were built in 1914–16, and aircraft of this type made the first Italian bombing raid of the war against Austro-Hungary on 20 August 1915. Nine other aircraft, designated Ca 2, had the central engine replaced by a 150 h.p. Isotta-Fraschini V-4B in-line engine. The Ca 1 and 2 continued to serve, latterly on night operations, until the appearance of the Ca 3 in 1917. The Ca 3 was generally similar to the Ca 1, having 3-bay, equal-span wings, a box-like nacelle and three polygonal rudders atop the tailplane. Much attention was paid to making the Capronis safe for taking off or landing on rough terrain, skids being fitted beneath the lower wingtips and tail and auxiliary wheels under the front of the nacelle to prevent a nose-over. The two pilots sat side by side in the nacelle, with a gunner/observer in the front cockpit armed with a Revelli machine-gun or a cannon; the unfortunate rear gunner occupied a cage-like open position behind the trailing edge of the top wing and directly above the pusher propeller. Powerplant of the Ca 3 comprised three 150 h.p. Isotta-Fraschini V-4B in-lines. Two hundred and seventy of these aircraft were built in Italy in 1916–18; they equipped well over a dozen squadriglie of the Corpo Aeronautica Militare, and one Italian Naval squadron in Albania. Eighty-six others, built under licence in France, served with two escadrilles of the French Aviation Militaire. Several Ca 3s were still in service at the Armistice. Variants of the basic Ca 3 included the Ca 3 Mod., with detachable outer-wing sections; one hundred and fifty-three examples were built during and after the war, some of them adapted to serve in an ambulance role.

The military designation Ca 4 was applied to a series of much larger triplanes, the first of which appeared in late 1917. Side-by-side seating for the two pilots was installed, and the front gunner's cockpit was retained; but in place of the rear gunner's cage separate positions were installed in each of the fuselage booms. The Ca 4 was powered initially by three 200 h.p. Isotta-Fraschinis, but their combined output was insufficient for an aeroplane of this size. Because of this and other shortcomings only three were built with this powerplant. They were followed in 1918 by twelve examples with 270 h.p. Isotta-Fraschinis and an oval-section nacelle with tandem pilot seating. These aircraft served with Italian Army and Navy Squadrons. The final production triplane variants were powered by Fiat, Isotta-Fraschini or Liberty engines of greater power, and the pilots' seats were situated side by side. A coffin-shaped container was suspended between the main undercarriage wheels that could hold 1,450 kg. (3,197 lb.) of bombs. Twenty-three were completed, six of them being supplied to the R.N.A.S. in 1918. The Ca 4 proved to be too slow for daylight bombing and was employed principally on night operations. The R.N.A.S. Ca 4s apparently were not used for combat purposes and were returned to Italy after the war. Variants included two which had a biplane tail unit incorporating a rearward-firing machine-gun position. One of these versions was intended for the R.N.A.S., but the aircraft were never delivered. One twin-engined variant, of which at least the prototype was completed, was a seaplane with twin sprung floats and intended to carry two torpedoes; it was powered by two 400 h.p. Liberty engines. It is thought that series production was planned, but few, if any, were completed.

The Ca 5 series marked a return to a biplane configuration, and were slightly bigger than the Ca 3s. First model in the series had three Fiat engines of 200 h.p. The wing-mounted pair were given frontal radiators, while the radiator for the middle engine was incorporated in the nose of the nacelle. War load was 540 kg. (1,190 lb.), and only two defensive machine-guns were carried. The initial version went into service early in 1918. Improved versions followed it, with three 200 h.p. Isotta-Fraschini, Fiat or Liberty engines. The Ca 5 operated mostly with Italian night-bomber squadrons in France during the last nine months of World War 1, although some were still flying on the Italian Front when the war ended. Total Italian production of Ca 5 variants reached two hundred and fifty-five, and a small batch were built by Esnault-Pelterie in France. Following the delivery of two Ca 5s to the United States, a further three of these aircraft were built in America before the war ended. Another type intended for production was a torpedo or bombing seaplane on twin Zari floats, powered by three Liberty engines. Licence production of the Ca 5 was started by Piaggio, but only ten were completed, and these were not delivered until after the Armistice.

Caproni bombers of one type or another were thus in constant service throughout the Italian participation in World War 1. Their load-carrying capabilities may not seem exceptional in relation to their size, but it must be remembered that the majority of their targets were at a great distance from their home bases,

involving long flights over hazardous mountain country. Because of their size they needed strong piloting, but their excellent flying qualities and powers of endurance were well suited to the conditions in which they were required to operate. Several civil cabin conversions were planned, some carrying up to 30 passengers, but none of them appears to have seen any commercial service. However, under the designation B.1, Breda built an 8-passenger version, and one of these aircraft made the inaugural scheduled flight between Milan and Rome on 29 January 1919.

60 **Siemens-Schuckert R types**
Marking the opposite extreme in size to its neat little D type fighters (see the *Fighters 1914–1919* volume), the Siemens-Schuckert Werke G.m.b.H. of Berlin and Nuremberg was also involved in manufacturing some of the largest German aircraft of World War 1. The company, originally noted for airship construction, had closed down its aircraft department in 1911, but reopened it in 1914, at first building small monoplanes. Its first large aeroplane, designed by Forssman, was apparently based upon earlier Sikorsky four-engined biplanes, and was begun in October 1914. Powered by four 110 h.p. Mercedes engines mounted singly on the lower mainplanes, and having a wing span of 78 ft. 9 in. (24.00 m.), it was completed and flown in the spring of 1915. It was, however, considerably underpowered, and the two inner engines were replaced

by 220 h.p. Mercedes D.IVs, the outer pair of 110 h.p. engines at the same time being remounted at mid-gap. Thus modified, it resumed trials in September 1915, and in April 1916 was eventually accepted for service use as a training aircraft. Meanwhile, in late 1914 the Idflieg had authorised the development of a new, 3-engined large biplane bomber designed by the brothers Bruno and Franz Steffen.

Construction of this aircraft, designated G.I.32/15, began in December 1914, and it made its first flight, from the Steffen works at Neumünster, in the following May. Its configuration was, to say the least, unusual. The unequal-span wings carried ailerons on the upper mainplanes only, but secondary ailerons were mounted between the upper and lower wings. The fuselage comprised a nose/cabin structure having polyhedral rear faces, mated to two triangular-section tapering booms (an upper and a lower) the purpose of which was to allow a wide field of fire to the rear. The lower boom incorporated the customary ventral tunnel, also for a rearward-firing gun. The tail assembly, supported primarily by the inverted-triangular upper boom, consisted of a tri-angular tailplane and rectangular elevator, beneath which were a central fin, two small outlying rudders, and two auxiliary elevators. All three Benz engines were mounted within the forward fuse-lage, where minor in-flight repairs or adjustments could be made, and their radiators occupied the entire frontal area of the nose. Power was transmitted via a clutch and gear system to a tractor propeller moun-ted on each of the inboard bays of interplane struts. Idflieg acceptance of the G.I.32/15, in July 1915, was accompanied by an order for six similar aircraft, to be designated G.33/15 to G.38/15. With the introduction of the Riesenflugzeug (giant aeroplane) category in November 1915 the designations were changed to R.I to R.VII; and again in March 1917 to R.1/15 to R.7/15 respectively.

The six new aircraft were in-tended originally to be powered by a trio of Maybach engines, but development problems with these units led instead to the use of 260 h.p. Mercedes D.IVas in R.II and R.VII, and 220 h.p. Benz Bz.IVs in R.III, IV, V and VI. These being of lower power than the intended installation, wing spans were correspondingly in-creased, compared with R.I, to 124 ft. 8 in. (38·00 m.) in R.II; 112 ft. 7½ in. (34·33 m.) in R.III and R.V; 123 ft. 4½ in. (37·60 m.) in R.IV; 109 ft. 5½ in. (33·36 m.) in R.VI; and 126 ft. 1½ in. (38·44 m.) in R.VII. Fuselage design and length also varied to some degree between the six. The R.II, the heaviest of the six at 18,651 lb. (8,460 kg.), was also the slowest, with a maximum speed of 68·4 m.p.h. (110 km./hr.); the other five could all manage top speeds of 81–82 m.p.h. (130–132 km./hr.).

In the event, only four of the SSW R types (R.IV to R.VII) were employed on operational duties, these serving in 1916–17 with Riesenflugzeugabteilung (Rfa) 501, based at Vilna, on the Eastern Front in Russia; R.II and R.III, like R.I, remained in Germany and were employed only for training, a function to which R.IV and R.VII also were later transferred. In February 1918 construction of two even larger R types was started by SSW, but of these only R.23/16 (R.VIII) was completed. Spanning 157 ft. 5¾ in. (48·00 m.) and powered by six 300 h.p. Basse und Selve BuS.IV engines, it had a gross weight of 35,053 lb. (15,900 kg.) and an estimated top speed of 77·7 m.p.h. (125 km./hr.); but, while undergoing ground testing in 1919, it was severely damaged by its propellers following a transmission failure, and never flew.

61 Zeppelin (Staaken) R types
Several German manufacturers produced Riesenflugzeug (giant aeroplane) designs during World War 1, and the most successful of these, though by no means the largest, were those produced by the Zeppelin Werke Staaken. Prior to its move to Staaken in mid-1916 the team responsible for these aircraft was based at the Versuchsbau Gotha-Ost (East Gotha Experimental Works), the first such design being started in November 1914. This was the V.G.O.I, which flew for the first time on 11 April 1915, powered by three 240 h.p. Maybach Mb.IV engines. One of these, mounted in the nose, drove a tractor propeller, while the other two, mounted midway between the wings, drove

pusher propellers. In the front of each of the wing nacelles was a small cockpit mounting twin machine-guns. Redesignated R.M.L.1, this machine was later employed on operations by the German Navy on the Eastern Front, where it was later joined by the V.G.O.II, a second machine of similar type. Both aircraft served with Rfa 500 (Riesenflugzeugabteilung) late in 1916, but they were seriously underpowered, and the V.G.O.I later returned to Staaken where it was refitted with five 245 h.p. Maybachs, two in each nacelle; it was later destroyed in a crash. An alternative attempt to provide sufficient power resulted in the V.G.O.III (later R.III after the introduction of the R category), in which six 160 h.p. Mercedes D.IIIs were installed. Two of these engines were paired in each nacelle to drive single pusher propellers, while the third pair were installed side by side in the nose to drive a tractor propeller. Armament was increased to five machine-guns.

The first aircraft in the series to have an R designation from the outset was the R.IV, which was basically a V.G.O.III airframe, but with the nacelle engines exchanged for four 220 h.p. Benz Bz.IVs. Up to seven machine-guns were carried by the R.IV, which entered service in July 1917 on the Eastern Front and was later transferred to the Western Front and used in raids on the United Kingdom. Work was also begun in 1916 on single examples of the R.V and R.VII, each powered by five 240 h.p.

Mb.IVs – a single one in the nose and a tandem-mounted tractor pair in each outer nacelle, the gun positions of which were relocated at the rear. A fifth machine-gun was carried in a Schwalbenest (swallow's nest) position above the top centre-section. The R.V and R.VII differed chiefly in their tailplane bracing; the former was accepted for service in September 1917 and used against London in 1918, while the latter was lost in a crash in August 1917 during delivery to its unit.

The only Zeppelin R type to go into series production was the R.VI, eighteen of which were completed, one by Zeppelin (Staaken), six by Aviatik, four by O.A.W. and seven by Schütte-Lanz. Fifteen of them were powered by four 260 h.p. Mercedes D.IVa engines, in tandem pairs each driving one tractor and one pusher propeller. With the elimination of the nose engine it was possible to install a front gun position with a ring mounting for two Parabellum weapons, and single dorsal and ventral guns were separately manned to the rear of the wings. Between these the two pilots sat side by side in an enclosed cabin. Three of the Aviatik machines, completed in 1918, had four 245 h.p. Maybachs, the cabin extended to the extreme nose and a large central vertical tail fin. The Staaken R.VI could carry internally up to eighteen 100 kg. P.u.W. bombs within the centre of the fuselage. Its maximum load was 2,000 kg. (4,409 lb.), though about half of this total was the usual average. Individual bombs of up to 1,000 kg.

(2,205 lb.) could be carried semi-recessed under the aircraft's belly. Deliveries of R.VIs began in June 1917, and from September they were actively engaged in bombing raids against targets in France and England, operating with Rfa 500 and 501. During their combat career only two R.VIs were shot down by the Allies, but another eight were written off in crashes. Two R.VIs were fitted experimentally with an additional engine, a 120 h.p. Mercedes D.II, driving a compressor to supercharge the main power plant and enable the bomber' to sustain its performance at greater heights.

Subsequent Zeppelin R types were built in small numbers only. They included three R.XIVs, one R.XIVa and three R.XVs all powered by five 245 h.p. Mb.IVs and armed with five machine-guns. These had three tractor and two pusher propellers and, therefore, no nacelle gun positions. The R.XVs were probably too late for operational service. Aviatik completed one example (of three ordered) of the R.XVI in October 1918, this having one 220 h.p. and one 550 h.p. Benz in each nacelle. Variants of the R.VI included the Type 8301 seaplane, three or four of which were built using R.VI wings and engine installations with an entirely new fuselage suspended mid-way between the wings and a tail assembly incorporating the large central fin of the final R.VIs. One of these machines was later fitted with a land undercarriage. The Type L seaplane, which was destroyed during trials, was essentially a standard D.IVa-powered R.VI mounted on twin floats some 13 m. (42 ft. 7⅞ in.) long.

62 Sikorsky Ilya Mouromets

The world's first four-engined aeroplane, the *Le Grand*, was designed by I. I. Sikorsky and G. I. Lavrov in 1913 and flew for the first time on 13 May that year. From it was developed an even larger aeroplane, the Ilya Mouromets, which was flown early in 1914 and powered by four 100 h.p. Argus engines. Fitted with a ski undercarriage, it carried a crew of five and had compartments in the rear fuselage for sleeping and eating. In February 1914 this aeroplane lifted 16 human passengers and a dog to an altitude of 2,000 m. (6,562 ft.) and remained in the air for 5 hours. In spring 1914 ten examples of a military version were ordered for the Imperial Russian Air Service; after the outbreak of war in August this order was increased substantially by the Central Military Technical Board, and eventually nearly eighty Ilya Mouromets bombers were built.

Production aircraft were built by the Russo-Baltic Waggon Factory (R.B.V.Z.) and appeared in five basic forms, all differing in dimensions, weights and powerplant. Inadequate supplies of aircraft engines posed a constant problem for the Russian aircraft industry, and several of the Sikorsky bombers were completed with inner engines of one rating and outer ones of another. About four Ilya Mouromets Type B were completed (two 135

h.p. and two 200 h.p. Salmson/ Canton-Unné). They were followed by thirty-three Type V. All but three of these machines had four 150 h.p. Sunbeam engines (a highly unsatisfactory unit); the others had two 125 h.p. and two 140 h.p. Argus engines. The twenty or so G-2s had four 150 h.p. RBVZ-6s; fifteen G-3s had a pair of these engines together with two 220 h.p. Renaults. The largest Mouromets, the E-1, was powered by four 220 h.p. Renaults. At an all-up weight of 7,000 kg. (15,432 lb.) the E-1 was also the fastest variant, with a maximum speed of 136·7 km./hr. (85 m.p.h.). Operational performance of the first pair of Mouromets bombers was so disappointing that the R.B.V.Z. was asked to suspend production. Fortunately, however, the type was reprieved, and under the command of Major-General M.V. Shidlovski (former chairman of the R.B.V.Z.) the Eskadra Vozdushnykh Korablei, or Squadron of Flying Ships, was formed specially to exploit and operate the subsequent aircraft. This was more than an ordinary bomber squadron: it was a completely self-contained unit which carried out its own test flying, training, overhaul and other activities as well.

From its base at Jablonna in Poland the E.V.K. made its first raid on 15 February 1915 over East Prussia, and from then until the Revolution in November 1917 this unit was responsible for some four hundred bombing raids over German and Lithuanian territory. During that time only one Ilya

Mouromets was lost to enemy air attack; this occurred on 12 September 1916, but not before the Mouromets's gunners had accounted for three of the enemy fighters. Two other machines were lost in crashes, and in February 1918 thirty were destroyed on their airfield at Vinnitza to prevent capture by the Germans.

Because of its size, the Ilya Mouromets needed plenty of attention on the ground and strong handling in the air; but it was a well-built aeroplane, capable of absorbing plenty of battle damage. It carried highly efficient bomb-sights of Russian design and manufacture which enabled it to score direct hits on well over 60 per cent of its targets. A typical bomb load was that carried by the G-2 and G-3, which ranged from 450–700 kg. (992–1,543 lb.). Normal defensive armament was three or four machine-guns, but up to seven could be fitted, including a turret in the tail. Basic crew, as in the Type B, was four men, but could be increased in proportion to the number of guns installed. The Ilya Mouromets also undertook long-range reconnaissance missions, for which it was ideally suited in the areas in which it operated. In December 1916 Tsar Nicholas II approved British and French requests to build the Ilya Mouromets under licence, but these options were not taken up.

63 Caudron G.III, G.IV and G.VI

Most nacelle-and-tailboom aeroplanes of 1914–19 were pusher biplanes; the Caudron G.III differed in having its engine at the front. It was developed from, and was similar to, the single-seat G.II which in 1913–14 was a familiar sight at many European air meetings. In its initial military form the G.IIIA.2 was a 2-seat corps reconnaissance and artillery observation aircraft used widely throughout the first half of World War 1 by the French, British, Belgian, Russian and Italian air forces. Most of the many hundreds of G.IIIs built were manufactured in France, but small quantities were built in the United Kingdom by the British Caudron Co. and in Italy A.E.R. built one hundred and seventy G.IIIs in 1915–16. The G.III was originally powered by an 80 h.p. engine, of Gnome, Le Rhône or Clerget manufacture, but a common installation in later machines was the 100 h.p. Anzani 10 C radial. The G.III had a useful endurance (4 hours), but was generally too slow and too vulnerable to be retained for long on observation duties. The French machines were withdrawn from the Front in mid-1916, but Italian G.IIIs continued to serve until March 1917 and the British models were not withdrawn from operational units until August 1917. As late as 1 January 1917 the R.F.C. was using Caudron G.IIIs, armed with small bombs and carrying a machine-gun in the front cockpit, for ground-strafing missions. The R.N.A.S. used a few of its G.IIIs for coastal patrol. One hundred and twenty-four G.IIIs were supplied to the R.N.A.S., and one hundred and nine to the R.F.C., and they served on every major front. Their withdrawal from front-line duty did not, however, mark the end of their career, for they became one of the most popular and familiar types of training aircraft to be used in the Allied air forces. In this role the aircraft was designated G.IIIE.2; one hundred and ninety-two E.2s were purchased by the A.E.F. in 1918. Most Caudron G.IIIs had warp-controlled wings, but ailerons were fitted to the top wings of some later aircraft.

The Caudron G.IV, which appeared in March 1915, was in essence a scaled-up version of the G.III, powered by two engines. Originally these were 80 h.p. Le Rhônes, with the 100 h.p. Anzani being introduced for later production aircraft; the vertical tail surfaces were increased to four. A free-firing Vickers or Lewis machine-gun was mounted in the front cockpit, and in its G.IVB.2 day bomber form the aircraft could carry a 100 kg. (220 lb.) bomb load. Some G.IVs were fitted with a second machine-gun, mounted over the top wing to fire to the rear. Although its bomb load was modest, the G.IV had a useful performance and a particularly good rate of climb; in service it proved to be a thoroughly reliable aircraft, as is shown by its adoption by the Italian Air Force for long-range flights across the Alps. It entered service with the French Aviation Militaire in November 1915, serving until the following autumn. In Italy A.E.R. built fifty-one G.IVs in 1916–17. The R.N.A.S.

received forty-three French-built G.IVs and twelve completed by the British Caudron Co. These were used in 1916 and early 1917 for day and night attacks on enemy seaplane and Zeppelin bases in Belgium by Nos. 4 and 5 Wings. Aircraft in French service included both B.2 and A.2 versions of the G.IV. In 1918 the A.E.F. purchased ten G.IVA.2s for use as trainers.

In summer 1916 a link between the G.IV and the later R-prefix bombers designed by René Caudron appeared in the form of the G.VI. This was a development of the G.IV, but incorporated many features, including the distinctive 'keeled' and covered fuselage, and single fin and rudder, of the Caudron R.4 and R.11. Powerplant for the G.VI was two Le Rhône rotary engines of 80, 110 or 120 h.p. The observer sat in the rear cockpit, in which there was a ring mounting for one or two defensive Lewis guns. The G.VI was apparently built only in an A.2 form, and in view of the imminence of the R.4 and R.11 it is probable that it was not built in substantial numbers. It has not been possible to provide a breakdown by types of French squadron allocations of Caudron G series aircraft, but in all the Aviation Militaire operated thirty-eight escadrilles equipped with these aircraft during World War 1.

64 Lohner L

The first flying-boats produced by the Jakob Lohner Werke of Vienna were the general-purpose E types, built in 1913. They were 2-seaters, with 85 h.p. Hiero engines, and in August 1914 one of these aircraft (E18) made the first World War 1 sortie by an Austrian aircraft. The later S types were unarmed training versions of the Type E. About two hundred, some of them converted Es, were in service during 1914–18; most of them had 85 h.p. Hieros, but some were fitted with 80 h.p. Oberursel rotaries.

In size and general configuration the Lohner L resembled the Type E, but was powered either by a 140 h.p. Hiero or by an Austro-Daimler of 140 or 180 h.p. A slender, elegant aeroplane with sweptback sesquiplane wings, the Lohner L seated a crew of two side by side, the observer occupying the right-hand seat and having a Schwarzlose machine-gun on a rotatable mounting. Up to 200 kg. (441 lb.) of bombs and/or depth charges could be carried. The Lohner L entered service in the second half of 1915, and it is thought that one hundred and sixty were completed by the parent company. To these may be added nine or ten similar machines built as Type Ms by the Naval Dockyard at Pola. About thirty-six examples were also completed of the Type R, a 3-seat reconnaissance variant of the Type L with photographic equipment instead of a bomb load.

The Lohner Ls were the most widely used flying-boats of the Austro-Hungarian Navy, and operated exclusively in the Adriatic area against Allied shipping and targets on the Italian mainland. It was an aircraft of this type (L40) that fell into Italian hands on 27 May

1915 and eventually gave rise to the long and successful range of Macchi-developed flying-boats. The Austrian Navy's most celebrated pilot, Lt. Gottfried Banfield, scored the first of his many aerial victories on 1 June 1916 while flying a Lohner L, and the general effectiveness of the type can be judged from the fact that only thirty of these aircraft were lost during the war, and only one each of the Types E, R and S. (Five Type Rs were owned in 1923 by Alfred Comte, at which time he founded the Luftverkehr und Sportfliegerschule in Zurich.) The illustration depicts one of two Lohner Ls from the Austrian Naval base at Kumbor that attacked the French Laubeuf-class submarine *Foucault* off the coast of Cattaro on 15 September 1916.

65 Franco-British Aviation flying-boats

The Franco-British Aviation Co. was almost entirely French in outlook and operation: its only claim to a dual nationality was an office in London, and even this tenuous connection had been severed by 1917. From 1913–15 the company built flying-boats of Lévêque design; none of these were purchased by the French government, but small numbers were exported to Austro-Hungary and Denmark. In 1915 the 2-seat F.B.A. Type B appeared, a development of the basic Lévêque design by Louis Schreck having an upswept rear hull with an oblong rudder and a 100 h.p. Gnome Monosoupape rotary engine driving a pusher propeller. This was built in some numbers for the Marine Nationale and the R.N.A.S. In addition to forty-four complete Type Bs (three of which it later transferred to the R.F.C.) the R.N.A.S. had twenty more of these aircraft completed by the Norman Thompson Flight Co. from French-built hulls, and a further sixty built entirely in England by the Gosport Aviation Co. None of the French-built machines survived the war, but twenty-four of the Gosport batch were still in existence in January 1919.

In April 1916 the Type B was followed by the Type C, generally similar except for a 130 h.p. Clerget engine. This was built for the French, Italian and Russian Navies, initially for coastal patrol and later, like the Type B, used for training.

The most widely built F.B.A. flying-boat, and possibly the most widely built flying-boat on either side during the war years, was the 3-seat Type H. This had a less swept-up rear hull, a high, strut-mounted tailplane and roughly oval rudder. It was not much bigger dimensionally than the Type C, but it had greater load-carrying capabilities and a Vee-type engine instead of the latter's rotary. Powerplants were Hispano-Suizas of various ratings or 160 h.p. Lorraine-Dietrichs. The Type H was built under licence in Italy by six manufacturers, following the supply of an initial batch from France. It says much for the merits of the F.B.A. that, despite the pre-eminence in Italy of the Macchi range of flying-boats, nine hundred and eighty-two

examples of the French design were built there. Most of them were powered by 160 h.p. Isotta-Fraschini V-4Bs and sported a small vertical fin. Armament consisted of a single machine-gun in the front cockpit. Four Italian-built Type Hs were presented to the R.N.A.S. and based at Otranto. The Type H served with the Marine Nationale, including the celebrated Escadrille de Dunkerque, and with the Belgian and Russian Navies. Some were still in service with Italian Squadriglie della Marina in Tripoli in 1922.

A development of the Type H, the F.B.A. Type S, had a 200 h.p. Hispano-Suiza, and increased bomb load of two 35 kg. or 50 kg. weapons. It featured an enlarged tail assembly, including a triangular vertical fin, and carried a 2- or 3-man crew. The Type S was in production for the final twelve months of World War 1 and saw widespread service with the Marine Nationale in the North Sea, English Channel and Mediterranean; a few also served with the Belgian Navy. One prototype was completed in 1918 of a Type S development: this retained the hull and powerplant of the Type S, allied to completely new wings and tail assemblies. Despite their widespread employment and undoubted usefulness as coastal patrol and anti-submarine aircraft, no record appears to have survived of French production figures for the individual F.B.A. types.

66 Sopwith Baby

One hundred and thirty-six military examples of the 1914 Sopwith

Schneider floatplane were built for the R.N.A.S., which used them widely for a variety of duties during the first half of World War 1. From this basic design was developed the Baby, which differed chiefly in having a more powerful rotary engine enclosed in a 'horseshoe' cowling. Five of the first one hundred Babies built by Sopwith had the same engine (100 h.p. Gnome Monosoupape) as the Schneiders, but the remaining ninety-five aircraft were fitted with 110 h.p. Clergets. This engine also powered sixty-one Babies built by Blackburn, twenty by Fairey and thirty by Parnall; the 130 h.p. Clerget was installed in one Sopwith-built machine, one hundred and fifteen by Blackburn, thirty by Fairey and one hundred by Parnall, thus bringing total Baby production to four hundred and fifty-seven aircraft. Sopwith aircraft were armed with a single Lewis machine-gun firing forward and upward at an angle through a small cut-out in the top wing; in other Babies this was replaced by a synchronised forward-firing Lewis mounted in front of the cockpit, except for forty of the Blackburn machines. This Blackburn batch carried Ranken darts or Le Prieur rockets for anti-Zeppelin attacks instead of a gun.

The Babies built by Fairey from 1916 were known as Hamble Babies, having been considerably redesigned by Fairey to have thicker wings with full-span trailing-edge flaps on all sections, an angular fin (similar to that of the Campania) and floats of improved hydrodynamic form. Fifty-six of the Parnall Babies were completed with Sopwith-type floats and tails and Fairey-type wings, and the remaining seventy-four were built as Hamble Baby Converts with a wheel-and-skid land undercarriage.

The Sopwith Baby served widely with the R.N.A.S. for most of 1917–18, at a dozen or more bases around the British coast and aboard eleven seaplane carriers operating in the North Sea and the Mediterranean. During the first half of 1917 they flew fighter patrols from Dunkirk, while in Italy, Egypt, Palestine and the Aegean they operated mainly in a bombing role. For bombing or anti-submarine work the Baby normally carried two 65 lb. bombs under the centre of the fuselage. Withdrawal of the Baby from front-line service began some time before the Armistice: the Hamble Baby Converts and several ex-operational Babies were employed in a training capacity. On 31 October 1918 there were eighty Babies of one kind or another on charge, but these were all officially declared obsolete in November. During the war period Babies were supplied to Canada (eight), France (nine), Japan (one), the Netherlands, and the U.S. Navy (one), and a few were also supplied to the Royal Norwegian Air Force after the end of the war.

67 Friedrichshafen FF33, FF39, FF49 and FF59

Serving from the spring of 1915 until the closing stages of World War 1, the Friedrichshafen range of 2-seat patrol floatplanes were probably the most extensively employed

German seaplanes of the war period; nearly five hundred examples of the four models listed above were completed. Most of them were armed, and their major duties included coastal and ocean patrol, fleet observation and co-operation and anti-submarine work. Some were based at coastal stations, operating in the North Sea and English Channel areas; others served aboard German seaplane carriers. The best-known example is the FF33E christened *Wölfchen* (Little Wolf), which was carried by the merchant raider *Wolf* in the Indian and Pacific Oceans and helped the German warship to account for twenty-eight Allied vessels.

The FF33 went into service in spring 1915 in replacement of another Friedrichshafen design, the FF29A, the first machines being six FF33As with back-to-front seating and 100 h.p. Mercedes D.I engines. They were followed by eleven FF33Bs, six with 120 h.p. D.II engines and five with 160 h.p. D.IIIs, in which the pilot more logically occupied the front cockpit. The first major production model was the FF33E, powered by a 150 h.p. Benz Bz.III, which became the standard installation on all later FF33 variants. The FF33E was also the first model to introduce wireless equipment. One hundred and sixty-two were built, plus a further three armed with a rear-mounted Parabellum machine-gun, which were redesignated FF33Fs. In 1917 the E model was transferred to the training role, its place being taken by the modernised and more effi-

cient FF33J, of which about a hundred were completed. Thirty modified Js were also built as FF33S trainers.

Before the FF33J, however, there had appeared a slightly smaller variant, with 2-bay wings and a ring-mounted Parabellum gun for the observer. This was the FF33H, produced as a seaplane fighter or escort to the unarmed FF33s in 1916; forty-five of these were built, L.V.G. and Sablatnig sharing with the parent company the manufacture of the E and H models. The most effective model of all was the FF33L, which was a slightly smaller development of the H with a spin-nered propeller and provision for a forward-firing second gun; it was more manoeuvrable and had a better performance than its predecessors. One hundred and thirty-five FF33Ls were built.

The FF39 was an interim design, which appeared in 1917 with a strengthened and refined fuselage, 200 h.p. Benz Bz.IV engine and rear-firing Parabellum; fourteen were completed. The principal Bz. IV-powered model, however, was the FF49, of which twenty-two FF49Bs and two hundred and eighteen FF49Cs were built by Friedrichshafen, L.F.G. and Sablatnig. The Bs were unarmed, but most Cs had a rear-firing Para-bellum and at least thirty of the late-production machines in 1918 had two guns fitted. Apart from the more powerful engine, the FF49 broadly resembled the FF33J except that it had balanced control surfaces. Before the war ended twenty examples were ordered of the FF59C, another Bz.IV-engined floatplane with a more compact fuselage and greater range than its predecessors. Friedrichshafen built forty-four seaplanes after the war, in 1918–19, but it is not known what types(s) these were. The only 'in service' figures available are those for FF33 variants in May 1917: these included one hundred and twenty-one Es, twenty-five Hs, thirty Js and one hundred and fourteen Ls.

APPENDIX 1

The research into the aircraft colour schemes illustrated in this volume is the work of Ian D. Huntley, A.M.R.Ae.S., whose studies of aircraft colours and markings have been made over a period of more than twenty years. Ian Huntley was one of a small team of experts formed from members of the Royal Aeronautical Society and the Society of Licensed Aircraft Engineers in 1958 to undertake full-scale restoration work on the aircraft of the Nash Collection, which was bought by the R.Ae.S. in December 1953. With the title Historic Aircraft Maintenance Group, this body began work at Hendon, transferring its activities later to the B.E.A. Engineering Base at London (Heathrow) Airport. After 1 April 1964 the aircraft were gradually dispersed to various R.A.F. stations in the United Kingdom for continued restoration, and are now on permanent loan to the Royal Air Force Museum at Hendon for display. Effectively, this meant that the official duties of the H.A.M.G. ceased towards the end of 1965, but Ian Huntley and A. S. Hughes, the H.A.M.G.'s Chief Engineer, continue to act as civilian consultants on the subject of historic aircraft restoration.

Soon after the move to Heathrow an appeal was made for information that would contribute towards restoring the various aircraft in authentic colour schemes, and a landslide of 'bits and pieces' arrived in response. In August 1961 a second similar appeal brought a second similar flood of information and material. Inevitably, much of it was too vague or contradictory, and the only satisfactory way to solve the problems and establish the true colour finishes was to trace the original paint specifications and to approach manufacturers to re-create paints and materials from them. Ian Huntley became a 'one-man Specifications Committee' charged with this task and with classifying and authenticating the material submitted. As a result he was in a unique position to advise on the completion of the colour illustrations in this volume, and the real hues of many colours can now be seen for the first time since World War 1.

Such research proves, if proof is needed, that the only really satisfactory method of recording and relaying colour information must be based on first-hand inspection of the colours concerned, whether *in situ* on present-day aircraft or in the form of re-created samples; these must then be related to a comprehensive dictionary of colours which gives a key 'code' for individual shades of a given colour. This is the formula adopted in preparing the illustrations in this series, for which we use as our main colour dictionary *The Methuen Handbook of Colour* by A. Kornerup and J. H. Wanscher.* This handbook gives a spectrum of colour variations that are especially well related to aircraft paint finishes through the years, and when correct colour values, using this handbook to code them, are compared with most existing verbal or pictorial representations of specific aircraft types, the need for a standardised scheme of reporting and portraying colour values is self-evident; and the inadequacy of mere verbal descriptions, such as 'dark green' or 'pale blue', is also woefully apparent – there are dozens of them. The need to have a standard system is especially urgent in the case of aircraft of the 1914–18 period, where the number of people with first-hand knowledge of these aircraft is diminishing rapidly.

There is still, unfortunately, an almost unbelievable lack even of good basic general knowledge about aircraft colour finishes – something like *eighty-five per cent* of the material submitted to the H.A.M.G. was either the result of guesswork or the perpetuation of a long-standing fallacy. Much of the guesswork undoubtedly arises from the fact that most photographs taken during the war and reproduced then or since were taken on film which was not colour-sensitive and which in any case gave only a black and white result. A little orthochromatic, and even less panchromatic, film was then available which, with appropriate colour filters, could give a more accurate tonal rendering of colours within the limits of a black and white medium. Uncertainty regarding the type of film used to take a particular photograph is therefore a contributory factor: one type, for example, may make a red rudder stripe appear darker than a blue one, while another type will give the reverse effect. All too often an inaccuracy arises, probably quite innocently, from an incorrect deduction made from such evidence; and 'for want of a nail' the error gradually gathers weight as more and more followers accept it and repeat it until it attains the status of an unassailable

* First published by Politikens Forlag, Copenhagen, in 1961, and by Methuen & Co., London, in 1963 (revised 1967).

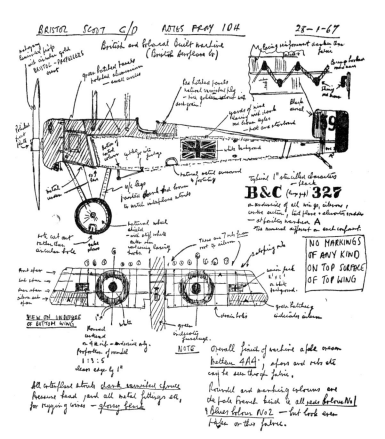

Typical sketch produced by Ian Huntley as a basic guide for artists
preparing the colour plates in this series.

fact. There is not the space here to discuss individual cases at length,
but one of the commonest misconceptions, which concerns the
British P.C.10 khaki finish of World War 1, is dealt with in some
detail in Appendix 2.

World War 1 was as much a forcing ground for the evolution of
aircraft protective finishes – in all senses – as it was for the design

of the machines themselves, and German and Italian aircraft, many of which had ply-covered fuselages, were able from a comparatively early date to employ disruptive camouflage schemes. Britain lagged somewhat behind the other powers in this technique, but by the time of the Armistice improvisation had been overtaken by a more serious study of the art of camouflage. In this respect the Salamander represents an interesting outcome of one such study. Up to 1917 use was made only of doping schemes that employed a first coating of clear shrinking dope, followed by a protective covering of pigmented varnish medium (a cellulose material with a similar base to clear dope but with its shrinking powers counteracted by the addition of a proportion of castor oil). During 1917, however, experiments showed that a pigmented dope not only gave an ideal fabric finish but saved time and eliminated the need to use such large quantities of cellulose material. From this it was established that, by using the ideal tropical sun-resisting pigment in the dope – P.C.12, a dark reddish-brown (as illustrated on pages 18 and 83 of the *Fighters 1914–1919* volume) – almost any finishing colour could be applied on top, all within the normal five coats, and yet maximum fabric protection was still maintained. This eventually led to the introduction of dark red-brown priming dope for use on fabric, a practice which is still in use today. Speculation naturally arose whether colours other than the standard dark brown could be used that would have a more concealing effect, and in summer 1918 various combinations of colour and pattern were studied to decide between 'dazzle' or 'splinter' schemes using bright and contrasting colours, and 'concealing' schemes made up of gently curving areas painted in dull, blending colours. Tests were carried out using various 'dummy' wings and, subsequently, B.E.2c, Camel, F.K.3 and Salamander aircraft for actual flight trials. The four matt colours used in the Salamander scheme were advertised in later years by Cellon Ltd. as 'Salamander colours', and several contractors building British observation aircraft were asked to prepare drawings showing the aircraft in these colours.

Other traps for the unwary exist when dealing with the 'lozenge' finishes adopted by the German and Austro-Hungarian air services. For one thing, there were probably more distinct patterns and colour combinations in printed schemes than is usually appreciated, quite apart from hand-painted schemes applied extempore by units in the field. The shapes of the 'lozenges' themselves varied from regular hexagons to irregular polygons, and generally a second fabric, of similar pattern but lighter tones, would be used for the undersides of the wings and horizontal tail surfaces. In one scheme, for example, the upper-surface and fuselage colours were Prussian blue, blue-green, dark ochre, sage green and dark violet; corresponding colours on the undersides were pink, blue, ochre, pale green and pale violet. Some lozenge fabrics were printed in as many as six or seven separate colours.

The error most commonly made, however, is in the incorrect *application* of a given scheme to an illustration or model, rather than the use of an inaccurate pattern. Thus, while the actual basic pattern may be quite correct, the *effect* is incorrect because it has been applied in the wrong direction. So far as the printed lozenge fabrics are concerned – obviously no hard and fast rules can be laid down for hand-painted schemes – the first stage was to evolve a unit pattern outline, and there were at least three of these in common use. This would then be engraved on rollers to print longitudinally on a standard roll of unbleached linen fabric so that the pattern was repeated along the length of the roll. Since the fabric was naturally much stronger across its width than along its length, the standard practice was to apply it chordwise to the flying surfaces – i.e. with the short fibres parallel to the wing main spar(s), the pattern repeating from leading edge to trailing edge or vice versa, and not spanwise from wing root to wingtip as is often supposed. The fabric, usually from 4–4½ ft. wide, was normally applied beginning at the centre-line of the upper wings or the roots of the lower wings and working outward towards the tips. This could vary on individual types, for example to avoid a seam between two strips of fabric coming in the way of an aileron control wire. Many German aircraft, mostly the larger types, had their wing fabric applied at 45 degrees to the leading edge, whereas British practice was to discourage this arrangement during the war period.

The above remarks apply of course to ex-works machines; repairs in the field would often have to be made with any odd length of fabric available, which would not necessarily be applied in the correct way or even be of the correct pattern. Movable flying surfaces – ailerons, elevators and rudders – and sometimes tailplanes did not always conform to standard practice. Because of their small areas and often irregular shapes, fabric might be applied to these components in whatever was the most convenient way, so that the pattern could run in any direction compared with that on the main airframe. Covering the fuselage was a relatively

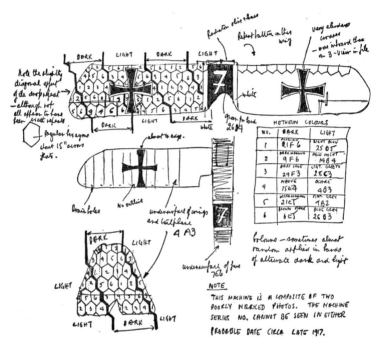

Austro-Hungarian hand-painted hexagons.

simple matter of making an 'envelope' of two, three or more longitudinal strips of fabric, depending on the size of the aeroplane, sewn together and laced up along the centre-line underneath. Sometimes ply-covered sections of aircraft – e.g. Albatros fighter fuselages or Gotha bomber noses – would be wrapped transversely in lozenge fabric to provide a hasty camouflage effect.

An interesting variation on German fabric finishes is the 'streaky' effect produced on some aircraft *circa* 1917 and excellently illustrated in the plate depicting the Fokker Dr.1. These aircraft came at a time when Germany was making every effort to use only cellulose for shrink-dope purposes and was evolving schemes to use dyes and other paint forms for its camouflage and markings. (The greatest shortage, incidentally, was of good red-pigmented materials, and explains why the use of red at this time was such a mark of the 'ace'. Only pilots of particular eminence could command the priority for materials in such short supply.) Over the yellowish (i.e. unbleached) linen Fokker tried applying a dark olive varnish, very sparingly, which gave a 'brushed-out' effect. This was then coated with a dark linseed-oil varnish which had the effect of transforming the dark olive to a brownish shade of green and the yellowish fabric that showed through it to a more orange shade.

These notes, brief as they are, show a few of the traps that exist for the student of aircraft colour schemes, and how easy it can be to fall into some of them. They will only be eradicated by more research, and by a wider publication of the results of that research. Many enthusiasts, in all parts of the world, are carrying out this kind of work with the same dedication and diligence that characterises Ian Huntley's efforts in this field. Sometimes the results of their labours are fortunate enough to get into print, but in all too many cases they do not. Through the medium of Blandford colour series it is hoped that the results of research of this kind can be made available economically to a wide circle of aviation enthusiasts who, for whatever reason, have a need for accurate reference on this subject. As already emphasised, verbal descriptions are especially valuable if they are based on first-hand knowledge or observation and can be related to a comprehensive colour dictionary – either the one already cited or a suitable alternative such as the U.S. Federal Standard publication F.S. 595a.

No single writer, historian or artist can hope to be a 'one-man encyclopaedia' of such a vast subject, and constructive help, be it in the form of fabric or paint samples, colour illustrations, verbal description of individual or national finishes, or any other form, will be welcomed – either by Ian Huntley, care of The Royal Aeronautical Society, 4 Hamilton Place, London W1V oBQ, or by the author, care of the publishers.

APPENDIX 2

by Ian D. Huntley, A.M.R.Ae.S.

The basic colour in which the upper surfaces of most British aircraft on the Western Front were finished has been referred to repeatedly in the past as 'khaki green' or even 'dark green'. The latter description is inaccurate, and the former sufficiently imprecise to mislead. The actual specification differed in constituent details over the four war years, but the early form, introduced as a varnish from 1916 onward, was mixed in a ratio of approximately 17 parts yellow ochre to 1 part lamp black (carbon black), by weight of dry pigment. This was not such an unbalanced mixture as it sounds, since the yellow ochre weighed fairly heavily while the lamp black was extremely light in weight. When mixed together the only possible pigmentation result is a khaki-brown shade, as discussed in detail later. What has given rise to the 'green' part of earlier descriptions is that, for protective purposes, this dry mixture was intermixed with cellulose acetate, oil varnish, or some other glossy liquid medium, producing an optical effect known as 'green shift' which gave the finished coat a tendency to look slightly greenish under certain light conditions. (All British finishes, except some of the late-war night colours, were highly glossy in their original state.) An ex-works aircraft could therefore show a tendency towards a greenish-brown shade – though still predominantly brown – but once the material had 'weathered' after the aircraft had been in service for a while the effective colour was a positive brown. Re-created paint samples and the inspection of actual fabric samples from contemporary aircraft bear this out.

In later years, as an aid to production at a time of materials shortage, the two original pigments were mixed in their original proportions and canned under the name 'Standard Khaki'. It was added straight from the can to the most readily available base medium, and its final coloration was accordingly dictated by the medium chosen; for example, mixing with an oil varnish would produce a greater degree of 'green shift' than mixing with cellulose acetate, and both shades could be observed on one airframe, the former finish applied to ply panels and the latter to upper-surface fabric. (An incidental point, often overlooked in describing or illustrating World War 1 colour schemes, is that often this dark finish was carried round and under the leading, and sometimes the trailing, edges of the flying surfaces for an inch or two, depending upon the size of the aeroplane, giving them an 'outlined' effect when seen from below.)

The British Khaki finishes

A protective coating or covering for the flimsy, fabric-covered flying surfaces of early aeroplanes was essential for two basic reasons: to keep the fabric stretched tautly over the main structure, and to prevent it from rotting under all conditions of use and weather. After various unsuccessful earlier experiments, an Advisory Committee for Aeronautics was set up in Britain in 1909 which, in conjunction with the Army (later Royal) Aircraft Factory, made a significant contribution towards solving this problem by evolving a series of P.C. (Protective Covering) varnishes. The Protective Covering studies were part of a series of experiments, started in early 1914, to find an ideal pigmentation that could be applied over clear-doped aeroplane fabric to shield it from the rapid rotting caused by the injurious (ultra-violet) rays of the sun. Most successful of the original P.C. series was P.C.10, then described as a dark khaki varnish, which afforded not only protection from the sun in a temperate climate but also a degree of camouflage when seen from above.

Patent rights on the P.C. series were taken out, and they became the only materials approved by the British War Office for use on the fabric of aircraft built for the Royal Flying Corps. The Admiralty's Air Department, being at that time a separate and autonomous organisation, chose not to be bound by the conditions imposed by the War Office, and freely purchased proprietary materials, including dopes and varnishes, which did not – and could not – conform to the patented P.C. series, in either constituent materials or colour, until R.F.C. and R.N.A.S. materials were standardised in 1916, following the formation of the joint-service Air Board. Before 1916, therefore, there were *two* forms of this protective finish: P.C.10 for aircraft built for the War Office, and Proprietary Khaki for aircraft built for the Admiralty.

Because of their 'freelance' nature, the Proprietary Khakis naturally varied in both chemical composition and hue, but the re-creation of many of these was facilitated by reference to published Admiralty formulae in which actual pigment proportions were given. Hence, in recent research to re-establish the nature and coloration of P.C.10, it was possible first to reproduce and eliminate a series of varnishes which were *not* P.C.10. Having done this, it was then necessary to isolate the original P.C.10 non-shrinking cellulose top-coat varnish from other finishing materials which, although using the pigments of P.C.10, were of a different chemical composition. (It is important here to realise two things. First, that the designation P.C.10 applied to the dry pigment used to colour the protective medium, and not to the finishing medium itself: in different chemical forms it was a constituent in at least four different forms of dope or varnish, producing in each a correspondingly different colour value. Second, that different media and systems of application over the years also resulted in different colour values.) The early varnishes incorporating P.C.10 pigments were applied directly to the fabric in three or four coats, followed by two or more top coats of clear, non-shrinking varnish. At a later stage, P.C.10 was applied in varnish form as two finishing top coats over five coats of clear, shrinking dope. The final P.C.10 dopes, using darker pigments, in greater proportions and in a different medium, were applied in three or four coats directly to the fabric.

Any assessment of P.C.10 colour values must, therefore, have as its basis the nature and proportions of the pigments involved. These were specified as natural oxide of iron (yellow ochre), darkened by the addition of a little lamp black (see opening paragraph). Ochre occurs in nature in a range of colours from dull yellowish-brown to light reddish-brown, depending upon the nature of any impurities in the soil where it is found and upon the proportion of ferric oxide (Fe_2O_3) which it contains; the greater the Fe_2O_3 content, the purer it is and the nearer it lies to the reddish-brown end of its colour range. Initially, the early P.C.10 varnishes called for a minimum ochre content of 30% Fe_2O_3, the first pigmented dopes for not less than 40%, and the later dopes not less than 60%. Although less critical to the final colour, the degree of purity of the carbon black pigment was also dictated by the P.C.10 specification.

Thus the early varnishes, having a low proportion of Fe_2O_3 in the pigment and being spread thinly on the fabric, resulted in a light olive-brown hue. The later dopes, with a higher percentage of pigment (which helped to save cellulose), appeared denser, more opaque, and of a more yellowish-brown colour. The introduction of P.C.10 pigments in linseed oil and long oil (copal type) varnishes, again in different proportions and strengths, produced further variations in final hue. It is the variety of application media – oils, varnishes, cellulose – which, with their optical effect of 'green shift' on a newly-finished aircraft, gave rise in the past to the oft-repeated 'dark green' or 'khaki-green' descriptions of aircraft finished in P.C.10 shades. At last, the exposure of this fallacy is becoming more widely recognised, although regrettably it is still perpetuated by some 'authorities' on the subject.

One other factor to emerge from the wartime use of these finishes was that a cellulose medium cannot be applied over an oil-based one (although the reverse was acceptable in an emergency). This necessitated a careful system of identifying various finishes by stencilling doping code letters on the finished surfaces, and the Air Board sought to standardise a single doping scheme for the fabric of all front-line aircraft, regardless of service. In the event, however, materials shortages and distribution and other problems prevented this ideal from being reached and, indeed, the doping code system became of increasing importance as more and more alternative doping and paint schemes came into being. The three main classes of doping/finishing schemes were as follows:

Class A
Using a clear, shrinking cellulose dope with a top coat of non-shrinking pigmented cellulose varnish. Introduced in April 1916 and remained in use throughout the remainder of the war. Consisted usually of five coats of clear dope and two of pigmented varnish (e.g. P.C.10, P.C.12, NIVO or black). When used initially in a Class A scheme, P.C.10 varnish could be applied also to metal and plywood components, and ex-works schemes usually called for such an application.

Class B
Using an opaque, shrinking cellulose dope with a top coat of clear, non-shrinking cellulose varnish. Introduced gradually during the

latter part of 1917. A much-improved scheme, consisting usually of three coats of pigmented dope and two top coats of clear varnish, the latter acting as a waterproofing agent. Finish lasted longer than that of Class A and was quicker to apply, but used greater quantities of basic pigment. Introduction of Pigmented Oil Varnishes (P.O.V.) was necessary for painting metal and plywood components, saving valuable cellulose while giving an oil finish to match cellulosed fabric. Partially phased out in 1918 in favour of Class C.

Class C
Using a waterproof, opaque, shrinking cellulose dope only. Introduced from early 1918, this was a much superior scheme giving a much longer-lasting finish, often with the application of only three coats. Like Class B, it saved basic cellulose but required much more pigment, solvents and softeners.

There were, of course, variations from standard. Some engine cowlings were left unpainted; in 1917 some aircraft appeared with P.C.10 cellulose on fabric upper surfaces and P.O.V. Standard Khaki (the official name of the P.C.10 P.O.V.) on the plywood and metal surfaces. During the early part of 1918, as Class B and C finishes called for greater quantities of basic pigment materials, a shortage of P.C.10 pigments led to the use of a dark grey P.O.V., or other shades of grey, as an alternative to P.C.10; and some aircraft, by mid-1918, displayed a mixture of grey P.O.V. cowlings and plywood surfaces with Class B finish on the wings only. No one scheme completely superseded another, which was why the 'finishing marks' on the fabric were so important.

Summary
The designation P.C.10 refers to the khaki-producing *pigment chemicals* used in early experiments. The actual range of colours resulting from the use of those pigments depended upon their purity, their proportions and the base medium with which they were mixed. The original specification called for this to be a nitro-cellulose (non-shrinking) varnish, but later specifications introduced acetate/nitro-cellulose (shrinking) dopes, spirit/oil varnishes (P.O.V.) and other media incorporating P.C.10 pigments, and each medium affected slightly the resulting coloration. Gradual weathering of aircraft in service affected this further still. Despite these possible

variations, the control exercised over paint finishes from April 1916 onward kept them all within a fairly well-defined avenue of colour, and the table below shows the approximate colour 'envelope' of Methuen reference numbers within which the great majority of shades can be said to fall. This table is based upon 48 original samples of fabric, and 32 reconstructed paint samples made from original specifications. The early-war Proprietary Khakis of Admiralty-sponsored aircraft were greener by comparison, and came generally within the Methuen range 3 F 8 to 4 F 8 .

P.C.10 covering range, from light khaki varnish to brownish P.O.V.

	A	B	C	D
FABRIC STATE	Lightest	Normal	Dark	Darkest
	Greenish-ochre	Greenish-brown	Brown-green	Almost all-brown
New*	3 E/F 7	4 F 7	4 F/G 7	4/5 F 6
Moderate wear	3 E/F 5	4 E/F 5	4 F/G 5	4/5 E/F 4
Well worn	3 E/F 4	4 E/F 4	4 F/G 4	4/5 F 2
Average	3 E/F 5/6	4 E/F 5/6	4 F/G 5/6	4/5 F 4/5

* Based on Air Board colour master.
Note. E or G values lighten or darken only marginally.

INDEX

The Pocket Encyclopaedia of World Aircraft in Colour

BOMBERS

PATROL AND TRANSPORT AIRCRAFT

1939–45

The Pocket Encyclopaedia
of World Aircraft in Colour

BOMBERS
PATROL AND TRANSPORT AIRCRAFT
1939-45

by
KENNETH MUNSON

Illustrated by
JOHN W. WOOD

Norman Dinnage
Frank Friend
Brian Hiley
William Hobson
Tony Mitchell
Jack Pelling

BLANDFORD PRESS
Poole   Dorset

First published in 1969
Copyright © 1969 Blandford Press Ltd.
Link House, West Street, Poole,
Dorset BH15 1LL
ISBN 0 7137 0379 2
Reprinted 1972
Reprinted 1975

Colour printed by The Ysel Press, Deventer, Holland
Text printed and books bound in England
by Richard Clay (The Chaucer Press), Ltd.,
Bungay, Suffolk

PREFACE

So many different types of aeroplane, old and new, conventional and bizarre, were involved in the war of 1939-45 that any selection for a volume of this size must necessarily be an arbitrary one. In this initial presentation, therefore, the selection has been governed primarily by the operational importance of the aircraft concerned, although some types have other claims for inclusion.

As before, our collective thanks are due to Ian D. Huntley for his invaluable specific knowledge and general guidance in the matter of aircraft colouring and markings. Also of considerable assistance have been the three invaluable volumes of *Markings and Camouflage Systems of Luftwaffe Aircraft in World War II*, by Karl Ries Jr. Grateful acknowledgment is also made of items published at various times by *The Aeromodeller, AiReview, Air Pictorial, Aviation Magazine International*, the *Journal of the American Aviation Historical Society, Flying Review International, Interconair*, the *IPMS Magazine* and Profile Publications Ltd. Individual help was again kindly given by Lt.-Col. N. Kindberg, of the Royal Swedish Air Force, and Jørgen Lundø, of Politikens Forlag, Copenhagen. Finally, my thanks go, as always, to Pamela Matthews for her considerable help in the preparation and checking of the manuscript.

Kenneth Munson

May 1969

INTRODUCTION

Most of the European nations involved in the war of 1939-45 had, during the latter half of the 1930s, embarked upon plans to expand and re-equip their air forces with more modern combat types. The natural process of evolution of new military aircraft was hastened by a belated recognition of the potential danger which existed in the form of the increasing might of the German *Luftwaffe*. However, by the outbreak of World War 2 Germany still possessed the strongest and most modern air force in Europe.

Germany had been categorically forbidden by the 1919 Treaty of Versailles to manufacture military aeroplanes, although the construction of light civil aircraft was allowed to continue on a modest scale. Most of the restrictions imposed by the Versailles Treaty were withdrawn in the 1926 Paris Air Agreement, and from then onward there began the re-establishment of a substantial aircraft industry, not only within Germany itself but in the form of new factories set up in Switzerland, the U.S.S.R. and elsewhere. The national airline, *Deutsche Lufthansa*, and the re-created *Luftsportverband*, ostensibly a private flying organisation, acted as a political cloak for new para-military activities whereby new bombers, fighters and transport aircraft were developed under the guise of fast 'air taxis', 'sporting' single-seaters and high-speed mailplanes. New military prototypes commonly appeared bearing civilian registration letters, but their quasi-civilian purpose was fairly apparent, and after Hitler came to power in 1933 little further attempt was made to preserve the pretence, although the practice of allocating civil registration marks to military prototypes continued. In 1935 the existence of the new *Luftwaffe* was confirmed officially when it was announced that *Reichsmarschall* Hermann Goering, the former Air Minister, had been appointed as its new Commander-in-Chief. After the German occupation of Austria in 1938 factories in that country were also utilised for the production of aeroplanes for the *Luftwaffe* and the output of combat aircraft for the German air force rose from some 300 a month at the end of 1935 to more than 1,000 a month by September 1939.

By comparison, the expansion programme embarked upon by the RAF before World War 2 was both modest and slow. Until 1936 the bomber force was composed principally of obsolescent biplanes or slow, ponderous monoplanes; but then, with the introduction of the 'shadow factory' programme, the extensive re-equipment of the RAF with more modern combat aircraft began, with the British motor-car industry geared to turn out aeroplanes to supplement those produced by the aircraft industry. In addition, substantial numbers of American types were ordered for the RAF by the British Purchasing Mission which visited the U.S.A. in 1938. Despite this augmented programme, however, on 3 September 1939 the RAF had no four-engined heavy bombers in service, and the total number of twin-engined medium bombers on charge at that time comprised only 226 Hampdens, 179 Wellingtons and 207 Whitleys. Of these, the Whitleys were already virtually obsolete, and only 169 Hampdens and 160 Wellingtons were with front-line squadrons. The light day bomber situation was slightly better, at least numerically, for there were 1,075 twin-engined Blenheims and 1,133 single-engined Battles on strength; but only half of these were with operational units, and the Battle was later to prove something of a disappointment. The Fleet Air Arm was in an even poorer state, its most modern fighter in September 1939 being the Sea Gladiator biplane. Seven new aircraft carriers had been ordered in 1938, but for the first three years or more of the war the best British torpedo-bomber-reconnaissance types that they had aboard them were also slow, vulnerable biplanes, and it is no small tribute to the quality of such aircraft as the Fairey Swordfish that it was capable of being flown with distinction and to good military effect for the major part of the war. Poland, France and the smaller European nations were, like Britain, still in the midst of their respective modernisation programmes when the war struck them. Each had excellent new types under development, but all too few were actually in service by the time they were needed.

The civil war which had broken out in Spain in 1936 had afforded an ideal opportunity for several European powers to send detachments of combat aircraft to that country, where they could gain valuable operational experience under genuine battle conditions. In the light of future events this was to prove something of a mixed blessing. In Spain, where they were generally opposed by aircraft older or technically inferior to those which they were flying themselves, the pilots of Germany's *Legion Condor* and Italy's *Aviazione Legionaria* were usually able to dispose of any aerial opposition with comparative ease. Bomber squadrons in particular were able to carry out raids with little or no fighter escort, since their opponents were either too few, too slow or too old to interrupt their progress seriously. The successful application of these tactics in Spain not unnaturally led the *Luftwaffe* to pursue similar tactics at the outset of World War 2, and in the initial advances across eastern and western Europe this policy continued to prove successful.

After the Dunkirk evacuation and the fall of France in 1940, the *Luftwaffe* began to increase its campaign of bombing raids against the United Kingdom as a preliminary softening-up process prior to the intended invasion of England. However, in the late summer of 1940 the *Luftwaffe* suffered its first serious defeat in the air when, in the Battle of Britain, operating without ground support and against superior fighter opposition, it failed to achieve the measure of air superiority required to allow the bomber force to achieve its objective. The success achieved by the RAF in the Battle of Britain gave the Allied air forces a valuable initial breathing space in which they were able to recover and remuster their strength before preparing first to withstand the continued German *blitzkrieg* and then to mount their own counter-bombing offensive.

Meanwhile, in June 1940 Italy had entered the war on the German side, and although the *Regia Aeronautica* possessed rather less modern warplanes than the *Luftwaffe*, it was still numerically a force to be reckoned with, having nearly 1,000 bombers and over 750 reconnaissance, transport and non-combatant types in its overall inventory. Germany did not immediately learn the lesson of the Battle of Britain, although one outcome was a marked increase in the defensive armament of her bomber fleet. The *Luftwaffe* continued daylight bombing attacks for quite some time afterwards; had it turned over immediately to a night bombing offensive while British night defences were still inadequate, the story might well have been a different one. As it was, Germany lost around 2,000 aircraft and 5,000 aircrew in

9

continued daylight attacks before switching to a night offensive. For a short time during 1940-41 Italian bombers based in Belgium gave some support to the *Luftwaffe* during day and night raids on British targets, but they achieved little success in this quarter, and were soon required to return home for operations in the Mediterranean area or in North Africa. A serious blow was dealt to the Italian war machine in November 1940 by the Fleet Air Arm, which brought off a remarkably successful attack on the Italian Fleet at Taranto, inflicting losses and damage almost as serious in their effect as those incurred just over a year later by the U.S. Navy when its ships at Pearl Harbor were attacked by the Japanese Naval Air Force. With one or two exceptions, Italian bombers of the war period were not an outstandingly successful breed. The only four-engined Italian bomber, the Piaggio P.108B, served only in small numbers, and, coincidentally, none of the multi-engined strategic bombers developed by Germany and Japan were successful operationally.

One of the biggest single factors in the ultimate downfall of Naziism was undoubtedly Hitler's decision in 1941 to invade the U.S.S.R. The Soviet Air Force had been another participant in the Spanish Civil War of 1936-39, and in 1938-39 was also engaged against the air forces of Japan during the Siberian border disputes. A major expansion and re-equipment programme for the Soviet Air Force was put in hand as a result of these campaigns, but at the time of the German invasion few new aircraft had been developed and put into service, and the Soviet Air Force, although strong numerically, did not possess large numbers of modern combat aircraft. The gap was bridged to a considerable extent after March 1941, when the U.S. Congress gave approval to the Lend-Lease Act, which permitted the donation of American aircraft to the Allied powers. By the end of 1942 several of the new Soviet-designed types had become available in quantity. Most of these were fighters or ground-attack aircraft; the bomber force was made up largely of the Ilyushin DB-3F and Tupolev SB-2, supplemented by such U.S. medium bomber types as the Douglas A-20 and North American B-25.

The U.S.A. had always been overtly sympathetic to the Allied cause, and the substantial numbers of American aircraft ordered before the war by the British Purchasing Commission were now augmented still further by the diversion to Britain of unfulfilled

French orders and by further supplies made under the Lend-Lease Act. When the U.S.A. itself was forced in December 1941 to become an active participant in the war the already large work load placed upon the American aircraft industry was increased by many more huge orders for combat aircraft for its own services, and several newly developed types were also earmarked for production. By a coincidence, U.S. and British strategists had each pursued, according to their own convictions, the evolution of specialised warplanes for certain roles which they considered vital. Fortuitously, these types largely complemented rather than overlapped one another when it came to the matter of pooling British and American production resources in a common war effort. Thus, the major U.S. effort was concentrated upon the production of long-range heavy bombers, patrol aircraft and transports. Nevertheless, considerable numbers of medium and light bombers were among the early supplies of Lend-Lease aircraft supplied to Britain and the U.S.S.R. The U.S. industry undertook the mass production of virtually all the transport aircraft required by the Allied powers, and at the outset nearly one-third of the total U.S. productive effort was devoted to the manufacture of transport types. The subsequent intermixture of aircraft between Britain and the U.S.A. resulted in a more comprehensive array of combat types than either country could probably have achieved by itself.

Japan's action in precipitating the U.S. entry into the war proved to be the final undoing of the Axis powers. The aircraft in service with the Japanese Army and Naval Air Forces at this time, like those of the other combatants, were largely those that had begun to enter service in the middle and late 1930s. Japan, too, had tested her military equipment under operational conditions and against a technically inferior adversary during conflicts throughout the 1930s with China and, later, with Siberia. The Japanese entry into the war was heralded by bomber types of the Japanese Naval Air Force, which flew from their parent aircraft carriers to attack the U.S. Fleet in Pearl Harbor early on the morning of 7 December 1941. Japan's subsequent activity during the war can be divided broadly into that on the mainland of south-east Asia, carried out chiefly by the Army Air Force, and that among the numerous island groups in the south-west Pacific, which was largely the responsibility of the Naval Air Force. So long as it retained its aircraft carriers, the Japanese Fleet was a formidable adversary; but, as the war progressed and its carrier fleet was gradually diminished and ultimately demolished, its power in the Pacific was reduced to negligible proportions. The Japanese Army overran the southern mainland of Asia so quickly at the outset of its offensive that its air force became very thinly spread over the vast area which it now had to cover, and eventually home production was unable to keep pace with even the normal combat wastage of aircraft for each service. America's vast output of transport aircraft was of particular value in south-east Asia, although naturally they figured largely in every major campaign of the war. Especially noteworthy was the maintenance of the supply routes across the Himalayas between India and China, without which the Allied forces in that theatre would have been hard pressed to maintain or advance their position. In April 1942 General 'Jimmy' Doolittle's small force of Mitchell bombers, taking off from the aircraft carrier *Hornet* to carry out a bombing attack on Tokyo, made world headlines. This operation was noteworthy for the fact that it took place at all, even though it was more of a morale-booster than an operation of great military value; but two months later, in June 1942, Japan suffered a really serious defeat in the Battle of Midway Island, in the course of which she lost four aircraft carriers and over 250 aircraft. The Battle of Midway was as much a key turning-point of the war in the Pacific as the Battle of Britain had been in the war in Europe.

Within a year of Pearl Harbor the number of aircraft in service with the U.S. forces had trebled, and most of this strength was serving abroad, to such an extent that it became necessary for the USAAF to loan some of its aircraft to the U.S. Navy so that the latter could maintain adequate maritime patrols over American home waters. One of the first steps taken by the USAAF was the establishment of the U.S. Eighth Air Force at bases in the United Kingdom, from where its Fortress and Liberator four-engined bombers could join with the RAF's Stirling, Halifax and Lancaster 'heavies' in carrying out round-the-clock day and night bombing of German targets. In the autumn of 1942 part of the Eighth was detached to form the basis of the U.S. Twelfth Air Force in North Africa. In 1943, after the successful conclusion of the North African campaign, first Sicily and then Italy were invaded. The bombing offensive against Germany continued, now with frequent thousand-bomber raids; and smaller, faster types, such as the Mosquito, were making their presence felt, both in the precision bombing of specialised targets and as pathfinders for the bigger bombers. Mosquitos also performed a considerable amount of photographic reconnaissance work, bringing back valuable intelligence pictures of the damage inflicted by the bombers. By this time, the British Fleet Air Arm was at last beginning to receive more modern monoplane fighters and bombers of British design, to augment the American types received earlier under Lend-Lease arrangements. One effect of the sustained bombing of Germany was the wholesale recall of *Luftwaffe* fighter squadrons from other fronts, from which they could ill be spared, to defend the German homeland; moreover, defensive fighters were now outnumbering bombers in the overall *Luftwaffe* establishment. Nevertheless, by cutting its reserves to negligible proportions, the *Luftwaffe* was still able to claim a first-line strength in mid-1943 of around 4,000 aircraft.

On 8 September 1943 the Italian forces under the command of Marshal Badoglio surrendered to the Allies, and the aircraft based in Italy became divided into two opposing camps. Those in that half of Italy which had still not been reached by the Allied advance were formed into the *Aviazione della Repubblica Sociale Italiana* and continued to fight alongside the *Luftwaffe*, while those in southern Italy became known as the Italian Co-Belligerent Air Force, which continued to fight with mixed Italian, American and British types on behalf of the Allied cause. Towards the end of 1943 the forthcoming invasion of the Continent was fore-shadowed by the setting up in November of the Allied Second Tactical Air Force, and by the increase in ground-attack raids against enemy targets. By the time the invasion came on 6 June 1944, day and night raids upon German-held targets were being made with comparative impunity, and valuable diversionary raids were made to distract enemy defence resources away from the invasion area. The invasion of Normandy itself involved one of the largest single troop movements in history, in which even the prodigious numbers of American transport aircraft were augmented by the use of many older bomber types to act as tugs for the troop-carrying gliders.

The invasion did not bring any decrease in the mass bombing

of German industrial areas, and among the later weapons devised for attacking such specialised targets as railway centres and viaducts was the tremendous 22,000-lb 'Grand Slam' bomb, which could be carried only by specially modified Lancasters. Germany, too, produced some last-minute weapons in the form of the *Vergeltungswaffen* (Reprisal Weapons) V1 and V2. The V1 flying bombs constituted a slight setback for a time in the autumn of 1944, but their measure was soon taken by the RAF's piston-engined Tempest and jet-engined Meteor fighters. Repeated attacks on their factories and launching sites finally disposed of the menace both from the V1 and from the V2 rocket missiles, which were used against Britain for a time during 1944-45. The hard-hit German aviation industry achieved a partial respite by an extensive dispersal of its factories and by setting up new plants underground, almost exclusively by now for the production of defensive fighters; but even these new aircraft were prevented from entering service in appreciable numbers by the continued attentions of Allied bombers to their factories and airfields. Among the types whose careers were thus affected was the Arado Ar 234, the first jet bomber to go into service anywhere in the world. The *Luftwaffe* suffered a final indignity by having its surviving aircraft virtually grounded for lack of fuel during the closing weeks of the European war.

From the end of 1944, once the end of the war in Europe was in sight, South-East Asia Command underwent a considerable expansion preparatory to a final all-out offensive in the Pacific theatre. After the end of the European war some twenty bomber squadrons were nominated as part of a new 'Tiger Force' which was to be dispatched to the Far East to supplement the existing bomber force; but this formation was still working up to operational level when Japan surrendered.

The successful American campaigns to recapture the Philippines and Marianas island groups in 1944 had marked the beginning of the final stage of the Pacific war, for after these actions Japanese sea power in the area was virtually non-effective, and the fanatical suicide attacks engaged in by Japanese Army and Navy pilots in their explosive-laden aircraft provided only a temporary, if serious, setback. The recapture of the Marianas islands of Saipan, Tinian and Guam by the U.S. Naval and Marine forces had at last given the Army Air Force the forward bases that it needed for its new B-29 Superfortress bombers to mount a regular series of attacks against targets within Japan itself, and in November 1944 over 100 Superfortresses raided Tokyo. Apart from the tremendous damage inflicted by such raids, the waters around Japan were heavily laid with mines to cut off external supply routes by sea. The last significant gestures by *Kamikaze* suicide pilots were made at Iwo Jima and Okinawa; and finally, it fell to the Superfortress to become the instrument for delivering the two atomic bombs on Hiroshima and Nagasaki which brought World War 2 to its end in August 1945.

THE COLOUR PLATES

As an aid to identification, the eighty colour plates which follow
have been arranged in an essentially visual order, within the
broad sequence: biplanes, single-engined monoplanes and multi-
engined monoplanes. The sole rocket-powered aircraft appears
last of all. The reference number of each type corresponds to the
appropriate text matter, and an index to all types illustrated
appears on pp. 162-3.

The 'split' plan view, adopted to give both upper and lower
surface markings within a single plan outline, depicts the colour
scheme appearing above and below either the port half or starboard half of the aircraft, according to whichever aspect is shown
in the side elevation. This should be borne in mind when studying,
for example, the plan views of U.S. aircraft, on which, normally,
the national insignia appear only on the port upper and starboard
lower surfaces of the wings.

1

Saunders-Roe-built Walrus II of No. 711 Squadron Fleet Air Arm, *ca.* spring 1941. *Engine:* One 775 h.p. Bristol Pegasus VI radial. *Span:* 45 ft. 10 in. (13.97 m.). *Length:* 37 ft. 7 in. (11.46 m.). *Height:* 15 ft. 3 in. (4.65 m.). *Normal take-off weight:* 7,200 lb. (3,266 kg.). *Maximum speed:* 135 m.p.h. (217 km./hr.) at 4,750 ft. (1,448 m.). *Operational ceiling:* 18,500 ft. (5,639 m.). *Range:* 600 miles (966 km.). *Armament:* One 0.303 in. Vickers K gun on Scarff ring in each of bow and mid-upper positions; light load of small bombs or depth charges beneath lower wings.

ALBACORE (U.K.)

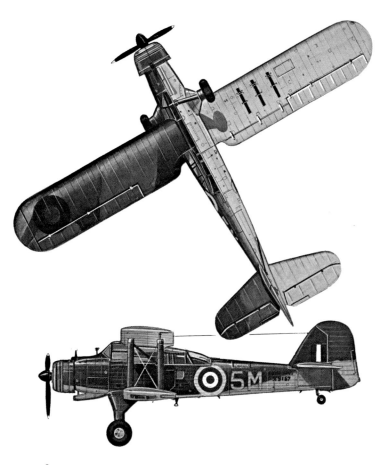

2

Fairey Albacore I of No. 826 Squadron, HMS *Formidable*, spring 1941. *Engine:* One 1,065 h.p. Bristol Taurus II radial. *Span:* 50 ft. 0 in. (15.24 m.). *Length:* 39 ft. 10 in. (12.14 m.). *Height:* 14 ft. 2¼ in. (4.32 m.). *Normal take-off weight:* 10,460 lb. (4,745 kg.). *Maximum speed:* 161 m.p.h. (259 km./hr.) at 4,000 ft. (1,219 m.). *Operational ceiling:* 20,700 ft. (6,310 m.). *Range with torpedo:* 930 miles (1,497 km.). *Armament:* One 0.303 in. machine-gun in starboard wing and two 0.303 in. Vickers K guns in rear cockpit; one 1,610 lb. (730 kg.) torpedo beneath fuselage or up to 2,000 lb. (907 kg.) or bombs beneath lower wings.

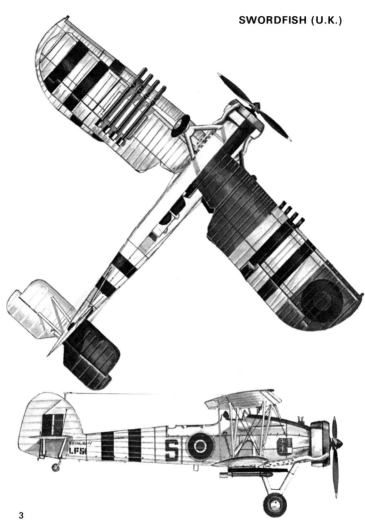

3

Fairey Swordfish II (unit unidentified) of the Fleet Air Arm, July 1944. *Engine:* One 690 h.p. Bristol Pegasus IIIM.3 radial. *Span:* 45 ft. 6 in. (13.87 m.). *Length:* 35 ft. 8 in. (10.87 m.). *Height:* 12 ft. 4 in. (3.76 m.). *Maximum take-off weight:* 7,510 lb. (3,406 kg.). *Maximum speed:* 138 m.p.h. (222 km./hr.) at 5,000 ft. (1,524 m.). *Operational ceiling:* 19,250 ft. (5,867 m.). *Typical range:* 546 miles (879 km.). *Armament:* One 0.303 in. Vickers machine-gun in upper engine cowling and one 0.303 in. Lewis or Vickers K gun in rear cockpit; eight 60 lb. (27 kg.). rocket projectiles beneath lower wings.

NORSEMAN (Canada)

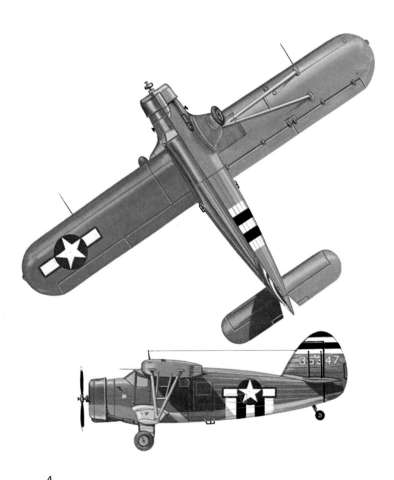

4

Noorduyn UC-64A Norseman of the USAAF, summer 1944. *Engine:* One 600 h.p. Pratt & Whitney R-1340-AN-1 Wasp radial. *Span:* 51 ft. 8 in. (15.75 m.). *Length:* 31 ft. 9 in. (9.68 m.). *Height:* 10 ft. 1 in. (3.07 m.). *Maximum take-off weight:* 7,400 lb. (3,357 kg.). *Maximum speed:* 165 m.p.h. (266 km./hr.) at 5,000 ft. (1,524 m.). *Operational ceiling:* 17,000 ft. (5,182 m.). *Typical range:* 600 miles (966 km.). *Armament:* None.

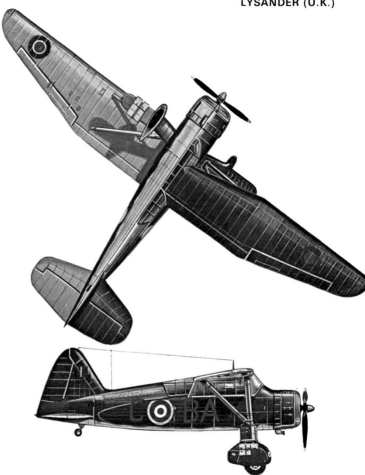

5

Westland Lysander ASR IIIA of No. 277 Squadron RAF, southern England, summer 1942. *Engine:* One 870 h.p. Bristol Mercury 30 radial. *Span:* 50 ft. 0 in. (15.24 m.). *Length:* 30 ft. 6 in. (9.30 m.). *Height:* 14 ft. 6 in. (4.42 m.). *Maximum take-off weight:* 6,318 lb. (2,866 kg.). *Maximum speed:* 212 m.p.h. (341 km./hr.) at 5,000 ft. (1,524 m.). *Operational ceiling:* 21,500 ft. (6,553 m.). *Typical range:* 500 miles (805 km.). *Armament:* One 0.303 in. Browning machine-gun in each wheel fairing; two more on movable mounting in rear of cabin.

FIESELER Fi 156 (Germany)

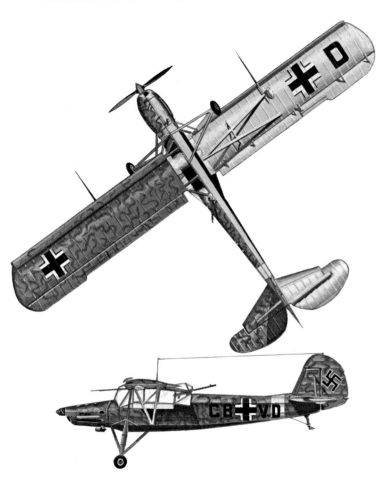

6
Fieseler Fi 156C-2 *Storch*, North Africa, *ca.* spring 1941. *Engine:* One 240 h.p.
Argus As 10C inverted-Vee type. *Span:* 46 ft. 9 in. (14.25 m.). *Length:* 32 ft.
5¾ in. (9.90 m.). *Height:* 10 ft. 0 in. (3.05 m.). *Normal take-off weight:* 2,923 lb.
(1,326 kg.). *Maximum speed:* 109 m.p.h. (175 km./hr.) at sea level. *Operational
ceiling:* 16,700 ft. (5,090 m.). *Maximum range with standard fuel:* 239 miles
(385 km.). *Armament:* One 7.9 mm. MG 15 machine-gun in rear of cabin.

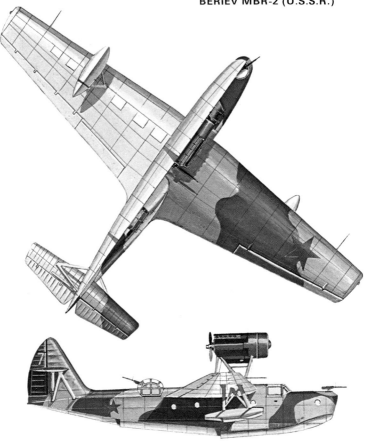

7

Beriev MBR-2 of the VVS-VMF (Soviet Naval Aviation), unit and date not determined. *Engine:* One 750 h.p. Mikulin AM-34N Vee type. *Span:* 62 ft. 4 in. (19.00 m.). *Length:* 44 ft. 3½ in. (13.50 m.). *Height:* approximately 14 ft. 9 in. (4.40 m.). *Maximum take-off weight:* 9,359 lb. (4,245 kg.). *Maximum speed:* 171 m.p.h. (275 km./hr.) at 6,560 ft. (2,000 m.). *Operational ceiling:* 16,080 ft. (4,900 m.). *Maximum range:* 932 miles (1,500 km.). *Armament:* One 7.62 mm. PV-1 machine-gun in open bow position and one 7.62 mm. ShKAS machine-gun in dorsal turret; up to 661 lb. (300 kg.) of bombs, mines or depth charges beneath the wings.

AICHI D3A (Japan)

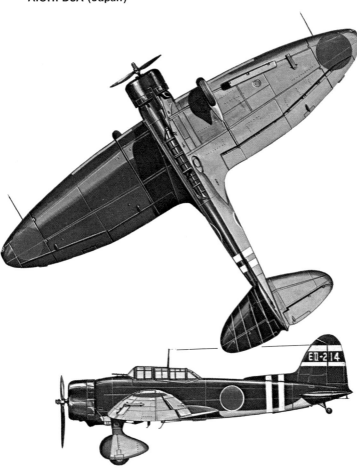

8

Aichi D3A1 Model 11 from the aircraft carrier *Zuikaku,* southern Pacific 1941–42. *Engine:* One 1,075 h.p. Mitsubishi Kinsei 44 radial. *Span:* 47 ft. 1½ in. (14.365 m.). *Length:* 33 ft. 5⅜ in. (10,195 m.). *Height:* 10 ft. 11⅞ in. (3.35 m.). *Normal take-off weight:* 8,047 lb. (3,650 kg.). *Maximum speed:* 242 m.p.h. (389 km./hr.) at 7,612 ft. (2,320 m.). *Operational ceiling:* 31,170 ft (9,500 m.). *Normal range:* 1,131 miles (1,820 km.). *Armament:* One 7.7 mm. machine-gun in each wing and one in rear cockpit; one 551 lb. (250 kg.) and two 130 lb. (60 kg.) bombs.

ARADO Ar 196 (Germany)

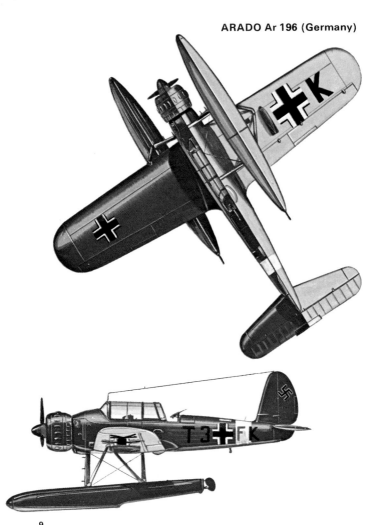

9

Arado Ar 196A-3 of 2/*Bordfl. Gruppe* 196, southern Italy, 1942. *Engine:* One 960 h.p. BMW 132K radial. *Span:* 40 ft. 8⅛ in. (12.40 m.). *Length:* 36 ft. 1⅛ in. (11.00 m.). *Height:* 14 ft. 4⅝ in. (4.40 m.). *Normal take-off weight:* 8,223 lb. (3,730 kg.). *Maximum speed:* 193 m.p.h. (310 km./hr.) at 13,120 ft. (4,000 m.). *Operational ceiling:* 23,000 ft. (7,020 m.). *Range:* 665 miles (1,070 km.). *Armament:* One 20 mm. MG FF cannon in each wing, two 7.9 mm. MG 17 machine-guns in rear cockpit and one in front fuselage; one 110 lb. (50 kg.) bomb beneath each wing.

NAKAJIMA B5N (Japan)

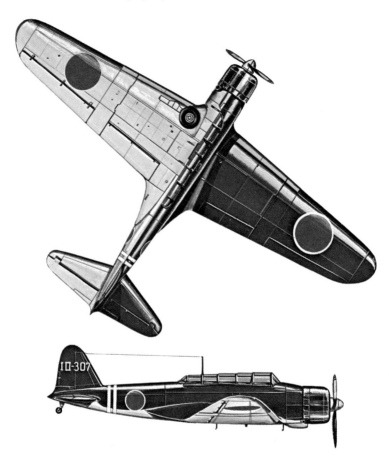

10

Nakajima B5N2 operating from the carrier *Zuikaku* during the Battle of the Coral Sea, May 1942. *Engine:* One 970 h.p. Nakajima Sakae 11 radial. *Span:* 50 ft. 11 in. (15.52 m.). *Length:* 33 ft. 9½ in. (10.30 m.). *Height:* 12 ft. 1⅜ in. (3.70 m.). *Maximum take-off weight:* 9,039 lb. (4,100 kg.). *Maximum speed:* 235 m.p.h. (378 km./hr.) at 11,810 ft. (3,600 m.). *Operational ceiling:* 27,100 ft. (8,260 m.). *Maximum range:* 1,075 miles (1,730 km.). *Armament:* Two 7.7 mm. machine-guns in upper engine cowling and one or two in rear cockpit; one 1,764 lb. (800 kg.) torpedo, or three 551 lb. (250 kg.) or 132 lb. (60 kg.) bombs, beneath the fuselage.

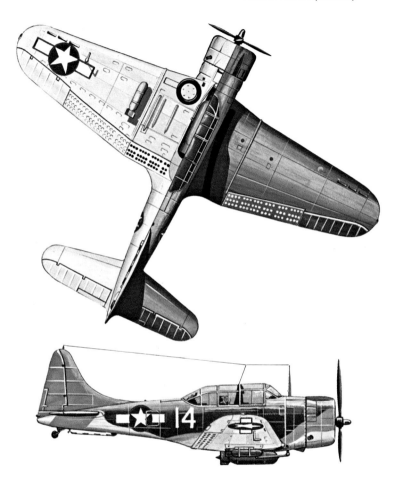

11

Douglas SBD-5 Dauntless of Squadron VB-5, USS *Yorktown*, August/
September 1943. *Engine:* One 1,200 h.p. Wright R-1820-60 Cyclone radial.
Span: 41 ft. 6 in. (12.65 m.). *Length:* 33 ft. 0 in. (10.06 m.). *Height:* 12 ft. 11 in.
(3.94 m.). *Maximum take-off weight:* 10,700 lb. (4,853 kg.). *Maximum speed:*
252 m.p.h. (406 km./hr.) at 13,800 ft. (4,200 m.). *Operational ceiling:* 24,300 ft.
(7,400 m.). *Range with 1,000 lb. (454 kg.) bomb load:* 1,115 miles (1,794 km.).
Armament: Two 0.50 in. machine-guns in front of fuselage, and two 0.30 in.
guns in rear cockpit; one 1,000 lb. (454 kg.) or 500 lb. (227 kg.) bomb beneath
fuselage, or two 100 lb. (45 kg.) bombs or two 250 lb. (113 kg.) depth charges
beneath the wings. 27

YOKOSUKA D4Y (Japan)

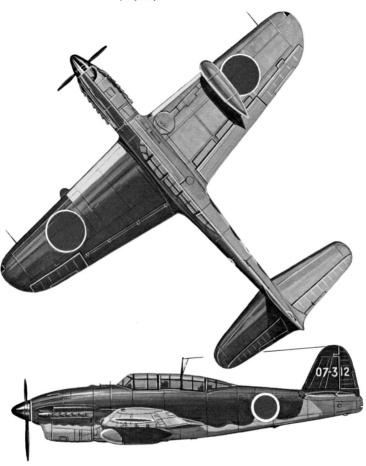

12

Yokosuka D4Y2 Model 12 *Suisei* of No. 107 Attack Squadron, No. 503 Air Corps, JNAF, 1944. *Engine:* One 1,400 h.p. Aichi Atsuta 32 inverted-Vee type. *Span:* 37 ft. 8½ in. (11.49 m.). *Length:* 33 ft. 6⅜ in. (10.22 m.). *Height:* 12 ft. 3¼ in. (3.74 m.). *Maximum take-off weight:* 9,597 lb. (4,353 kg.). *Maximum speed:* 366 m.p.h. (589 km./hr.) at 17,225 ft. (5,250 m.). *Operational ceiling:* 35,170 ft. (10,720 m.). *Normal range:* 749 miles (1,205 km.). *Armament:* Two 7.7 mm. machine-guns in upper engine cowling and one in rear cockpit; one 551 lb. (250 kg.) bomb internally and one 66 lb. (30 kg.) bomb beneath each wing.

13

Eastern-built TBM-3 Avenger of Air Group 38, US Navy, August 1945. *Engine:* One 1,900 h.p. Wright R-2600-20 Cyclone radial. *Span:* 54 ft. 2 in. (16.51 m.). *Length:* 40 ft. 0⅛ in. (12.19 m.). *Height:* 16 ft. 5 in. (5.00 m.). *Maximum take-off weight:* 18,250 lb. (8,278 kg.). *Maximum speed:* 267 m.p.h. (430 km./hr.) at 15,000 ft. (4,572 m.). *Operational ceiling:* 23,400 ft. (7,132 m.). *Maximum range:* 2,530 miles (4,072 km.). *Armament:* One 0.50 in. machine-gun in each wing and one in dorsal turret; one 0.30 in. machine-gun in upper engine cowling and one in ventral position; one 22-in. torpedo or one 2,000 lb. (907 kg.) bomb internally. Provision for rocket projectiles beneath each wing.

SUKHOI Su-2 (U.S.S.R.)

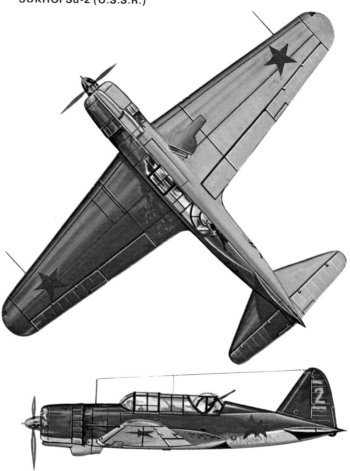

14

Sukhoi Su-2 of an unidentified operational training unit of the Soviet Air Force, 1943. *Engine:* One 1,000 h.p. M-88B radial. *Span:* 46 ft. 11 in. (14.30 m.). *Length:* 33 ft. 7½ in. (10.25 m.). *Height:* approx. 12 ft. 3¾ in. (3.75 m.). *Maximum take-off weight:* 9,645 lb. (4,375 kg.). *Maximum speed:* 283 m.p.h. (455 km./hr.) at 14,435 ft. (4,400 m.). *Operational ceiling:* 28,870 ft. (8,800 m.). *Range with 882 lb. (400 kg.) bomb load:* 746 miles (1,200 km.). *Armament:* Four 7.62 mm. ShKAS machine-guns in wings and one in dorsal turret; up to 1,323 lb. (600 kg.) of bombs.

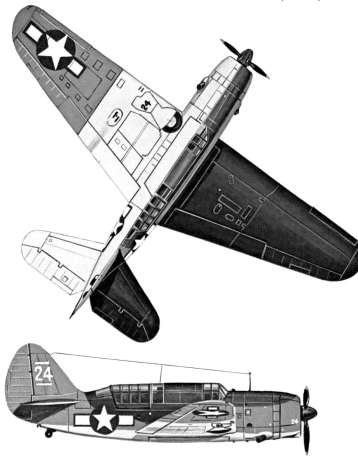

15

Curtiss SB2C-1C of Squadron VB-8, USS *Bunker Hill*, June 1944. *Engine:* One 1,700 h.p. Wright R-2600-8 Cyclone radial. *Span:* 49 ft. 8⅝ in. (15.15 m.). *Length:* 36 ft. 8 in. (11.18 m.). *Height:* 14 ft. 9 in. (4.50 m.). *Normal take-off weight:* 14,760 lb. (6,695 kg.). *Maximum speed:* 281 m.p.h. (452 km./hr.) at 12,400 ft. (3,780 m.). *Operational ceiling:* 24,700 ft. (7,529 m.). *Maximum range:* 1,895 miles (3,050 km.). *Armament:* One 20 mm. cannon in each wing and two 0.30 in. machine-guns in rear of cabin; one 1,000 lb. (454 kg.) bomb internally.

NAKAJIMA B6N (Japan)

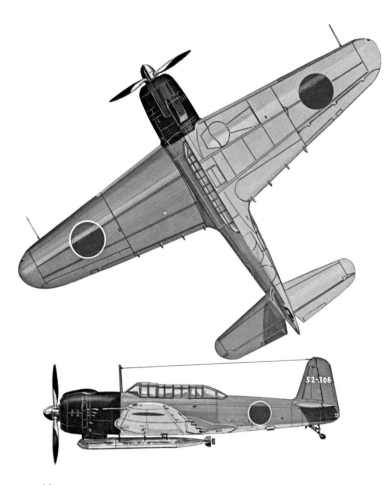

16

Nakajima B6N2 *Tenzan* of the 752nd Air Corps, JNAF, June 1944. *Engine:* One 1,850 h.p. Mitsubishi Kasei 25 radial. *Span:* 48 ft. 10⅝ in. (14.90 m.). *Length:* 35 ft. 7½ in. (10.86 m.). *Height:* 12 ft. 5⅝ in. (3.80 m.). *Maximum take-off weight:* 12,456 lb. (5,650 kg.). *Maximum speed:* 299 m.p.h. (482 km./hr.) at 16,080 ft. (4,900 m.). *Operational ceiling:* 29,660 ft. (9,040 m.). *Maximum range:* 1,644 miles (2,646 km.). *Armament:* One 7.7 mm. machine-gun in port wing, one in rear cockpit and one in ventral position; one 1,764 lb. (800 kg.) torpedo or six 220 lb. (100 kg.) bombs beneath the fuselage.

BARRACUDA (U.K.)

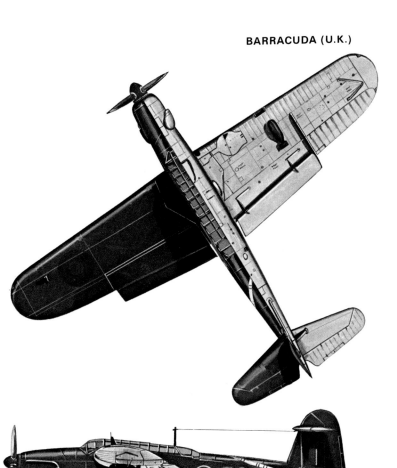

17

Fairey Barracuda II of No. 829 Squadron, HMS *Victorious* during attack on the *Tirpitz*, July 1944. *Engine:* One 1,600 h.p. Rolls-Royce Merlin 32 Vee type. *Span:* 49 ft. 2 in. (14.99 m.). *Length:* 39 ft. 9 in. (12.12 m.). *Height:* 15 ft. 1 in. (4.60 m.). *Maximum take-off weight:* 14,100 lb. (6,395 kg.). *Maximum speed:* 228 m.p.h. (367 km/hr.) at 1,750 ft. (533 m.). *Operational ceiling:* 16,600 ft. (5,060 m.). *Range with torpedo:* 686 miles (1,104 km.). *Armament:* Two 0.303 in. Vickers K guns in rear of cabin; one 1,620 lb. (735 kg.) torpedo or one 1,000 lb. (454 kg.) bomb beneath fuselage, or four 450 lb. (204 kg.) depth charges or six 250 lb. (113 kg.) bombs beneath the wings.

BATTLE (U.K.)

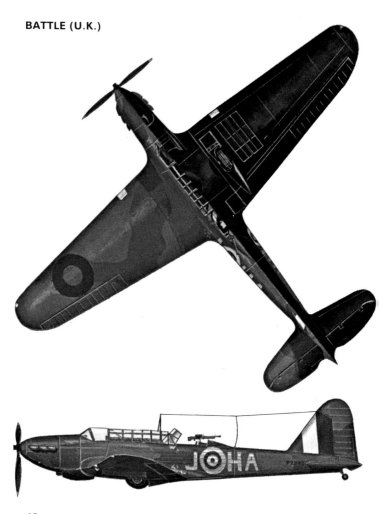

18

Fairey Battle II of No. 218 Squadron, after its re-formation in the UK ,in June 1940. *Engine:* One 1,030 h.p. Rolls-Royce Merlin II Vee type. *Span:* 54 ft. 0 in. (16.46 m.). *Length:* 42 ft. 1¾ in. (12.85 m.). *Height:* 15 ft. 6 in. (4.72 m.). *Normal take-off weight:* 10,792 lb. (4,895 kg.). *Maximum speed:* 257 m.p.h. (414 km./hr.) at 15,000 ft. (4,572 m.). *Operational ceiling:* 25,000 ft. (7,620 m.). *Maximum range:* 1,000 miles (1,609 km.). *Armament:* One 0.303 in. Browning machine-gun in starboard wing and one 0.303 in. Vickers K gun in rear of cabin; normal warload of four 250 lb. (113 kg.) bombs within the wings.

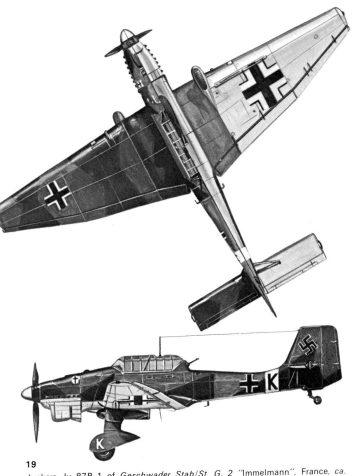

19

Junkers Ju 87B-1 of *Geschwader Stab/St. G. 2 "Immelmann"*, France, *ca.* summer 1940. *Engine:* One 900 h.p. Junkers Jumo 211A-1 inverted-Vee type. *Span:* 45 ft. 3¼ in. (13.80 m.). *Length:* 36 ft. 5 in. (11.10 m.). *Height:* 12 ft. 8½ in. (3.87 m.). *Normal take-off weight:* 9,370 lb. (4,250 kg.). *Maximum speed:* 242 m.p.h. (390 km./hr.) at 13,410 ft. (4,400 m.). *Operational ceiling:* 26,250 ft. (8,000 m.). *Range with 1,102 lb (500 kg.) bomb load:* 342 miles (550 km.). *Armament:* One 7.9 mm. MG 17 machine-gun in each wing and one 7.9 mm. MG 15 gun in rear of cabin; one 1,102 lb. (500 kg.) or 551 lb. (250 kg.) bomb beneath fuselage and up to four 110 lb. (50 kg.) bombs beneath the wings.

NAKAJIMA C6N (Japan)

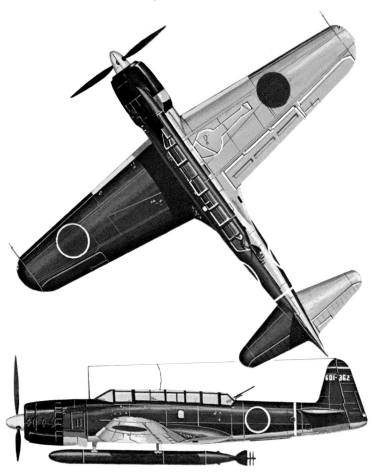

20

Nakajima C6N1-1B Model 21 *Saiun* from the carrier *Zuikaku*, 1944. *Engine:* One 1,990 h.p. Nakajima Homare 21 radial. *Span:* 41 ft. $0\frac{1}{8}$ in. (12.50 m.). *Length:* 36 ft. $5\frac{3}{4}$ in. (11.12 m.). *Height:* 12 ft. $11\frac{7}{8}$ in. (3.96 m.). *Maximum take-off weight:* 11,596 lb. (5,260 kg.). *Maximum speed:* 395 m.p.h. (635 km./hr.) at 19,685 ft. (6,000 m.). *Operational ceiling:* 37,070 ft. (11,300 m.). *Maximum range:* 2,855 miles (4,595 km.). *Armament:* One 7.92 mm. machine-gun in rear of cabin.

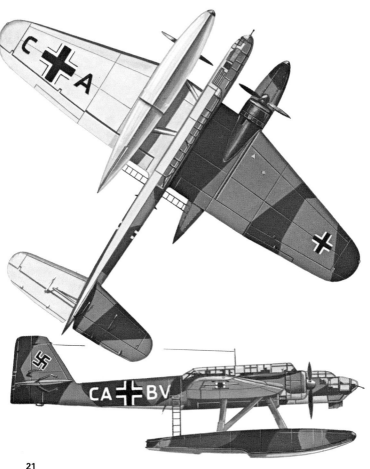

21

Heinkel He 115B-1, ex works with factory flight test codes, 1939-40. *Engines:*
Two 970 h.p. BMW 132K radials. *Span:* 73 ft. 1 in. (22.28 m.). *Length:* 56 ft.
9 in. (17.30 m.). *Height:* 21 ft. 7¾ in. (6.60 m.). *Maximum take-off weight:*
22,928 lb. (10,400 kg.). *Maximum speed:* 203 m.p.h. (327 km./hr.) at 11,155 ft.
(3,400 m.). *Operational ceiling:* 17,060 ft. (5,200 m.). *Maximum range:* 2,082
miles (3,350 km.). *Armament:* Single 7.9 mm. MG 15 machine-guns in nose
and dorsal positions; five 551 lb. (250 kg.) bombs, or two such bombs and one
1,764 lb. (800 kg.) torpedo or one 2,028 lb. (920 kg.) sea mine.

WELLINGTON (U.K.)

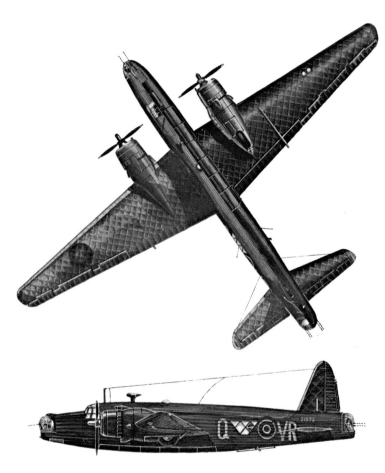

22

Vickers Wellington III of No. 419 Squadron RCAF, 1941-42. *Engines:* Two 1,500 h.p. Bristol Hercules XI radials. *Span:* 86 ft. 2 in. (26.26 m.). *Length:* 64 ft. 7 in. (19.68 m.). *Height:* 17 ft. 6 in. (5.33 m.). *Maximum take-off weight:* 29,500 lb. (13,381 kg.). *Maximum speed:* 255 m.p.h. (410 km./hr.) at 12,500 ft. (3,810 m.). *Operational ceiling:* 19,000 ft. (5,791 m.). *Range with 1,500 lb. (680 kg.) bomb load:* 2,200 miles (3,541 km.). *Armament:* Two 0.303 in. machine-guns in nose turret, four in tail turret and two in beam positions; up to 4,500 lb. (2,041 kg.) of bombs internally.

HEINKEL He 111 (Germany)

23

Heinkel He 111H-3 of III/KG.53 during the Battle of Britain, summer 1940.
Engines: Two 1,200 h.p. Junkers Jumo 211D-1 inverted-Vee type. *Span:* 74 ft.
1¾ in. (22.60 m.). *Length:* 53 ft. 9⅝ in. (16.40 m.). *Height:* 13 ft. 1½ in. (4.00 m.).
Normal take-off weight: 24,912 lb. (11,300 kg.). *Maximum speed:* 258 m.p.h.
(415 km./hr.) at 16,400 ft. (5,000 m.). *Operational ceiling:* 25,590 ft. (7,800 m.).
Range with maximum bomb load: 758 miles (1,220 km.). *Armament:* One 20
mm. MG FF cannon in ventral gondola, and five 7.9 mm. MG 15 machine-guns
in nose, dorsal, ventral and beam positions; up to 4,409 lb. (2,000 kg.) of bombs
internally.

39

ANSON (U.K.)

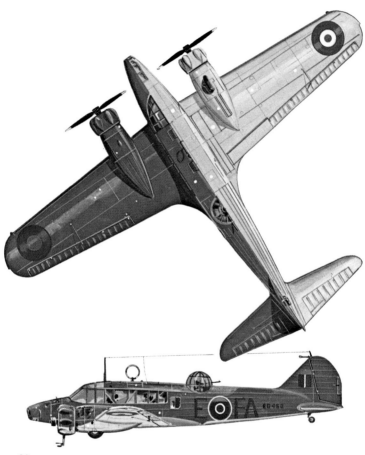

24

Avro Anson ASR I of No. 281 Squadron RAF, late 1943. *Engines:* Two 350 h.p. Armstrong Siddeley Cheetah IX radials. *Span:* 56 ft. 6 in. (17.22 m.). *Length:* 42 ft. 3 in. (12.88 m.). *Height:* 13 ft. 1 in. (3.99 m.). *Maximum take-off weight:* 8,000 lb. (3,629 kg.). *Maximum speed:* 188 m.p.h. (303 km./hr.) at 7,000 ft. (2,134 m.). *Operational ceiling:* 19,000 ft. (5,791 m.). *Range:* 790 miles (1,271 km.). *Armament:* One 0.303 in. machine-gun on port side of front fuselage and one in dorsal turret.

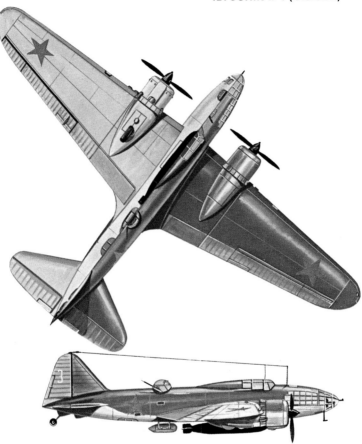

25

Ilyushin II-4 (DB-3F) of the VVS-VMF (Soviet Naval Aviation), Baltic Sea area, *ca.* 1941-42. *Engines:* Two 1,100 h.p. M-88B radials. *Span:* 70 ft. $4\frac{1}{8}$ in. (21.44 m.). *Length:* 48 ft. $6\frac{5}{8}$ in. (14.80 m.). *Height:* approximately 13 ft. 9 in. (4.20 m.). *Maximum take-off weight:* 22,046 lb. (10,000 kg.). *Maximum speed:* 255 m.p.h. (410 km./hr.) at 21,000 ft. (6,400 m.). *Operational ceiling:* 29,530 ft. (9,000 m.). *Maximum range with 2,205 lb.* (*1,000 kg.*) *bomb load:* 2,647 miles (4,260 km.). *Armament:* Three 7.62 mm. ShKAS or 12.7 mm. BS machine-guns, one each in nose, dorsal and ventral positions; 2,205 lb. (1,000 kg.) of bombs internally, plus one 2,072 lb. (940 kg.) 45-36-AN or -AV torpedo or up to 3,307 lb. (1,500 kg.) of bombs beneath the fuselage.

MARTIN 167 (U.S.A.)

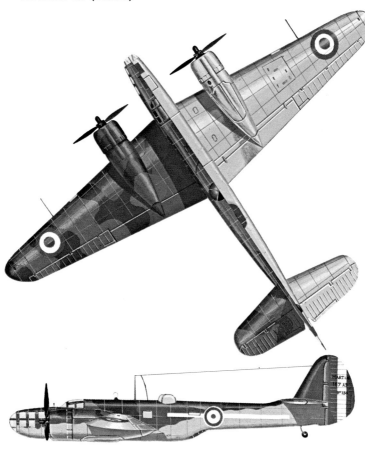

26

Martin 167A-3 (Model 167F) of the *Armée de l'Air* (unit unknown), France, *ca.* March/April 1940. *Engines:* Two 1,050 h.p. Pratt & Whitney R-1830-S1C3-G Twin Wasp radials. *Span:* 61 ft. 4 in. (18.69 m.). *Length:* 46 ft. 8 in. (14.22 m.). *Height:* 10 ft. 1 in. (3.07 m.). *Normal take-off weight:* 15,297 lb. (6,939 kg.). *Maximum speed:* 304 m.p.h. (489 km./hr.) at 14,000 ft. (4,267 m.). *Operational ceiling:* 29,500 ft. (8,992 m.). *Maximum range:* 1,300 miles (2,092 km.). *Armament:* Two 0.30 in. machine-guns in each wing and one each in dorsal and ventral positions; up to 1,250 lb. (567 kg.) of bombs internally.

BLENHEIM (U.K.)

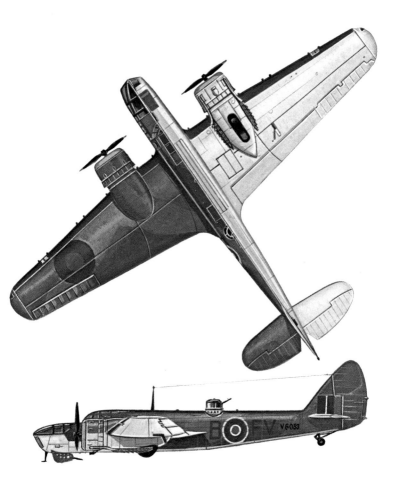

27

Rootes-built Blenheim IVL of No. 13 OTU, RAF, fitted with leading-edge balloon-cable cutters, *ca.* August 1942. *Engines:* Two 920 h.p. Bristol Mercury XV radials. *Span:* 56 ft. 4 in. (17.17 m.). *Length:* 42 ft. 9 in. (13.04 m.). *Height:* 12 ft. 10 in. (3.91 m.). *Maximum take-off weight:* 14,400 lb. (6,531 kg.). *Maximum speed:* 266 m.p.h. (428 km./hr.) at 11,800 ft. (3,597 m.). *Operational ceiling:* 27,000 ft. (8,230 m.). *Maximum range:* 1,950 miles (3,138 km.). *Armament:* One 0.303 in. Vickers K gun in nose, two 0.303 in. Browning machine-guns in dorsal turret and two in fairing beneath nose; up to 1,000 lb. (454 kg.) of bombs internally.

43

BEAUFIGHTER (U.K.)

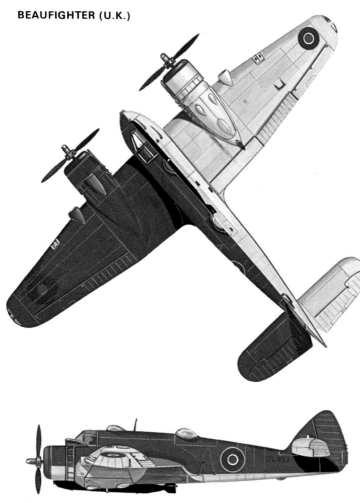

28

Bristol Beaufighter TF VIC of Coastal Command Development Unit, RAF *ca.* March/April 1943. *Engines:* Two 1,670 h.p. Bristol Hercules VI or XVI radials. *Span:* 57 ft. 10 in. (17.63 m.). *Length:* 41 ft. 4 in. (12.60 m.). *Height:* 15 ft. 10 in. (4.83 m.). *Maximum take-off weight:* 23,884 lb. (10,834 kg.). *Maximum speed:* 312 m.p.h. (502 km./hr.) at 14,000 ft. (4,267 m.). *Operational ceiling:* 26,000 ft. (7,925 m.). *Normal range:* 1,540 miles (2,478 km.). *Armament:* Four 20 mm. Hispano cannon in nose, three 0.303 in. Browning machine-guns in each wing, and one 0.303 in. Vickers K gun in dorsal position; one 1,605 lb. (728 kg.). torpedo beneath fuselage.

BEAUFORT (U.K.)

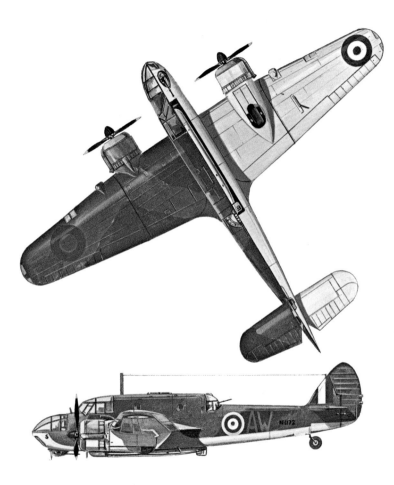

29

Bristol Beaufort I of No. 42 Squadron RAF, March 1941. *Engines:* Two 1,130 h.p. Bristol Taurus VI radials. *Span:* 57 ft. 10 in. (17.63 m.). *Length:* 44 ft. 2 in. (13.46 m.). *Height:* 14 ft. 3 in. (4.34 m.). *Maximum take-off weight:* 21,228 lb. (9,628 kg.). *Maximum speed (with torpedo):* 225 m.p.h. (362 km./hr.) at 5,000 ft. (1,524 m.). *Operational ceiling:* 16,500 ft. (5,029 m.). *Maximum range:* 1,600 miles (2,575 km.). *Armament:* Two 0.303 in. Vickers K guns in dorsal turret and one in port wing, plus one 0.303 in. rear-firing Browning machine-gun beneath nose; up to 1,000 lb. (454 kg.) of bombs internally and 500 lb. (227 kg.) externally, or one 1,605 lb. (728 kg.) torpedo semi-internally.

45

MOSQUITO (U.K.)

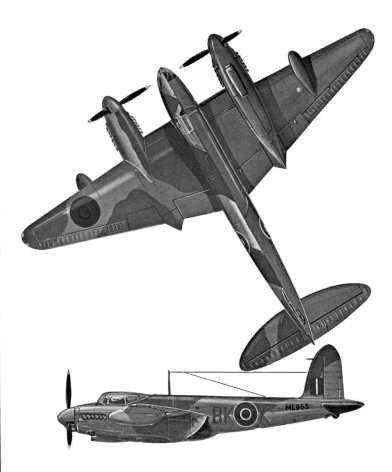

30

De Havilland Mosquito B XVI of No. 571 (Pathfinder) Squadron RAF, spring 1944. *Engines:* Two 1,680 h.p. Rolls-Royce Merlin 72 or 76 Vee type. *Span:* 54 ft. 2 in. (16.51 m.). *Length:* 40 ft. 6 in. (12.34 m.). *Height:* 15 ft. 3½ in. (4.66 m.). *Normal take-off weight:* 19,093 lb. (8,660 kg.). *Maximum speed:* 408 m.p.h. (656 km./hr.) at 26,000 ft. (7,925 m.). *Operational ceiling:* 37,000 ft. (11,278 m.). *Range with maximum bomb load:* 1,370 miles (2,205 km.). *Armament:* No guns; maximum bomb load of 4,000 lb. (1,814 kg.).

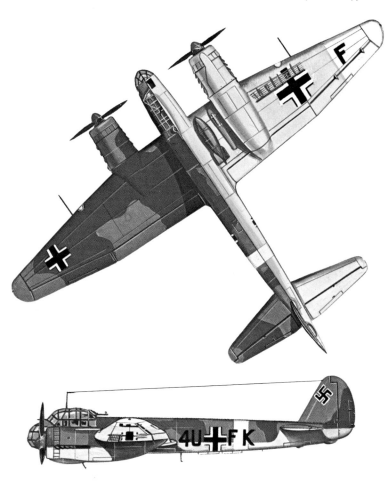

31

Junkers Ju 88A-4/Trop. of 2(F)/123, Western Desert, summer 1942. *Engines:* Two 1,340 h.p. Junkers Jumo 211J inverted-Vee type. *Span:* 65 ft. 7⅜ in. (20.00 m.). *Length:* 47 ft. 2⅞ in. (14.40 m.). *Height:* 15 ft. 11 in. (4.85 m.). *Maximum take-off weight:* 30,865 lb. (14,000 kg.). *Maximum speed:* 269 m.p.h. (433 km./hr.) at 14,765 ft. (4,500 m.). *Operational ceiling:* 26,900 ft. (8,200 m.). *Normal range:* 1,112 miles (1,790 km.). *Typical armament:* Nine 7.9 mm. MG 81 machine-guns, two in extreme nose, one in front of pilot, two in rear of cabin, and two forward and two aft in under-nose cupola; 1,102 lb. (500 kg.) of bombs internally and up to 2,205 lb. (1,000 kg.) externally.

47

BOSTON (U.S.A.)

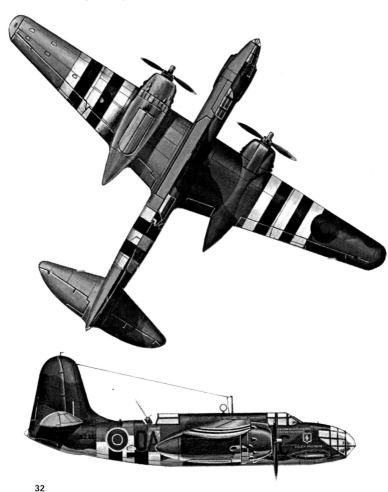

32

Douglas Boston IIIA of No. 342 (Lorraine) Squadron FAFL, summer 1944.
Engines: Two 1,600 h.p. Wright R-2600-23 Cyclone radials. *Span:* 61 ft. 4 in.
(18.69 m.). *Length:* 47 ft. 3 in. (14.40 m.). *Height:* 17 ft. 7 in. (5.36 m.).
Maximum take-off weight: 24,500 lb. (11,113 kg.). *Maximum speed:* 342 m.p.h.
(550 km./hr.) at 13,000 ft. (3,962 m.). *Operational ceiling:* 24,250 ft. (7,391 m.).
Range with maximum bomb load: 1,050 miles (1,690 km.). *Armament:* Two
0.303 in. Browning machine-guns on each side of nose, and two in dorsal
position, plus one 0.303 in. Vickers K gun in ventral position; up to 2,000 lb.
(907 kg.) of bombs internally.

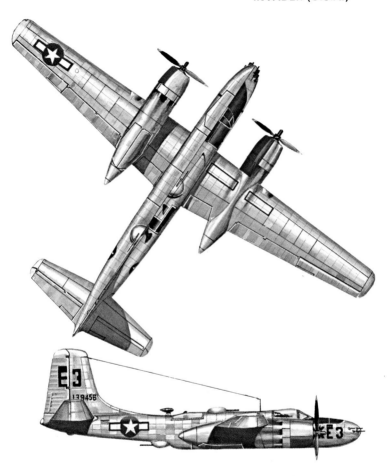

33

Douglas A-26B Invader of the US Ninth Air Force, ETO 1944-45. *Engines:* Two 2,000 h.p. Pratt & Whitney R-2800-27 or -71 Double Wasp radials. *Span:* 70 ft. 0 in. (21.34 m.). *Length:* 50 ft. 0 in. (15.24 m.). *Height:* 18 ft. 6 in. (5.64 m.). *Maximum take-off weight:* 35,000 lb. (15,876 kg.). *Maximum speed:* 355 m.p.h. (571 km./hr.) at 15,000 ft. (4,572 m.). *Operational ceiling:* 22,100 ft. (6,736 m.). *Range with maximum bomb load:* 1,400 miles (2,253 km.). *Armament:* Ten 0.50 in. machine-guns, six in nose and two each in dorsal and ventral turrets; up to 4,000 lb. (1,814 kg.) of bombs internally.

BALTIMORE (U.S.A.)

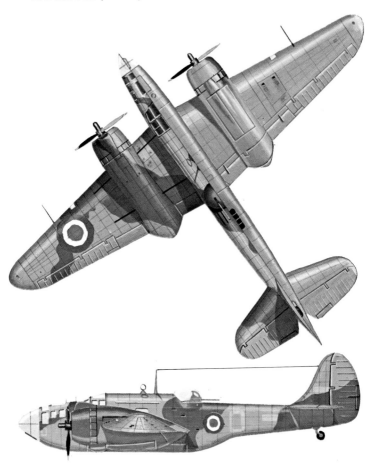

34

Martin Baltimore IV, ex-RAF machine seconded to the *Stormo Baltimore* of the Italian Co-Belligerent Air Force, *ca.* November 1944. *Engines:* Two 1,660 h.p. Wright R-2600-19 Double-Row Cyclone radials. *Span:* 61 ft. 4 in. (18.69 m.). *Length:* 48 ft. 6 in. (14.78 m.). *Height:* 17 ft. 9 in. (5.41 m.). *Maximum take-off weight:* 23,000 lb. (10,433 kg.). *Maximum speed:* 302 m.p.h. (486 km./hr.) at 11,000 ft. (3,353 m.). *Operational ceiling:* 24,000 ft. (7,315 m.). *Range with 1,000 lb. (454 kg.) bomb load:* 1,082 miles (1,741 km.). *Armament:* Two 0.50 in. machine-guns in dorsal turret, two 0.303 in. machine-guns in each wing and up to six 0.30 in. machine-guns in ventral positions; up to 2,000 lb. (907 kg.) of bombs internally.

MARAUDER (U.S.A.)

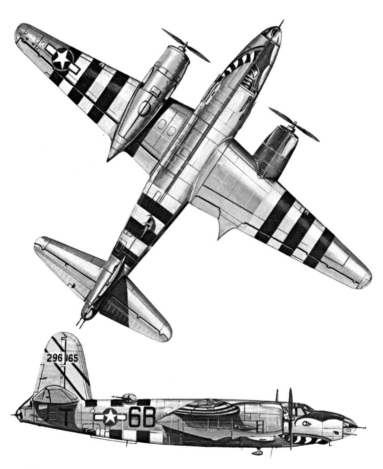

35

Martin B-26B-55 Marauder of the 598th Bomber Squadron, 397th Bomber Group, US Ninth Air Force, June 1944. Engines: Two 1,920 h.p. Pratt & Whitney R-2800-43 Double Wasp radials. *Span:* 71 ft. 0 in. (21.64 m.). *Length:* 58 ft. 3 in. (17.75 m.). *Height:* 21 ft. 6 in. (6.55 m.). *Maximum take-off weight:* 37,000 lb. (16,783 kg.). *Maximum speed:* 282 m.p.h. (454 km./hr.) at 15,000 ft. (4,572 m.). *Operational ceiling:* 21,700 ft. (6,614 m.). *Range with 3,000 lb. (1,361 kg.) bomb load:* 1,150 miles (1,851 km.). *Armament:* Eleven 0.50 in. machine-guns, in dorsal and tail turrets (two each), beam positions (one each), nose (one) and external nose blisters (two each side), plus one 0.30 in. gun in extreme nose; up to 5,200 lb. (2,359 kg.) of bombs.

51

PZL P.37 (Poland)

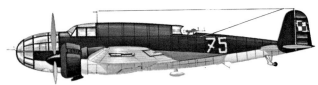

36

PZL P.37 Łoś B, possibly an aircraft of *Dyon* X/I, 1st Air Regiment, Warsaw 1939.
Engines: Two 918 h.p. PZL-built Bristol Pegasus XX radials. *Span:* 58 ft. 8¾ in.
(17.90 m.). *Length:* 42 ft. 3⅞ in. (12.90 m.). *Height:* 16 ft. 8 in. (5.08 m.).
Normal take-off weight: 18,739 lb. (8,500 kg.). *Maximum speed:* 273 m.p.h.
(440 km./hr.) at 12,140 ft. (3,700 m.). *Operational ceiling:* 19,685 ft. (6,000 m.).
Range with 3,880 lb. (1,760 kg.) bomb load: 1,616 miles (2,600 km.). *Armament:*
Single 7.7 mm. KM Wz.37 machine-guns in each of nose, dorsal and ventral
positions; normal warload of twenty 243 lb. (110 kg.) bombs in wing centre-
section; maximum permissible load of 5,688 lb. (2,580 kg.).

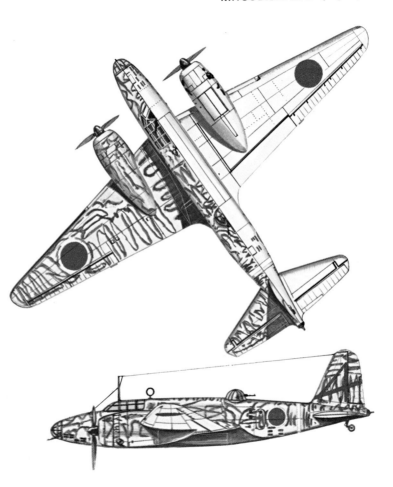

37
Mitsubishi Ki-21-IIb Model 2B of the 1st Squadron, 14th Group JAAF,
Philippines, 1944. *Engines:* Two 1,500 h.p. Mitsubishi Ha-101 radials. *Span:*
73 ft. 9$\frac{7}{8}$ in. (22.50 m.). *Length:* 52 ft. 6 in. (16.00 m.). *Height:* 15 ft. 11 in.
(4.85 m.). *Normal take-off weight:* 21,407 lb. (9,710 kg.). *Maximum speed:*
302 m.p.h. (486 km./hr.) at 15,485 ft. (4,720 m.). *Operational ceiling:* 32,810 ft.
(10,000 m.). *Normal range:* 1,678 miles (2,700 km.). *Armament:* One 12.7 mm.
Type 1 machine-gun in dorsal turret, five 7.7 mm. Type 89 machine-guns (one
each in nose, tail, ventral and two beam positions); up to 2,205 lb. (1,000 kg.) of
bombs internally.

MITSUBISHI G4M (Japan)

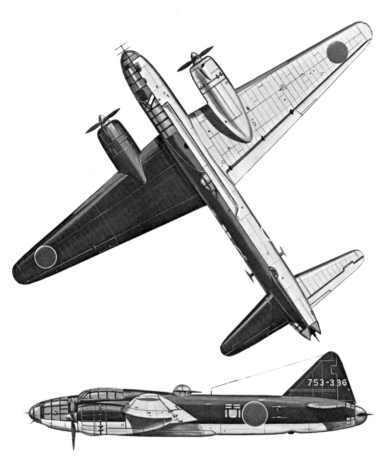

38

Mitsubishi G4M2a Model 24 of the 753rd Air Corps JNAF, Philippines, autumn 1944. *Engines:* Two 1,850 h.p. Mitsubishi Kasei 25 radials. *Span:* 81 ft. 7⅞ in. (24.89 m.). *Length:* 64 ft. 4⅞ in. (19.63 m.). *Height:* 13 ft. 5⅞ in. (4.11 m.). *Maximum take-off weight:* 33,069 lb. (15,000 kg.). *Maximum speed:* 272 m.p.h. (437 km./hr.) at 15,090 ft. (4,600 m.). *Operational ceiling:* 29,365 ft. (8,950 m.). *Normal range:* 1,497 miles (2,410 km.). *Armament:* Four 20 mm. Type 99 cannon (one each in dorsal, tail and two beam positions), and one 7.7 mm. Type 97 machine-gun in nose; up to 2,205 lb. (1,000 kg.) of bombs internally or one 1,764 lb. (800 kg.) torpedo.

MITSUBISHI Ki-67 (Japan)

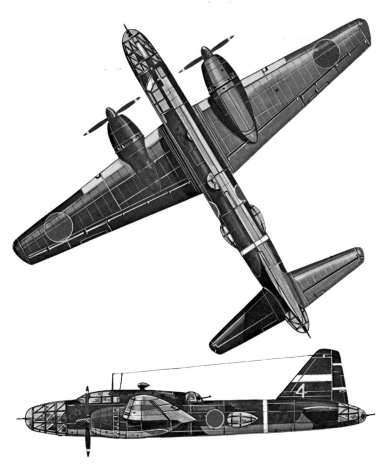

39

Mitsubishi Ki-67-lb Model 1B *Hiryu* of the JAAF (unit unidentified), 1945.
Engines: Two 1,900 h.p. Mitsubishi Ha-104 radials. *Span:* 73 ft. 9⅞ in. (22.50 m.).
Length: 61 ft. 4¼ in. (18.70 m.). *Height:* 18 ft. 4½ in. (5.60 m.). *Normal take-off
weight:* 30,346 lb. (13,765 kg.). *Maximum speed:* 334 m.p.h. (537 km./hr.) at
19,980 ft. (6,090 m.). *Operational ceiling:* 31,070 ft. (9,470 m.). *Normal range:*
1,740 miles (2,800 km.). *Armament:* One 20 mm. Ho-5 cannon in dorsal turret,
four 12.7 mm. Type 1 machine-guns (one each in nose, tail and two beam
positions); up to 1,764 lb. (800 kg.) of bombs internally.

NAKAJIMA Ki-49 (Japan)

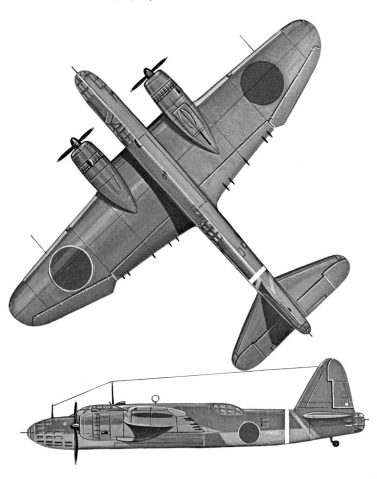

40

Nakajima Ki-49-IIa Model 2A *Donryu* of the 3rd Squadron, 95th Group JAAF, 1944-45. *Engines:* Two 1,450 h.p. Nakajima Ha-109-II radials. *Span:* 66 ft. 7¼ in. (20.30 m.). *Length:* 53 ft. 1¾ in. (16.20 m.). *Height:* 13 ft. 11⅜ in. (4.25 m.). *Normal take-off weight:* 23,545 lb. (10,680 kg.). *Maximum speed:* 304 m.p.h. (490 km./hr.) at 16,405 ft. (5,000 m.). *Operational ceiling:* 26,770 ft. (8,160 m.). *Normal range:* 1,491 miles (2,400 km.). *Armament:* One 20 mm. cannon in dorsal turret, and five 7.92 mm. machine-guns in nose, tail, ventral and beam positions; up to 2,205 lb. (1,000 kg.) of bombs internally.

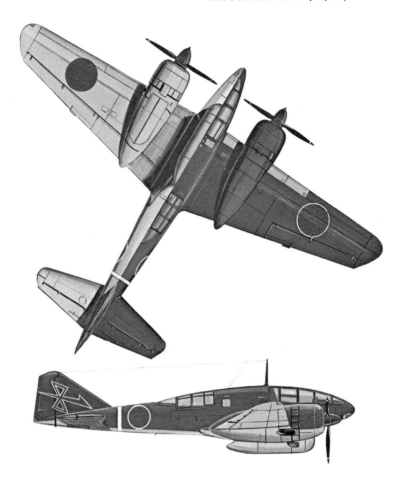

41

Mitsubishi Ki-46-III Model 3 of the 2nd Squadron, 81st Group JAAF, Burma 1944. *Engines:* Two 1,500 h.p. Mitsubishi Ha-112-II radials. *Span:* 48 ft. 2¾ in. (14.70 m.). *Length:* 36 ft. 1 in. (11.00 m.). *Height:* 12 ft. 8¾ in. (3.88 m.). *Maximum take-off weight:* 14,330 lb. (6,500 kg.). *Maximum speed:* 391 m.p.h. (630 km./hr.) at 19,685 ft. (6,000 m.). *Operational ceiling:* 34,450 ft. (10,500 m.). *Maximum range:* 2,485 miles (4,000 km.). *Armament:* None.

YOKOSUKA P1Y (Japan)

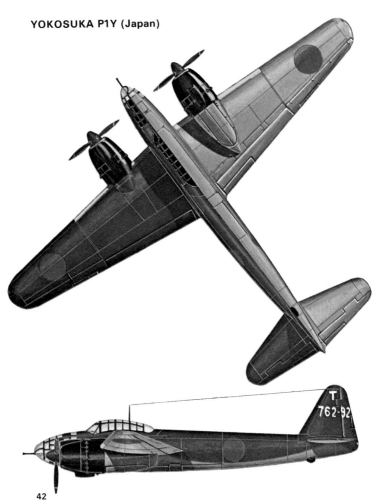

42

Yokosuka P1Y1 Model 11 *Ginga* of No. 262 Bomber Squadron, 762nd Air
Corps JNAF, 1944-45. *Engines:* Two 1,820 h.p. Nakajima Homare 11 radials.
Span: 65 ft. 7⅜ in. (20.00 m.). *Length:* 49 ft. 2½ in. (15.00 m.). *Height:* 14 ft. 1¼ in.
(4.30 m.). *Maximum take-off weight:* 29,762 lb. (13,500 kg.). *Maximum speed:*
345 m.p.h. (556 km./hr.) at 19,360 ft. (5,900 m.). *Operational ceiling:* 33,530 ft.
(10,220 m.). *Range:* 2,728 miles (4,390 km.). *Armament:* One 20 mm. cannon
in nose, one 12.7 mm. machine-gun in dorsal position; up to 1,102 lb. (500 kg.).
of bombs internally, and further small bombs, or one 1,874 lb. (850 kg.). or
1,764 lb. (800 kg.) torpedo, externally.

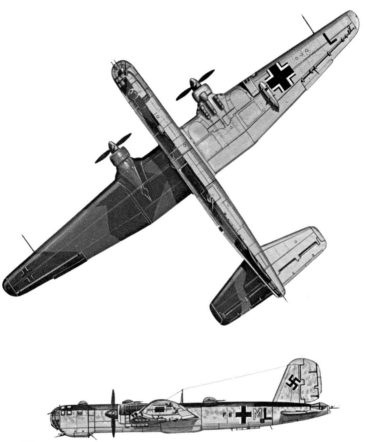

43

Heinkel He 177A-5/R7 *Greif* of *Stäffel* 6, II/KG.40, Bordeaux-Mérignac, *ca.*
November 1943. *Engines:* Two 2,950 h.p. Daimler-Benz DB 610 (coupled DB
605) radials. *Span:* 103 ft. 1¾ in. (31.44 m.). *Length:* 72 ft. 2⅛ in. (22.00 m.).
Height: 21 ft. 0 in. (6.40 m.). *Normal take-off weight:* 59,966 lb. (27,200 kg.).
Maximum speed: 303 m.p.h. (488 km./hr.) at 20,010 ft. (6,100 m.). *Operational
ceiling:* 49,870 ft. (15,200 m.). *Maximum range with two Hs 293 missiles:*
3,107 miles (5,000 km.). *Armament:* One 20 mm. MG 151 cannon in front of
under-nose cupola and one in tail; two 13 mm. MG 131 machine-guns in
forward dorsal barbette and one in rear dorsal turret; and one 7.9 mm. MG 81
gun in nose and two in rear of under-nose cupola; up to 2,205 lb. (1,000 kg.)
of bombs internally and two mines, torpedos or missiles externally.

CURTISS C-46 (U.S.A.)

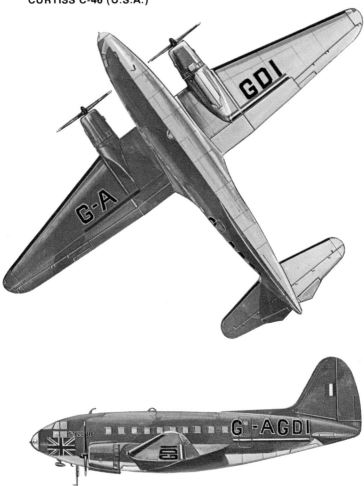

44

Curtiss CW-20 *St. Louis* (prototype for C-46 series), as delivered for operation by BOAC, December 1941. *Engines:* Two 1,700 h.p. Wright 586-C14-BA2 Double-Row Cyclone radials. *Span:* 108 ft. 1 in. (32.94 m.). *Length:* 76 ft. 4 in. (23.27 m.). *Height:* 21 ft. 9 in. (6.63 m.). *Maximum take-off weight:* 45,000 lb. (20,412 kg.). *Maximum speed:* 240 m.p.h. (386 km./hr.) at sea level. *Operational ceiling:* 26,900 ft. (8,199 m.). *Normal range with 4,621 lb. (2,096 kg.) payload:* 2,000 miles (3,219 km.). *Armament:* None.

45
Douglas C-53C Skytrooper of the USAAF, El Kabrit, spring 1943. *Engines:* Two
1,200 h.p. Pratt & Whitney R-1830-92 Twin Wasp radials. *Span:* 95 ft. 0 in.
(28.96 m.). *Length:* 64 ft. 5½ in. (19.65 m.). *Height:* 16 ft. 11 in. (5.16 m.).
Maximum take-off weight: 29,300 lb. (13,290 kg.). *Maximum speed:* 210 m.p.h.
(338 km./hr.) at 8,800 ft. (2,682 m.). *Operational ceiling:* 24,100 ft. (7,346 m.).
Normal range: 1,350 miles (2,173 km.). *Armament:* None.

CATALINA (U.S.A.)

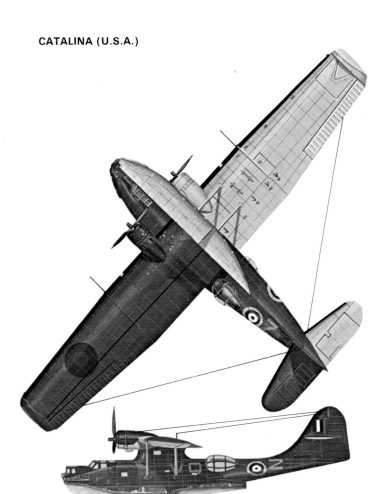

46

Consolidated Catalina I (PBY-5) of No. 209 Squadron RAF which spotted the *Bismarck* on 26 May 1941. *Engines:* Two 1,200 h.p. Pratt & Whitney R-1830-S1C3-G Twin Wasp radials. *Span:* 104 ft. 0 in. (31.70 m.). *Length:* 63 ft. 10½ in. (19.47 m.). *Height:* 18 ft. 10⅜ in. (5.76 m.). *Normal take-off weight:* 27,080 lb. (12,283 kg.). *Maximum speed:* 190 m.p.h. (306 km./hr.) at 10,500 ft. (3,200 m.). *Operational ceiling:* 24,000 ft. (7,315 m.). *Maximum range:* 4,000 miles (6,437 km.). *Armament:* Six 0.303 in. Vickers guns, one in bow, two in each side blister and one in ventral tunnel aft of hull step; up to 2,000 lb. (907 kg.) of bombs.

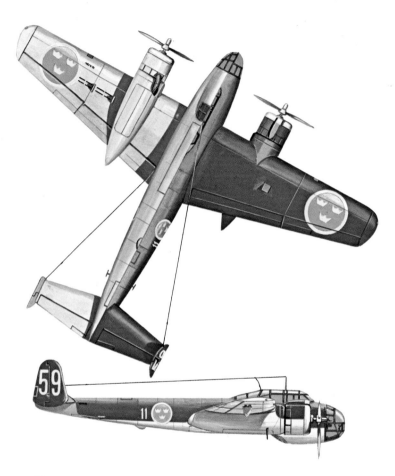

47

Saab-18A (B 18A) of F 11 Wing (3rd Division), *Kungl. Svenska Flygvapnet,*
1944-45. *Engines:* Two 1,065 h.p. SFA-built Pratt & Whitney R-1830-S1C3-G
Twin Wasp radials. *Span:* 55 ft. 9¼ in. (17.00 m.). *Length:* 43 ft. 4⅞ in. (13.23 m.).
Height: 14 ft. 3¼ in. (4.35 m.). *Normal take-off weight:* 17,946 lb. (8,140 kg.).
Maximum speed: 289 m.p.h. (465 km./hr.) at 19,685 ft. (6,000 m.). *Operational
ceiling:* 26,250 ft. (8,000 m.). *Maximum range:* 1,367 miles (2,200 km.).
Armament: One 13.2 mm. machine-gun in rear of crew cabin and one in rear of
under-nose fairing, and one 7.9 mm. gun in starboard side of nose; up to 3,307 lb.
(1,500 kg.) of bombs.

DORNIER Do 217 (Germany)

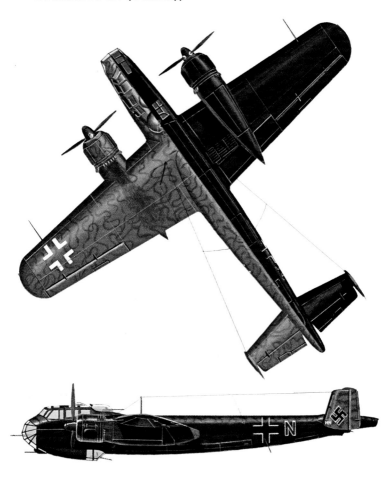

48

Dornier Do 217E-2 of 5/KG.6, France, early 1943. *Engines:* Two 1,580 h.p. BMW 801 M radials. *Span:* 62 ft. 4 in. (19.00 m.). *Length:* 56 ft 9⅛ in. (17.30 m.). *Height:* 16 ft. 4⅞ in. (5.00 m.). *Normal take-off weight:* 33,069 lb. (15,000 kg.). *Maximum speed:* 320 *m.p.h.* (515 km./hr.) at 17,060 ft. (5,200 m.). *Operational ceiling:* 24,610 ft. (7,500 m.). *Maximum range:* 1,429 miles (2,300 km.). *Armament:* One 15 mm. MG 151 cannon in nose, one 13 mm. MG 131 machine-gun in dorsal turret and one in rear of under-nose cupola, one 7.9 mm. MG 15 gun in nose and one each side in rear of cabin; up to 5,512 lb. (2,500 kg.) of bombs internally and 3,307 lb. (1,500 kg.) externally.

64

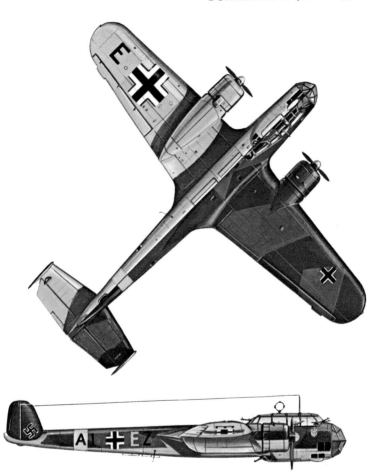

49

Dornier Do 17Z-2 of 15/KG.53 (*Kroaten*), Eastern Front, September 1942.
Engines: Two 1,000 h.p. Bramo Fafnir 323P radials. *Span:* 59 ft. 0⅝ in. (18.00 m.).
Length: 51 ft. 9⅝ in. (15.79 m.). *Height:* 14 ft. 11½ in. (4.56 m.). *Normal take-off
weight:* 18,872 lb. (8,560 kg.). *Maximum speed:* 224 m.p.h. (360 km./hr.) at
13,120 ft. (4,000 m.). *Operational ceiling:* 22,965 ft. (7,000 m.). *Maximum
range with 1,102 lb. (500 kg.) bomb load and auxiliary fuel:* 721 miles (1,160
km.). *Armament:* Six 7.9 mm. MG 15 machine-guns: one in nose, one in front
of cabin, one each side in rear of cabin, one aft of cabin and one in ventral
position; up to 2,205 lb. (1,000 kg.) of bombs internally.

WHITLEY (U.K.)

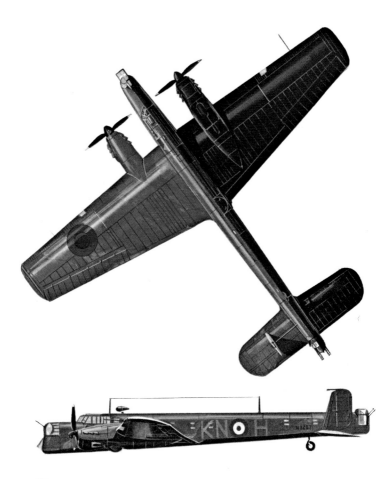

50

Armstrong Whitworth Whitley V of No. 77 Squadron RAF, April 1940. *Engines:* Two 1,075 h.p. Rolls-Royce Merlin X Vee type. *Span:* 84 ft. 0 in. (25.60 m.). *Length:* 70 ft. 6 in. (21.49 m.). *Height:* 15 ft. 0 in. (4.57 m.). *Normal take-off weight:* 33,500 lb. (15,196 kg.). *Maximum speed:* 230 m.p.h. (370 km./hr.) at 16,400 ft. (5,000 m.). *Operational ceiling:* 26,000 ft. (7,925 m.). *Maximum range:* 2,400 miles (3,862 km.). *Armament:* One 0.303 in. Vickers gun in nose turret and four 0.303 in. Browning machine-guns in tail turret; up to 7,000 lb. (3,175 kg.) of bombs internally.

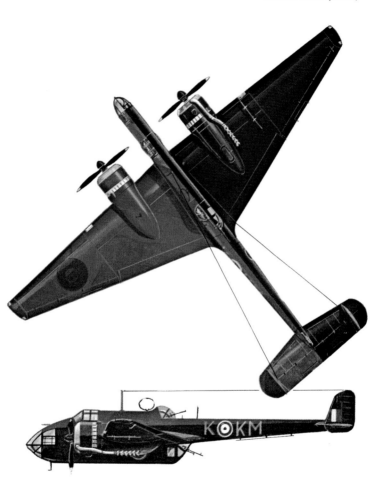

HAMPDEN (U.K.)

51

Handley Page Hampden I of No. 44 (Rhodesia) Squadron RAF, summer 1941. *Engines:* Two 980 h.p. Bristol Pegasus XVIII radials. *Span:* 69 ft. 2 in. (21.08 m.). *Length:* 53 ft. 7 in. (16.33 m.). *Height:* 14 ft. 4 in. (4.37 m.). *Normal take-off weight:* 18,756 lb. (8,508 kg.). *Maximum speed:* 265 m.p.h. (426 km./hr.) at 15,500 ft. (4,724 m.). *Operational ceiling:* 22,700 ft. (6,919 m.). *Range with maximum bomb load:* 1,095 miles (1,762 km.). *Armament:* Six 0.303 in. Vickers K guns (two in nose and two each in dorsal and ventral positions); up to 4,000 lb. (1,814 kg.) of bombs internally.

FIAT B.R.20 (Italy)

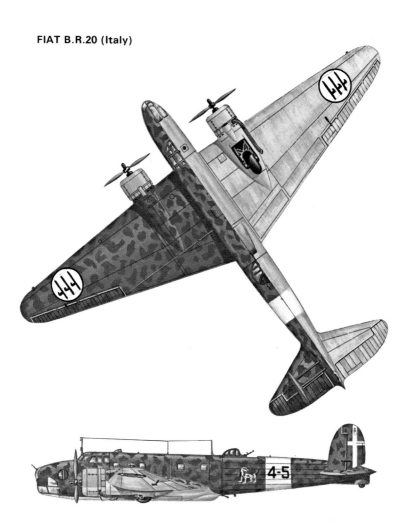

52

Fiat B.R.20M *Cicogna* of the 4° *Squadriglia*, 11° *Gruppo*, 13° *Stormo B.T.*, northern Italy, autumn 1940. *Engines:* Two 1,000 h.p. Fiat A.80 RC 41 radials. *Span:* 70 ft. 8⅞ in. (21.56 m.). *Length:* 55 ft. 0¾ in. (16.78 m.). *Height:* 15 ft. 7 in. (4.75 m.). *Normal take-off weight:* 23,038 lb. (10,450 kg.). *Maximum speed:* 267 m.p.h. (430 km./hr.) at 13,120 ft. (4,000 m.). *Operational ceiling:* 22,145 ft. (6,750 m.). *Range:* 1,243 miles (2,000 km.). *Armament:* One 12.7 mm. Breda-SAFAT machine-gun in dorsal turret and three 7.7 mm. Breda-SAFAT guns (one each in nose, tail and ventral positions); up to 3,527 lb. (1,600 kg.) of bombs internally.

68

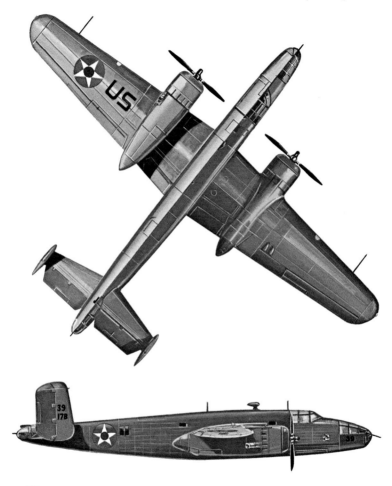

53

North American B-25A of the 34th Bomber Squadron, 17th Bombardment Group USAAC, summer 1941. *Engines:* Two 1,700 h.p. Wright R-2600-9 Cyclone radials. *Span:* 67 ft. 7 in. (20.60 m.). *Length:* 54 ft. 1 in. (16.48 m.). *Height:* 15 ft. 9 in. (4.80 m.). *Maximum take-off weight:* 27,100 lb. (12,292 kg.). *Maximum speed:* 315 m.p.h. (507 km./hr.) at 15,000 ft. (4,572 m.). *Operational ceiling:* 27,000 ft. (8,230 m.). *Range with maximum bomb load:* 1,350 miles (2,173 km.). *Armament:* One 0.50 in. machine-gun in tail, and three 0.30 in. guns (one in nose and one in each beam position); up to 3,000 lb. (1,361 kg.) of bombs internally.

69

HUDSON (U.S.A.)

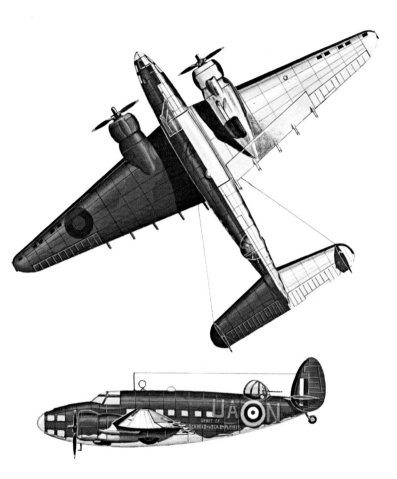

54

Lockheed Hudson III of No. 269 Squadron RAF, winter 1941-42. *Engines:* Two 1,200 h.p. Wright GR-1820-G205A Cyclone radials. *Span:* 65 ft. 6 in. (19.96 m.). *Length:* 44 ft. 4 in. (13.51 m.). *Height:* 11 ft. 10½ in. (3.62 m.). *Maximum take-off weight:* 20,000 lb. (9,072 kg.). *Maximum speed:* 255 m.p.h. (410 km./hr.) at 5,000 ft. (1,524 m.). *Operational ceiling:* 24,500 ft. (7,468 m.). *Maximum range:* 2,160 miles (3,476 km.). *Armament:* Seven 0.303 in. machine-guns (two each in nose and dorsal turret, one in each beam position, and one in ventral position); up to 750 lb. (340 kg.) of bombs.

VENTURA (U.S.A.)

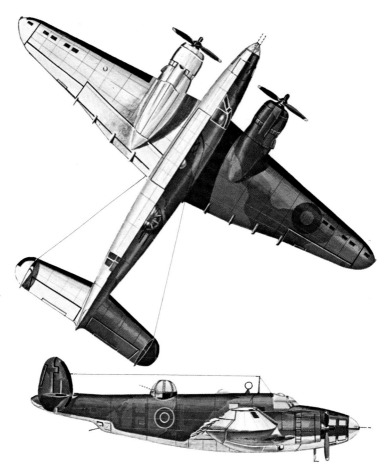

55

Lockheed Ventura I of No. 21 Squadron RAF, summer/autumn 1942. *Engines:*
Two 2,000 h.p. Pratt & Whitney GR-2800-S1A4-G Double Wasp radials.
Span: 65 ft. 6 in. (19.96 m.). *Length:* 51 ft. 5 in. (15.67 m.). *Height:* 11 ft. 10½ in.
(3.62 m.). *Maximum take-off weight:* 26,000 lb. (11,793 kg.). *Maximum
speed:* 312 m.p.h. (502 km./hr.) at 6,800 ft. (2,073 m.). *Operational ceiling:*
25,200 ft. (7,681 m.). *Range with maximum bomb load:* 1,000 miles (1,609 km.).
Armament: Two 0.50 in. machine-guns in nose, six 0.303 in. machine-guns
(two each in nose, dorsal turret and ventral position); up to 2,500 lb. (1,134 kg.)
of bombs internally.

LODESTAR (U.S.A.)

56

Lockheed C-60A Lodestar of the USAAF, 1943-44. *Engines:* Two 1,200 h.p. Wright R-1820-87 Cyclone radials. *Span:* 65 ft. 6 in. (19.96 m.). *Length:* 49 ft. 9⅞ in. (15.19 m.). *Height:* 11 ft. 10½ in. (3.62 m.). *Normal take-off weight:* 18,500 lb. (8,392 kg.). *Maximum speed:* 266 m.p.h. (428 km./hr.) at 17,000 ft. (5,182 m.). *Operational ceiling:* 27,000 ft. (8,230 m.). *Maximum range with full load:* 1,660 miles (2,672 km.). *Armament:* None.

57

Armstrong Whitworth Albemarle ST I of No. 297 Squadron RAF, June 1944. *Engines:* Two 1,590 h.p. Bristol Hercules XI radials. *Span:* 77 ft. 0 in. (23.47 m.). *Length:* 59 ft. 11 in. (18.26 m.). *Height:* 15 ft. 7 in. (4.75 m.). *Maximum take-off weight:* 36,500 lb. (16,556 kg.). *Maximum speed:* 265 m.p.h. (426 km./hr.) at 10,500 ft. (3,200 m.). *Operational ceiling:* 18,000 ft. (5,486 m.). *Normal range:* 1,300 miles (2,092 km.). *Armament:* Four 0.303 in. machine-guns in dorsal turret.

EXPEDITER (U.S.A.)

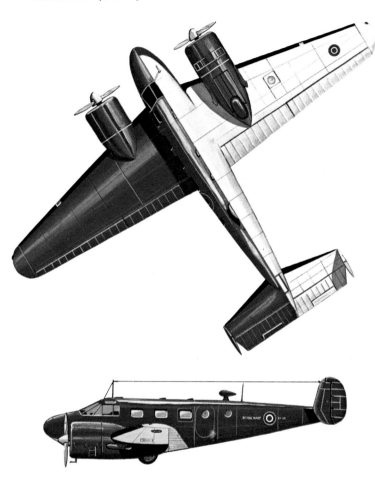

58

Beech Expediter II (UC-45F) of the Royal Navy, personal transport of Vice-Admiral Sir Dennis Boyd, 1945. *Engines:* Two 450 h.p. Pratt & Whitney R-985-AN-1 Wasp Junior radials. *Span:* 47 ft. 7¾ in. (14.52 m.). *Length:* 34 ft. 2¾ in (10.43 m.). *Height:* 9 ft. 4 in. (2.84 m.). *Normal take-off weight:* 7,500 lb. (3,402 kg.). *Maximum speed:* 223 m.p.h. (359 km./hr.) at sea level. *Operational ceiling:* 27,000 ft. (8,230 m.). *Maximum range:* 1,200 miles (1,931 km.). *Armament:* None.

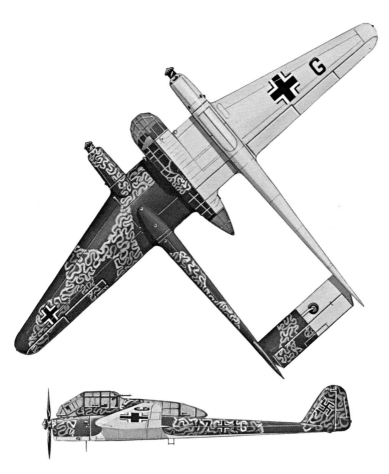

59

Focke-Wulf Fw 189A-2 of 1(H)/32 serving with *Luftflotte* 5, Eastern Front
(White Sea area) October 1942. *Engines:* Two 465 h.p. Argus As 410A-1
inverted-Vee type. *Span:* 60 ft. 4¾ in. (18.40 m.). *Length:* 39 ft. 4½ in. (12.00 m.).
Height: 10 ft. 2 in. (3.10 m.). *Normal take-off weight:* 8,708 lb. (3,950 kg.).
Maximum speed: 217 m.p.h. (350 km./hr.) at 7,870 ft. (2,400 m.). *Operational
ceiling:* 23,950 ft. (7,300 m.). *Normal range:* 416 miles (670 km.). *Armament:*
Four 7.9 mm. MG 81 machine-guns (two in dorsal position and two in rear of
nacelle), and one 7.9 mm. MG 17 gun in each wing root; four 110 lb. (50 kg.)
bombs beneath the wings.

BLOHM und VOSS Bv 138 (Germany)

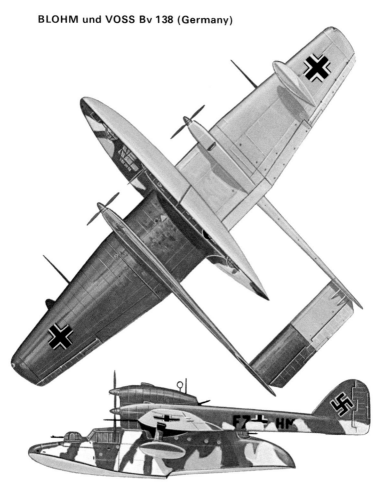

60

Blohm und Voss Bv 138C-1 of an unidentified *Aufklärungsgruppe* (Reconnaissance Group), possibly in the Baltic Sea area, *ca.* 1942-43. *Engines:* Three 880 h.p. Junkers Jumo 205D vertically-opposed diesel type. *Span:* 88 ft. 7 in. (27.00 m.). *Length:* 65 ft. 1½ in. (19.85 m.). *Height:* 19 ft. 4¼ in. (5.90 m.). *Normal take-off weight:* 31,967 lb. (14,500 kg.). *Maximum speed:* 171 m.p.h. (275 km./hr.) at 6,560 ft. (2,000 m.). *Operational ceiling:* 16,400 ft. (5,000 m.). *Maximum range:* 2,760 miles (4,355 km.). *Armament:* Two 20 mm. MG 151 cannon (one each in bow and rear turrets), one 13 mm. MG 131 machine-gun aft of central engine, and provision for one 7.9 mm. MG 15 gun in starboard side of hull; three or six 110 lb. (50 kg.) bombs or four 331 lb. (150 kg.) depth charges beneath starboard centre-section.

CANT. Z.506B (Italy)

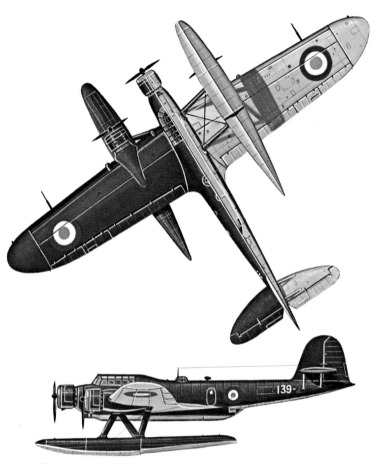

61

C.R.D.A. Cant. Z.506B *Airone* Serie XII, formerly of the 139° *Squadriglia da Ricognizione Marittima,* in the insignia of the Italian Co-Belligerent Air Force, 1943–44. *Engines:* Three 750 h.p. Alfa Romeo 126 RC 34 radials. *Span:* 86 ft. 11¼ in. (26.50 m.). *Length:* 63 ft. 1⅞ in. (19.25 m.). *Height:* 24 ft. 5⅜ in. (7.45 m.). *Maximum take-off weight:* 28,008 lb. (12,705 kg.). *Maximum speed:* 217 m.p.h. (350 km./hr.) at 13,120 ft. (4,000 m.). *Operational ceiling:* 24,000 ft. (7,320 m.). *Range with 2,094 lb. (950 kg.) bomb load:* 1,243 miles (2,000 km.). *Armament:* One 12.7 mm. Scotti machine-gun in dorsal turret, one 7.7 mm. Breda-SAFAT machine-gun in ventral position and one in each beam position; up to 2,645 lb. (1,200 kg.) of bombs.

JUNKERS Ju 52/3m (Germany)

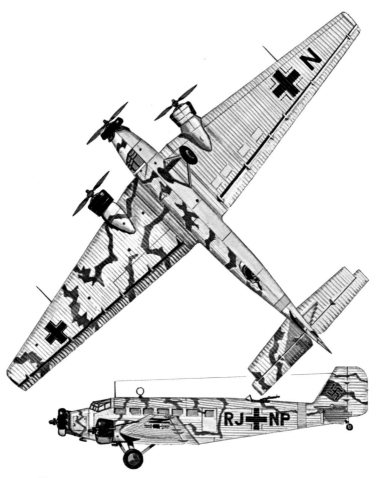

62

Junkers Ju 52/3m of *Kampffliegerschüle* Thorn, winter 1942–43. *Engines:* Three 830 h.p. BMW 132T radials. *Span:* 95 ft. 11½ in. (29.25 m.). *Length:* 62 ft. 0 in. (18.90 m.). *Height:* 14 ft. 9⅛ in. (4.50 m.). *Maximum take-off weight:* 24,317 lb. (11,030 kg.). *Maximum speed:* 190 m.p.h. (305 km./hr.) at 8,200 ft. (2,500 m.). *Operational ceiling:* 18,045 ft. (5,500 m.). *Range with 2,205 lb. (1,000 kg.) payload:* 808 miles (1,300 km.). *Armament:* One 13 mm. MG 131 machine-gun in dorsal position and two 7.9 mm. MG 15 guns firing through passengers' windows.

CANT. Z.1007 (Italy)

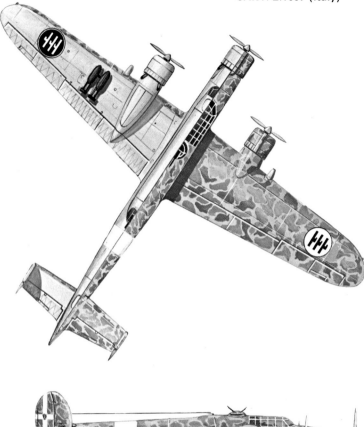

63

C.R.D.A. Cant. Z.1007*bis Alcione* of the 211° *Squadriglia B.T.,* Mediterranean area 1941–42. *Engines:* Three 1,000 h.p. Piaggio P.XI*bis* RC 40 radials. *Span:* 81 ft. 4⅜ in. (24.80 m.). *Length:* 60 ft. 2⅜ in. (18.35 m.). *Height:* 17 ft. 1½ in. (5.22 m.). *Maximum take-off weight:* 30,029 lb. (13,621 kg.). *Maximum speed:* 283 m.p.h. (455 km./hr.) at 17,220 ft. (5,250 m.). *Operational ceiling:* 24,610 ft. (7,500 m.). *Range with maximum bomb load:* 1,367 miles (2,200 km.). *Armament:* One 12.7 mm. Breda-SAFAT machine-gun in dorsal turret, one in ventral position and one 7.7 mm. gun in each beam position; up to 4,409 lb. (2,000 kg.) of bombs internally.

SAVOIA-MARCHETTI S.M.79 (Italy)

64

Savoia-Marchetti S.M.79-II *Sparviero* of the 59° *Squadriglia*, 33° *Gruppo*, 11° *Stormo B.T.*, Cyrenaica November 1940. *Engines:* Three 1,000 h.p. Piaggio P.XI RC 40 radials. *Span:* 69 ft. 6⅝ in. (21.20 m.). *Length:* 53 ft. 1¾ in. (16.20 m.). *Height:* 15 ft. 11 in. (4.60 m.). *Normal take-off weight:* 25,133 lb. (11,400 kg.). *Maximum speed:* 295 m.p.h. (475 km./hr.) at 13,120 ft. (4,000 m.). *Operational ceiling:* 27,890 ft. (8,500 m.). *Range with maximum bomb load:* 1,243 miles 2,000 km.). *Armament:* Three 12.7 mm. Breda-SAFAT machine-guns (one above pilot's cabin, one in dorsal position, one in ventral gondola), and one 7.7 mm. Lewis gun amidships to fire to port or starboard; up to 2,756 lb. (1,250 kg.) of bombs internally.

80

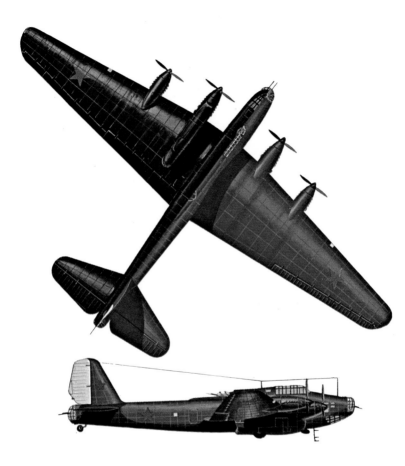

65

Petlyakov Pe-8 of the Soviet Air Force, used for communications between
Moscow and the UK, 1942. *Engines:* Four 1,350 h.p. Mikulin AM-35A Vee
type. *Span:* 131 ft. 0⅜ in. (39.94 m.). *Length:* 73 ft. 8⅝ in. (22.47 m.). *Height:*
20 ft. 0⅛ in. (6.10 m.). *Maximum take-off weight:* 73,469 lb. (33,325 kg.).
Maximum speed: 272 m.p.h. (438 km./hr.) at 24,935 ft. (7,600 m.). *Operational
ceiling:* 31,988 ft. (9,750 m.). *Maximum range with 4,409 lb. (2,000 kg.) bomb
load:* 3,383 miles (5,445 km.). *Armament:* One 20 mm. ShVAK cannon in each
of the dorsal and tail turrets, one 12.7 mm. Beresin machine-gun in the rear of
each inboard engine nacelle, and two 7.62 mm. ShKAS guns in nose turret; up
to 8,818 lb. (4,000 kg.) of bombs internally.

81

STIRLING (U.K.)

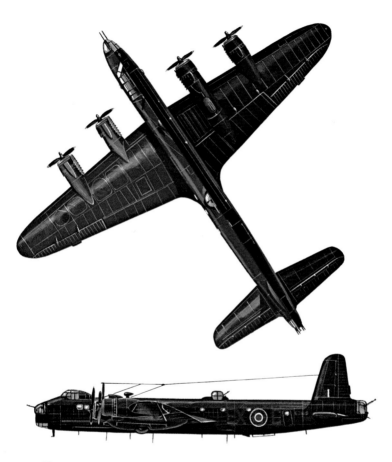

66

Short Stirling B III of No. 199 Bomber Support Squadron RAF, autumn 1944. *Engines:* Four 1,650 h.p. Bristol Hercules XVI radials. *Span:* 99 ft. 1 in. (30.20 m.). *Length:* 87 ft. 3 in. (26.59 m.). *Height:* 22 ft. 9 in. (6.93 m.). *Maximum take-off weight:* 70,000 lb. (31,751 kg.). *Maximum speed:* 270 m.p.h. (435 km./hr.) at 14,500 ft. (4,420 m.). *Operational ceiling:* 17,000 ft. (5,182 m.). *Range with 3,500 lb. (1,588 kg.) bomb load:* 2,010 miles (3,235 km.). *Armament:* Two 0.303 in. Browning machine-guns in each of nose and dorsal turrets, and four more in tail turret; up to 14,000 lb. (6,350 kg.) of bombs internally.

FOCKE-WULF Fw 200 (Germany)

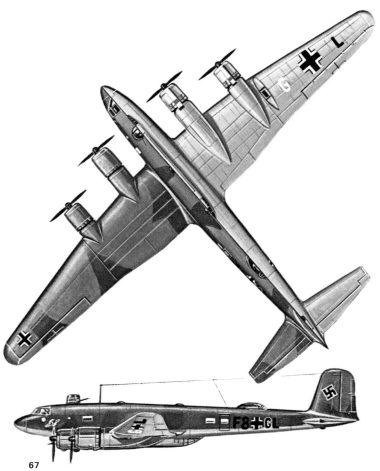

67

Focke-Wulf Fw 200C-3/U1 *Condor* of I/KG.40 operating with *Fliegerführer Atlantik,* summer 1941. *Engines:* Four 1,200 h.p. Bramo 323R-2 Fafnir radials. *Span:* 107 ft. 9½ in. (30.855 m.). *Length:* 76 ft. 11½ in. (23.46 m.). *Height:* 20 ft. 8 in. (6.30 m.). *Maximum take-off weight:* 50,045 lb. (22,700 kg.). *Maximum speed:* 207 m.p.h. (333 km./hr.) at 15,750 ft. (4,800 m.). *Operational ceiling:* 19,030 ft. (5,800 m.). *Range (standard fuel):* 2,206 miles (3,550 km.). *Armament:* One 20 mm. MG 151/20 cannon in the front of the ventral gondola, one 15 mm. MG 151 machine-gun in forward dorsal turret, and three 7.9 mm. MG 15 guns (one in the rear of the ventral gondola and one in each beam position); up to 4,630 lb. (2,100 kg.) of bombs internally and externally.

FORTRESS (U.S.A.)

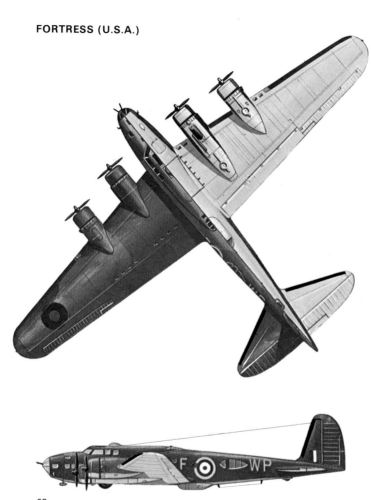

68

Boeing Fortress I (B-17C) of No. 90 Squadron RAF Bomber Command, summer 1941. *Engines:* Four 1,200 h.p. Wright R-1820-666C Cyclone radials. *Span:* 103 ft. 9⅜ in. (31.63 m.). *Length:* 67 ft. 10½ in. (20.69 m.). *Height:* 15 ft. 4½ in. (4.68 m.). *Normal take-off weight:* 47,500 lb. (21,546 kg.). *Maximum speed:* 325 m.p.h. (523 km./hr.) at 25,000 ft. (7,620 m.). *Operational ceiling:* 36,700 ft. (11,186 m.). *Maximum range:* 3,500 miles (5,633 km.). *Armament:* Six 0.50 in. Browning machine-guns (two each in dorsal and ventral positions, one in each beam position) and one 0.30 in. gun in nose; up to 4,000 lb. (1,814 kg.) of bombs internally.

69

Douglas-built Boeing B-17F-60-DL of the 390th Bombing Group, US Eighth Air Force, UK 1943–45. *Engines:* Four 1,200 h.p. Wright R-1820-97 Cyclone radials. *Span:* 103 ft. 9$\frac{3}{8}$ in. (31.63 m.). *Length:* 74 ft. 8$\frac{7}{8}$ in. (22.78 m.). *Height:* 19 ft. 2$\frac{1}{2}$ in. (5.85 m.). *Normal take-off weight:* 55,000 lb. (24,948 kg.). *Maximum speed:* 299 m.p.h. (481 km./hr.) at 25,000 ft. (7,620 m.). *Operational ceiling:* 37,500 ft. (11,431 m.). *Range with 6,000 lb.* (2,722 kg.) *bomb load:* 1,300 miles (2,092 km.). *Armament:* Eight or nine 0.50 in. Browning machine-guns (two in forward dorsal turret, one in rear dorsal position (optional), two in ventral turret, two in tail turret and one in each beam position), and one 0.30 in. gun in nose; maximum permitted short-range load of 12,800 lb. (5,806 kg.) of bombs internally and 8,000 lb. (3,629 kg.) externally.

SUPERFORTRESS (U.S.A.)

70

Boeing B-29 Superfortress of the 795th Bomber Squadron, 468th Bomber Group, US 20th Air Force, CBI theatre early autumn 1944. *Engines:* Four 2,200 h.p. Wright R-3350-23 Cyclone radials. *Span:* 141 ft. 3 in. (43.05 m.). *Length:* 99 ft. 0 in. (30.18 m.). *Height:* 27 ft. 9 in. (8.46 m.). *Maximum take-off weight:* 135,000 lb. (61,235 kg.). *Maximum speed:* 357 m.p.h. (575 km./hr.) at 30,000 ft. (9,144 m.). *Operational ceiling:* 33,600 ft. (10,241 m.). *Range with 10,000 lb. (4,536 kg.) bomb load:* 3,250 miles (5,230 km.). *Armament:* One 20 mm. M2 cannon and two 0.50 in. machine-guns in tail turret; eight other 0.50 in. guns, two each in fore and aft dorsal and ventral turrets; up to 20,000 lb. (9,072 kg.) of bombs internally. **86**

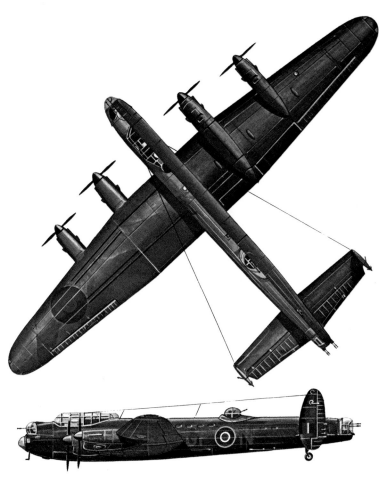

71
Avro Lancaster B I of No. 1661 Conversion Unit RAF, February 1944. *Engines:* Four 1,280 h.p. Rolls-Royce Merlin XX or 22 Vee type. *Span:* 102 ft. 0 in. (31.09 m.). *Length:* 69 ft. 4 in. (21.13 m.). *Height:* 19 ft. 7 in. (5.97 m.). *Maximum take-off weight:* 68,000 lb. (30.844 kg.). *Maximum speed:* 287 m.p.h. (462 km./hr.) at 11,500 ft. (3,505 m.). *Operational ceiling:* 24,500 ft. (7,467 m.). *Range with 12,000 lb. (5,443 kg.) bomb load:* 1,730 miles (2,784 km.). *Armament:* Eight 0.303 in. Browning machine-guns (two each in nose and dorsal turrets, four in tail turret); up to 18,000 lb. (8,165 kg.) of bombs internally.

HALIFAX I (U.K.)

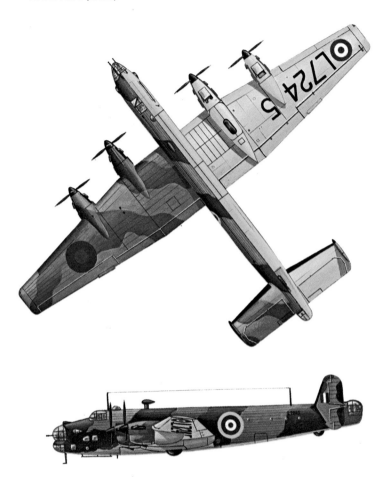

72

Handley Page Halifax second prototype (representative of Mk I configuration), *ca.* September 1940. *Data apply to production Mk I Series I. Engines:* Four 1,075 h.p. Rolls-Royce Merlin X Vee type. *Span:* 98 ft. 10 in. (30.12 m.). *Length:* 70 ft. 1 in. (21.36 m.). *Height:* 20 ft. 9 in. (6.32 m.). *Maximum take-off weight:* 55,000 lb. (24,948 kg.). *Maximum speed:* 265 m.p.h. (426 km./hr.) at 17,500 ft. (5,334 m.). *Operational ceiling:* 22,800 ft. (6,949 m.). *Range with 5,800 lb. (2,631 kg.) bomb load:* 1,860 miles (2,993 km.). *Armament:* Two 0.303 in. Browning machine-guns in nose turret, four others in tail turret and (on some aircraft) two in beam positions; up to 13,000 lb. (5,897 kg.) of bombs internally.

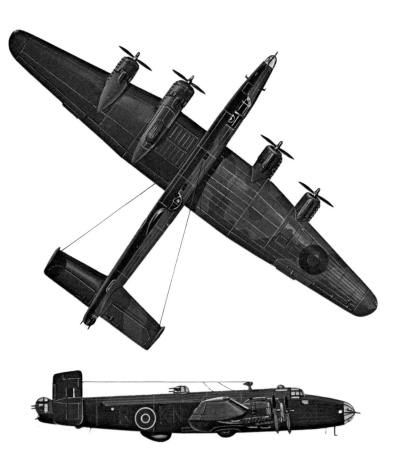

73

Handley Page Halifax B III of No. 77 Squadron RAF Bomber Command, 1944. *Engines:* Four 1,615 h.p. Bristol Hercules XVI radials. *Span:* 104 ft. 2 in. (31.75 m.). *Length:* 71 ft. 7 in. (21.82 m.). *Height:* 20 ft. 9 in. (6.32 m.). *Normal take-off weight:* 54,400 lb. (24,675 kg.). *Maximum speed:* 282 m.p.h. (454 km./hr.) at 13,500 ft. (4,115 m.). *Operational ceiling:* 24,000 ft. (7,315 m.). *Range with maximum bomb load:* 1,030 miles (1,658 km.). *Armament:* Eight 0.303 in. Browning machine-guns (four each in dorsal and tail turrets) and one 0.303 in. Vickers K gun in nose; up to 13,000 lb. (5,897 kg.) of bombs internally.

LIBERATOR (U.S.A.)

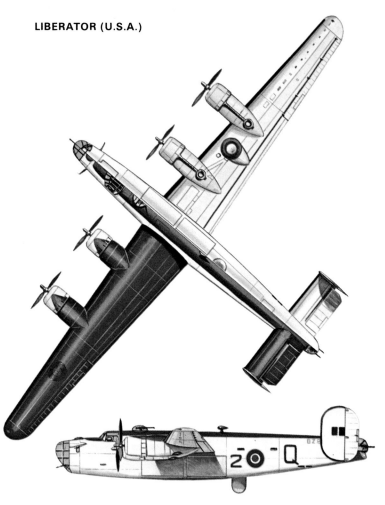

74

Consolidated Liberator GR III (B-24D) of RAF Coastal Command, late 1943. *Engines:* Four 1,200 h.p. Pratt & Whitney R-1830-43 Twin Wasp radials. *Span:* 110 ft. 0 in. (33.53 m.). *Length:* 66 ft. 4 in. (20.22 m.). *Height:* 17 ft. 11 in. (5.46 m.). *Maximum take-off weight:* 64,000 lb. (29,030 kg.). *Maximum speed:* 303 m.p.h. (488 km./hr.) at 25,000 ft. (7,620 m.). *Operational ceiling:* 32,000 ft. (9,754 m.). *Maximum range:* 4,600 miles (7,403 km.). *Armament:* Two 0.50 in. Browning machine-guns in dorsal turret, and seven 0.303 in. Browning guns (one in nose, four in tail turret and one in each beam position); up to 8,000 lb. (3,629 kg.) of bombs internally.

LIBERATOR (U.S.A.)

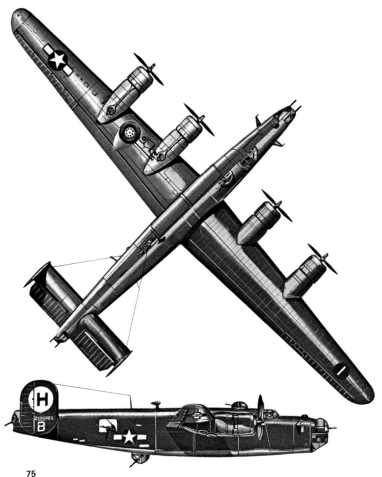

75

Convair B-24J-95-CO of the 448th Bombardment Group, US Eighth Air Force, UK *ca.* spring 1944. *Engines:* Four 1,200 h.p. Pratt & Whitney R-1830-65 Twin Wasp radials. *Span:* 110 ft. 0 in. (33.53 m.). *Length:* 67 ft. 2 in. (20.47 m.). *Height:* 17 ft. 7½ in. (5.37 m.). *Normal take-off weight:* 56,000 lb. (25,401 kg.). *Maximum speed:* 290 m.p.h. (467 km./hr.) at 25,000 ft. (7,620 m.). *Operational ceiling:* 28,000 ft. (8,534 m.). *Range at maximum overload weight of 64,500 lb. (29,257 kg.), including 5,000 lb. (2,268 kg.) bomb load:* 2,100 miles (3,380 km.). *Armament:* Ten 0.50 in. Browning machine-guns (two each in nose, tail, dorsal and ventral turrets and one in each beam position); normally up to 5,000 lb. (2,268 kg.) of bombs internally.

SUNDERLAND (U.K.)

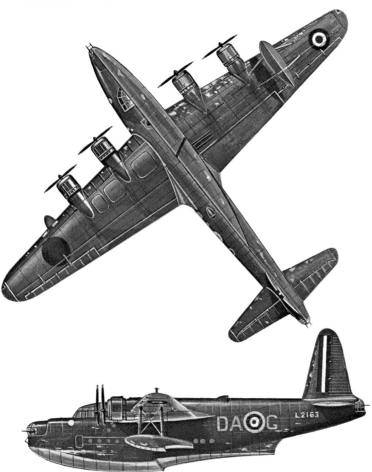

76

Short Sunderland I of No. 210 (GR) Squadron RAF Coastal Command, 1940.
Engines: Four 1,010 h.p. Bristol Pegasus XXII radials. *Span:* 112 ft. 8 in.
(34.34 m.). *Length:* 85 ft. 8 in. (26.11 m.). *Height:* 32 ft. 10½ in. (10.02 m.).
Normal take-off weight: 44,600 lb. (20,230 kg.). *Maximum speed:* 210 m.p.h.
(338 km./hr.) at 6,500 ft. (1,981 m.). *Range with maximum load:* 1,780 miles
(2,865 km.). *Armament:* Four 0.303 in. Browning machine-guns in tail turret,
one 0.303 in. Vickers K or Lewis gun in nose turret, and two Vickers K guns
amidships; up to 2,000 lb. (907 kg.) of bombs internally.

KAWANISHI H8K (Japan)

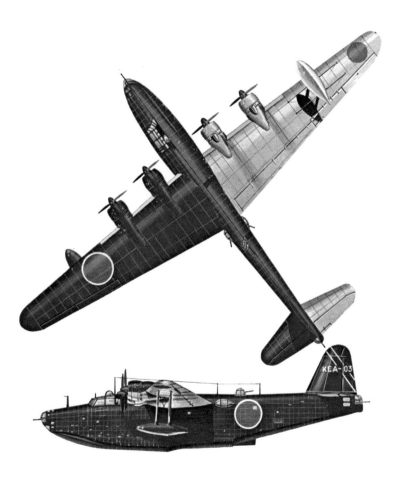

77

Kawanishi H8K2 Model 12 of the JNAF Combined Maritime Escort Force, *ca.* 1944-45. *Engines:* Four 1,850 h.p. Mitsubishi Kasei 22 radials. *Span:* 124 ft. 8 in. (38.00 m.). *Length:* 92 ft. $3\frac{1}{2}$ in. (28.13 m.). *Height:* 30 ft. $0\frac{1}{4}$ in. (9.15 m.). *Maximum take-off weight:* 71,650 lb. (32,500 kg.). *Maximum speed:* 290 m.p.h. (467 km./hr.) at 16,400 ft. (5,000 m.). *Operational ceiling:* 28,770 ft. (8,770 m.). *Maximum range:* 4,474 miles (7,200 km.). *Armament:* Two 20 mm. cannon in each of nose and tail turrets, one 20 mm. cannon in dorsal turret, and four 7.7 mm. machine-guns in beam blisters and on flight deck; up to eight 551 lb. (250 kg.) bombs or two 1,764 lb. (800 kg.) torpedos.

KAWANISHI H6K (Japan)

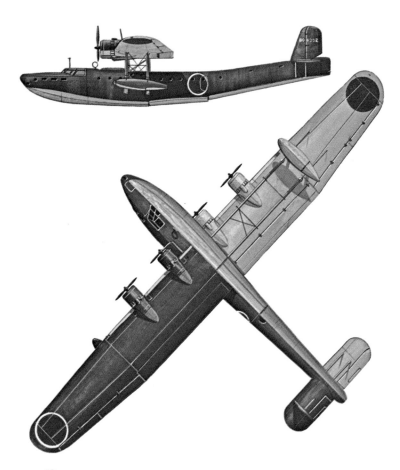

78

Kawanishi H6K4-L transport of No. 801 Air Corps JAAF, 1942. *Engines:* Four 1,070 h.p. Mitsubishi Kinsei 46 radials. *Span:* 131 ft. 2¾ in. (40.00 m.). *Length:* 84 ft. 1 in. (25.63 m.). *Height:* 20 ft. 6⅞ in. (6.27 m.). *Normal take-off weight:* 37,479 lb. (17,000 kg.). *Maximum speed:* 211 m.p.h. (340 km./hr.) at 13,120 ft. (4,000 m.). *Operational ceiling:* 31,530 ft. (9,610 m.). *Maximum range:* 2,535 miles (6,080 km.). *Armament (H6K4 patrol version only):* One 20 mm. cannon in tail turret, four 7.7 mm. machine-guns (one each in bow, dorsal and two beam positions); up to 3,527 lb. (1,600 kg.) of bombs internally or two 1,764 lb. (800 kg.) torpedos externally.

MESSERSCHMITT Me 323 (Germany)

79

Messerschmitt Me 323D-1 (unit unknown), Eastern Front 1942–43. *Engines:* Six 990 h.p. Gnome-Rhône 14N 48/49 radials. *Data apply to Me 323D-6.* *Span:* 181 ft. 1¼ in. (55.20 m.). *Length:* 93 ft. 4½ in. (28.46 m.). *Height:* approximately 27 ft. 6 in. (8.38 m.). *Normal take-off weight:* 95,901 lb. (43,500 kg.). *Maximum speed:* 137 m.p.h. (220 km./hr.) at sea level. *Maximum payload:* 24,251 lb. (11,000 kg.). *Typical range:* 696 miles (1,120 km.). *Armament:* Five 13 mm. MG 131 machine-guns firing through apertures in nose-loading doors and from dorsal positions.

OHKA (Japan)

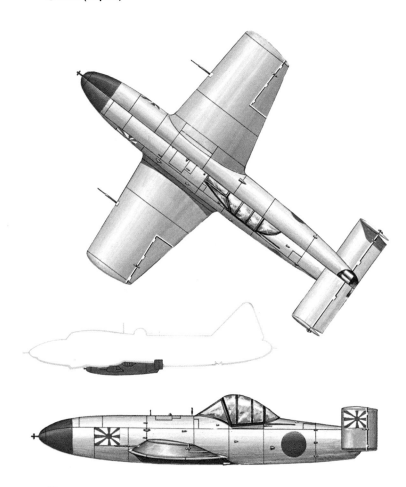

80

Yokosuka MXY-7 *Ohka* Model 11 piloted bomb, exhibited in the Indian Air Force Museum, New Delhi. *Engine:* One 1,764 lb. (800 kg.) st Type 4 Model 20 solid-propellant rocket motor. *Span:* 16 ft. $4\frac{7}{8}$ in. (5.00 m.). *Length:* 19 ft. $10\frac{7}{8}$ in. (6.07 m.). *Height:* approximately 3 ft. $11\frac{1}{4}$ in. (1.20 m.). *Maximum weight:* 4,718 lb. (2,140 kg.). *Maximum level speed:* 534 m.p.h. (860 km./hr.). *Maximum diving speed:* 621 m.p.h. (1,000 km./hr.). *Range:* 55 miles (88 km.).

1 Supermarine Walrus

Originally in the Fleet reconnaissance role, and later as an air/sea rescue aeroplane, the Walrus amphibious flying boat was one of the best known sights in the wartime skies, especially those over British home waters. The Walrus could trace its lineage back to the Seagull amphibians of the 1920s, and when the prototype (K 4797) first appeared it was known as the Seagull V. It first flew on 21 June 1933, powered by a 635 hp Bristol Pegasus IIM.2 radial engine driving a pusher propeller. Twenty-four Seagull V's were ordered by the Australian Government, and a further twelve, to Specification 2/35, by the Fleet Air Arm, to whom it was known as the Walrus. In the following year Specification 37/36 was issued to cover another two hundred and four Walrus I's, and additional contracts followed later. Three from FAA orders were diverted to the Irish Army Air Corps in 1939. The metal-hulled Walrus I was delivered to FAA units from July 1936, initial allocations being made to battleships, cruisers and other warships equipped with catapults. These units were combined in January 1940 as No 700 Squadron, whose total aircraft strength included forty-two Walruses. Other Fleet-spotter squadrons to employ the Walrus included Nos 711, 712 and 714. From 1941 onward the Walrus was also employed increasingly by the Royal Air Force as an air/sea rescue amphibian, a task which it performed with distinction until the end of the war.

Seven RAF squadrons in Britain and four in the Middle East operated the Walrus in this role. From the two hundred and eighty-eighth machine onward production was undertaken by Saunders-Roe at Cowes with the designation Walrus II. The Saro-built aircraft had wooden hulls and Pegasus VI engines, and most of the ASR squadrons were equipped with this version. Despite its archaic appearance, the Walrus was a more rugged aeroplane than it seemed, and operated with utter reliability in sharply contrasted climates. Some operating in the Argentine were retired as recently as 1966.

2 Fairey Albacore

Two prototypes of the Albacore were built, to the requirements of Specification S.41/36 for a three-seat torpedo/spotter/reconnaissance aircraft for the FAA. The first of these (L 7074) flew on 12 December 1938, and production began in 1939 of the initial order for ninety-eight, placed in May 1937. When production ended in 1943 this total had increased to eight hundred and one. Early production Albacores, like the prototypes, were powered by Bristol Taurus II engines, but the 1,130 hp Taurus XII was installed in later batches; otherwise the 'Applecore' underwent comparatively little modification during its wartime career. This began with the formation of No 826 Squadron of the FAA specially to operate the Albacore, and the first dozen were officially accepted in mid-March 1940. The first operational sorties were made some ten weeks later, and in 1941 Albacores began to equip carrier-based FAA squadrons as well as those at shore stations. They subsequently gave extensive service in home waters and in the Mediterranean and Middle East theatres of war, until the arrival of Barracuda monoplane torpedo-bombers during 1943. At the peak of their career they equipped fifteen FAA squadrons, and figured in such major campaigns as the Battles of Cape Matapan and El Alamein, and the Allied landings in Sicily and at Salerno. When the last FAA squadron to fly Albacores (No 841) disbanded late in 1943 its aircraft were taken over by the Royal Canadian Air Force, in whose service they helped to keep the sea lanes open during the Allied invasion of Normandy in June 1944. Thus the Albacore, originally brought into being to replace the Fairey Swordfish, served alongside its sister aeroplane throughout its career and was actually retired from British service before the Swordfish.

3 Fairey Swordfish

Fortunately for the wartime Royal Navy, the loss of the Fairey T.S.R.I prototype in an accident in September 1933 was not sufficient to deter the Fairey Aviation Co from following it with a second, slightly larger development, the T.S.R.II. Designed, as its initials indicated, for the torpedo/spotter/reconnaissance role, the T.S.R.II (K 4190) was the true prototype of the later Swordfish and made its first flight on 17 April 1934. Delivery of production Swordfish to the FAA began

in July 1936, the first recipient being No 825 Squadron. These were built to Specification S.38/34 and had the Pegasus IIIM.3 as powerplant. As an alternative to the 1,610 lb (730 kg) torpedo which it was designed to carry beneath the fuselage, the Swordfish I could carry a 1,500 lb (680 kg) mine in the same position or a similar total weight of bombs distributed under the fuselage and lower wings. Thirteen FAA squadrons were equipped with Swordfish at the outbreak of World War 2, a figure which was later almost doubled. At first they were employed largely on convoy or fleet escort duties, but in April 1940 the first major torpedo attack was made by Swordfish from HMS *Furious* during the Norwegian campaign, and their duties soon extended to include mine-laying. Their most notable achievement was the destruction of three battleships, two destroyers, a cruiser and other warships of the Italian Fleet at Taranto on 10-11 November 1940, for the loss of only two Swordfish. The next variant was the Mk II, which appeared in 1943 and was built with metal-covered lower wings, enabling it to carry rocket projectiles. Later Mk II's were fitted with Pegasus XXX engines of 820 hp, and these also powered the Mk III, identifiable by its ASV radar housing beneath the front fuselage. Swordfish from all three Marks underwent conversion to Mk IV for service with the Royal Canadian Air Force; these were provided with enclosed cockpits. A substantial number of Mk I's were converted as twin-float seaplanes for service aboard catapult-equipped warships. The Swordfish was in action until less than four hours before the German surrender was signed, but after the war in Europe ended it was swiftly retired, the last FAA squadron disbanding on 21 May 1945. Total Swordfish production (including the prototype T.S.R.II) amounted to six hundred and ninety-two by Fairey and one thousand six hundred and ninety-nine by Blackburn. The Swordfish was universally known as the 'Stringbag' to all associated with it. Its lengthy and successful career, outlasting that of the Albacore which was meant to replace it, was a tribute to its excellent flying qualities, robust construction and uncomplaining adaptability.

4 **Noorduyn Norseman**

The first example of this Canadian 'bush' transport was completed in January 1935, and was then operated by Dominion Skyways, which later became a part of Canadian Pacific Air Lines. During the next five years Noorduyn sold only seventeen more of these aircraft, to commercial operators and to the Royal Canadian Mounted Police. Following the outbreak of World War 2, however, demand for military versions of this 9-seat utility transport increased spectacularly, both the RCAF and the USAAF placing orders. The former ordered thirty-eight Norseman Mk IV for radio and navigational training under the Empire Air Training Scheme. The USAAF, after evaluating seven

YC-64 Norsemen delivered in mid-1942, placed orders early in the following year for seven hundred and forty-six C-64A (later UC-64A) production aircraft; under Lend-Lease, thirty-four of these went to the RCAF as the Norseman VI, and forty-three others to various other Allied air forces; three others were diverted to the U.S. Navy with the designation JA-1. Plans for Aeronca also to build the C-64A were cancelled, but six C-64B floatplanes were ordered for the Engineering Corps, these all being delivered in 1943. Interchangeable wheel, ski or twin-float landing gear was available for all Norseman aircraft; the type was used by the U.S. forces mainly as a passenger or freight transport, but other duties included those of communications or casualty evacuation. Production of the Norseman by Noorduyn continued until 1946, when it was taken over by the Canadian Car and Foundry Company. The last of nine hundred and eighteen Norsemen was completed in January 1960. The post-war commercial version, the Norseman V (described in the *Private Aircraft* volume in this series), continues to be used in substantial numbers, alongside many demilitarised C-64A's.

5 **Westland Lysander**

Evolved to Specification A.39/34 for a 2-seat Army co-operation aeroplane, the Lysander was destined to play a far from passive role in the forthcoming war, and drew attention to its capabilities as early as

November 1939, when a Lysander shot down an He 111 bomber over France. The first of two Lysander prototypes (K 6127) flew on 15 June 1936, and in the following September one hundred and forty-four were ordered for the RAF under Specification 36/36. Deliveries, to No 16 Squadron, began in June 1938, and on 3 September 1939 the RAF had on charge sixty-eight Lysander Mk I and one hundred and ninety-five Mk II. Ultimately, one hundred and sixty-nine Mk I and four hundred and forty-two Mk II were completed. These differed principally in powerplant, the Mk I having an 890 hp Bristol Mercury XII and the Mk II a 905 hp Perseus XII. During wartime production of the Mks III (two hundred and sixty-seven) and IIIA (four hundred and forty-seven) many of these were built, and many earlier Lysanders converted, for service as target tugs. But the Lysander was to serve with distinction in roles of more direct value than these, notably those of air/sea rescue and agent-dropping. Here the low flying speeds and remarkable STOL characteristics of the Lysander provided a unique performance, especially for landing in and taking off from small fields or roads in Occupied Europe while fulfilling its 'cloak and dagger' role. Up to six bombs could be carried attached to the wheel fairings. All except the Mk IIIA carried only a single 0·303 in Lewis or Browning gun in the rear cockpit, but experimental versions with two 20-mm cannon or a four-gun Boulton Paul

turret were evolved in 1939. Other experimental Lysanders included the Steiger-wing P 9105, a converted Mk II, and the short-fuselage, tandem-wing project produced in 1941 by modifying the original prototype. Lysander production at Yeovil ended in January 1942, but an additional seventy-five Mk II and two hundred and fifty Mk III were built in Canada by the National Steel Car Corporation. Lysanders were supplied to Egypt (twenty), Eire (six), Finland (nine) and Turkey (thirty-six), and also served with the Free French and various Commonwealth air forces.

6   **Fieseler Fi 156 Storch** (**Stork**) Germany's counterpart to the Westland Lysander, the Fieseler Storch was also of pre-war design, three of the five prototypes being flown during 1936. A small pre-series batch of Fi 156A-o's was followed by the initial production model, the A-1, in 1938. No examples were completed of the Fi 156B, a projected civil version, and production continued with the Fi 156C series. The Fi 156C-o, which appeared early in 1939, introduced a defensive MG 15 machine-gun, mounted in a raised section at the rear of the 3-seat cabin, and was followed by C-1 staff transport and C-2 observation versions. All models thus far had been powered by Argus As 10C engines, but most of the multi-purpose C-3's built were fitted with the As 10P version of this engine. Detail improvements introduced during the production life of the C-3 were incorporated in

its successor, the C-5, which was able to carry such optional items as three 110-lb (50-kg) bombs, a 298-lb (135-kg) mine, a pod-mounted reconnaissance camera or an auxiliary drop-tank with which its range was increased to 628 miles (1,010 km). Final models were the Fi 156D-0 (As 10C) and Fi 156D-1 (As 10P), with increased cabin space and enlarged doors to permit the loading of a stretcher. From 1942 until the end of the war the C-5 and D-1 were the principal models in production. The Fi 156E-0 was a successful but experimental-only version with caterpillar-track landing gear for operation on rough or soft terrain. The Storch's remarkable STOL qualities enabled it to take off and land in extremely short distances, due to the full-span Handley Page wing leading-edge slats, and the slotted flaps and ailerons extending over the entire trailing edge. The wings could be folded back alongside the fuselage. Wartime production of the Storch, which amounted to two thousand five hundred and forty-nine aircraft, was transferred during 1944 to the Mraz factory in Czechoslovakia (which built sixty-four) and to the Morane-Saulnier works at Puteaux. The Storch served with the *Luftwaffe*, the *Regia Aeronautica* and in small numbers with the air forces of Bulgaria, Croatia, Finland, Hungary, Rumania, Slovakia and Switzerland. Both companies continued to build the type after the war, the Mraz version being known as the K-65 Cap (Stork) and the French version as the Criquet

(Locust). The Fi 256 was a wartime Puteaux-built prototype for an enlarged 5-seat development.

7 Beriev MBR-2

In many ways the MBR-2 was to the Soviet Navy what the Supermarine Walrus was to the RAF and Fleet Air Arm, both types enjoying long production lives and service careers. The MBR-2 was designed by Georgi M. Beriev and flown in 1931, the functional letters in its designation indicating *Morskoi Blizhnii Razvedchik*, or Naval Short Range Reconnaissance. The prototype was powered by an imported BMW VI.Z engine of 500 hp, and it was a licence-built development of this, the 680 hp M-17B, which powered the initial production version of the flying boat in 1934. This version carried a crew of four or five, with the two pilots seated side by side in an open cockpit; had open gun positions in the bow and midway along the top of the fuselage, each with a PV-1 machine-gun on a movable mounting; and was characterised by a square-topped fin and rudder. The flying boat, which became a standard Soviet Naval Aviation type during 1935, could also be fitted with a fixed wheel or ski landing gear, to enable it to operate from land or ice-covered waters. In 1934 an 8-passenger commercial version, designated MP-1, was put into service on internal routes by Aeroflot, and an MP-1T freighter counterpart appeared two years later. In 1935, however, an extensive redesign had been carried out by Beriev, based upon the installation of the more powerful Mikulin AM-34N engine. Other major changes included the provision of a manually operated dorsal turret, an enclosed crew cabin and larger, redesigned vertical tail surfaces. This version, sometimes referred to as the MBR-2*bis*, remained in production until 1941, and saw extensive service throughout World War 2. Many were still in service for fishery patrol and similar duties ten years later, and a few may still be flying today. The AM-34N-powered civil version was designated MP-1*bis* and entered Aeroflot service in 1937, after the prototype had been used to establish several distance and load-to-altitude records for women pilots.

8 Aichi D3A

Aichi was one of three companies to compete, in 1936, for the Imperial Japanese Navy's 11-Shi requirement for a new carrier-borne dive bomber, and its design showed strongly the influence of current German products by Heinkel, with whom the Japanese Navy had a clandestine agreement. Aichi's design was awarded a development contract, and entered production in 1937 as the D3A1 Model 11, or Type 99 carrier-based dive bomber. The Model 11 remained in production until August 1942; it was a standard JNAF type at the time of the attack on Pearl Harbor (in which it took part), and in April 1942 the British carrier *Hermes* and the cruisers *Cornwall* and *Dorsetshire* were sunk in the Indian Ocean by D3A1's. A single 250 kg bomb could

be carried on a ventral cradle which was swung forward and downward to clear the propeller during delivery, and a 60 kg bomb could be attached to each outer wing section. After delivering its bombs the D3A1 was sufficiently well armed and manoeuvrable to put up a creditable fight against the Allied fighters then in service. Four hundred and seventy-eight D3A1's were built, production then continuing with the D3A2 Model 22 until January 1944, when eight hundred and sixteen D3A2's had been completed. The D3A2 introduced cockpit and minor airframe improvements, but differed chiefly in having a 1,300 hp Kinsei 54 engine which raised the maximum speed to 266 mph (428 kmh) at 18,540 ft (5,650 m). Normal and maximum take-off weights of this model were 8,378 lb (3,800 kg) and 9,088 lb (4,122 kg) respectively, and the maximum range 1,572 miles (2,530 km). Both the D3A1 and the D3A2 (which were code named 'Val' by the Allies) figured prominently in the major Pacific battles, including those of Santa Cruz, Midway and the Solomon Islands; but increasing losses, both of aircraft and of experienced pilots, progressively reduced their contribution to the Japanese war effort, and during the second half of the Pacific War they were encountered much less often. Some were converted as single-seat suicide attack aircraft, and a number of D3A2's were adapted for the training role with the designation D3A2-K.

9 Arado Ar 196

Possessing a general appearance similar to many of the Arado biplanes of the immediate pre-war years, the Arado Ar 196 monoplane entered service in the month preceding the outbreak of World War 2. Its design had been started some years earlier, as a replacement for the obsolescent Heinkel He 60 catapult biplanes then carried by German capital ships, and during 1938 two twin-float prototypes (the Ar 196V1 and V2), and two others (the V3 and V4) with one centrally mounted main float, were flown. Towards the end of 1938 production was started at Warnemünde of the Ar 196A-1. Apart from replacement of the 880 hp BMW 132Dc radial (which had powered all four prototypes) by the more powerful BMW 132K, the Ar 196A-1 basically resembled the V2 prototype, the smaller fin and horn-balanced rudder of the V1 having been discarded in favour of a more typical Arado empennage. The Ar 196A-1 was armed with single forward- and rearward-firing 7·9 mm MG 17 machine-guns, one fixed in the front fuselage and the other on a flexible mount in the aft cockpit. The Ar 196A-1's, twenty-six of which were completed during 1939, were deployed chiefly aboard such major warships as the *Bismarck*, *Gneisenau*, *Graf Spee*, *Lützow*, *Scharnhorst* and *Scheer*, and at shore-based training establishments. In 1940 the initial version began to be joined by the principal production version, the Arado Ar 196A-3. This had improved internal equipment, but was notable chiefly for its augmented armament. When they first entered service the Ar 196A-3's operated from newly acquired bases in France, and were frequently used against Allied anti-submarine patrols in the Biscay area until countered by the appearance of the Beaufighter. Thereafter they themselves were used for anti-submarine patrols, and for convoy escort and reconnaissance, from seaplane shore bases in the Mediterranean theatre (notably Crete). The only other known operational version was the Ar 196A-5, which differed from the A-3 simply in internal equipment. Sixty-nine examples of this model were completed by Fokker in the Netherlands during 1943-44. Production by Arado, which ceased in 1943, amounted to four hundred and one aircraft, the great majority of which were the A-3 model. A further twenty-three A-3's were completed in 1942-43 by the Sud-Ouest factory at St Nazaire in Vichy France. *Luftwaffe* units employing the Ar 196 included *Seeaufklärungsgruppen* 125 and 126 and *Bordfliegergruppe* 196. Small numbers of Ar 196A-3's were also in service in the Adriatic during the war, with the air forces of Rumania and Bulgaria. The Ar 196V3, with its central main float and outer stabilising floats, was intended to serve as prototype for a proposed Ar 196B production model following this configuration, but which proved to be unnecessary. The V4 was used for armament trials.

10 Nakajima B5N

The B5N was designed by Nakajima to a 10-Shi (1935) requirement by the JNAF for a carrier-based attack bomber. It exhibited several advanced features for its time, and its design was influenced in no small part by the Northrop 5A, an example of which had arrived in Japan in 1935. The prototype B5N1 flew for the first time in January 1937, and was a clean-looking 2/3-seat monoplane with mechanically folding wings, Fowler-type landing flaps and a fully retractable main undercarriage. Its 770 hp Hikari 3 radial engine was installed beneath a neat NACA cowling, and on test the prototype aircraft exceeded the performance specification in many respects. The B5N1 Model 11 entered production late in 1937, and saw combat service in the Sino-Japanese conflict that preceded Japan's entry into World War 2. The B5N1 was armed with a single defensive machine-gun at the rear. Production of the B5N1 was simplified by adopting manual instead of mechanical wing-folding, and by substituting slotted flaps for the Fowler type. Late production aircraft (designated Model 12) were fitted with 985 hp Sakae 11 engines. A prototype appeared in December 1939 of the B5N2 Model 23, a torpedo bomber version powered by a 1,115 hp Sakae 21 engine. This was armed with two forward-firing guns and one or two guns in the rear cockpit; and it could carry an 18 in torpedo or bombs under the fuselage. The B5N2 entered JNAF service in 1940, and both variants were concerned in the attack on Pearl Harbor in December 1941. Subsequently they were responsible for the destruction of several other major U.S. carriers during the early part of the war. The B5N, known by the Allied code name 'Kate', was encountered operationally as late as June 1944, when a number were engaged in the Marianas Islands campaign. For a year or more, however, the B5N had been obsolescent, and indeed several B5N1's were withdrawn from operations and converted to B5N1-K trainers soon after the B5N2 began to enter service. More than one thousand two hundred 'Kates' were completed, some of them by Aichi, before the B5N began to be superseded by its newer and faster stablemate, the B6N Tenzan. A number of B5N's were, however, employed as suicide aircraft in the final stages of the war.

11 Douglas SBD Dauntless

Evolution of the Dauntless began in 1934, when a Northrop team under Ed Heinemann based a new Navy dive-bomber design on the company's Army A-17A. Designated XBT-1, it flew in July 1935, and in February 1936 fifty-four BT-1's with 825 hp R-1535-94 engines were ordered. The last of these was completed as the XBT-2, with a 1,000 hp R-1820-32 engine. With further modifications, notably to the landing gear and vertical tail contours, this was redesignated XSBD-1 when Northrop was absorbed by Douglas on 31 August 1937. At about this time the perforated dive flaps, a distinctive Dauntless feature, were introduced. Delivery of fifty-seven SBD-1's to the Marine Corps began in mid-1940. Simultaneously, the U.S. Navy ordered eighty-seven SBD-2's with additional fuel, protective armour and autopilots. Both versions were armed with two 0·30 in machine-guns in the upper engine cowling and a single 0·30 in gun in the rear cockpit. Bombs up to 1,000 lb (454 kg) in size could be carried on an under-fuselage cradle; maximum bomb load was 1,200 lb (544 kg). Delivery of SBD-2's, from November 1940, was followed from March 1941 by one hundred and seventy-four SBD-3's, with R-1820-52 engines and 0·50 in front guns. The two models were standard U.S. Navy carrier-borne dive-bombers at the time of Pearl Harbor; subsequently, the Navy received a further four hundred and ten SBD-3's. In May 1942 SBD pilots from the USS *Lexington* and *Yorktown* were credited with forty of the ninety-one enemy aircraft lost during the Battle of the Coral Sea; a month later, at Midway, SBD's from the *Enterprise, Hornet* and *Yorktown* sank the Japanese carriers *Akagi, Kaga* and *Soryu* and put the *Hiryu* out of action. Their own attrition rate was the lowest of any U.S. carrier aircraft in the Pacific, due largely to an outstanding ability to absorb battle damage, and the Dauntless at this time did more than any other type to turn the tide of the war in the Pacific. Later, Dauntlesses continued the war from the decks of escort carriers, flying anti-submarine or close-support missions with depth charges or rocket projectiles. In October 1942 delivery began of seven hundred and eighty SBD-4's fitted with radar and radio-navigation equipment. They were followed by the major production model, the SBD-5, with increased engine power. To the two thousand nine hundred and sixty-five SBD-5's for the U.S. Navy were added sixty SBD-5A's, built to an Army contract but delivered instead to the Marine Corps. One SBD-5, with a 1,350 hp R-1820-66 engine, acted as a prototype for the four hundred and fifty SBD-6's which completed Dauntless production in July 1944. Overall production amounted to five thousand nine hundred and thirty-six, the balance consisting of one hundred and sixty-eight A-24's and six hundred and fifteen A-24B's for the USAAF, delivered from June 1941. These corresponded to the SBD-3 and -3A, SBD-4 and SBD-5 respectively, but had new tailwheels, internal equipment changes and no arrester gear. The Army machines were not flown with a great degree of combat success, and were used chiefly for training or communications. The Royal New Zealand Air Force received eighteen SBD-3's, twenty-seven SBD-4's and twenty-three SBD-5's. Thirty-two SBD-5's were supplied to the French Navy, and between forty and fifty A-24B's to the *Armée de l'Air*; but the latter, like their U.S. Army counterparts, were employed mainly on second-line duties. Nine SBD-5's were delivered to the British Fleet Air Arm, but were not used operationally.

12   Yokosuka D4Y Suisei (Comet)

When the prototype D4Y1 made its first flight in November 1940 it became the first Japanese Navy aircraft since 1932 to fly with an in-line engine. The Navy's 1937 specification, to which it was designed, had called for a 2-seat, carrier-based dive bomber with a range of 920-1,380 miles (1,480-2,220 km) and a speed as fast as the A6M2 Zero fighter. Yokosuka's design proposed an aeroplane with a comparatively small airframe, in which the minimal frontal area of an in-line engine was an important factor. The prototype was powered by an imported Daimler-Benz DB 600G of 960 hp; production D4Y1's by the 1,200 hp Aichi Atsuta 21. Apart from five hundred completed by the Hiro Naval Air Arsenal, Aichi also built all of the two thousand three hundred and nineteen D4Y's that were produced. The D4Y1 Model 11 entered production early in 1941, but when various structural weaknesses became apparent during service this was supplanted by the strengthened D4Y2 with the Atsuta 32 engine. Delivery of Atsuta engines, however, fell behind the airframe production date, and gave rise to the D4Y3 Model 33, in which a change was made to the 1,560 hp Mitsubishi Kinsei 62 radial engine. Some loss of performance with this engine was accepted as the price for virtual elimination, in the D4Y3, of undercarriage retraction difficulties and other problems encountered in earlier models. The Suisei first appeared operationally in a reconnaissance role, designated D4Y1-C, when aircraft from the carrier *Soryu* took part in the Battle of Midway Island. The D4Y2 was used initially as a dive bomber, but by the time of the Marianas campaign in September 1944 – its first major action – this also (as the D4Y2-C) had become used for reconnaissance. By the time the radial-engined D4Y3 appeared, Japanese carrier losses were such that the 'Judy' (as the D4Y was coded by the Allies) operated almost equally from shore bases. During the final year of the war there appeared the D4Y4 Model 43, a single-seat conversion of the D4Y3 adapted for suicide attacks with 1,764 lb (800 kg) of high explosive on board; and a number of Model 12's were converted to D4Y2-S emergency night fighters for home defence in 1945. These had one or two 20 mm cannon placed behind the rear cockpit to fire obliquely forward and upward.

13   Grumman TBF Avenger

The Avenger was a pre-war design, two XTBF-1 prototypes of which were ordered by the U.S. Navy in April 1940. The first of these made its maiden flight on 1 August 1941, by which time a substantial first order had been placed. The first production TBF-1's were delivered to Squadron VT-8 late in January 1942, and the Avenger made its combat debut early in the following June at the Battle of Midway. The aircraft had typical Grumman lines, the most noticeable feature being the very deep fuselage, which enabled the torpedo or bomb load to be totally enclosed. The TBF-1C had two wing-mounted 0·50 in machine-guns in addition to the nose, dorsal and ventral guns of the original TBF-1, and could carry auxiliary drop-tanks. Both models were 3-seaters and were powered by the 1,700 hp R-2600-8 engine. Up to December 1943 Grumman built two thousand two hundred and ninety-three TBF-1/-1C Avengers, including the two original prototypes, one XTBF-2 and one XTBF-3. Four hundred and two of them were supplied to the Royal Navy as Avenger Mk I's (= TBF-1B) and sixty-three to the RNZAF. The British aircraft were briefly known as Tarpons, but the U.S. name was later standardised. Meanwhile, in the U.S.A. production had also begun in September 1942 by the Eastern Aircraft Division of General Motors, which built two thousand eight hundred and eighty-two as the TBM-1 and -1C. Three hundred and thirty-four of these went to the Royal Navy as Avenger II's. The 'dash two' variant was not built by either company, but Eastern completed a prototype and four thousand six hundred and sixty-four TBM-3's with uprated Cyclone engines and their wings strengthened to carry rocket projectiles or a radar pod. Two hundred and twenty-two of these became the British Avenger III. Further strengthening of the airframe produced the XTBM-4, but production of this model was cancelled when the war ended. This did not, however, end the Avenger's long and productive career: those

of the U.S. Navy were not finally retired until 1954, and post-war variants served with some foreign naval air forces for several years after this. During the major part of World War 2 the Avenger was the standard U.S. Navy torpedo-bomber, operating alike from carriers or shore bases, mostly in the Pacific theatre.

14 **Sukhoi Su-2**
While a member of the Tupolev design collective, Pavel Sukhoi designed a low-wing, single-engined bomber designated ANT-51. Test flights of this aeroplane, which began in August 1937, were disappointing, but Sukhoi continued to develop the basic concept after establishing his own design bureau early in 1939. Three prototypes were completed and flown, with 950 hp M-87A, M-87B and M-88 engines respectively, and the third version was accepted for production in 1940 with the functional designation BB-1. The production BB-1 had a well-armoured cockpit and crew of two, and the internal weapons bay could, if necessary, contain the entire 1,323 lb (600 kg) bomb load. More usually, however, the internal load was restricted to 882 lb (400 kg), the remaining weapons (bombs or rocket projectiles) being distributed under the wings. Early in 1941 the uprated M-88B engine began to be installed, and with the revision of the Soviet designation system the BB-1 became known as the Su-2. During the early period of the Nazi attack on the U.S.S.R. the Su-2 was in fairly widespread use, but it was

no match for the *Luftwaffe's* superior fighters, and after about a hundred Su-2's had been completed (some with twin dorsal guns) an attempt was made to improve its performance to bridge the gap until the Ilyushin Il-2 became available in quantity. Protective crew armour was increased, but the major alteration was the introduction of the 1,400 hp Shvetsov M-82 engine, which became the standard powerplant until production ceased during the latter half of 1942. Despite the numbers produced, the installation of the M-82 engine proved a retrograde step, for, while it improved the Su-2's performance on paper, its higher installed weight upset the aircraft's handling characteristics. Combat losses continued to be high, and the Su-2 was withdrawn from operational units from 1942 onward. An Su-2 re-engined with a 2,100 hp M-90 radial was test-flown in 1941 with the designation Su-4. A much superior development was the ground-attack Su-6, but as a contemporary of the already-established Il-2, this did not go into large-scale production.

15 Curtiss SB2C Helldiver

The XSB2C-1 Helldiver prototype, following its first flight on 18 December 1940, was lost in a crash early in the following year – an inauspicious beginning to the career of perhaps the most successful dive bomber ever to enter U.S. Navy service. The initial Navy order, placed in November 1940, was later increased until nine hundred and seventy-eight SB2C-1's had been completed, the first of which was delivered in June 1942. They were succeeded by one thousand one hundred and twelve SB2C-3's, two thousand and forty-five SB2C-4's and nine hundred and seventy SB2C-5's. The SB2C-3 had the 1,900 hp R-2600-20 model of the Cyclone engine, while the SB2C-4 introduced search radar in an under-wing fairing and provision for an external warload of 1,000 lb (454 kg) of bombs or eight 5 in rocket projectiles. The SB2C-5 was essentially a longer-range variant of the -4. Nine hundred Helldivers purchased by the USAAF, and built by Curtiss and Douglas with the Army title A-25A Shrike, were mostly transferred to the Marine Corps as SB2C-1A's. Starting in the summer of 1943 the Canadian Car and Foundry Co built eight hundred and ninety-four SBW-1, -3, -4 and -5 Helldivers, including twenty-six supplied to the British Fleet Air Arm. Fairchild in Canada contributed three hundred SBF-1, -3 and -4 versions to bring the overall Helldiver production total to seven thousand two hundred aircraft. The British machines were not used on active service, but the American Helldivers, perpetuating the name given to Curtiss's earlier SBC biplane dive bomber, played a prominent part in the Pacific war, operating from the USS *Bunker Hill*, *Enterprise*, *Essex*, *Independence* and other carriers. Their first major action was the Rabaul campaign in November 1943, and they took part in virtually every major naval/air action during the rest of the war. One SB2C-1 was fitted experimentally with twin floats as the XSB2C-2, and an SB2C-5 with 2,100 hp R-2600-22 engine became the sole XSB2C-6, but neither version went into production.

16 Nakajima B6N Tenzan

Just as Nakajima's earlier B5N attack bomber had exhibited superiority over most of its Allied contemporaries, so did its successor, the B6N, despite the engine troubles encountered early in its career. Only the lack of a carrier fleet and sufficient experienced pilots by the JNAF prevented the B6N from being a more serious threat to Allied shipping during the later part of the war. The powerplant chosen for the B6N1, which flew in prototype form in March 1942, was the 1,870 hp Nakajima Mamori II. Despite the bulk of this powerful two-row radial engine, it was installed in a close-fitting cowling that did little to mar the outstandingly clean lines of the B6N design. However, the engine was prone to overheating and vibration, which eventually caused the B6N1 Model 11 to be withdrawn from production, though not from service. It was superseded by the B6N2 Model 12, powered by the more reliable Mitsubishi Kasei 25, which offered a lighter installed weight and more straightforward maintenance for only a slight reduction in output. The B6N was named Tenzan by the Japanese, after a Chinese mountain, and in the Allied code naming system was known as 'Jill'. The B6N1 carried dorsal and ventral machine-guns,

the latter gun being extended into the airstream after the torpedo had been releasedt, to discourage anti-aircraft fire from the ship just attacked. In the B6N2 an additional forward-firing gun was provided in one wing. To avoid fouling the bombs or torpedo, the oil cooler was offset to port on the lower portion of the engine cowling. First combat appearance of the Tenzan was in December 1943, when a group of B6N1's attacked a U.S. task force off the Marshall Islands, but most of the one thousand two hundred and sixty-eight Tenzans built at Nakajima's Handa and Koizumi factories were B6N2's. This version made its first operational appearance in the Marianas campaign in June 1944, and was encountered again in engagements in the Caroline and Solomon Islands groups and at Iwo Jima. Tenzans carrying ASV radar attacked Allied naval concentrations off Kyushu in March 1945, and from April to June 1945 the JNAF mounted a considerable torpedo and suicide attack campaign with Tenzans against Allied ships in the vicinity of Okinawa.

17 Fairey Barracuda

The ungainly form of the Barracuda, and its 'Christmas-tree' appearance when bedecked with torpedos, bombs, lifeboats, radar arrays and the like, were the direct outcome of the exacting Specification S.24/37 to which it was designed. It was the first British carrier-based monoplane torpedo bomber of all-metal construction, yet its high, strut-braced tailplane and large, Fairey-Youngman trailing-edge flaps might have suggested to the uninitiated a less sophisticated design than was actually the case. Abandonment of the intended Rolls-Royce Exe engine delayed the trials of the first prototype (P 1767), which eventually flew on 7 December 1940 with a 1,260 hp Merlin 30. Priority afforded to other types of aircraft then delayed production, the first Barracuda I not being flown until 18 May 1942. Thirty of this model were completed (including five by Westland), and they were followed by one thousand six hundred and eighty-eight Barracuda II's with the uprated Merlin 32, which permitted higher operating weights but slightly reduced the overall performance. The Barracuda I's were used chiefly for trials or conversion training, the first operational unit being No 827 Squadron, which received the Mk II in January 1943. First combat action was with No 810 Squadron during the Salerno landings eight months later. In service, the Barracuda was more often employed as a dive bomber than with a torpedo, and it was in this role that forty-two Barracudas, from four Squadrons aboard the carriers *Victorious* and *Furious*, carried out the attack on the *Tirpitz* in *Kaafioord* in northern Norway in April 1944, scoring fifteen direct hits on the German battleship with armour-piercing 500 lb and 1,000 lb bombs for the loss of only three Barracudas. Later that month Barracudas from *Illustrious* carried out the type's first combat action in the Pacific theatre. Final wartime

version was the Mk III, with a ventral ASV radome for anti-submarine patrols but otherwise generally similar to the Mk II. Fairey built six hundred and seventy-five Mk II's, Blackburn seven hundred, Boulton Paul three hundred and Westland thirteen. Four hundred and sixty Mk III's were built by Fairey, and three hundred and ninety-two by Boulton Paul. One Mk II was re-engined with a 1,850 hp Griffon VII as prototype for the unarmed Mk V (the Mk IV was not built), and this aircraft (P 9976) flew on 16 November 1944. Thirty production Mk V's, with tail surfaces and other features extensively redesigned, were built by Fairey, with 2,020 hp Griffon 37's, but were not completed until after the war and served mainly as trainers.

18 Fairey Battle

Often, when a particular aeroplane type is utilised as a flying test-bed for a variety of experimental engines, such employment is an indication that its general handling qualities are rather above the average. Such was the case with the Battle, several examples of which were employed in this fashion to air-test various engines of up to 2,000 hp. This was a considerable increase over the 1,030 hp of the Merlin I that powered the prototype (K 4303) when it made its first flight on 10 March 1936. The Battle was designed by Marcel Lobelle to Specification P.27/32 for a 2-seat day bomber to replace the Hawker Hart biplane, and an initial order for one hundred and fifty-five Battles, to Specification P.23/35, was placed before the prototype had flown. The first production Battle was completed in June 1937, and the bomber – now a 3-seater – was one of the types chosen for large-scale priority production as part of the RAF expansion programme. Under the 'shadow factory' scheme Austin Motors shared the production with Fairey, and on 3 September 1939 the RAF had well over a thousand Battle Mks I-III on charge. (Production Battles were powered successively by Merlin Mk I, II, III or V engines, and took their own Mark numbers from that of the engine. This famous engine series first entered production as the powerplant for the Battle.) Ultimately, Fairey built one thousand one hundred and fifty-six Battles, and Austin one thousand and twenty-nine; an additional eighteen were completed before the war by Avions Fairey in Belgium. First RAF deliveries were made to No 63 Squadron in May 1937, and on 2 September 1939 ten Battle squadrons flew to France as part of the Advanced Air Striking Force. Normal bomb load was stowed in four cells in the wings, but this could be increased to a maximum of 1,500 lb (680 kg) by carrying extra bombs on under-wing racks. Many brave actions were fought by Battle crews, but the bomber was already outdated by the time the war started and was no match for the *Luftwaffe* fighters ranged against it. Consequently, it was soon withdrawn to non-combatant duties, such as operational training and

target towing. In the former role it flew also with the air forces of Australia, Canada and South Africa, and pre-war exports also included twenty-nine for the Turkish Air Force. The type was finally withdrawn from RAF service in 1949.

19 **Junkers Ju 87**
The United States and Germany, in particular, were enthusiastic proponents of the dive bomber during the later 1930s and the early part of World War 2. This particular species of warplane seemed to be typified in the Ju 87, whose ugly lines and wailing engine struck an especial note of terror in the skies above Poland, France and the Low Countries in 1939–40. Design of the Ju 87, by Dipl-Ing Pohlmann, started in 1933, and the first prototype flew early in 1935. This was powered by a Rolls-Royce Kestrel engine and had rectangular twin fins and rudders, but the Ju 87V2, flown in the following autumn, had a single tail and a 610 hp Junkers Jumo 210A engine, and was more representative of the production aircraft to follow. A pre-series batch of Ju 87A-0's was started in 1936, and in the spring of 1937 delivery began of the Ju-87A-1 initial production model, followed by the generally similar A-2. About two hundred A series were built before, in the autumn of 1938, there appeared the much-modified Ju 87B. Powered by the Jumo 211, this had an enlarged vertical tail, redesigned crew canopy and new-style cantilever fairings over the main legs of

the landing gear. Both the A and B models were sent for service with the Condor Legion in Spain in 1938, but by the outbreak of World War 2 the A series had been relegated to the training role, and the three hundred and thirty-six aircraft in front-line service were all Ju 87B-1's. The fighter superiority of the *Luftwaffe* ensured the Ju 87 a comparatively uninterrupted passage in 1939-40, but opposition during the Battle of Britain was much sterner, and losses of the Ju 87 were considerably heavier. Nevertheless, production of the B series continued into 1941, and substantial numbers were supplied to the *Regia Aeronautica*, and to the air forces of Bulgaria, Hungary and Rumania. In production alongside the B series was the long-range Ju 87R, which from 1940 was used for anti-shipping and other missions. Before the war small numbers were also completed of the Ju 87C, a version of the B with arrester hook, folding wings and other 'navalised' attributes. This was planned for service aboard the carrier *Graf Zeppelin*, but the ship was never completed, and the few Ju 87C-0's built served with a land-based unit. Others laid down as C-1's were completed as B-2's. After the setbacks in the Battle of Britain the Ju 87B continued to serve in the Mediterranean and North Africa. Its subsequent development and employment was mainly in the close-support role or as a trainer; these versions are described in the companion volume *Fighters, Attack and Training Aircraft 1939–45.*

20 **Nakajima C6N Saiun (Colourful Cloud)**
The Saiun was designed by Yasuo Fukuda to a 17-Shi (1942) requirement for a carrier-based reconnaissance aircraft. Originally, Fukuda contemplated the use of two 1,000 hp radial engines mounted in tandem, but a single, small-diameter Homare engine, which promised to develop around 2,000 hp, was chosen instead. To shorten the Saiun's development period, no less than twenty-three prototypes were ordered, and many of these were completed by the end of 1943. Several of the prototypes were assigned to active units as part of the test programme, and it was they that made the aircraft's operational debut. The Saiun, to which the Allies gave the code name 'Myrt', was first encountered in June 1944, when a number of these aircraft made a reconnaissance of the U.S. task force assembling for the attack on the Marianas Islands. Later the Saiun also reconnoitred the force being assembled to attack Saipan. Series production of the Saiun, as the C6N1 Model 11, began in 1944, the first deliveries to JNAF units being made in August. By the end of the war Nakajima's Handa and Koizumi factories had built four hundred and ninety-eight Saiuns, but their service career was delayed and interrupted by continual troubles with the problematical Homare engine, and they were not met in large numbers. The light armament of the reconnaissance version reflected the aircraft's ability to outpace and outclimb most of

the late-war Allied fighters, but those converted for other roles were more comprehensively equipped. The C6N1-S was a home defence night fighter, with a crew of two and twin 20 mm cannon fixed in the rear fuselage to fire obliquely forward and upward. The C6N1-B was a 3-seat torpedo bomber conversion. Two prototypes were also completed of an improved reconnaissance variant, the C6N2 Model 22, powered by the 2,000 hp Homare 24 engine. The final development, designated C6N3 Saiun-Kai, was to have been powered by a Hitachi 92 engine, but this had only reached the project stage when the war ended.

21 Heinkel He 115

It was to be expected that Ernst Heinkel, designer of several fine marine aircraft during World War 1, should produce one of the leading seaplanes of the 1939-45 conflict. The first He 115 prototype (D-AEHF) flew in 1936, being modified later for attempts on the prevailing world seaplane speed records, eight of which it captured on 20 March 1938. The definitive production aircraft was fore-shadowed by the third and fourth prototypes, with an extensively glazed nose and long 'greenhouse' canopy, and, in the latter case, no wire bracing for the twin floats. Ten pre-production He 115A-0's and thirty-four He 115A-1's were completed in 1937 and 1938 respectively, the latter having an MG 15 gun in the nose as well as the observer's dorsal gun. The A-2 was the export

equivalent of the *Luftwaffe's* A-1, and was sold to Norway (six) and Sweden (ten). The first large-scale domestic version, the He 115A-3, was soon followed by the He 115B series, comprising ten B-0's and fifty-two B-1/B-2's. These had increased fuel capacity and could carry one of Hitler's much-vaunted 'secret weapons', the magnetic mine, in addition to their internal bomb load. With these they caused considerable havoc to Allied shipping during the early years of the war. In 1940–41 there appeared the He 115C series, of which the C-0, C-1 and C-2 sub-types had an extra forward-firing 20 mm MG 151 cannon in a fairing under the nose. On some aircraft, a 7·9 mm MG 17 gun was installed in each wing root as well. The C series concluded with eighteen C-3 minelayers and thirty C-4 torpedo bombers, the latter having the dorsal MG 15 as its only defensive gun. One He 115A-1 was re-engined with 1,600 hp BMW 801C radials and equipped with five machine-guns and a cannon to become the He 115D; but although this was used operationally, no production of the D series was undertaken. In fact, all production was halted for a time, but was resumed in 1943–44 to build one hundred and forty-one examples of the E-0 and E-1 variants, bringing the overall total to about four hundred aircraft. These were similar to earlier models except for variations in armament. Two of the Norwegian A-2's, which escaped to Britain after the invasion of Norway in 1940, were later employed in RAF colours to transport Allied agents between Malta and North Africa.

22   Vickers Wellington

On 3 September 1939 the RAF had one hundred and seventy-nine Wellingtons on strength, rather less than the number of Hampdens or Whitleys, but these three types bore the brunt of Bomber Command's operations during the early part of the war until the arrival of the four-engined heavy bombers from 1941. The Wellington went on to outstrip both of its contemporaries, an ultimate total of eleven thousand four hundred and sixty-one being built before production ceased in October 1945. After being withdrawn from Bomber Command in 1943, Wellingtons began a second career with Coastal Command as maritime reconnaissance aircraft, at home and in the Middle and Far East; others were employed briefly as transports and (after the war) as aircrew trainers. The 'Wimpey' was designed to Specification B.9/32, the prototype (K 4049) flying on 15 June 1936. Considerable redesign of the fuselage and vertical tail was evident in the production aircraft, ordered to Specification 29/36. The first of these was flown on 23 December 1937, and the first Wellington squadron was No 9, which received its aircraft in October 1938. Those in service when war broke out were Pegasus-engined Mks I or IA, but the most numerous early model was the Mk IC, of which two thousand six hundred and eighty-five were built. Prototypes had also flown before the war

of the Merlin-engined Mk II and the Mk III with Bristol Hercules radials. Wellingtons of Nos 9 and 149 Squadrons, in company with Blenheims, carried out the RAF's first bombing attack of the war when they bombed German shipping at Brunsbüttel. From mid-December 1939 they were switched to night bombing only, joining in the first raid on Berlin late in August 1940. In the following month they made their Middle East debut, and appeared in the Far East from early 1942. By this time the Mk III (one thousand five hundred and nineteen built) was the principal service version, although two squadrons operated the Twin Wasp-engined Mk IV. The first general reconnaissance version for Coastal Command, the Mk VIII, appeared in the spring of 1942. Three hundred and ninety-four, with similar engines to the Mk IC, were built. They were followed by substantial batches of the Mks XI, XII, XIII and XIV, with differing versions of the Hercules and variations in operational equipment. Overseas, the Wellington maintained its combat role, the Mk X in particular (three thousand eight hundred and four built) serving with the Middle East Air Forces as well as with Bomber Command. Wellingtons of No 40 Squadron made a bombing attack on Treviso, Italy, as late as March 1945. Other Wellingtons were converted as torpedo bombers, mine-layers and transports, and a special variant designated D.W.1 was fitted with a large electro-magnetic 'de-gaussing' ring to trigger off enemy mines. The light but extremely strong geodetic method of the Wellington's construction not only enabled it to carry a creditable bomb load but was capable of withstanding a considerable amount of battle damage without failure.

23 Heinkel He 111

In one form or another, the He 111's service career extended over more than thirty years, an outstanding tribute to the design, evolved by the Günter brothers early in 1934. Of the original four prototypes, the first was flown on 24 February 1935, and the second and fourth were completed ostensibly as civilian transports. Bomber production was heralded in the summer of 1935 by the He 111V4 and a pre-series batch of He 111A-0's, but their BMW engines provided insufficient power, and the first major type was the He 111B, with DB 600-series engines. This was one of the most successful types to serve with the Condor Legion in Spain, where it was fast enough to fly unescorted. To preserve supplies of DB 600's for fighter production, the He 111D did not enter large-scale production, the next major versions being the Jumo-powered He 111E and F. The latter employed the revised, straight-tapered wings originally evolved for the proposed commercial G model. Both E and F models also served in Spain, and after the Civil War the surviving He 111's became a part of the Spanish Air Force. Production of the variants so far mentioned had reached nearly a thousand by the outbreak of World War 2, but a new

model had also made its appearance. This was the He 111P, whose extensively glazed, restyled front section, with its offset ball turret in the extreme nose, became characteristic of all subsequent variants. It was built in comparatively small numbers, again because of the use of Daimler-Benz engines, but its Jumo-powered counterpart, the He 111H, became the most widely used series of all, well over five thousand being built before production ended in 1944. Reflecting their rough reception during the Battle of Britain, successive H and subsequent types appeared with progressive increases in defensive armament, the number of crew members being increased to five or six according to the number of guns. Although most extensively used in its intended role as a medium bomber, the He 111H carried a variety of operational loads during its service. The H-6 was particularly effective as a torpedo bomber, carrying two of these weapons usually, while other H sub-types became carriers for the Hs 293 glider bomb and the FZG-76 (V1) flying bomb. More bizarre variants included the H-8 fitted with balloon-cable cutters, and the He 111Z *Zwilling* (Twin) glider tug, a union of two H-6 airframes linked by a new centre-section supporting a fifth Jumo engine. The H-23 was an 8-seat paratroop transport. German production, of all versions, was well in excess of seven thousand. Licence-built He 111H-16's, designated C.2111, were built in Spain by CASA, and served with the

Spanish Air Force until well into the 1960s.

24 Avro Anson

Design of the Anson twin-engined coastal reconnaissance monoplane was based upon that of the Avro 652 commercial 6-seater, and was known as the Avro 652A. The military prototype (K 4771) was flown on 24 March 1935, and in the following summer Specification 18/35 was issued to cover the initial contract for one hundred and seventy-four Anson Mk I's for Coastal Command. The first Ansons were delivered to No 48 Squadron in March 1936. By the outbreak of war the RAF had seven hundred and sixty serviceable Anson I's, equipping ten squadrons of Coastal Command and sixteen of Bomber Command, and production was still continuing. Strictly, by then they were obsolescent, and from 1940 began to be replaced by Whitleys and imported American Hudsons, but some continued to serve in the general reconnaissance role until 1942, while others carried out air/sea rescue duty with Coastal Command squadrons over an even longer period. Almost from the outset, the Anson had also been envisaged as an aircrew trainer, and it was essentially the impetus given by the gigantic Empire Air Training Scheme of 1939 that led ultimately to the manufacture of eight thousand one hundred and thirty-eight Ansons in Britain by 1952 (including six thousand seven hundred and four Mk I's), and a further two thousand eight hundred and eighty-two under the super-

vision of Federal Aircraft Ltd in Canada. Canadian-built Ansons, differing principally in powerplant, comprised the Mk II (330 hp Jacobs L-6BM), and the Mks V and VI (both with 450 hp Pratt & Whitney R-985-AN 14B). As an interim measure, two hundred and twenty-three British-built Mks III (Jacobs) and IV (Wright Whirlwind) were supplied to Canada. Anson trainers subsequently served with all major Commonwealth air forces, as well as those of Egypt, Finland, Greece, Ireland and the U.S. Army. Anson I's later converted for ambulance or light transport duty included one hundred and four as Mk X's, ninety as Mk XI's and twenty as Mk XII's. An additional two hundred and twenty-one aircraft were built as Mk XII's from the outset. The Mks XI and XII both featured the taller cabin that also characterised the post-war Avro XIX civil transport version.

25 Ilyushin Il-4

The most widely used Soviet bomber of the war years, the Il-4 began its career under the design bureau designation TsKB-26 in 1935; its military or functional designation was DB-3, the letters indicating *Dalnii Bombardirovchtchik* or Long-Range Bomber. It was chosen for development, in preference to the contemporary DB-2 designed by Pavel Sukhoi, in its slightly modified TsKB-30 form, and delivery of production DB-3's began in 1937. The initial production DB-3, a manoeuvrable aeroplane despite its size and weight, was characterised by its squarish, blunt nose, and was powered by two 765 hp M-85 radial engines; 960 hp M-86 engines replaced these in later production batches. Armament consisted of single hand-operated 7·62 mm ShKAS machine-guns in nose and dorsal turrets, with a third gun firing down through a trap in the rear fuselage floor. Some aircraft of the original type saw service during World War 2, although by then the current version was the DB-3F (for *Forsirovanni* = boosted), design of which had started in 1938. This was at first powered by 950 hp M-87A engines and later by the more powerful M-88B, but the chief structural difference lay in the complete redesign of the nose section. This was now longer, more streamlined, well provided with windows, and instead of the DB-3's angular turret its gun was provided with a universal joint mounting. The DB-3F entered production after completing its acceptance trials in June 1939, and during the following year (when it was redesignated Il-4) large numbers were built. As a result of the war, strategic materials became in short supply, and deliveries of M-87A engines could not be maintained at an adequate rate. Further redesign therefore took place, in which several of the fuselage components, and later the outer wing panels, were manufactured from wood instead of metal; and by mid-1942 the M-88B engine was introduced as the standard powerplant. Output then increased steadily until 1944, when Il-4 production ceased. The bomber

served extensively throughout the war with both the Soviet Air Force and Soviet Navy, and it was a force of Il-4's from the latter service which carried out the first long-range attack by Soviet aircraft on Berlin on the night of 8 August 1941. Subsidiary duties included reconnaissance and glider training.

26 Martin 167 Maryland

The slim, twin-engined monoplane that the British services came to know as the Maryland was evolved in 1938 to enter a USAAC design competition ultimately won by the Douglas DB-7. One prototype of the Martin 167W was ordered by the U.S. Army as the XA-22, and this aircraft (NX 22076) made its first flight on 14 March 1939. No U.S. orders were forthcoming, but in 1939 the French Government placed total orders for two hundred and fifteen for the *Armée de l'Air*. These had the Martin export designation 167F and the French military designation 167A-3. The first 167F flew in August 1939, and deliveries began in October. Probably no more than one-third of those ordered were delivered to France, where they were in action against the German advance in the spring of 1940. After the fall of France several of the survivors were operated by the Vichy Air Force during 1940-41. At least five are known to have escaped to serve with the Royal Air Force, and delivery of a further seventy-six from the original French orders was also diverted to the RAF. These received the name Maryland Mk I, and almost all of them were employed by bomber and reconnaissance squadrons in the Middle East. A further one hundred and fifty, with British equipment and a different mark of Twin Wasp engine, were ordered by the British Purchasing Mission as the Maryland Mk II. The clean but unusually slender lines of the Martin 167 led *The Aeroplane* to remark, in September 1940, that it 'is nice as an aeroplane but a little cramped as a fighting machine'. Nevertheless, the Maryland was comparatively fast for a twin-engined machine, especially when relieved of the necessity to carry a bomb load, and made a useful reconnaissance type during the middle years of the war. A reconnaissance by RAF Marylands preceded the Fleet Air Arm's November 1940 assault on the Italian Fleet at Taranto, and in May 1941 a Maryland of the Fleet Air Arm (which received a few of the RAF machines) first brought the news of the movement of the *Bismarck* which led to the action in which the German warship was sunk. Seventy-two of the final batch of Maryland II's were re-allocated to serve with four squadrons of the South African Air Force.

27 Bristol Blenheim

Developed from the Bristol 142 *Britain First*, the Blenheim twin-engined medium bomber first appeared in production form as the short-nosed Blenheim Mk I, whose prototype (K 7033) first flew on 25 June 1936. By that time an initial contract had already been placed, and the first Blenheim I's were delivered in March 1937 to No 114 Squadron. One thousand two hundred and eighty Mk I's were built, and at the outbreak of World War 2 one thousand and seven of these were on RAF charge, including one hundred and forty-seven completed as Mk IF fighters with a ventral pack of four Browning guns. Most of the bombers were serving in the Middle and Far East, home squadrons of the RAF having already begun to re-equip with the long-nosed Mk IV bomber, one hundred and ninety-seven of which were on strength at 3 September 1939. From the eighty-first machine onward these were designated Blenheim IVL, the suffix indicating a longer range by virtue of additional wing fuel tanks. With Mercury XV engines replacing the 840 hp Mercury VIII's of the Blenheim I, the Mk IV was better armed and had a slightly improved performance over its predecessor. One thousand nine hundred and thirty Mk IV's were completed. By contrast, the performance of the final British variant, the Mk V, was disappointing. This version was redesigned to meet Specification B.6/40, and in 1941 one Mk VA day bomber prototype and one close-support Mk VB were built by Bristol. Rootes Securities Ltd built nine hundred and forty-two examples, mostly as the Mk VD (a 'tropical' version of the VA), but including a proportion of Mk VC dual-control trainers. Combat losses of the Mk VD were heavy, and it was quickly replaced by US Baltimores and

Venturas. During their career Blenheims served with every operational command of the RAF and in every theatre of the war. Pre-war exports included Blenheim I's for Finland, Rumania, Turkey and Yugoslavia. The Mk I was built under licence in Yugoslavia, and both the Mks I and IV in Finland. In Canada, Fairchild built six hundred and seventy-six Blenheims for the Royal Canadian Air Force, by whom they were designated Bolingbroke Mks I to IV.

28 Bristol Beaufighter

The Beaufighter was originally designed as a fighter, and the principal variants to serve in this capacity are described in the companion volume *Fighters, Attack and Training Aircraft 1939–45*. Its design was, however, based to a large extent upon the Beaufort torpedo bomber, and although the torpedo-carrying models were officially designated TF (Torpedo Fighter), it was considered more appropriate to include them in this volume for purposes of comparison with other types performing a similar function. The first torpedo-dropping experiments were made in 1942 with X 8065, a standard Beaufighter VIC (the Coastal Command version) adapted to carry a standard British or U.S. torpedo beneath the fuselage. Thereafter an experimental squadron was formed, which achieved its first combat success off Norway in April 1943. The so-called 'Torbeau' proved an effective torpedo bomber while retaining enough of its former performance to

carry out its other coastal duties of escort fighter and reconnaissance. Sixty Mk VI's on the production line were completed as ITF (Interim Torpedo Fighters), but two new variants soon began to appear. These were the TF Mk X torpedo bomber and the non-torpedo-carrying Mk XIC, both with 1,770 hp Hercules XVII engines. The TF Mk X, two thousand two hundred and five of which were built, had AI radar installed in a characteristic nose 'thimble' fairing, and a dorsal fin extension was introduced on later production batches. It could carry a heavier torpedo than the Mk VI (ITF), or could, alternatively, be equipped with two 250 lb (113 kg) bombs and eight rocket projectiles beneath the wings. The Mk VI (ITF) aircraft were later re-engined and brought up to Mk X standard. Three hundred and sixty-four Beaufighter Mk 21's were built for the RAAF by the Government Aircraft Factories at Fishermen's Bend and Mascot, NSW. Except for Hercules XVIII engines and four 0·50 in wing guns in place of the six Brownings, these were generally similar to the RAF's Mk X. It was they upon whom their Japanese opponents bestowed the respectful nickname of 'Whispering Death'. In spite of its later designation, the Mk XIC was only an interim model pending large-scale delivery of the Mk X, and only one hundred and sixty-three were built.

29 Bristol Beaufort

The Type 152 proposals submitted in April 1936 were designed to meet two Air Ministry Specifications: M.15/35 for a torpedo bomber, and G.24/35 for a general reconnaissance aeroplane. Detail design work began in March 1937. The prototype (L 4441) first flew on 15 October 1938, powered by two 1,065 hp Bristol Taurus II radials in place of the Perseus originally planned. Specification 10/36 was framed to cover production aircraft, seventy-eight of which had been ordered in September 1936, and the Beaufort I entered production in 1939. Initially this was armed with one 0·303 in machine-gun in the port wing and two in the dorsal turret; later, a rear-firing gun was added in an off-set blister beneath the nose, and some aircraft also had twin K guns in the nose and two others in beam positions. Bristol built nine hundred and sixty-five Beaufort I's, first deliveries being made to No 22 Squadron, Coastal Command. In January 1940 a Beaufort from this unit came close to sinking the battle cruiser *Gneisenau* in Brest harbour on 6 April 1941, and Beauforts of No 86 Squadron played an important part in trying to prevent the 'Channel dash' by the *Gneisenau*, *Scharnhorst* and *Prinz Eugen* early in 1942. Other RAF Beaufort squadrons in the United Kingdom and Mediterranean included Nos 39, 42, 47, 203, 217, 415 and 489. They remained in service until replaced by torpedo-carrying Beaufighters in 1943, their duties including mine-laying. At the outset the Beaufort had also been chosen for production in Australia. In November 1940 one aircraft was flown with 1,200 hp

Pratt & Whitney R-1830-S1C3G Twin Wasp engines, becoming the prototype for four hundred and fifteen similarly powered Beaufort II's for the RAF. Many of these were completed, and others later converted, as operational trainers, with a dorsal turret faired over. Another Twin-Wasp engined prototype was flown in Australia in May 1941, and up to August 1944 seven hundred Beauforts were built there. These comprised fifty Mk V, thirty Mk VA, forty Mk VI, sixty Mk VII and five hundred and twenty Mk VIII. These differed chiefly in the engine variant or equipment fitted, though the enlarged fin introduced on the Mk VII later became standard on all Australian Beauforts. They served with the RAAF in the Solomons, Timor, New Guinea and several other Pacific battle areas. In November 1944 forty-six aircraft were converted into Mk IX troop transports. A Mk III was proposed, but not built, with Merlin XX engines and Beaufighter 'long-range' outer wing sections; one Mk IV was completed, with 1,750 hp Taurus engines.

30 De Havilland Mosquito

One of the outstandingly versatile aeroplanes of any era, the D.H.98 Mosquito was first conceived, in 1938, as a day bomber fast enough to outrun enemy fighters and thus carry no armament. Not until March 1940 was firm official interest shown in the design, fifty then being ordered. Three prototypes were built, the first and second of these

(W4050 and W4051) being completed in bomber and photo-reconnaissance configuration respectively. They flew on 25 November 1940 and 10 June 1941. The initial fifty aircraft included ten PR Mk I and ten B Mk IV, and the first operational Mosquito sortie was flown by an aircraft of the former batch on 20 September 1941. The B IV's entered service with No 105 Squadron in May 1942, and two hundred and seventy-three Mk IV's were eventually built. In addition to three de Havilland factories in the United Kingdom, contributions to overall Mosquito production were also made by Airspeed (one hundred and twenty-two), Percival (two hundred and forty-five) and Standard Motors (one hundred and sixty-five). De Havilland built altogether five thousand and seven Mosquitos, four thousand four hundred and forty-four of them during the war period. In addition, two hundred and eight (Mks 40–43) were built by de Havilland Australia, and one thousand one hundred and thirty-four (Mks VII, 20–22 and 24–27) by de Havilland Canada. Wartime Mosquito production totalled six thousand seven hundred and ten, with a further one thousand and seventy-one completed after VJ-day. Mosquitos quickly established a reputation for their excellent flying qualities, their unequalled talent for destroying pin-point targets, and for having easily the lowest loss rate of any aircraft in service with Bomber Command. Mosquito IV's originally equipped the Pathfinder Force, which later employed also the high-altitude Mk IX and the second most numerous variant, the Mk XVI; and photo-reconnaissance counterparts of these three Marks constituted the principal wartime PR variants of the Mosquito. From early in 1944 the most popular Mosquito weapon was the 4,000 lb (1,814 kg) 'block-buster' bomb, carried in a specially bulged bomb bay retrospectively fitted to all Mks IX and XVI and several Mk IV's. About one thousand two hundred Mosquito XVI's were built, and were later flown with auxiliary pinion fuel tanks to increase their range. The NF Mk II, FB Mk VI and other fighter and fighter-bomber variants are described in the *Fighters, Attack and Training Aircraft 1939–45* volume.

31 Junkers Ju 88

The most adaptable German warplane of World War 2, and among the most widely used, the Ju 88 was evolved to a 1937 requirement issued by the RLM for a fast, well-armed multi-purpose aeroplane. The first prototype (D-AQEN) was flown on 21 December 1936, powered by two 1,000 hp DB 600A in-line engines. The second prototype was essentially similar, but in the third the powerplant was a pair of Jumo 211A engines, and the Jumo was to power the majority of Ju 88's subsequently built. The characteristic multi-panelled glazed nose section first appeared on the fourth prototype. A pre-series batch of Ju 88A-0's were completed during the summer of 1939, and delivery of the first Ju 88A-1 production models began in September. The A series continued, with very few gaps, through to the A-17, and included variants for such specialised roles as dive bombing, anti-shipping strike, long range reconnaissance and conversion training. Probably the most common model was the A-4, which served both in Europe and North Africa. This was the first version to incorporate modifications resulting from operational experience gained during the Battle of Britain; it had extended-span wings, Jumo 211J engines, increased bomb load and defensive armament. Twenty Ju 88A-4's were supplied to Finland, and others to the *Regia Aeronautica*. The Ju 88B, evolved before the outbreak of war, followed a separate line of development to become the Ju 188, and the next major production model, chronologically, was the Ju 88C fighter series. The Ju 88D (over one thousand eight hundred built as D-1, D-2 and D-3) was a developed version of the A-4 for the strategic reconnaissance role. Next bomber series was the Ju 88S, powered by 1,700 hp BMW 801G radials (in the S-1), 1,810 hp BMW 801TJ's (S-2) or 1,750 hp Jumo 213E-1's (S-3). Apart from powerplant, the S sub-types were basically similar to one another, and differed from the earlier bombers in having a smaller, fully rounded glazed nose. They were less heavily armed, and carried a smaller bomb load, but performance compared with the A and D series was considerably better. The Ju 88T-1 and T-3 were

photo-reconnaissance counterparts of the S-1 and S-3. Production of bomber and reconnaissance variants of the Ju 88 totalled ten thousand seven hundred and seventy-four, just over 60 per cent of the overall total. Other major versions are dealt with in the *Fighters, Attack and Training Aircraft 1939-45* volume. Towards the end of the war many Ju 88 airframes ended their days rather ignominiously as the explosive-laden lower portion of *Mistel* composite attack weapons, carrying a Bf 109 or Fw 190 pick-a-back fashion to guide them on to their targets.

32 **Douglas DB-7 series**
Douglas submitted its Model 7A design in a 1938 U.S. Army competition for a twin-engined attack bomber, and was authorised to build prototypes for evaluation. The first appeared as the improved Model 7B, with 1,100 hp Twin Wasp engines and a tricycle undercarriage, first flying on 26 October 1939. First customer was France, which ordered one hundred in February 1939; the first U.S. orders, for one hundred and eighty-six A-20's and A-20A's, followed three months later. These, with the manufacturer's designation DB-7, had a narrower but deeper fuselage. The first DB-7 was flown on 17 August 1939, with 1,050 hp Twin Wasps. On 14 October French DB-7 orders were increased to two hundred and seventy, the second batch to have uprated engines; six days later a further hundred were ordered, designated DB-7A and having 1,600 hp

Wright Cyclones. Little more than a hundred DB-7's had been delivered before the fall of France in 1940, and the remainder were diverted to Britain. The DB-7's were initially named Boston I and II by the RAF, but later converted into Havoc I fighters; the DB-7A's became Havoc II. In February 1940 Britain ordered one hundred and fifty DB-7B's (not to be confused with the original Model 7B). These were similar to the DB-7A, but with seven 0·303 in guns instead of the latter version's six 7·5 mm guns. The RAF ultimately received seven hundred and eighty-one, named Boston III. Nine hundred and ninety-nine A-20B's were built for the U.S. Army. Features of the RAF's Boston III were incorporated into eight hundred and eight A-20C's for the USAAF. Of these, two hundred and two went to the RAF designated Boston IIIA. Next major U.S. variant was the A-20G, two thousand eight hundred and fifty being built with the 'solid' nose of the fighter variants and bomb-carrying capacity later increased to 4,000 lb (1,814 kg). Production batches of the A-20G varied in armament, and some carried a ventral fuel tank. The four hundred and twelve A-20H's were similar apart from their 1,700 hp Twin Wasp engines. A one-piece moulded transparent nose characterised the A-20J (four hundred and fifty built) and A-20K (four hundred and thirteen built), known in the RAF as the Boston IV and V. Overall production of the DB-7 'family', including the Havoc fighter models, totalled seven thousand three hundred and eighty-five, and came to an end in September 1944. Almost half of this output went to the U.S.S.R., but USAAF and RAF variants served in all theatres of the war, undertaking a wide range of operational duties beyond those for which they were designed. Small quantities were employed by the U.S. Navy, and by the air forces of Brazil and Canada.

33 Douglas A-26 Invader

Although nowadays best known for its operational service in Korea, the Congo and Vietnam, the Douglas Invader's design was actually begun in January 1941, well before the U.S. entered World War 2. It was initiated as a successor to the Douglas A-20 Havoc, and in June 1941 the USAAF ordered three prototypes. The first of these was flown on 10 January 1942, but each was completed to a different configuration. The original XA-26 was an attack bomber, with a 3,000 lb (1,361 kg) internal bomb load, twin guns in its transparent nose section and two others in each of the dorsal and ventral turrets; the XA-26A, a night fighter, had a solid radar-carrying nose, four cannon in a ventral tray and four 0·50 in guns in the upper turret; while the XA-26B had a shorter nose mounting a single 75 mm cannon. In the initial production model, the A-26B, the armament was changed yet again (see caption on page 49), and the bomb load increased. Later production batches introduced R-2800-79 engines with water injection, boosting the power and performance at altitude, the number of nose guns was increased to eight, and additional gun-packs, rocket projectiles or 2,000 lb (907 kg) of bombs could be carried beneath the wings. To concentrate the firepower even more, the dorsal guns could be locked forward and fired by the pilot. Five hundred and thirty-five water-injection A-26B's were built, following the initial eight hundred and twenty by Douglas's Long Beach and Tulsa factories. The Invader made its European operational debut in the autumn of 1944, and its first Pacific appearance early in 1945. The A-26C, which appeared in 1945, also saw limited service before the war ended. This had the twin-gun transparent 'bombardier' nose, but was otherwise similar to the B model. With the arrival of VJ-day, large numbers of Invader orders were cancelled, but even so, one thousand and ninety-one A-26C's were completed. In Europe alone, A-26 series aircraft flew over eleven thousand sorties and dropped more than eighteen thousand tons of bombs for the loss of sixty-seven aircraft in combat; curiously, despite their formidable firepower, they destroyed only seven enemy aircraft during this period. After the war, redesignated in the B-26 series after the Martin Marauder was withdrawn in 1958, they became a standard post-war USAF type, and the latest models continue to serve in Vietnam some twenty-five years after their first operational mission.

34   Martin Baltimore

The Baltimore was designed specifically to British requirements, to provide an improved successor to the Martin 167 operated by the RAF as the Maryland. It appeared as the Martin 187, the first production aircraft (there was no separate prototype) flying on 14 June 1941, some thirteen months after the RAF had placed an order for four hundred. These were built as Baltimore Mks I (fifty), II (one hundred) and III (two hundred and fifty), all being similarly powered and having four wing guns and one rearward-firing and four-downward-firing ventral guns. Only the dorsal armament distinguished them, the Mks I and II having single and twin Vickers K guns respectively, while the Mk III had a Boulton Paul four-gun turret. The Baltimore was given the USAAF designation A-30, although none served with the American forces. Lend-Lease supplies included two hundred and eighty-one Baltimore IIIA's (identical to the Mk III), two hundred and ninety-four Mk IV's and six hundred Mk V's, bringing overall manufacture to one thousand five hundred and seventy-five before production ended in May 1944. The Baltimore IV (illustrated) replaced the Boulton Paul turret by a twin-gun Martin turret, and the Baltimore V was similar except for the up-rated 1,700 hp R-2600-29 engines. The Baltimore, like the Maryland, served exclusively in the Middle East theatre, where it equipped several squadrons of the RAF from the spring of 1942 onward. Two squadrons of the South African Air Force were also equipped with them, and several were operational in the Balkans area, especially over Yugoslavia, with the *Stormo Baltimore* of the Italian Co-Belligerent Air Force in 1944-45. A few others were handed over to the Royal Navy for non-operational duties.

35 Martin B-26 Marauder

Finishing the war with a combat loss rate of less than 1 per cent, the Marauder more than vindicated its early reputation as a 'widow maker', which arose chiefly from the high accident rate created by inexperienced pilots handling an unfamiliar and unusually heavy aeroplane. As the Martin 179, its design was entered for a 1939 U.S. Army design competition and was rewarded by an immediate order for two hundred and one aircraft without the usual prototype preliminaries. The first B-26, flown on 25 November 1940, exhibited a modest armament, compared with later models, of only five defensive guns. Delivery to USAAC units began in 1941, in which year there also appeared the B-26A, with heavier calibre nose and tail guns, provision for extra fuel tanks in the bomb bay and for carrying a torpedo beneath the fuselage. One hundred and thirty-nine B-26A's were completed, making their operational debut from Australian bases in the spring of 1942. The B-26 also appeared in action from Alaskan and North African bases. Then followed the B-26B, with uprated engines and increased armament. Of the one thousand eight hundred and eighty-three built, all but the first six hundred and forty-one B-26B's also introduced a new, extended-span wing and taller tail. The B-26B made its operational debut in Europe in May 1943, subsequently becoming one of the hardest-worked Allied medium bombers in this theatre. One thousand two hundred and ten B-26C's were built, essentially similar to the later B models. These were succeeded by the B-26F (three hundred built), in which the wing incidence was increased with the purpose of improving take-off performance and reducing the accident rate. The final model was the B-26G, which differed only slightly from the F; nine hundred and fifty G models were completed, the last being delivered in March 1945. Of the overall U.S. production supplies to the RAF under Lend-Lease included fifty-two B-26A's (as Marauder I's), two hundred B-26F's (Marauder II) and one hundred and fifty B-26G's (Marauder III). Many other Marauders were completed for the USAAF as AT-23 or TB-26 trainers, and some for the U.S. Navy as JM-1's.

36 PZL P.37 Łoś (Elk)

This elegant Polish medium bomber was among the best of its type to appear in the 1930s, but lack of appreciation of its qualities by the Army authorities controlling aircraft procurement for the Polish Air Force denied it the commercial and operational successes that it deserved. The original design, by Jerzy Dabrowski, received approval from the Department of Aeronautics in October 1934, and was developed under the designation P.37. In August 1935 work began on two flying prototypes and a static test airframe, and the P.37/I flew late in June 1936 with two 873 hp Polish-built Bristol Pegasus XIIB engines. This prototype, and nine of the first ten similarly powered Łoś A production aircraft, had a single fin and rudder. The P.37/II prototype, and all other production Łoś bombers, had a twin-tail assembly. The P.37/II, which flew in April 1937, was prototype for the Łoś B, differing principally in its more powerful Pegasus XX engines and an ingenious cantilever main landing gear. Orders were placed for twenty more Łoś A's and one hundred and fifty Łoś B's, the majority to be delivered by 1 April 1939. Delivery of the Łoś B began in autumn 1938, when the existing Łoś A's were fitted with dual controls and transferred to operational conversion training with No 213 Squadron. The Army used devious means to denigrate the P.37's operational worth, cutting back military orders for the Łoś B in April 1939 when only a hundred had been completed. The P.37/II was refitted with several alternative engines, including the Gnome-Rhône 14N.1 of 970 hp and the 14N.20/21 of 1,050 hp, which were intended for use in the proposed Łoś C and Łoś D export models. Before the outbreak of war PZL had received encouraging orders from Bulgaria, Rumania, Turkey and Yugoslavia; and had good prospects of further sales or licences in Belgium, Denmark, Estonia and Greece. However, none of these aircraft were delivered, and the Polish Air Force itself had only some ninety Łoś bombers on charge when the war began. Of these, thirty-six were with Nos 211, 212, 216 and 217 Squadrons of the Tactical Air Force's Bomber Brigade which had been formed in the previous summer. In the second week of fighting nine more were acquired, but twenty-six of the forty-five operational machines were lost during the sixteen days before the U.S.S.R. invaded Poland from the east. The surviving aircraft, with twenty-seven others from Brzesc airfield, were withdrawn to Rumania, in whose colours subsequently fought against Soviet forces. Variants included an abortive heavy fighter project with an eight-gun 'solid' nose, and the P.49/I Miś (Teddy Bear). The latter, incomplete when the war started, was the prototype for a more powerful and more heavily armed bomber version.

37 **Mitsubishi Ki-21**
The Ki-21 won an exacting design competition initiated by the Japanese Army Air Force early in 1936, and the first of five prototypes was completed in November of that year. With improved fields of fire for the defensive guns, and 850 hp Nakajima Ha-5-*Kai* engines replacing the Mitsubishi Kinsei Ha-6's of the first prototype, it was accepted for initial production as the Ki-21-Ia, or Type 97 heavy

bomber. It entered JAAF service in 1937, and in 1938 Nakajima began to contribute to the production programme, delivering its first Ki-21 in August. The Model 1A was quickly succeeded by the Model 1B (Ki-21-Ib), into which were built modifications resulting from combat experience during the fighting with China. Increases were made in protective armour for the crew, defensive armament and the sizes of the flaps and bomb bay. The Model 1C (Ki-21-Ic) had increased fuel and an extra lateral gun. A wider-span tailplane was introduced on the Model 2A (Ki-21-IIa). Mitsubishi began the development of this late in 1939, replacing the former power-plant by 1,490 hp Ha-101 engines. The Ki-21 was a standard Army bomber at the time of Pearl Harbor, and was subsequently encountered in Burma, Hong Kong, India, Malaya, the Netherlands East Indies and the Philippines. Under the Allied code-naming system, the Ki-21 was known as 'Sally', although the name 'Gwen' was briefly allocated to the Model 2B (Ki-21-IIb) before it was recognised as a Ki-21 variant. The Model 2B was the final production variant of this now-obsolescent bomber, recognisable by the turret replacing the dorsal 'greenhouse' of the earlier models. With its appearance, many earlier Ki-21's were withdrawn either for training or for conversion to MC-21 transports. Shortly before the war ended, nine Ki-21's were made ready as assault transports at Kyushu, to transfer demolition troops to Okinawa, but only one

reached its target. Production came to an end in September 1944 after one thousand seven hundred and thirteen had been built by Mitsubishi, plus three hundred and fifty-one by Nakajima (up to February 1941). Just over five hundred transport counterparts of the Ki-21 were built by Mitsubishi, designated MC-20 in their civil form and Ki-57 (code-name 'Topsy') in military guise. Proposals for a Ki-21-III version were shelved in favour of the Ki-67.

38 Mitsubishi G4M

The G4M was evolved to a 'range-at-all-costs' specification, issued by the Japanese Navy in 1937 for a twin-engined medium bomber. Kiro Honjo, who led the design team, could only accomplish this by packing so much fuel into the wings that no armour protection could be provided for the fuel tanks or the crew. Then, after the prototype G4M1 had flown in October 1939, Mitsubishi were instructed to adapt the design for bomber escort duties, with increased armament and a crew of ten. Thirty G6M1's, as this version was known, had been built and service tested before the JNAF admitted their performance was inadequate and abandoned the project. The aircraft subsequently served as G6M1-K trainers and later still as G6M1-L2 troop transports. By the end of March 1941, however, fourteen more G4M1 bombers had been flown, and in April this version was accepted for service with the JNAF as the Model 11 land-based attack bomber. The G4M1 had a single 20 mm tail gun, with 7·7 mm guns in each of the nose, ventral and dorsal positions; powerplant was two 1,530 hp Mitsubishi Kasei 11 radials. The G4M1 was used by Japan in pre-war operations in south-east China, and by the time of her entry into World War 2 there were some one hundred and eighty G4M1's in service with the JNAF. They scored a number of early successes, but the 1,100 gallons (5,000 litres) of unprotected fuel in their tanks made them extremely vulnerable and the bomber soon became known to U.S. gunners as the 'one-shot lighter'. Three months after particularly heavy losses in the Solomons campaign of August 1942, Mitsubishi began work on the G4M2 Model 22. This had an improved armament, and 1,850 hp Kasei 21 engines with methanol injection; the fuel capacity was increased, but still the tanks remained unprotected. Nevertheless, the G4M2 became the major production model, appearing in five other versions: the G4M2a Model 24 (bulged bomb doors, Kasei 25 engines); G4M2b Model 25 (Kasei 27's); G4M2c Model 26 (total of two 20 mm and four 7·7 mm guns); G4M2d (for flight-testing the Ne-20 turbojet engine); and the G4M2e Model 24-J (four 20 mm guns and one 7·7 mm). Model 24-J's were later adapted as carriers for the Ohka suicide aircraft. Late in 1943, in the face of continuing heavy losses, Mitsubishi built sixty examples of the G4M3a Model 34 and G4M3b Model 36. These carried a reduced fuel load of 968

gallons (4,400 litres), in fully protected tanks, in a much-re-designed wing. Total production of G4M's (Allied code name 'Betty') amounted to two thousand four hundred and seventy-nine aircraft, many of which were converted to 20-seat troop transports towards the end of the war. Flight trials of a G4M3c Model 37, with exhaust-driven superchargers were partially completed before VJ-day; another project, the G4M4, was abandoned.

39 Mitsubishi Ki-67 Hiryu (Flying Dragon)

Design of the Ki-67, led by Dr Hisanojo Ozawa, began late in 1941 to a JAAF specification issued early that year. The first prototype was flown at the beginning of 1943, and by the end of that year fifteen Ki-67's had been completed. The Hiryu showed a considerable advancement over earlier Army bombers, not only in performance but in the degree of armour protection afforded to the crew members and the fuel installation. It was ordered into production in Model 1A form (Ki-67-Ia) early in 1944, and began to enter service during the summer. First combat appearance of the Ki-67 (code-named 'Peggy' by the Allies) was during the Battle of the Philippine Sea, where it was flown by Army crews but operated as a torpedo bomber under the direction of the Japanese Navy. The Model 1A was soon supplanted in production by the Model 1B (Ki-67-Ib), in which the former's flush-mounted beam guns were replaced by transparent blisters. By the end of the war

Mitsubishi had built six hundred and six Hiryus, while others had been completed by Kawasaki (ninety-one), Nippon Hikoki (twenty-nine) and the Army Air Arsenal (one). The majority of Ki-67's operated from Kyushu, and were encountered during the final year of the war in the Iwo Jima, Marianas and Okinawa battle areas, among others. Some became test-beds for the proposed Ki-67-II (two 2,500 hp Ha-214 engines), but this was still incomplete when the war ended. One development that did materialise was the Ki-109 'heavy' fighter. This replaced the originally proposed Ki-69 escort fighter version of the Hiryu, and the later Ki-112 project of 1943. Two Model 1B bombers were assigned early in 1944 to the Tachikawa Army Air Arsenal, where they were converted to mount a 75 mm Type 88 cannon in the nose, the only other armament being a 12·7 mm tail gun. Twenty of these 4-seat fighters were built, but Mitsubishi's inability to deliver any of the Ha-104ru turbo-supercharged engines intended for them caused them to be fitted with the same non-supercharged units as the bomber versions. With these they were unable to reach the combat altitude necessary to carry out the task for which they had been built – interception of the B-29 Superfortress bombers attacking Japan.

40 Nakajima Ki-49 Donryu

The first prototype Ki-49 was flown in August 1939, having been designed to a JAAF specification issued at the end of the preceding year. It was followed by a second prototype, each being powered by Nakajima Ha-5B engines. The Ki-49 had been evolved as a replacement for the Mitsubishi Ki-21, with the object of overcoming the slow speed and poor defensive armament of the latter; but the prototypes proved less than 20 mph (32 kmh) faster than the Ki-21, had a poor operational ceiling and were armed only with a single 20 mm cannon and two 7·92 mm machine-guns. Some improvement was made in subsequent prototypes, and in the Ki-49-I Model 1 which entered production in the late spring of 1940, by installing 1,250 hp Ha-41 engines. One hundred and twenty-nine Ki-49-I's were built at Ota, and the name Donryu was bestowed by the manufacturer, after the well-known Shinto shrine there. (A colloquial translation of Donryu is 'Dragon Swallower'.) In the Allied coding system the Ki-49 was known as 'Helen'. The Ki-49-IIa, the next production version, had three additional 7·92 mm guns; in the Ki-49-IIb all five machine-guns were of 12·7 mm calibre. Six hundred and forty-nine Ki-49-II's were built by Nakajima, fifty by Tachikawa and a small number by Mansyu. The parent company also completed six examples of a Ki-49-III, with 2,500 hp Ha-117 engines, but this version was not developed, and production of the Donryu ceased in December 1944. First operational appearance of the Ki-49-I was on 19 February 1942, when a force of them attacked Port Darwin in Australia from New

Guinea. The Ki-49-II, which entered service in the following September, was encountered in the China-Burma-India theatre, the Netherlands East Indies, Formosa and the Philippines. After the Leyte Island campaign, in which many were lost, they were extensively used for suicide attacks, though some were employed for mine detection and coastal patrol. A Ki-49, carrying Emperor Hirohito's envoy to Okinawa to sign the surrender agreement on 19-20 August 1945, made the last flight of the war by a JAAF aircraft. Such was the insistence on engine power and defensive armament that the Ki-49 inevitably suffered from having a small bomb load and inadequate range. Three Ki-58 fighter prototypes, based on the Ki-49-IIa, were built with five 20 mm and three 12·7 mm guns; and two Ki-49-III's were converted as formation leaders with the designation Ki-80.

41 Mitsubishi Ki-46

The Ki-46, in terms of aerodynamics and performance one of the best Japanese aircraft to serve during World War 2, was designed by Tomio Kubo to a JAAF requirement issued in December 1937. The specification was a rigorous one, for a fast, high altitude, long range, twin-engined reconnaissance aeroplane capable of speeds more than 50 mph (80 km/hr) faster than the latest western single-engined fighters. These demands were met by ingenious weight-saving and excellent streamlining, and the first prototype, powered by 875 hp

Mitsubishi Ha-26-I engines, was flown in November 1939. The aircraft entered immediate production as the Ki-46-I, or Army Type 100 Model 1 Command Reconnaissance monoplane. The initial thirty-four aircraft were similarly powered, and were armed with a single 7·7 mm Type 89 machine-gun on a movable mounting in the rear cabin. They were used mostly for service trials and crew training, the main production version being the Ki-46-II Model 2, which first flew in March 1941. One thousand and ninety-three Model 2's were built, with 1,080 hp Ha-102 engines providing enhanced performance. Delivery of these began in July 1941, initially to JAAF units in Manchuria and China. The Ki-46 (code named 'Dinah' by the Allies) subsequently appeared in virtually every theatre of the Pacific war. A few Ki-46-II's were also used by the Japanese Navy, and others were converted in 1943 to Ki-46-II-Kai operational trainers, with a second, raised cockpit behind the pilot's cabin. In December 1942 two prototypes were flown of the Ki-46-III, and six hundred and nine Model 3's were completed. The Ki-46-IIIa featured a modified nose canopy, eliminating the former step in front of the pilot's cabin, carried additional fuel and dispensed with the dorsal gun. Four prototypes were also built in 1945 of the Ki-46-IVa, basically similar but with turbo-supercharged Ha-112-IIru engines, but no production was undertaken. The entire one thousand seven hundred and forty-two Ki-46's were built by Mitsubishi at Nagoya and, later, at Toyama. In 1944, however, a substantial quantity of Model 3's began to be converted to Ki-46-III-Kai fighters by the Army Aeronautical Research Institute at Tachikawa for Japanese home defence. Conversion involved a 'stepped' nose, broadly similar to the original one, housing two 20 mm Ho-5 cannon and, between the front and rear crew cabins, a 37 mm Ho-203 cannon fixed to fire forward and upward. The Ki-46-IIIb, of which a few were built for ground attack, was similar, but omitted the dorsal cannon. Projected fighter variants included the Ki-46-IIIc (twin Ho-5's) and Ki-46-IVb (two nose-mounted Ho-5's).

42 Yokosuka P1Y1 Ginga (Milky Way)

The Ginga, code-named 'Frances' by the Allies, was evolved to a Japanese Navy 15-Shi (1940) requirement for a land-based bomber and dive bomber, though the first of several prototypes was not flown until early 1943. Designated Y-20, it was a handsome, well-built aeroplane with retractable under-wing air brakes. With its construction simplified and additional armour protection for the crew, the bomber was accepted for the JNAF as the P1Y1 Model 11. Production was undertaken by the Nakajima factories at Koizumi and Fukushima, which had built nine hundred and six Ginga bombers by the end of the war; delivery to combat units began in spring 1944. The Ginga was employed chiefly

from land bases in Japan, especially from the island of Kyushu. In place of the usual single dorsal gun, some aircraft had a turret mounting twin 12·7 mm or 20 mm guns. Despite excellent flying qualities, the Ginga's operational career was restricted by the lack of skilled production staff, efficient pilots and fuel. Difficulties were also encountered with the Homare engines, which had been installed at the direction of the Navy. At Okinawa, many Gingas were employed as suicide aircraft. Kawanishi, invited to develop a night-fighter version of the Ginga, decided to replace the troublesome Homare with the more reliable Mitsubishi Kasei 25 radial of 1,850 hp. Kawanishi proposed two new variants – the P1Y2 bomber and the P1Y2-S night fighter – but preference was given to the latter type. A prototype was flown in June 1944, and ninety-six production aircraft, designated P1Y2-S Model 26 Kyokko (Aurora), were built. They carried elementary AI radar, and were armed with three 20 mm cannon, one on a movable mounting in the rear cabin and the other pair fixed to fire forward and upward from amidships. Despite Japan's urgent need of a strong home defence, the P1Y2-S had still only reached trials units when the war ended. The only operational night fighters were a few P1Y1-S conversions of Nakajima-built bombers. Some of these had a hand-operated dorsal turret with two 20 mm cannon, but none carried radar. One Ginga was used in 1945 to flight-test the Ne-20 turbojet engine. A further night fighter, P1Y3-S with 1,990 hp Homare engines, was projected but not built; and another proposed variant, the Ginga-Kai, was to have acted as parent aircraft for the Model 22 version of the Ohka suicide aircraft.

43 Heinkel He 177 Greif (Griffin)

The fact that the He 177 was the only German long-range strategic bomber to go into series production during World War 2 was doubtless due chiefly to the official indecision and political interference with its development that gave little chance of its initial design faults being satisfactorily overcome before it was pressed into service. Had it been permitted a natural and uninterrupted development, its story might have been very different, for it was basically a conventional design in all but one respect. This was the radical decision to employ pairs of coupled engines, each pair in a single nacelle, driving a single propeller. It was designed to a 1938 specification for a dual-purpose heavy bomber and anti-shipping aircraft, and was, unbelievably, required to be stressed for dive bombing. The first prototype, flown on 19 November 1939, just managed to keep within the overall weight limits of the specification, but service variants of the He 177 became progressively heavier. More ominous, however, was the curtailment of the first flight due to engine overheating, which was to plague the He 177 throughout its career. Eight prototypes were completed,

followed by thirty-five pre-production He 177A-0's built by Arado and Heinkel and one hundred and thirty Arado-built He 177A-1's. The early aircraft in this batch were used for further trials, and after a brief and unhappy operational debut the remainder were also withdrawn from service. From late 1942 they were replaced by one hundred and seventy Heinkel-built A-3's and eight hundred and twenty-six A-5's, which had longer fuselages and repositioned engine nacelles. Main combat area of these models was the Eastern Front, where the bomber's use also for ground-attack produced some interesting variations in armament. Other He 177A's were employed as transports, and certain variants were equipped to carry Hs 293 or FX 1400 missiles externally. A few A-6's were built, but by now attention was being diverted to developing the *Greif* with four separately mounted engines. When the German forces evacuated Paris the prototype He 274A (formerly the He 177A-4) was still awaiting its first flight at the Farman factory at Suresnes. One He 177A-3 airframe became the four-engined He 277, to which Heinkel gave the false designation He 177B to overcome official disapproval of the re-engined design. This flew late in 1943 with four 1,730 hp DB 603A engines, followed by two more prototypes and a small production batch, but these did not enter squadron service.

44 Curtiss C-46 Commando

Designed by Curtiss-Wright in 1936 as a 36-seat commercial airliner designated CW-20, the prototype of this capacious transport (NX 19436) first flew on 26 March 1940. It was evaluated by the U.S. Army, under the designation C-55, but was then restored to civil standard and purchased by BOAC, who named it *St Louis* and operated it as a 24-seater between Gibraltar and Malta and on longer routes. The USAAF ordered an initial twenty-five, further modified and having 2,000 hp Pratt & Whitney R-2800-43 Twin Wasp engines, for service as C-46 troop and freight transports. Originally named Condor III, the C-46 was later renamed Commando, and was produced in substantial numbers for the USAAF and U.S. Navy. The two major production models were the C-46A (one thousand four hundred and ninety-one built) and C-46D (one thousand four hundred and ten), the former having a single, large loading door while the latter had double freight doors and a remodelled nose section. The B, C, G, H, K and L variants were experimental models that did not go into production, the other Army models being the single-door C-46E (seventeen built) and double-door C-46F (two hundred and thirty-four built). These were counterparts to the A and D models, with R-2800-75 instead of -51 engines. One hundred and sixty R5C-1's (corresponding to the C-46A) were also built for the U.S. Marine Corps, with whom they performed invaluable supply and casualty evacuation duties. The Army aircraft, employed predominantly in the Far East, became

famous for their round-the-clock flights across the Himalayas to keep open the supply routes between Burma and China. They first appeared in Europe in March 1945, when they were used to drop paratroops during the Rhine crossing. Compared with the civil prototype, the military Commando could airlift up to 40 troops, 33 stretcher cases or a 10,000 lb (4,536 kg) payload of freight or military equipment.

45 Douglas C-47 Skytrain series

First Douglas Commercial transports to be acquired by the U.S. services were a number of DC-2's (Army C-32A and C-34, Navy R2D-1), followed by thirty-five C-39's with DC-2 fuselages and the DC-3's tail surfaces and outer wing panels. The principal wartime versions of the DC-3 were the Twin Wasp-engined C-47 Skytrain, C-53 Skytrooper and the Navy R4D series, differing in minor detail only, except for their function. The first nine hundred and fifty-three C-47's were troop or cargo transports; they were followed in 1942 by four thousand nine hundred and ninety-one C-47A's, and from 1943 by three thousand one hundred and eight C-47B's, all by Douglas. One hundred and thirty-three TC-47B's were also built, for training duties. The Skytrooper, as its name implied, was specifically a troop transport, of which Douglas produced one hundred and ninety-three C-53's, eight C-53B's, seventeen C-53C's and one hundred and fifty-nine

C-53D's from 1941 to 1943. Seventeen C-117A VIP transports were delivered in 1945. Commercial airline DST's (Douglas Sleeper Transports) or DC-3's impressed for war service included thirty-six with designations C-48 to C-48C, one hundred and thirty-eight C-49 to C-49K, fourteen C-50 to C-50D, one C-51, five C-52 to C-52C, two C-68 and four C-84. The Sky-trooper preceded the C-47 into service (October 1941), despite its higher designation number; the first Skytrains were delivered in January 1942. More than one thousand two hundred were supplied under Lend-Lease to the RAF, by whom they were known as Dakota Mks I to IV. They first entered service with No 31 Squadron in Burma in June 1942. Additional roles included casualty evacuation and glider towing. Total wartime production of military DC-3's, which ended in August 1945, amounted to ten thousand one hundred and twenty-three, mostly built by Douglas. Nor was this all: in addition to about seven hundred supplied to the U.S.S.R. under Lend-Lease, the Soviet engineer Boris Lisunov spent some time at Douglas prior to initiating pro-duction of a Soviet-built version known as the Li-2 (formerly PS-84). Some two thousand were built in the U.S.S.R., including some with a gun turret just above and behind the crew cabin. Licence production was also undertaken in Japan, where Showa built three hundred and eighty L2D2's and L2D3's for the JNAF (code-named 'Tabby' by the Allies) and Nakajima completed a further seventy.

46 Consolidated PBY Catalina

First flown as the XP3Y-1 on 21 March 1935, the Consolidated Model 28 was the first U.S. military flying boat with cantilever wings. Sixty were ordered as PBY-1's in 1935, deliveries (to Squadron VP-11F) beginning in October 1936. Fifty PBY-2's followed in 1937-38, and in the latter year three PBY-3's and a manufacturing licence were sold to the U.S.S.R. The Soviet version, designated GST, was powered by M-62 engines. Orders for the U.S. Navy continued with sixty-six PBY-3's and thirty-three PBY-4's, the latter introducing the prominent lateral observation blisters that characterised most subsequent versions. The RAF received one Model 28-5 for evalu-ation in July 1939, resulting in an order for fifty aircraft similar to the U.S. Navy's PBY-5. The RAF name Catalina was subsequently adopted for the PBY's in USN service. During 1940 the RAF doubled its original order, and others were ordered by Australia (eighteen), Canada (fifty), France (thirty) and the Netherlands East Indies (thirty-six). Of the U.S. Navy's original order for two hundred PBY-5's, the final thirty-three were completed as PBY-5A amphibians, and an additional one hundred and thirty-four were ordered to -5A standard. Twelve later became RAF Catalina III's, and twelve more were included in the NEI contract. Seven hundred and fifty-three PBY-5's were built, and seven hundred and ninety-four PBY-5A's, fifty-six of the latter for the USAF as OA-10's. Lend-Lease supplies to Britain included two hundred and twenty-five PBY-5B's (Catalina IA) and ninety-seven Catalina IVA's with ASV radar. Production continued with the tall-finned Naval Aircraft Factory PBN-1 Nomad (one hundred and fifty-six, most of which went to the U.S.S.R.) and the similar PBY-6A amphibian (two hundred and thirty-five, including seventy-five Army OA-10B's and forty-eight for the U.S.S.R.). Canadian Vickers-built amphibians went to the USAAF (two hundred and thirty OA-10A's) and RCAF (one hundred and forty-nine Cansos). Boeing (Canada) production included two hundred and forty PB2B-1's (mostly as RAF Catalina IVB's), seventeen RCAF Catalinas, fifty tall-finned PB2B-2's (RAF Catalina VI) and fifty-five RCAF Cansos. Total U.S./Canadian production of PBY models was three thousand two hundred and ninety, to which were added several hundred GST's built in the U.S.S.R.

47 Saab-18

The Saab-18 originated, under the project designation L 11, as a twin-engined recconaissance aircraft, two prototypes being ordered in November 1939 and February 1940. By the time the first of these flew on 19 June 1942 changing tactical requirements had caused it to be developed primarily as a light day bomber and dive bomber. In general configuration it closely resembled the Dornier Do 215 bomber, except that the crew cabin was offset to port to improve the pilot's downward vision. With 1,065 hp Twin Wasp engines, the prototype had been somewhat underpowered; nevertheless, in July 1942 production was started of an initial batch of sixty aircraft with these engines, and these began to enter *Flygvapnet* service in June 1944 in B 18A bomber and S 18A reconnaissance forms. On 10 June 1944 the prototype was flown of the B 18B, powered by two of the 1,475 hp Daimler Benz DB 605B in-line engines which by then were being licence-built in Sweden for the Saab-21 fighter. The production B 18B's, one hundred and twenty of which were completed, did not enter service until after the war (1946). They had a maximum internal bomb load of 3,307 lb (1,500 kg), a fixed armament of one 7·9 mm and two 13·2 mm guns, ejection seats for the pilot and navigator, and provision for carrying rocket projectiles beneath the wings. The final production version was the T 18B, whose prototype was flown on 7 July 1945; sixty-two were built. Originally intended as a torpedo-bomber, the T 18B served finally in the attack role, carrying a two-man crew and armed with one 57 mm Bofors gun and two 20 mm cannon. This version remained in service until 1956.

48 Dornier Do 217

A substantial number of Do 217 prototypes were built, the first of them flying in August 1938 and generally resembling a scaled-up Do 215B. All of the first six incorporated a novel four-leaf air brake, opening umbrella-style in operation and forming an extension of the rear fuselage when retracted. This feature proved troublesome to operate and was discarded on later models. First major series was the Do 217E, which entered production in 1941 following service trials with a small pre-series batch of Do 217A-0's in the preceding year. Numerous E sub-types appeared, powered by various models of the BMW 801 radial engine and differing in armament and other equipment. The Do 217E-5 carried additional radio gear for launching and guiding two underwing Hs 293 missiles. Many E-2's later became Do 217J night fighters. The next bomber series, with a redesigned and even more bulbous nose than its predecessors, was the Do 217K (1,700 hp BMW 801D). The K-2 and K-3 sub-types could carry special anti-shipping weapons beneath extended wings of 81 ft 4$\frac{3}{8}$ in (24·80 m) span. In-line engines – 1,750 hp DB 603A's – appeared in the Do 217M series, many of which were also converted later for night fighting as the Do 217N. Final production model, a reconnaissance version, was the Do 217P (also with DB 603A's), but only six of these were built. The Do 217W (or Do 216) twin-float torpedo bomber project remained uncompleted, and only prototypes were completed of the much-developed Do 317. Total output of Do 217 variants reached one thousand seven hundred and

thirty, all except three hundred and sixty-four of these being bomber models. The Do 217 night fighters are described in the *Fighters, Attack and Training Aircraft 1939–45* volume.

49 **Dornier Do 17 and Do 215**
The Do 17 was evolved originally as a 6-passenger, high-speed mailplane for Deutsche Luft hansa, the Do 17V1 first prototype making its maiden flight in the autumn of 1934. Three single-finned prototypes were built for DLH, but the extreme slimness of the aeroplane was its commercial undoing, the narrow fuselage demanding extraordinary agility by passengers in order to reach their seats. However, the RLM decided to evaluate the design in its efforts to procure a new medium bomber for the *Luftwaffe*. Further prototypes were ordered, the first of them (Do 17V4) setting the future design pattern by having twin fins and rudders. The specially stripped Do 17V8, with boosted engines, created a considerable stir at the Zürich International Military Aircraft Competition in July 1937, when its performance clearly outshone even the best of the single-seat fighters being displayed. By this time two production versions of the aircraft were already in *Luftwaffe* squadron service, and in 1938 joined the Condor Legion in the Spanish Civil War. These were the Do 17E-1 bomber, with 750 hp BMW VI engines and a 1,764 lb (800 kg) bomb load, and its reconnaissance-bomber counterpart, the Do 17F-1. Impressed by the V8's performance at Zürich, the Yugoslav Govern-

ment ordered twenty of an export version, designated Do 17K and powered by 986 hp Gnome-Rhône 14N radials, which improved both speed and range. This model was later licence-built in Yugoslavia, and when Germany invaded the country in April 1941 seventy were in service; the few that survived the fighting were allocated to the Croatian Air Force after the Nazi occupation. To maintain the Do 17's performance in relation to contemporary fighters, two new production models appeared with supercharged engines. These were the Do 17M (900 hp Bramo 323A) and Do 17P series (865 hp BMW 132N), otherwise generally corresponding to the E and F models. Two experimental series, the Do 17R and Do 17S, between them gave rise to the Do 17U, a pathfinder bomber with DB 600A engines, and then to the Do 17Z. The latter, with Bramo 323A or 1,000 hp Bramo 323P's, featured a more angular, bulbous front fuselage, and over five hundred Z models were built for bombing, reconnaissance and training. Two of the pre-production Do 17Z-0's, redesignated Do 215V1 and V2, became foreign demonstrators with Bramo and Gnome-Rhône engines respectively. The only foreign order received was from Sweden, for eighteen Do 215A-1's with DB 601A engines, but these were taken over by the *Luftwaffe* before delivery. They were followed by one hundred and one Do 215B's, most of which were similar except for the B-5, a night fighter/intruder version with a six-gun 'solid' nose. Development subsequently continued as the Do 217, described separately.

50 Armstrong Whitworth Whitley

Oldest of the three standard RAF twin-engined bombers at the outbreak of World War 2, the Whitley was designed to Specification B.3/34, and the first prototype (K 4586) was flown on 17 March 1936. Thirty-four Mk I Whitleys were built, powered by 795 hp Armstrong Siddeley Tiger IX radial engines, and the first deliveries were made to No 10 Squadron in March 1937. Late-production Mk I's introduced dihedral on the wings, which became standard for all subsequent machines. The forty-six Mk II's were followed by eighty Mk III's with 920 hp Tiger VIII engines and a retractable ventral turret aft of the wing trailing-edge. A change was made to in-line engines in the Mks IV and IVA, thirty-three and seven of which were completed with 1,030 hp Merlin IV and 1,145 hp Merlin X engines respectively. Merlin X's were also adopted for the main wartime version, the Mk V, of which one thousand four hundred and sixty-six were produced. This was redesigned with a longer fuselage and tail fins of a modified shape. One hundred and forty-six Whitley VII's were produced for general reconnaissance work with Coastal Command, having increased range and carrying ASV radar for anti-shipping patrols. A number of Mk V's were later converted to Mk VII standard. Strictly speaking, the Whitley was obsolete as a bomber by the outbreak of war, when the RAF had two hundred and seven (mostly Mks I to IV) on charge; and its first operational missions were leaflet-dropping and security patrols. However, in company with Hampdens, Whitleys made the first bombing raid of the war on German soil on 19-20 March 1940, and in June 1940 became the first British bombers to attack a target in Italy. Their front-line career ended late in 1942, when even the reconnaissance versions were withdrawn, but they continued to serve for the remainder of the war in the valuable, if less glamorous, roles of troop and freight transport and glider tug. Fifteen Whitley V's were converted for freighter duties with BOAC in the spring of 1942, but (except for one casualty) were returned to the RAF by 1943.

51 Handley Page Hampden

Following the Whitley and Wellington, the Hampden was the third of Britain's trio of twin-engined medium bombers to enter service, two hundred and twenty-six being on RAF strength on 3 September 1939, serving with ten squadrons. Designed to the same Specification (B.9/32) as the Wellington, the first of the two Hampden prototypes (K 4240) flew for the first time on 21 June 1936. An initial order, for one hundred and eighty Hampden Mk I's to Specification 30/36, followed two months later, and these began to be delivered from September 1938, the first recipient being No 49 Squadron. In production Hampdens the rather ugly square-

cut nose section was replaced by a curved Perspex moulding, the rear gun installations were modified and Pegasus XVIII's replaced the original Pegasus P.E.5S(a) engines. Even with these improvements, the Hampden was a disappointment operationally, the field of fire being very limited and the extremely narrow fuselage produced excessive fatigue for the 4-man crew. Later attempts to mitigate the bomber's defensive shortcomings by fitting twin guns in each of the rearward-firing positions improved the situation only marginally. Nevertheless, Hampdens continued in operational service with Bomber Command, principally on night bombing raids or minelaying, until September 1942, and many of them continued in service as torpedo bombers or reconnaissance aircraft with Coastal Command for a year or more after this. During their service Hampdens took part in the first bombing raids on Berlin and in the first of the 1,000-bomber raids on Cologne. One thousand two hundred and seventy Hampdens were built in the United Kingdom by Handley Page (five hundred) and English Electric (seven hundred and seventy). In Canada, Canadian Associated Aircraft Ltd also completed one hundred and sixty in 1940–41. Two Hampdens were re-engined with 1,000 hp Wright GR-1820-G105A Cyclones as prototypes for a Mk II version, but this did not go into production. Concurrently with the first RAF order, however, a contract had also been placed for one hundred of a variant with 1,000 hp Napier Dagger in-line engines, named Hereford; this order was later increased to one hundred and fifty. These were built by Short Bros & Harland, but due to powerplant problems, many of these were later re-engined to become Hampdens. Those that remained as Herefords served with operational training units only.

52 Fiat B.R.20 Cicogna (Stork)

The B.R.20 (indicating *Bombardamento Rosatelli*, after its designer) was evolved in 1935 to provide the *Regia Aeronautica* with a fast, well-armed light bomber. The prototype's first flight, on 10 February 1936, was soon followed by the initial production B.R.20, with 1,000 hp Fiat A.80 RC 41 engines and various detail modifications. The first of these entered service with the 13° *Stormo Bombardamento Terrestre* in September 1936. Before the outbreak of World War 2 Fiat also built two B.R.20L, these being demilitarised models for international competitions and record flights. From the summer of 1937, B.R.20 bombers became engaged in the Spanish Civil War, and in June 1940 this type equipped four bomber *Stormi*, some two hundred and fifty having been built up to that time. Meanwhile, late in 1939 the prototype had been flown of the B.R.20M (for *Modificato*), an improved version characterised chiefly by its somewhat longer fuselage, better-contoured nose section and strengthened wings. About sixty of these were in service in June 1940, and series production continued until summer 1942, at

which time five hundred and eighty had been completed. The majority of these were built as B.R.20M's; at least a hundred were B.R.20's, but many of these aircraft were later brought up to B.R.20M standard. They were used regularly during the early part of the war for bombing duties in the Mediterranean area, the Eastern Front, and, briefly, with the *Corpo Aereo Italiano* based in Belgium for attacks on the United Kingdom. By the end of 1942, when they began to be replaced by later types, their main duties were coastal reconnaissance and convoy patrol, and many others were employed as operational trainers. Late in 1940 Fiat flight-tested the first prototype of a much redesigned model designated B.R.20bis, and a second was flown in 1942. This version had increased armament and bomb load, installed in a considerably refined fuselage with a nose section reminiscent of the Heinkel He 111 and He 115. The use of 1,250 hp Fiat A.82 RC 32 engines gave a marked increase in performance, but only a dozen or so of this model appear to have reached squadron service. In 1938 eighty-five B.R.20's were supplied to Japan, where they were used by the JAAF as an interim type in China pending quantity deliveries of the Mitsubishi Ki-21.

53 North American B-25 Mitchell

North American Aviation was awarded an immediate production contract for its NA-62 design, without the usual preliminary prototypes, and the first B-25 was flown on 19 August 1940. By the end of the year twenty-four had been delivered, all except the first nine having the gull-winged appearance that was a characteristic of the bomber. They were followed in 1941 by forty B-25A's, then by one hundred and nineteen B-25's with dorsal and ventral gun turrets. First operational unit was the 17th Bombardment Group, which began to receive its B-25's in 1941. Production continued with one thousand six hundred and nineteen B-25C's and two thousand two hundred and ninety B-25D's from early 1942, and in April that year B-25B's flying off the USS *Hornet* made their epic raid on Tokyo. The B-25E and F were experimental models, production continuing with the B-25G, which carried two 0·50 in guns alongside a 75 mm cannon in a new 'solid' nose. Four hundred and five B-25G's were built, and a hundred and seventy-five earlier Mitchells were modified to carry a total of ten 0·50 in guns. An even more heavily armed 'gunship' was the B-25H, one thousand of which were produced with the 75 mm nose cannon and fourteen 0·50 in guns; this entered operational service in February 1944, joining the earlier multi-gunned Mitchells on anti-shipping strikes in the Pacific battle areas. Final production model, the B-25J (four thousand three hundred and eighteen built), reverted to the standard bomber nose, but retained the forward placing of the dorsal turret introduced on the H model. Mitchells in U.S. service operated predominantly in the Pacific war

zone, but large numbers were supplied elsewhere during the war. Two hundred and forty-eight B-25H's and four hundred and fifty-eight B-25J's were transferred to the U.S. Navy from 1943 as PBJ-1H's and -1J's, most being operated by Marine Corps squadrons. Eight hundred and seventy Mitchells of various models were supplied to the U.S.S.R. under Lend-Lease; twenty-three Mitchell I's (B-26B) and five hundred and thirty-eight Mitchell II's (B-25C and D) were received by the RAF; and others were supplied to Brazil (twenty-nine), China (one hundred and thirty-one) and the Netherlands (two hundred and forty-nine).

54 Lockheed Hudson

The Hudson was evolved at short notice, in 1938, to meet a British requirement for a coastal reconnaissance aircraft to supplement the Anson. Essentially, it was a militarised version of the Model 14 commercial airliner that had flown in July 1937, and an initial RAF order was placed for two hundred. The first of these was flown on 10 December 1938; deliveries of Hudson I's to Britain began in February 1939, the first recipient being No 224 Squadron. On arrival, many were fitted with twin-gun Boulton Paul turrets. On the outbreak of war the RAF had seventy-eight Hudsons on strength, and on 8 October 1939 one of them destroyed the first German aircraft to fall to RAF guns in the war. Lockheed supplied three hundred and fifty Hudson I's and twenty similar Hudson II's before introducing the Mk III, with more powerful Cyclone engines and ventral and beam guns. Four hundred and twenty-eight of this version were ordered. The only other direct purchases were three hundred and nine Hudson V's with 1,200 hp Twin Wasp engines. Many other Hudson's reached the RAF under Lend-Lease, however. These included three hundred and eighty-two Cyclone-engined Mk IIIA's, and thirty Mk IV's and four hundred and fifty Mk VI's with Twin Wasp engines. In 1941 the Hudson was given USAAF designations: A-28 for the Twin Wasp version and A-29 for the models with Cyclone engines. Eighty-two A-28's and four hundred and eighteen A-29's went to the USAAF, except for twenty A-28's that were transferred to the U.S. Navy with the designation PBO-1. In service with Squadron VP-82, one of these became the first U.S. aircraft of the war to destroy a German submarine. The Hudson continued in front-line service with Coastal Command until 1943-44, but undertook a variety of wartime duties that included agent-dropping, transport and operational training.

55 Lockheed Ventura

As the Hudson was evolved from the commercial Lockheed Model 14, so was the Ventura a militarised form of the larger Model 18, also instigated at the request of the British Purchasing Commission in 1940. The initial RAF contracts were for six hundred and seventy-five aircraft,

of which the first one hundred and eighty-eight were delivered from summer 1942 as Ventura Mk I's, following the first flight on 31 July 1941. They entered service with No 21 Squadron of Bomber Command in October 1942 and made their first operational sorties early in the following month. The Ventura II and Lend-Lease IIA which followed had a different variant of Double Wasp engines, an increased bomb load of 3,000 lb (1,361 kg) and two additional guns in the fuselage. However, the Ventura was less successful in daylight operations than had been hoped, and deliveries were halted after about three hundred had been delivered. The remaining IIA's were acquired by the USAAF as B-34's, and more than three hundred others from previous RAF contracts became B-34A Lexington bombers or B-34B navigation trainers with the USAAF. The proposed Ventura III (B-37) with Wright Cyclone engines was cancelled after delivery of only eighteen of the U.S. Army's order for five hundred and fifty, and subsequent production concentrated upon the PV-1 model for the U.S. Navy, ordered in September 1942. This model had R-2800-31 Double Wasps, a 'solid' nose, six defensive guns, provision for external drop tanks and the ability to carry depth charges or a torpedo as an alternative to bombs. One thousand six hundred PV-1's were built, three hundred and fifty-eight of which went to RAF Coastal Command and several Commonwealth air forces as Ventura GR Mk V's. Twenty-seven of the Ventura II's originally intended for Britain were acquired by the U.S. Navy and designated PV-3 (PV-2 being the designation already allotted to a Ventura development known as the Harpoon).

56 Lockheed Lodestar

The pre-war Model 18 Lodestar commercial transport was selected by the U.S. Army for wartime production, three hundred and twenty-five being built as standard Army and Navy paratroop transports with the designation C-60A. A proposed freighter version with large cargo-loading doors was to have been built in even larger numbers, but this contract was cancelled. However, a variety of assorted civil Model 18's were acquired for war service under several separate designations. Those in USAAF service included thirty-six C-56 to C-56E; thirteen C-57 and seven C-57A; ten C-59; thirty-six C-60; and one C-66. The U.S. Navy designations R50-1, -2, -5 and -6 correspond to the USAAF's C-56, C-59, C-60 and C-60A, while the R5O-3 and -4 were 4-seat and 7-seat executive transports respectively. Many of the impressed commercial Model 18's were returned to their former owners during 1943-44, very few remaining in service beyond this date. Although not in service in great numbers, the Lodestar performed a wide range of duties that included troop and cargo transport, casualty evacuation and glider training. More than two dozen civil Lodestars were also impressed into service with the RAF, to whom

Lend-Lease deliveries included ten Mk IA and seventeen Mk II. Twenty aircraft corresponding to the American C-56B version were supplied to the Royal Netherlands Indies Army Air Corps.

57 Armstrong Whitworth Albemarle

The A.W.41 Albemarle was designed by Armstrong Whitworth to Air Ministry Specification B.18/38, for a twin-engined medium bomber of mixed wood and metal construction that could be contracted extensively to firms outside the aircraft industry. Two prototypes were completed by Armstrong Whitworth, and the first flight was made by the second of these (P 1361) on 20 March 1930. Completion of the entire production run of six hundred aircraft was entrusted to A. W. Hawkesley Ltd at Gloucester, but only the first thirty-two (designated Mk I Series 1) were completed as bombers. For this role they were to have had a 6-man crew, including two gunners to man the four-gun dorsal turret and the retractable 'dustbin'-type, two-gun ventral turret; the dorsal turret was offset slightly to port to simplify access to the rear fuselage. The Albemarle, although it also had a fixed, shock-absorbing tailwheel, was the first British military aircraft with a retractable nosewheel undercarriage to enter service. The first production aircraft was completed in December 1941, but the Albemarle never served in its intended role, and these thirty-two aircraft were instead converted for transport duties. Deliveries began to No 295 Squadron at Harwell in January 1943. Subsequent Albemarles were designated ST (Special Transport) or GT (General Transport), and were completed as follows: ninety-nine ST Mk I, sixty-nine GT Mk I, ninety-nine ST Mk II, forty-nine ST Mk V, one hundred and thirty-three ST Mk VI and one hundred and seventeen GT Mk VI. These were further subdivided into Series according to variations of equipment or role. The eight ST Mk I Series 1's had only twin dorsal guns, with a sliding hood over them; the fourteen ST Mk I Series 2's had Malcolm glider-towing gear; the ST Mk VI's were Series 1's with a starboard side rear freight door; and the GT Mk VI's were Series 2's with additional radio equipment and no dorsal armament. The Mk II could operate as a 10-man paratroop transport, and the Mk V (otherwise similar to the Mk II) was fitted with fuel jettison equipment. All were powered by Bristol Hercules XI engines, though there was a project for a Merlin-engined Mk III, and one Mk IV was completed with 1,600 hp Wright R-2600-A5B Double Cyclones. Other RAF squadrons to operate the Albemarle included Nos 296 and 297 (in the United Kingdom and in North Africa), and No 570; small numbers also served with Nos 161 and 511, and some (ten?) Albemarles were supplied to the Soviet Air Force. Large numbers took part in the Allied landings in Sicily (July 1943), Normandy (June 1944) and at Arnhem (September 1944).

58 **Beech UC-45 Expediter**
This was the military version of the pre-war Beech Model 18, one of the most adaptable twin-engined aeroplanes ever built: developed versions are still in production, and operate in all parts of the world. First military orders were placed before Pearl Harbor, the U.S. Army ordering eleven 6-seat C-45's (Model B18S) and twenty 8-seat C-45A's in 1940-41. Also in 1941 came the first orders for a 5-seat navigation trainer version, the AT-7 Navigator, five hundred and seventy-seven of which were ultimately delivered. The first mass-produced military transport version was the C-45B, basically the same as the A but with interior layout modified to Army requirements. Two hundred and twenty-three C-45B's were produced for the USAAF, one hundred and twenty-one similar aircraft were supplied to Britain under Lend-Lease as Expediter Mk I's. Five went to the Royal Navy, the remainder to the RAF. The 'Utility Cargo' designation first appeared on the two UC-45C's adopted by the USAAF; the two UC-45D's and six UC-45E's were 5-seaters similar to the AT-7 and -7B trainers. Major production transport was the 7-seat UC-45F, one thousand one hundred and thirty-seven of which were delivered to the U.S. Army from 1944. An additional two hundred and thirty-six were supplied to the RAF, and sixty-seven to the Fleet Air Arm, by whom they were known as the Expediter II. Subsequent trainers included seven AT-7A's, with convertible twin float or ski

landing gear, and nine AT-7B's, which were basically 'winterised' AT-7's. Five of this model were supplied to the RAF. Final USAAF variant was the AT-7C, with R-985-AN-3 engines; five hundred and forty-nine were completed. A development of the AT-7 for bombing training was the AT-11 Kansas, one thousand five hundred and eighty-two of which were completed; thirty-six were later converted to AT-11A's for navigation training. Many Expediters were used by the U.S. Navy, with JR (Utility Transport) series designations: the Navy's JRB-1, -2, -3 and -4 corresponded to the Army C-45, C-45A, C-45B and UC-45F respectively. Navy counterpart to the AT-7 was the SNB-2. Several other aircraft served as USAAF photographic aircraft, with the name Discoverer. These included fourteen F-2's, thirteen F-2A's (converted from transport models) and forty-two F-2B's.

59 Focke-Wulf Fw 189 Uhu (Owl)

The Fw 189 was designed originally to a 1937 specification for a tactical reconnaissance aircraft. The Fw 189V1 prototype (D-OPVN), first flown in July 1938, was an unorthodox aeroplane, with two 430 hp Argus As 410 engines mounted in slender booms that also carried the tail assembly. The crew members were accommodated in an extensively glazed central nacelle. A second and third prototype were completed to generally similar configuration, the Fw 189V2 carrying guns and external bomb racks. The first series version to go into production was the Fw 189B dual-control trainer, three B-0's and ten B-1's being completed in 1939-40. Production of the first reconnaissance series began in the spring of 1940, ten Fw 189A-0 pre-series aircraft being followed by the A-1, the better-armed A-2 and a smaller quantity of A-3 trainers. First deliveries to the *Luftwaffe* were made in the autumn of 1940, but it was not until the end of the following year that the Fw 189 began to appear in front-line units in any numbers. Thereafter the *Uhu*, as it was known to its crews, became employed in increasing numbers, especially on the Eastern Front. It was popular with those who flew it, and its delicate appearance belied what was in fact an adaptable, manoeuvrable and sturdily built aeroplane. Production of the Fw 189A series was undertaken by the parent company, which built one hundred and ninety-seven, excluding prototypes; at the Aero factory in Czechoslovakia, which built three hundred and thirty-seven; and at Bordeaux-Mérignac in France, where two hundred and ninety-three were completed. Small numbers were supplied to the air forces of Hungary and Slovakia. Meanwhile, in 1939 the Fw 189V1 had been reflown after being modified to have a very small but heavily armoured central nacelle seating two crew members. This and the generally similar Fw 189V6 were prototypes for a proposed attack version, the Fw 189C, but the latter did not go into production. The float-fitted Fw 189D, the Fw 189E with Gnome-

Rhône engines, and the more powerful Fw 189G were all projects that did not come to fruition, but a small number of Fw 189F-1's, with 580 hp As 411 engines, did become operational.

60 Blohm und Voss Bv 138

A product of Hamburger Flugzeugbau, the aircraft division of the Blohm und Voss shipbuilding company, the prototype of this three-engined flying boat was designated Ha 138V1 when it made its first flight on 15 July 1937. A second prototype, with a modified hull and tail surfaces, was flown on 6 November 1937, both being powered by 600 hp Junkers Jumo 205C engines. In 1938 the 'Ha' designations were discarded, the third machine to be completed being designated Bv 138A-01. This was the first of six pre-production aircraft, embodying a much-enlarged hull, redesigned booms and tail, and a horizontal wing centre section. Production began late in 1939 of twenty-five similar Bv 138A-1's, intended for well-equipped, long-range maritime patrol duties, but this initial version was not a conspicuous success, and the first pair were actually employed as 10-passenger transports in Norway. It made its combat debut in October 1940, at about which time the A-1 was beginning to be replaced by the Bv 138B-1, twenty-one of which were built with a turret-mounted nose cannon, a similar gun in the rear of the hull and 880 hp Jumo 205D engines. The major version in service was the Bv 138C-1, two hundred and twenty-seven of which were produced between 1941 and 1943. The C-1, with more efficient propellers and a 13 mm upper gun, offered slightly better performance and defence than its predecessor. Despite an indifferent start to its career, the Bv 138 eventually proved to be both robust and versatile, and was employed with increasing effect both on convoy patrol in Arctic waters and, in association with the U-boat patrols, on anti-shipping missions over the North Atlantic and the Mediterranean. A few were also converted for sweeping or 'degaussing' minefields (these were designated Bv 138MS), and many more were adapted for launching from catapults.

61 C.R.D.A. Cant. Z.506B Airone (Heron)

The Z.506 first appeared as a 12-passenger commercial transport, the prototype (I-CANT) making its first flight in 1936 with Pratt & Whitney Hornet engines. Small batches of Z.506A's (760 hp Cyclones) and Z.506C's (750 or 800 hp Alfa Romeos) were delivered, from 1936 to 1938, to the Italian airline Ala Littoria, during which time successively improved world records for speed, distance and payload-to-height were established by various machines. Meanwhile, in July 1936 the prototype was handed over to the Italian Air Ministry, leading to the evolution of a bomber/torpedo bomber version, the Z.506B. This carried a crew of five and had a redesigned fuselage whose chief features were a raised cockpit, seating the two pilots in tandem; a ventral gondola, incorporating a forward bomb aimer's position, the bomb bay and a rear defensive gun position; and a strut-braced tailplane. The bomb bay could accommodate two 1,102 lb (500 kg) bombs, various combinations of smaller bombs up to a total of 1,984 lb (900 kg) or a single 1,764 lb (800 kg) torpedo. A pair of Breda-SAFAT 12·7 mm machine-guns were installed in a retractable Breda M.1 dorsal turret. The Z.506B Serie I entered production at Monfalcone in 1937, thirty-two being completed and delivered to the *Regia Aeronautica* during 1938. Some of these joined Italy's *Aviazione Legionaria* in Spain at the end of that year, where they were employed primarily for rescue or reconnaissance missions. By June 1940 production at Monfalcone had reached ninety-five Serie I and later models, others had been completed by Piaggio at Finalmarina, and Z.506B's in Italian service included twenty-nine of an order for thirty placed by the Polish Government in 1938. Principal Airone formations in 1940 were the 31° *Stormo da Bombardamento Marittimo* at Elmas (Sardinia) and the 35° *Stormo B.M.* at Brindisi. The Airone was active in its primary role during the early part of the war, but after the Greek islands campaign of 1941 all aircraft of this type were diverted to maritime patrol duties of various kinds, serving, *inter alia*, with the 139°, 147°, 170° and 199° *Squadriglie da Ricognizione Marittima*. After the Italian capitulation, twenty-three Z.506B's became part of the *Raggruppamento Idro* (seaplane group) of the Co-Belligerent Air Force based at Taranto. By this time the principal service variant was the Serie XII, the gross weight of which had been raised by improvements in bomb-carrying capacity (to 2,645 lb = 1,200 kg) and defensive armament. It has not been possible to establish individual details of intermediate Serie numbers, nor of overall Airone production. The only other wartime variant identified was the Z.506S (for Soccorso = help), a conversion of the Z.506B for air/sea rescue. Some of these served in *Luftwaffe* colours, five were among the Co-Belligerent Air Force's acquisitions in 1943, and a further twenty conversions were made by Siai-Marchetti after the war for the reconstituted *Aeronautica Militare Italiano*, with which they served until 1959.

62 Junkers Ju 52/3m

Although it first entered military service as a bomber, it is as a transport aeroplane that the Ju 52/3m began and ended its career. Developed from the single-engined Ju 52 flown in October 1930, the first of the Ju 52/3m trimotors made its maiden flight in 1932, and for several pre-war years they were used widely by Deutsche Lufthansa and other airlines, notably in South America. Several hundred were delivered to the *Luftwaffe* in 1934-35 in bomber configuration, but they were regarded only as interim equipment, pending the arrival of such types as the He 111 and Do 17. Thus, in their first operational role, in the Spanish Civil War of 1936-39, they were employed principally as troop transports. The early production models were powered by 600 hp BMW 132A engines; the first version to introduce the higher-powered BMW 132T was the Ju 53/3mg5e. Principal production model was the Ju 52/3mg7e, with enlarged cabin doors, autopilot and other detail improvements; this could be fitted out either as an 18-seat troop transport or as an ambulance with provision for 12 stretchers. In these two roles the Ju 52/3m served for many years with the *Luftwaffe*, by whom it was popularly known as 'Iron Annie'. Their best-known action came with the invasion of Norway in April 1940, in which nearly six hundred of these transports were engaged. Almost as many were in action during the invasion of France and the Low Countries, and in both campaigns well over a quarter of the Junkers transports involved were lost. Nevertheless, they continued to figure prominently in such subsequent Nazi campaigns as those in Greece, Libya and Crete. Other duties undertaken by the Ju 52/3m during its *Luftwaffe* career included those of supply transport and glider tug, and some aircraft were fitted with electromagnetic 'de-gaussing' rings for clearing minefields. Most models had provision for interchangeable wheel, ski or float landing gear. Overall production of the Ju 52/3m between 1934 and 1944, including civil models, amounted to four thousand eight hundred and forty-five aircraft. Of these, two thousand eight hundred and four were built in Germany between 1939 and 1945. Many pre-war commercial Ju 52/3m's were impressed for military service, and when the war was over several hundred were allocated to many foreign airlines, assisting them to re-establish their pre-war services until more modern types became available. A few remain in airline service today.

63 C.R.D.A. Cant. Z.1007 Alcione (Kingfisher)

The most important wartime contemporary of the S.M.79 Sparviero was another trimotor bomber, the Z.1007 designed by Ing Filippo Zappata. The first prototype flew towards the end of 1937, others following during the ensuing year and a half, and the Z.1007 entered production in 1939. The early aircraft for the *Regia Aeronautica* carried a light defensive armament of four 7·7 mm guns, and were powered by 840 hp Isotta-Fraschini Asso IX RC 35 Vee-type engines, installed in annular cowlings that gave them the appearance of being radials. This initial version was soon followed by the principal model, the Z.1007*bis*, in which a change was made to 1,000 hp Piaggio radials, resulting in a considerably improved performance. This version had increases in wing span and overall length, and a strengthened undercarriage, all permitting it to operate at higher gross weights; and defensive armament was improved. Eighty-seven Alcioni were in service when Italy entered the war. Of all-wood construction, the Alcione was unusual in being built in both single- and twin-finned forms; production was undertaken by IMAM

(Meridionali) and Piaggio, as well as by CRDA. As an alternative to its internal load, the Z.1007*bis* could carry a pair of 450 mm (17·7 in) torpedos under the fuselage, and the type was also employed for reconnaissance. The Alcione saw most of its wartime service in the Mediterranean area and North Africa, but also served on the Eastern Front, standing up well to extremes of climate despite its wooden construction. A later version, the Z.1007*ter*, appeared in *Regia Aeronautica* service towards the end of 1942. It had 1,175 hp Piaggio P.XIX engines and a reduced bomb load, but was not built in substantial numbers. The parallel Z.1015, with 1,500 hp Piaggio P.XII RC 35 engines, was likewise surpassed by the promise of an even better design, the Z.1018, which had flown in 1940.

64 Savoia-Marchetti S.M.79 Sparviero (Hawk)

The S.M.79, designed by Alessandro Marchetti, originated as the prototype (I-MAGO) of an 8-seat commercial transport, making its first flight in October 1934. Several record flights, with various powerplants, were made in 1935-36, leading to the completion of the second prototype as a military bomber, powered by three 780 hp Alfa Romeo 126 RC 34 engines. This entered production as the S.M.79-I Sparviero, characterised by the dorsal hump which caused it to be nicknamed *il Gobbo* (the hunchback) when it entered service. The 8° and 111° *Stormi Bombardamento Veloce* (High Speed Bomber Groups)

achieved some considerable success with their Sparvieri during the Spanish Civil War, and forty-five S.M.79-I's were ordered in 1938 by Yugoslavia. In 1937 service trials were begun of the S.M.79-I equipped to carry one 450 mm (17·7 in) torpedo, and later two, beneath the fuselage. These trials indicated that, with more powerful engines, the Sparviero could easily carry two of these weapons externally, and in October 1939 production began of the S.M.79-II, to equip the *Squadriglie Aerosiluranti* (Torpedo Bomber Squadrons) of the *Regia Aeronautica*. Apart from one batch with 1,030 hp Fiat A.80 RC 41 engines, all S.M.79-II's were powered by the Piaggio P.XI radial. Production was sub-contracted to Macchi and Reggiane factories, and in June 1940 there were nearly six hundred Sparvieri, of both models, in Italian service. The S.M.79 was active during World War 2 throughout the Mediterranean area, in North Africa and the Balkan states, its duties including torpedo attack, conventional bombing, reconnaissance, close-support and, eventually, transport and training. After the Italian surrender in 1943 about three dozen continued to fly with the Co-Belligerent Air Force, while the pro-German *Aviazione della RSI* employed several S.M.79-III's. This was a cleaned-up version, without the ventral gondola, and had a forward-firing 20 mm cannon. The S.M.79B was a twin-engined export model, with an extensively glazed nose, and was first flown in 1936. It was built for Brazil (three), Iraq (four) and Rumania (forty-eight), each version with a different power-plant. The Rumanian I.A.R. factories also built the S.M.79B under licence with Junkers Jumo 211D in-line engines. Overall Italian production of S.M.79 variants, including export models, reached one thousand three hundred and thirty before output ceased in 1944.

65 **Petlyakov Pe-8**
The Pe-8 was evolved to meet a 1934 Soviet Air Force specification for a long range heavy bomber, and originally bore the designation ANT-42, indicating that it was a product of the A.N. Tupolev design bureau. Its military designation was TB-7. When the Soviet designation system was changed at the end of 1940 credit was given to Vladimir Petlyakov, who had led the team responsible for its design. The proto-type bomber first flew on 27 December 1936, with 1,100 hp Mikulin M-105 engines, and later trials were conducted with an M-100 engine mounted in the fuselage to drive a supercharger for the four propulsion engines. Late in 1939, when the TB-7 entered production at Kuznets, it was powered by AM-35A engines, which did not require this clumsy arrangement in order to maintain the bomber's excellent speed-at-altitude performance. The aircraft entered service during 1940, and in the summer of 1941 carried out their first major attack of the war when a formation of Pe-8's raided Berlin. They continued to make similar deep-penetration raids behind the German lines. Mean-while, attempts to improve the design had begun early in 1941 with the installation of M-30B diesel engines, whose greater fuel economy offered an even longer range. Unfortunately, this powerplant proved unsatisfactory in other ways, and trials with M-82 radials revealed an unacceptable loss of performance; eventually, the withdrawal from production of the AM-35A led to the installation, from 1943, of M-82FN fuel-injection radial engines in production Pe-8's. This version introduced various aero-dynamic improvements, evolved by I. F. Nyezval after Petlyakov's death in 1942, and the nacelle gun instal-lations were omitted. Design changes and powerplant difficulties were chiefly responsible for Pe-8 pro-duction coming to an end in 1944, the total number built being com-paratively small by Soviet wartime standards. In 1942 one Pe-8 made a flight of more than 11,000 miles (17,700 km) from Moscow to Washington and back via Scotland, Iceland and Canada.

66 **Short Stirling**
The Stirling was a victim of its own Specification (B.12/36), because of which its wings were of such low aspect ratio that its operational ceiling was limited and its bomb bay could take no single weapon larger than 2,000 lb (907 kg) in size. The prototype (L 7600), preceded in 1938 by flight trials of the P.31 half-scale wooden prototype, made its first flight on 14 May 1939. It crashed on landing, but a second machine (L 7605) was flown on

3 December 1939. In May 1940 the first production Stirling Mk I made its maiden flight, and deliveries of this version began in August 1940 to No 7 Squadron. The initial order for one hundred Stirlings was soon increased, and after the 1939 Munich crisis stood at one thousand five hundred. Hercules XI engines of 1,595 hp in the Mk I replaced the 1,375 hp Hercules II's of the two prototypes. Two conversions were made as Mk II prototypes, with 1,600 hp Wright R-2600-A5B Cyclone engines, but this model never went into production. The major service version was the Mk III, which in addition to Hercules XVI engines introduced a new-style dorsal gun turret. Two Mk III's were converted in 1943 as Mk IV prototypes, the latter version being produced for both paratroop transport and glider towing duties. The Mk IV was basically similar to the Mk III, except for the removal of some or all gun turrets and having, in the paratrooper version, an exit hatch aft of the bomb bay. The final version, the Mk V, was an unarmed passenger or cargo transport with a fuselage rear-loading door and an extended nose section which hinged sideways to provide an additional loading facility. Short Bros built five hundred and thirty-two Mk I, six hundred and eighteen Mk III, four hundred and fifty Mk IV and one hundred and sixty Mk V; in addition, one hundred and ninety-one Mk I and four hundred and twenty-nine Mk II were completed by Austin Motors. The Stirling I first went into action on 10 February 1941, with an attack on an oil storage depot at Rotterdam, and throughout 1942 began mounting the heavy bombing of enemy targets later continued by the Halifax and Lancaster by night and the U.S. Fortress and Liberator by day. It figured in the first and many subsequent thousand-bomber raids, and was the first Bomber Command type fitted with the 'Oboe' blind-bombing device. Before their transfer to less belligerent duties in the later war years many Stirlings also carried out minelaying duties.

67 **Focke-Wulf Fw 200 Condor**
The Fw 200V1 prototype (D-AERE *Saarland*), which first flew on 27 July 1937, was designed by Dr Kurt Tank as a 26-passenger commercial transport for Deutsche Lufthansa, and prior to World War 2 the Fw 200A and Fw 200B also served with Danish and Brazilian operators. Two other prototypes were acquired by the RLM, later becoming personal transports for Hitler and his staff, but the first suggestion to employ the Condor for maritime patrol came from Japan. None of the aircraft ordered by Japan were in fact delivered, but the Condor was adapted, as the Fw 200C, for ocean patrol and bombing duties with the *Luftwaffe*. In spite of this it was as a military transport that the Fw 200C was first employed operationally, during the invasion of Norway in the spring of 1940. Early production Fw 200C's were powered by 830 hp BMW 132H engines and carried a crew of 5, but with successive variations in armament the crew later

increased to 7 men, and from the Fw 200C-3 onward Bramo 323R engines became the standard power-plant. The Fw 200C-1 first entered service in the maritime role towards the end of 1940, with *Kampfgeschwader* 40, followed by the C-2 and C-3 models during 1941. The principal sub-type was the C-4, with more advanced radar and radio equipment, which entered production early in 1942. Subsequent variants included the C-6 and C-8, adapted to carry two Hs 293 guided missiles. The latter was the final military variant, a total of two hundred and seventy-six Condors (including prototypes) having been built when production ended early in 1944. Considering the small quantity built, the Condor established a considerable reputation as a commerce raider during the early war years, operating independently or in conjunction with U-boat patrols against the Allied convoys. It was not ideally suited to the rigours of maritime warfare, however, and many were lost through structural failure when indulging in strenuous manoeuvres. When its initial successes began to diminish after the appearance of the CAM ships and such Allied types as the Beaufighter and Liberator, it was progressively transferred to the transport role for which it had first been designed.

68 & 69 **Boeing B-17 Flying Fortress**

In service from beginning to end of the U.S. participation in World War 2, the B-17 was evolved in 1934 for a USAAC design competition for an offshore anti-shipping bomber. In 1935 the prototype was completed, as the Boeing 299, and flew for the first time on 28 July 1935, powered by four 750 hp Pratt & Whitney Hornet engines. A change of power-plant, to 1,000 hp Wright Cyclones, was specified for the thirteen Y1B-17's and one Y1B-17A that were then ordered for evaluation; after trials, these were placed in service as the B-17 and B-17A respectively. The initial production batch comprised thirty-nine B-17B's, with modified nose, larger rudder and internal improvements. They were followed by thirty-eight B-17C's (higher-powered Cyclones and revised armament), twenty of which were supplied to the Royal Air Force in 1941 as the Fortress Mk I. The B-17D, forty-two of which were ordered for the USAAF, was generally similar, and most American C's were later converted to D standard. It was the B-17E which first introduced the huge, sail-like fin and rudder that characterised all subsequent Fortresses, and the much-improved defensive armament on this model included, for the first time, a tail gun turret to cover the blind spot to the rear of the bomber. Five hundred and twelve B-17E's were built by Boeing, including forty-five which became the Fortress IIA of the RAF. American B-17E's, serving in the United Kingdom, made the first raids on European targets by the U.S. Eighth Air Force in August 1942, and this version also served extensively in the Pacific theatre. The next model, the B-17F, was sub-contracted to Douglas and Lockheed-Vega factories which, with Boeing, built three thousand four hundred and five. Nineteen of these were supplied to the RAF as the Fortress II, and forty-one others were converted to F-9 series photographic reconnaissance aircraft. The same three companies combined to build eight thousand six hundred and eighty examples of the last production model, the B-17G; eighty-five of these became Fortress III's with RAF Coastal Command and ten others were converted to F-9C's. The B-17G was characterised chiefly by its 'chin' turret with two additional 0·50 in machine-guns, a feature later added to many B-17F's in service. Forty-eight B-17G's were allocated to the U.S. Navy and Coast Guard, with whom they performed ASR or early warning patrol duties; these aircraft were designated PB-1G or PB-1W respectively, the latter having large ventral radomes. About fifty other Flying Fortresses, adapted to carry a lifeboat under the fuselage, were redesignated B-17H and employed on air/sea rescue work. The Flying Fortress's principal sphere of activity during World War 2 was in Europe, where the E, F and G models were the mainstay of the U.S. heavy day bomber attacks on enemy targets.

70 **Boeing B-29 Superfortress**
Design of the Superfortress began well before America's entry into World War 2, when the Boeing Model 345 was evolved to a USAAC requirement of February 1940 for a 'hemisphere defense weapon'. In

August 1940 two prototypes, designated XB-29, were ordered by the USAAF, and the first one was flown on 21 September 1942. It was a much larger aeroplane than Boeing's earlier B-17 Fortress, and was characterised by its circular-section, pressurised fuselage and remote-controlled gun turrets. Powerplant was four 2,200 hp Wright R-3350-13 Cyclone radial engines. By the time of the first flight, nearly seventeen hundred B-29's had been ordered. The first pre-production YB-29 Superfortress flew on 26 June 1943, and squadron deliveries began in the following month to the 58th Bombardment Wing. The first operational B-29 mission was carried out on 5 June 1944, and the first attack upon a target in Japan on 15 June 1944. It was during this month that the Superfortresses moved to the bases in the Marianas Islands, from whence they subsequently mounted a steadily increasing bombing campaign against the Japanese homeland. Apart from the direct damage caused by this campaign, it was responsible for many Japanese aircraft from other Pacific battle fronts being withdrawn for home defence duties, although comparatively few types were capable of indulging in effective combat at the altitudes flown by the American bombers. Superfortresses also carried out extensive minelaying in Japanese waters; a hundred and eighteen others became F-13/F-13A photo-reconnaissance aircraft. Finally, two B-29's brought the war to its dramatic close with the dropping of atomic bombs on Hiroshima and Nagasaki on 6 and 9

August 1945. Shortly after VJ-day over five thousand Superfortresses were cancelled, but when B-29 production ended early in 1946 the three Boeing factories had completed two thousand seven hundred and fifty-six B-29's and B-29A's; in addition, six hundred and sixty-eight B-29's were manufactured by Bell, and five hundred and thirty-six B-29's by Martin. Three hundred and eleven of the Bell machines were converted to B-29B's with reduced armament.

71 Avro Lancaster

The Lancaster was a direct development of Avro's unsuccessful Manchester twin-engined bomber, its prototype (BT 308) being originally the Manchester III, complete with triple tail unit, modified by the installation of four 1,130 hp Merlin X engines in place of the two Vulture engines of the Manchester. This prototype flew on 9 January 1941, being followed just over nine months later by the first production Mk I, of which delivery began (to No 44 Squadron) shortly after Christmas 1941. The first Lancaster combat mission came on 2 March 1942, and the first bombing raid, on Essen, followed eight days later. The Lancaster I, fitted successively with Merlin XX, 22 or 24 engines, remained the only version in service throughout 1942 and early 1943, and an eventual total of three thousand four hundred and forty Mk I's were completed by Avro, Armstrong Whitworth, Austin Motors, Metropolitan-Vickers and Vickers-Armstrongs. Avro completed two prototypes for the Lancaster II, powered

by 1,725 hp Bristol Hercules radial engines as a safeguard against possible supply shortage of Merlins. In the event no such shortage arose, but three hundred production Lancaster II's were built by Armstrong Whitworth. The other principal version, the Lancaster III, was powered by Packard-built Merlin 28, 38 or 224 engines; apart from a modified bomb-aimer's window, this exhibited few other differences from the Mk I. Most of the three thousand and twenty Mk III's completed were built by Avro, but one hundred and ten were manufactured by Armstrong Whitworth and one hundred and thirty-six by Metropolitan-Vickers. The Mark numbers IV and V applied to extensively redesigned models that eventually became the Lincoln, while the small batch of Mk VI's were Mk III's converted to Merlin 85 or 87 engines in redesigned cowlings. The final British variant was the Mk VII, one hundred and eighty being built by Austin with Martin dorsal turrets mounting twin 0·50 in guns. In Canada, Victory Aircraft Ltd manufactured four hundred and thirty Lancaster X's, which had Packard-Merlin 28's and were essentially similar to the Mk III. The Lancaster's bomb-carrying feats were legion. It was designed originally to carry bombs of 4,000 lb (1,814 kg) in size, but successive modifications to the bomb bay produced the Mk I (Special) capable of carrying first 8,000 lb (3,629 kg) and then 12,000 lb (5,443 kg) weapons, and culminating in the 22,000 lb (9,979 kg) 'Grand Slam' armour-piercing weapon designed by Barnes Wallis. This remarkable engineer also designed the skipping bomb carried by the Lancasters of No 617 Squadron in their epic raid on the Moehne and Eder dams on 17 May 1943.

72 & 73 **Handley Page Halifax**
The H.P.57 came into being as a redesign of the twin-Vulture-engined H.P.56 evolved to meet Air Ministry Specification P.13/36, after it had become apparent that the Vulture would be unsatisfactory. The H.P.57 was a much-enlarged design, drawn up around four Rolls-Royce Merlin engines, and the first of two prototypes (L 7244) was flown on 24 September 1939, by which time an initial contract had already been placed. Deliveries of the Halifax Mk I, to No 35 Squadron, began in November 1940, and the bomber made its operational debut in a raid on Le Havre on the night of 11-12 March 1941. The early machines became known as Mk I Series I, being followed by the Mk I Series II with a higher gross weight and Series III with increased fuel tankage. The first major modification appeared in the Mk II Series I, with its two-gun dorsal turret and uprated Merlin XX engines. The Mk II Series I (Special) had a fairing in place of the nose turret, and the engine exhaust muffs omitted; the Series IA first introduced the drag-reducing moulded Perspex nose that became a standard Halifax feature, had a four-gun dorsal turret, and Merlin 22 engines. Variants of the Mk II Series I (Special) and Series IA, with Dowty landing gear instead of the standard Messier gear, were designated Mk V Series I (Special) and Series IA. One thousand nine hundred and sixty-six Mk II's and nine hundred and fifteen Mk V's were built. One other important modification appearing in the Mk II Series IA was the introduction of larger, rectangular vertical tail surfaces, designed to overcome serious control difficulties experienced with earlier models. The Perspex nose and rectangular fins characterised all subsequent Halifaxes, whose only serious drawback now was a lack of adequate power. Thus, in the Mk III, which appeared in 1943, the Merlin powerplant was abandoned in favour of Bristol Hercules radial engines. The Mk III became the most numerous Halifax variant, two thousand and ninety-one being built. The Mk IV was a project that remained uncompleted, the next operational models being the Mks VI and VII, the former powered by 1,675 hp Hercules 100, while the latter reverted to the Hercules XVI as used in the Mk III. These were the final bomber versions, and compared with earlier models were built in relatively small numbers. Halifax production ended with the Mk VIII supply transport and Mk IX paratroop transport, the final aircraft being delivered in November 1946. Six thousand one hundred and seventy-six Halifaxes had then been built, by a widely sub-contracted wartime programme that included English Electric, Fairey, Rootes Motors and the London Aircraft Production Group as well as the parent company. The Halifax re-

mained in service with Bomber Command throughout the war, making its last operational sortie on 25 April 1945. Its work included many special-duty missions, including agent-dropping and radar countermeasures, and it also served in the Middle East. After the war Halifaxes remained in service for a time with Coastal and Transport Commands, the last flight being made by a Coastal Command GR Mk VI in March 1952.

74 & 75 Consolidated B-24 Liberator

To the Liberator go the distinctions of being built in greater numbers and more variants than any other U.S. aircraft of World War 2, and of serving in more combat theatres, over a longer period, than any heavy bomber on either side. It originated as the Consolidated Model 32, a major feature of which was the exceptionally high aspect ratio Davis wing that gave the Liberator its prodigious range. Allied to this was the deep, capacious fuselage that enabled the aircraft to carry a large bomb load and also made it eminently suitable as a transport. The sole XB-24 prototype flew on 29 December 1941, followed by seven YB-24 service trials aircraft and thirty-six production B-24A's. One hundred and twenty were also ordered by the French Government, but these were diverted to Britain, the first few being designated LB-30 or -30A and used by BOAC for transatlantic ferry flying. Twenty others went to RAF Coastal Command as Liberator I's, equipped with an early form of ASV

radar. The first B-24A deliveries to the USAAF were made in June 1941, followed by nine B-24C's with turbo-supercharged engines and revised armament. The first U.S. version actually to serve in the bomber role was the B-24D, which was essentially similar to the B-24C except for its R-1830-43 engines and increased gross weight. Production of the B-24D, including ten by Douglas, totalled two thousand seven hundred and thirty-eight. Two hundred and sixty were supplied to the RAF as the Liberator III and IIIA (the former having Boulton Paul gun turrets), plus a further one hundred and twenty-two, fitted with 'chin' and ventral radar fairings and Leigh airborne searchlights, which served with Coastal Command as the Liberator Mk V. In mid-1943 those USAAF B-24D's engaged on anti-submarine patrol were transferred to the U.S. Navy, by whom they were redesignated PB4Y-1. Seven hundred and ninety-one B-24E's were built by Convair (as Consolidated was now known), Douglas and the Ford Motor Co, distinguishable from the D model chiefly by their modified propellers; while North American contributed four hundred and thirty B-24G's, some of them with a powered gun turret installed in the nose. An Emerson nose turret and R-1830-65 engines characterised the B-24H, three thousand one hundred of which were completed by Convair, Douglas and Ford. These three companies, plus North American, then manufactured six thousand six hundred and seventy-eight B-24J's, with

155

a Motor Products nose turret and a ventral Briggs ball turret. One thousand two hundred and seventy-eight B-24J's became the RAF's Liberator Mk VI bomber and Mk VII for general reconnaissance. Nine hundred and seventy-seven were delivered to the U.S. Navy, also receiving the designation PB4Y-1 and having, in most cases, radar in place of the ventral turret. Other armament variations characterised the B-24L (one thousand six hundred and sixty-seven by Convair and Ford) and B-24M (two thousand five hundred and ninety-three, from the same factories). Ford had completed seven examples of the single-finned YB-24N, and forty-six similar RY-3's which were delivered to the U.S. Navy, when further contracts (for over five thousand B-24N's) were cancelled in May 1945. The Liberator, although sharing a substantial part of the bombing of Europe with its contemporary, the Boeing Fortress, was even more prominent in the Pacific theatre, where its excellent range was particularly valuable. It also gave considerable service as a transport aircraft, two hundred and seventy-six B-24D-type aircraft being completed as C-87's for this role; close on one hundred Liberators of various types were adapted as F-7 series photo-reconnaissance aircraft; and others were utilised as cargo transports, tanker aircraft and flying classrooms. In addition to those serving with the U.S. forces and the RAF, considerable numbers also operated with the Canadian and other Commonwealth air forces.

When Liberator production ended on 31 May 1945 the total output of all variants had reached eighteen thousand one hundred and eighty-eight aircraft.

76 Short Sunderland

The Sunderland, eventually to become the RAF's longest-serving operational aircraft, was first delivered to No 230 Squadron in Singapore early in June 1938. Its design, based upon the successful C Class 'Empire' flying boats of Imperial Airways, was evolved to Specification R.2/33, and the prototype (K 4774) was flown on 16 October 1937 with 950 hp Pegasus X engines. With Pegasus XXII's and revised nose and tail armament, the Sunderland Mk I entered production in 1938, and by 3 September 1939 forty were in service with four RAF squadrons. Ninety Mk I's were eventually completed, including fifteen by Blackburn. This company also built five of the forty-three Sunderland II's which, from the end of 1941, began to replace the Mk I's in service. The Mk II introduced Pegasus XVIII engines, with two-stage superchargers, a twin-gun Botha-type dorsal turret in place of the 'midships gun ports, an improved tail turret and ASV radar. Rising operating weights now necessitated redesign of the hull planing bottom, and the Mk II on which this was tested thus became the prototype for the chief production model, the Sunderland III. The first Short-built Mk III flew on 15 December 1941; the parent company eventually produced two hundred and eighty-six Mk III's, while a further one hundred and seventy were built by Blackburn. It was No 10 Squadron of the Royal Australian Air Force which first experimented with a group of four machine-guns in the nose of the Sunderland III. This proved so successful, both against enemy submarines and aircraft, that many Sunderlands were subsequently operated with this total armoury of ten guns, their bristling defence earning them the respectful nickname *Stachelschwein* (porcupine) from their German adversaries. The designation Sunderland IV was given originally to a larger, heavier development with 1,700 hp Bristol Hercules engines, eight 0·50 in machine-guns and two 20 mm cannon. In the event, only two prototypes and eight production aircraft were built; they were given the new type name Seaford, but after a brief service appearance were later converted into Solent commercial transports for BOAC. Final military variant was the Mk V (one hundred built by Shorts and fifty by Blackburn), with 1,200 hp Pratt & Whitney R-1830-90 Twin Wasps as powerplant and improved ASV equipment. The Sunderland V entered service in February 1945, and was the last version to serve with the RAF, finally retiring in 1958. Sunderlands exported post-war to the French *Aéronavale* (nineteen) and the RNZAF (sixteen) served until 1960 and 1966 respectively.

77 Kawanishi H8K

The 13-Shi (1938) specification to which Dr Kikuhara designed the first prototype H8K1 was an exacting one, and in its initial trials early in 1941 the flying boat gave little indication of its future promise, having a lack of stability on the water and a marked tendency to 'porpoise'. Various modifications were made to this and the three pre-production H8K1's of 1941, all of which were powered by 1,530 hp Mitsubishi Kasei 11 engines. As finally accepted for production in February 1942, the H8K1 Model 11 had a deeper hull, with a more efficient planing bottom, and enlarged vertical tail surfaces. Thirteen production H8K1's were built at Kohnan. They carried a crew of 10 and were armed, like the pre-series machines, with a single 20 mm tail gun, one 20 mm and two 7·7 mm guns in the nose turret and a 7·7 mm gun in each of the beam blisters. Operational debut of 'Emily', as the H8K was later dubbed by the Allies, was made by the three pre-series H8K1's. These made an abortive attack on Pearl Harbor early in March 1942, flying from the Marshall Islands and refuelling from submarine tankers *en route*. The production H8K1 was an excellent hydrodynamic design, with a performance equal or superior to any other flying boat in service during the war. In 1943 it was superseded by the H8K2 Model 12, with more powerful Kasei 22 engines and increased armament. This was employed throughout the Pacific theatre, its maximum endurance of nearly 27 hours enabling it to carry out extremely long range maritime patrol, bombing and reconnaissance duties. Late production H8K2's carried ASV radar in the bow, the beam observation blisters being omitted. One hundred and twelve H8K2's were completed during 1943-45, plus thirty-six examples of a transport version, the H8K2-L Model 32 Sei-Ku (Clear Sky). This could carry up to sixty-four passengers, or a mixed load of passengers and cargo. It was recognisable by double rows of fuselage windows and a reduced armament of a single 13 mm and 20 mm gun respectively in the nose and tail. The first prototype H8K1, re-engined in 1943 with Kasei 22's and converted to a passenger layout, served as the trials aircraft for this version. Two H8K3 Model 22's were essentially late production H8K2's fitted experimentally with retractable wing-tip floats (originally planned for the first prototype) and a retractable dorsal turret. Later they were re-engined with Kasei 25b's and were redesignated H8K4 Model 23. Neither went into production, and the projected H8K4-L Model 33 transport was never completed.

78 Kawanishi H6K

One of the most efficient Japanese aircraft of the late 1930's, the Kawanishi H6K flying boat was designed to a JNAF specification of 1934, and three of the five prototypes had flown by the end of 1936. Two of these, and one other machine, had their original 840 hp Nakajima Hikari 2 engines replaced later by 1,000 hp Mitsubishi Kinsei 43's, in which form they were delivered to the JNAF for squadron service in January 1938 under the designation H6K1. The fifth machine served as prototype for the initial production version, the H6K2 Model 11, nine more of which were built. The designation H6K3 was allocated to the next two aircraft, which were completed as transports. They were later restyled H6K2-L, and a total of eighteen was eventually delivered to Japan Air Lines as 16-seat commercial and military transports. The early military models flew operationally with the JNAF during the Sino-Japanese conflict, but by the outbreak of World War 2 the principal version in service was the H6K4 Model 22. Initially, this had been built with Kinsei 43 engines, but from August 1941 the standard powerplant became the more powerful Kinsei 46, permitting higher operating weights. Sixty-six Model 22's, later code-named 'Mavis' by the Allies, were in JNAF service at the time of Pearl Harbor, and eventually between two and three times this number were completed, several of them as H6K4-L transports. An attempt to prolong the flying boat's career resulted in the H6K5 Model 23, with 1,300 hp Kinsei 53 engines, but the satisfactory evolution of the later H8K from the same stable rendered such a course unnecessary, and only a comparatively small number of H6K5's were built. Most 'Mavis' flying boats ended their careers in the transport role, but by the end of 1943 they had virtually disappeared from service. A total of two hundred and seventeen H6K's, of all versions, were built.

79 Messerschmitt Me 323

Messerschmitt's huge transport glider, the Me 321 *Gigant*, had been produced only in small numbers before it was realised that the need to use rocket assistance and three twin-engined Bf 110's to get it into the air was uneconomical. Ing Degel of Messerschmitt was therefore given, early in 1941, the task of evolving from it an aeroplane that could take off under its own power. His solution, calculated also to avoid making demands upon German engine production, was to install Gnome-Rhône 14N engines, already in production in Occupied France. At first it was supposed that four of these engines would suffice, and ten prototypes were completed to this configuration. The first, designated Me 323V1, was flown in April 1941, but it soon became apparent that four engines were inadequate, and in August 1941 the first of five six-engined prototypes was flown. When manufacture of the Me 321 glider ended in January 1942, the six-engined Me 323 entered production. The initial model was the Me 323D-1, of which just over two dozen were built. One example was also completed of the Me 323D-2, to compare the merits of two-blade wooden propellers with the three-blade metal ones of the D-1. The D-1's five MG 131 machine-guns remained the minimum basic armament of the main production model, the Me 323D-6. However, additional weapons were often carried, and there were reports of some Me 323's with as many as eighteen machine-guns on board. In 1943 one hundred and forty

Me 323D-6's were built, and Messerschmitt delivered nineteen examples of the Me 323E-1, whose basic armament included a power-operated turret, mounting a 20 mm MG 151 cannon, installed above the centre engine nacelle on each wing. In 1944, before having to devote its resources to the Me 262 jet fighter, Messerschmitt had begun production of the Me 323F-1, powered by Gnome-Rhône 14R engines. Production was then transferred to the Zeppelin plant at Friedrichshafen, where a few F-1's were re-engined in mid-1944 with 1,340 hp Jumo 211F engines, but little further output was undertaken. The Me 323 was an invaluable supply transport on the Eastern Front, where it first appeared, but in North Africa and elsewhere its slow speed and difficult handling made it an easy prey for Allied fighters. After heavy losses during the evacuation of Tunisia little more was heard of this huge aeroplane, and further projected versions remained uncompleted.

80 Yokosuka MXY-7 Ohka (Cherry Blossom)

Most Japanese *Kamikaze* (Divine Wind) suicide air attacks were made by existing service aircraft adapted for the purpose, but one aircraft developed specifically for this role was also met operationally. This was the Ohka piloted flying bomb, developed to a project initiated by the Japanese Naval Air Research and Development Centre and evolved by the Yokosuka Naval Air Arsenal. Design work began in August 1944, priority production by several factories starting in September. The only version to reach combat status was the Model 11, seven hundred and fifty-five of which were built up to March 1945. Powered by a three-barrelled rocket motor and carrying a 2,645 lb (1,200 kg) warhead in the nose, the Ohka was attached beneath the belly of a G4M2e parent aircraft, the bomb doors of which were removed in order to accommodate it. The Ohka was carried to about 50 miles (80 km) from its target, when it was launched from a height usually around 27,000 ft (8,200 km) at an airspeed of some 200 mph (320 km/hr) to complete its journey alone. The pilot maintained it in a glide towards the target, using the rocket motor only for the last few miles and the ultimate steep dive. Fifty Ohka Model 11's were aboard the carrier *Shinano* when it was sunk by U.S. forces *en route* to the Philippines in November 1944. The aircraft was first encountered operationally on 21 March 1945, when sixteen Ohkas, with their parent aircraft and an escort of thirty Zero fighters, were intercepted while making for a U.S. task force about 300 miles (480 km) from Kyushu. All of the Ohka-carrying bombers, and half of the escorting fighters, were destroyed without a single weapon being launched. Sub-

sequently, about three hundred Ohkas were allocated to the Okinawa area; probably no more than a quarter of these were launched at Allied targets, but these were enough to persuade their victims, at least, that perhaps the code name *Baka* (Japanese for 'fool') bestowed by the U.S. Navy was after all something of a misnomer. The only other version built in quantity was the Model 22, about fifty of which were completed. This had a 13 ft 6¼ in (4·12 m) wing span, was 22 ft 6⅞ in (6·88m) long, and had a gross weight of 3,197 lb (1,450 kg) including a 1,323 lb (600 kg) warhead. Powerplant was a TSU-11 jet engine, the compressor of which was driven by a 110 hp Hatsukaze piston-engine to provide 441 lb (200 kg) of thrust. The intended parent aircraft was the P1Y1 Ginga, but the Ohka 22 had a disappointing performance and did not go into service. The Model 33, proposed in April 1945, was incomplete when the war ended. Intended for air-launching from the G8N1 Renzan four-engined bomber, it would have had a 1,047 lb (475 kg) st Ne-20 turbojet and a warhead comparable to the Model 11. Project studies were also made for Models 43A (with folding wings) and 43B, to be launched from submarine-based and land-based catapults respectively.

INDEX

Heinkel	He 111	23	39	115
	He 115	21	37	113
	He 177 Greif	43	59	132
Ilyushin	Il-4 (DB-3F)	25	41	116
Junkers	Ju 52/3m	62	78	146
	Ju 87	19	35	111
	Ju 88	31	47	121
Kawanishi	H6K	78	94	158
	H8K	77	93	157
Lockheed	Hudson	54	70	140
	Lodestar	56	72	142
	Ventura	55	71	141
Martin	A-30 Baltimore	34	50	124
	B-26 Marauder	35	51	125
	Model 167 Maryland	26	42	117
Messerschmitt	Me 323	79	95	159
Mitsubishi	G4M	38	54	127
	Ki-21	37	53	126
	Ki-46	41	57	130
	Ki-67 Hiryu	39	55	128
Nakajima	B5N	10	26	104
	B6N Tenzan	16	32	109
	C6N Saiun	20	36	112
	Ki-49 Donryu	40	56	129
Noorduyn	Norseman	4	20	99
North American	B-25 Mitchell	53	69	139
Petlyakov	Pe-8 (TB-7)	65	81	149
PZL	P.37 Łoś	36	52	125
Saab	Saab-18	47	63	135
Savoia-Marchetti	S.M.79 Sparviero	64	80	148
Short	Stirling	66	82	149
	Sunderland	76	92	156
Sukhoi	Su-2	14	30	107
Supermarine	Walrus	1	17	97
Vickers	Wellington	22	38	114
Westland	Lysander	5	21	99
Yokosuka	D4Y Suisei	12	28	106
	MXY-7 Ohka	80	96	159
	P1Y1 Ginga	42	58	131